THE OFFICIAL

1995
BLACKBOOK
PRICE GUIDE OF
UNITED STATES
POSTAGE
STAMPS

SEVENTEENTH EDITION

BY MARC HUDGEONS, N.L.G.

"The Scott Catalogue Numbers are used herein under license from Scott Publishing Co., the copyright owner. All rights thereto are reserved under the Pan American and Universal Copyright Conventions."

HOUSE OF COLLECTIBLES • NEW YORK

Sale of this book without a front cover may be unauthorized. If this book is coverless, it may have been reported to the publisher as "unsold or destroyed" and neither the author nor the publisher may have received payment for it.

Important Notice. All of the information, including valuations, in this book has been compiled from the most reliable sources, and every effort has been made to eliminate errors and questionable data. Nevertheless, the possibility of error, in a work of such immense scope, always exists. The publisher will not be held responsible for losses which may occur in the purchase, sale, or other transaction of items because of information contained herein. Readers who feel they have discovered errors are invited to *write* and inform us, so they may be corrected in subsequent editions. Those seeking further information on the topics covered in this book are advised to refer to the complete line of *Official Price Guides* published by the House of Collectibles.

© 1994 by Random House, Inc.

This is a registered trademark of Random House, Inc.

All rights reserved under International and Pan-American Copyright Conventions.

Published by: House of Collectibles
201 East 50th Street
New York, New York 10022

Distributed by Ballantine Books, a division of Random House, Inc., New York, and simultaneously in Canada by Random House of Canada Limited, Toronto.

Manufactured in the United States of America

ISSN: 0195-3559

ISBN: 0-876-37930-7

Cover design by Kristine Mills
Cover photo: 1894 First Bureau issue, courtesy of Ivy, Shreve & Mader Auction Galleries, New York. Photo imaging © George Kerrigan

Seventeenth Edition: July 1994

10 9 8 7 6 5 4 3 2 1

TABLE OF CONTENTS

OFFICIAL BOARD OF CONTRIBUTORS

Mr. Armin R. Crowe
Mr. Steven Levine
Mr. Bob Dumaine
Mr. Harry Miller
Mr. Frank Wells

Mr. Al Zimmerman
Mr. Don McDowell
Mr. Don Sagar
Mr. Ernest A. Kehr
Mr. Jack Williams

The publisher also wishes to express special thanks to Mr. Armin R. Crowe at the Collectors Institute, Ltd., Omaha, Nebraska 68144, and for the special help provided by *Linn's Stamp Journal*. The designs for the stamps issued from 1978 to date are copyrighted by the U.S. Postal Service and are used by permission from the U.S. Postal Service.

NOTE TO READERS

All advertisements appearing in this book have been accepted in good faith, but the publisher assumes no responsibility in any transactions that occur between readers and advertisers.

MARKET REVIEW

Activity in U.S. stamp collecting continues to increase as the U.S. economy improves. While most collectors over the past years have been very selective in their purchases, substantial growth and activity in the marketplace indicate that many collectors are concentrating on a wider variety of stamp issues.

Philatelic shows and auctions have also served to spark greater interest and activity. It appears most collectors are upgrading their collections. Look for the prices of higher grades to increase in value over the next year. Select and purchase the finest grades your budget will allow. Remember, the supply of quality stamps is steady and will hold or increase in value while the lesser grades are more subject to price fluctuation.

Nineteenth- and twentieth-century stamps have increased in value on the average of 5 percent to 8 percent, while airmail stamps have increased 8 percent to 10 percent over last year's prices. These increases, although minor, reflect a welcome and healthy demand for the most common stamp issues by collectors who seek to complete their collections and albums. Try to deal in stamps that are accurately graded. The price ranges for these stamps will vary only slightly. Remember that stamps that are selling for well under their currently traded value are often misgraded or misrepresented.

The U.S. Postal Service has been very active over the past year regarding new stamp releases. This is important in many ways. They are doing an excellent job in the subject selection and quality of design presentation of these new stamps. The quality of these new stamps appeals to and serves to stimulate new collectors. The best example is the Elvis Presley stamp released the early part of last year. Millions of these stamps have been produced and purchased both for use and collections. Another new release that is currently receiving an unprecedented amount of press is the "Bill Pickett" stamp in the "Legends of the West" series. Regardless of the outcome, this stamp has sparked a tremendous interest in the field of stamp collecting.

New releases by the U.S. Postal Service will always be the most important aspect in the field of collecting. As the number of new collectors increase in time, many will go on to collect older issues and will produce a broader base for the entire stamp-collecting hobby.

THE STORY OF U.S. STAMPS

The world's first postage stamps were issued by Great Britain in 1840 and pictured its new queen, Victoria, then 21 years old. It was not until 1847 that the U.S. released postage stamps, but prior to that time some city postmasters issued stamps of their own. These very valuable stamps, known as "postmaster provisionals," were used in St. Louis, New York, Annapolis and a number of other cities.

The first federally released postage stamps comprised a 5¢ denomination picturing Benjamin Franklin and a 10¢ showing George Washington. Their size was very similar to that of modern non-commemoratives and they had gummed backs, just like our stamps. The chief difference was that they carried no little holes or perforations between each specimen on a sheet, to aid in separation. Instead they had to be cut apart with scissors or creased and torn by hand. These stamps are called "imperforates," or "without perforations." All stamps in those days, including Europe's, were made in this way. The U.S. did not start perforating its stamps until 1857, ten years later.

Imperforates rank today as the hobby's aristocrats, its elder statesmen and foremost classics. They have long been dear to the hearts of collectors, and not merely on grounds of their antiquity. Some specialists maintain that these issues, every one of them bearing a statesman's portrait, are more elegantly engraved than any of their descendants. In addition, they can be found (with luck and the necessary cash) in super specimens that put ordinary perforated stamps to shame. When a stamp is perforated, every one on the sheet is of identical size. Some sheets may be better centered than others, depending on how the paper is fed, but no specimens will be physically larger than any others. With imperforates, it's quite another matter. The cutting was never done very evenly. Some specimens were cropped or cut into by scissor wielders and left with margins so immense that portions of all the surrounding stamps are visible. These are called jumbo margin copies and the prices collectors will give for them are often astronomic, provided the condition is otherwise good. It is not at all unusual for one of these oversized beauties to command three or four times the normal sum. Collectors must take care though, because in philately, as in most other things, all that sparkles is not necessarily diamonds. Larcenous persons have been known to take very ordinary average stamps and add fake margins.

Not all imperforates are equally easy (or hard) to get with four full margins. This is all a matter of how closely together they were printed on the sheet. The cutter is less apt to make a mistake if the stamps are further apart on the sheet. Scott's #11, the 3¢ 1851, is by far the most difficult to find with full margins. It also happens to be the least expensive imperforate, thanks to the enormous quantities printed. While the usual specimen will fetch only $8–$10 used, a jumbo margin #11 has no trouble selling for $20, $30 or more.

The second series of imperforates, issued from 1851 to 1856, comprised values from 1¢ to 12¢. There were five stamps, with Washington appearing on three of them; the other two portraits of Franklin and Jefferson. In 1857 the same group of stamps was released again, this time with perforations and three high values: a 24¢ and 90¢ pictured Washington, and a 30¢ portrayed Franklin. The 90¢ stamp was not exceeded in face value until the Columbian Exposition series in 1893. Because very little mail required the paying of so much postage, most specimens of the 90¢, 1857–1861 that went to private hands never got on letters. Consequently, this stamp is much more difficult to find used than unused, a rare circumstance for a U.S. issue. Needless to say, counterfeit cancels exist.

There was no question by this time that postage stamps had scored a big success. Any doubts or complaints that some users may have had about them at the beginning had long since vanished. Certain persons became so fond of stamps that they began saving them, used as well as unused, and thus the hobby of philately was born. For the government, stamps brought greater economy to the postal service than anticipated. They also allowed mail to travel faster. There was just one problem: some people were abusing the system. During the Civil War, and shortly thereafter, it became apparent that many stamps were going through the mails twice or more. People were cleaning off the cancels and using them again. This may have been done by individuals but, more likely, it was a large-scale operation in which used stamps were cleaned in wholesale quantities and sold to business houses and other volume mailers at a discount. The government was being bilked out of thousands of dollars, but there seemed no solution until a plan was devised to use "grills" on the faces of stamps in 1867. These were networks of tiny embossed dots which weakened the paper and would, presumably, cause it to break apart if any attempt was made at erasing the cancel.

After just two years the grill was dropped, but it had appeared on enough stamps in that short time to provide philatelists with an intriguing subspecialty. Not all the grills were alike. They differed in size and style and collecting them is quite a sport.

The year 1869 marked the first year of U.S. pictorial stamps that portrayed things or events rather than portraits. They cannot really be termed commemoratives in the modern sense, but they were extremely pictorial. Subjects included a pony express rider, a rail locomotive, panoramas of the landing of Columbus, the signing of the Declaration of Independence, and others. This series also presented the first stamps to be printed in more than one color. Multicolor printing was no small operation in those days. It required two separate plates; one consisting of frames to be printed in one color, and the other central designs to be printed in a different color. The sheets were fed through one press, allowed to dry, then fed into the next to receive the final printing. As the feeding was done by hand, human error occasionally occurred. A few sheets were fed upside down the second time around, resulting in the first, but not the most famous, U.S. inverts, or stamps with upside down centers. These are very valuable and seldom offered on the market. The king of all United States inverts is a twentieth-century stamp, the 24¢ airmail of 1918. This small stamp has a central design of a Curtiss Jenny single engine plane. It was printed 100 to a sheet. On the day it was issued, a Washington, D.C. collector, William T. Robey, took a few minutes from his lunch hour to go into the local post office and buy a sheet. He had no intention of using the stamps but merely wanted them for his collection. After putting down his $24 he received what appeared to be a normal sheet, but after looking closer, Mr. Robey found that on every stamp the airplane was upside down. This incident stirred a furor of considerable proportion. The government was embarrassed since it had claimed that the old 1869 inverts could not happen again with its new machinery and rigid controls. It tried, without success, to buy the sheet back from Robey. Meanwhile it notified postmasters around the country to check their stocks for further error sheets. No more were found, and when it became evident that Robey's sheet was the only one in existence he began receiving substantial offers from collectors and dealers. The offers seemed tempting and he finally sold his treasure for $15,000 to Eugene Klein of Philadelphia, a prominent dealer. Klein immediately resold the sheet to Col. Edward H. R. Green of New York, the legendary collector who also owned the only five known specimens of the 1913 Liberty nickel. It is believed Green paid at least $17,500 for this philatelic morsel, a huge sum in those days but only about one third as much as each of the 100 stamps are now individually worth. Green broke up the sheet into blocks, selling most of them and recovering his entire cost. Several single specimens were subsequently lost; one was supposed to have disappeared into a vacuum cleaner while Green's housekeeper was tidying up.

FACTORS BEHIND STAMP PRICES

The collector value (or "market value") of any stamp rests with a variety of factors. Philately becomes a bit less mysterious when one understands the forces at work in the stamp marketplace.

A beginner will normally presume that expensive stamps are expensive because of rarity. Certainly there is a great deal of talk about stamp rarities within the hobby, and so it is natural enough to ascribe high prices to the phenomenon of rarity. In fact, rarity is only one of several factors that influence stamp prices, and the influence it carries is not particularly clear-cut.

In this book you will note some stamps (mostly among the early regular issues) with values of $1,000, $2,000, and even higher. Obviously these stamps are rarer than those selling for $10 or $15. But once having said that, we have virtually summed up our useful knowledge of rarity and its effect on prices. A comparison of prices, between stamps in roughly similar ranges of value, does not indicate which is the rarer. A stamp selling for $1,000 is not necessarily rarer than one selling for $500. A $10,000 stamp may actually be more abundant than one which commands $5,000. This hard-to-comprehend fact of philatelic life prevails because of the other factors involved in determining a stamp's price. If rarity were the only factor, one could, of course, easily see which stamps are the rarest by the prices they fetch.

The word "rare" is an elixir to many collectors, not only of stamps but other collectors' items. Sellers are well aware of this, and seldom fail to sprinkle the word liberally in their sales literature. There is no law against calling a stamp rare, as this represents a personal opinion more than anything else and opinions are allowable in advertising. Unfortunately, there is no standard definition for rarity. Does "rare" mean just a handful of specimens in existence, with one reaching the sales portals once in five years? Does it mean 100 in existence, or 1,000, or some other number? Since stamps are—today, at any rate—printed in the multimillions, a thousand surviving specimens might seem a very tiny total to some people. Further complicating this situation is the fact that the specific rarity of most stamps cannot be determined, or even estimated, with any hope of accuracy. The quantities printed are recorded for most of our stamps, going back even into the nineteenth century, but the quantity *surviving* of any particular stamp is anyone's guess. It is obvious that a stamp that goes through the auction rooms once a year is fairly rare, but this provides no sound basis for guessing the number of specimens in existence. That could only be accomplished if some sort of grand census could be taken, and all specimens tallied. This, of course, is nothing but a pipe dream. Some collectors would not participate in such a census; some might be unaware that it was being conducted. Then, too, there are many scarce or rare stamps in hands other than those of collectors, such as dealers and museums. Additionally, there could be (and probably are) existing specimens of rare stamps yet to be discovered, as fresh discoveries are made periodically in the hobby through attic cleaning and the like.

In terms of influence on price, rarity is outdistanced somewhat by *popularity*. Some stamps, for one reason or other, are simply more popular than others. They have a sort of innate appeal for hobbyists, either through reputation, exquisite designing, circumstances of issue, oddity, or various other potential reasons. These stamps sell out rapidly from the stocks of dealers, while some stamps that are supposedly scarcer will linger in stock albums for ages and ages waiting to tempt a customer. It is no wonder, then, that the prices of popular stamps rise more quickly than those that are scarce but not in brisk demand. The Columbian series typifies the effect of popularity on stamp values. If stamp prices were fixed by scarcity alone, none of the Columbians would be selling for nearly as much. Much of their value derives from their overwhelming popularity with collectors of U.S. stamps. It would be safe to say, in fact, that *all* of the Columbians from the lowest face value to the $5, are more plentiful than other U.S. stamps selling for precisely the same sums. Every dealer has Columbians in stock, and quite a few dealers have the high value of the set, too. They are not "hard to get." But they *are* very costly.

Popularity, of course, does not remain constant forever. There are shifts in philatelic popularity, usually slight but occasionally extreme. The popularity of commemoratives as a whole versus regular issues as a whole can change from time to time. Then, too, there are swings of popularity for airmails, first day covers, blocks, coil pairs, mint sheets, and all other philatelic material. A climb or decline in the price of any philatelic item is often an indication of the forces of popularity at work. Then there are activities of investors to consider, whose buying habits seldom reflect those of the pure collector. A great deal of buying by investors in any short period of time (such as occurred during 1979 and 1980, and to less extent in 1981) can make prices seem well out of balance.

Also on the subject of prices, it is important for the beginner to realize that arithmetic is usually futile when dealing with stamp values. You cannot determine the price of one philatelic item by knowing the value of a similar one. This can best be shown by the relative values of singles and blocks of four. A block of four is, as one would expect, worth *more* than four times as much as single specimens of that stamp. It is not just four specimens of the stamp, but four of them *attached*, which lends added scarcity and appeal. The difficulty lies in trying to use mathematics to determine a block's value. Some blocks are worth five times as much as the single stamp; some six times; some ten times as much or even more. Almost all blocks—except very common ones—will vary somewhat in value, in relation to the value of the individual stamp. There is no satisfactory explanation for this, other than the presumption that some blocks are scarcer than others or just in greater demand than others.

In the case of common philatelic items, the value hinges greatly on the method of sale. If you want to buy one specimen of a common cover, you may have to pay $1.50. But if you were willing to buy a hundred common first day covers *of the dealer's choice*, you could very likely get them for $75 or 75¢ each. Buying in quantity, and allowing the dealer to make the selections, can save a great deal of money. Of course one may then ask: What is the real value of those covers? Is it $1.50 or 75¢? The only answer is that it depends on how you buy!

If this article seems to raise a great many questions without supplying many answers, it will, hopefully, serve to show that stamp collecting is not bound to rigid formulas. What happens in the stamp market is largely beyond prediction, or precise explanation. This, indeed, is one of the exciting aspects of the hobby.

STAMP COLLECTORS' TERMINOLOGY

Adhesives—A term given to stamps that have gummed backs and are intended to be pasted on articles and items that are to be mailed.

Aerophilately—The collecting of airmail or any form of stamps related to mail carried by air.

Airmail—Any mail carried by air.

Albino—An uncolored embossed impression of a stamp generally found on envelopes.

Approvals—Stamps sent to collectors. They are examined by the collector, who selects stamps to purchase and returns balance with payment for the stamps he retained.

Arrow Block—An arrow-like mark found on blocks of stamps in the selvage. This mark is used as a guide for cutting or perforating stamps.

As-is—A term used when selling a stamp. It means no representation is given as to its condition or authenticity. Buyers should beware.

Backprint—Any printing that may appear on reverse of stamp.

Backstamp—The postmark on the back of a letter indicating what time or date the letter arrived at the post office.

Bantams—A miniature stamp given to a war economy issue of stamps from South Africa.

Batonne—Watermarked paper used in printing stamps.

Bicolored—A two-color printed stamp.

Bisect—A stamp that could be used by cutting in half and at half the face value.

Block—A term used for a series of four or more stamps attached at least two high and two across.

Bourse—A meeting or convention of stamp collectors and dealers where stamps are bought, sold, and traded.

Cachet—A design printed on the face of an envelope, generally celebrating the commemoration of a new postage stamp issue. Generally called a first day cover.

Cancellation—A marking placed on the face of a stamp to show that it has been used.

Cancelled to Order—A stamp cancelled by the government without being used. Generally remainder stamps or special issues. Common practice of Russian nations.

Centering—The manner in which the design of a stamp is printed and centered upon the stamp blank. A perfectly centered stamp would have equal margins on all sides.

Classic—A popular, unique, highly desired or very artistic stamp. Not necessarily a rare stamp, but one sought after by the collector. Generally used only for nineteenth-century issues.

Coils—Stamps sold in rolls for use in vending machines.

Commemorative—A stamp issued to commemorate or celebrate a special event.

Crease—A fold or wrinkle in a stamp.

Cut Square—An embossed staple removed from the envelope by cutting.

Dead Country—A country no longer issuing stamps.

Demonetized—A stamp no longer valid for use.

Error—A stamp printed or produced with a major design or color defect.

Essay—Preliminary design for a postage stamp.

Face Value—The value of a stamp indicated on the face or surface of the stamp.

Frank—A marking on the face of an envelope indicating the free and legal use of postage. Generally for government use.

Fugitive Inks—A special ink used to print stamps, which can be rubbed or washed off easily, to eliminate erasures and forgeries.

General Collector—One who collects all kinds of issues and all types of stamps from different countries.

Granite Paper—A type of paper containing colored fibers to prevent forgery.

Gum—The adhesive coating on the back of a stamp.

Handstamped—A stamp that has been handcancelled.

Hinge—A specially gummed piece of glassine paper used to attach a stamp to the album page.

Imperforate—A stamp without perforations.

Inverted—Where one portion of a stamp's design is inverted or upside down from the remainder of the design.

Local Stamps—Stamps that are only valid in a limited area.

Margin—The unprinted area around a stamp.

Miniature Sheet—A smaller than usual sheet of stamps.

Mint Condition—A stamp in original condition as it left the postal printing office.

Mirror Print—A stamp error printed in reverse as though looking at a regular stamp reflected in a mirror.

Multicolored—A stamp printed in three or more colors.

Never Hinged—A stamp in original mint condition never hinged in an album.

Off Paper—A used stamp that has been removed from the envelope to which it was attached.

On Paper—A used stamp still attached to the envelope.

Original Gum—A stamp with the same or original adhesive that was applied in the manufacturing process.

Pair—Two stamps unseparated.

Pen Cancellation—A stamp cancelled by pen or pencil.

Perforation Gauge—A printed chart containing various sizes of perforation holes used in determining the type or size of perforation of a stamp.

Perforations—Holes punched along stamp designs allowing stamps to be easily separated.

Philatelist—One who collects stamps.

Pictorial Stamps—Stamps that bear large pictures of animals, birds, flowers, etc.

Plate Block Number—The printing plate number used to identify a block of four or more stamps taken from a sheet of stamps.

Postally Used—A stamp that has been properly used and cancelled.

Precancels—A stamp that has been cancelled in advance. Generally used on bulk mail.

Reissue—A new printing of an old stamp that has been out of circulation.

Revenue Stamp—A label or stamp affixed to an item as evidence of tax payment.

Seals—An adhesive label that looks like a stamp, used for various fund raising campaigns.

Se-tenant—Two or more stamps joined together, each having a different design or value.

Sheet—A page of stamps as they are printed, usually separated before distribution to post offices.

Soaking—Removing used stamps from paper to which they are attached by soaking in water. *(NOTE: Colored cancels may cause staining to other stamps.)*

Souvenir Sheet—One or more specially designed stamps printed by the government in celebration of a special stamp.

Splice—The splice made between rolls of paper in the printing operation. Stamps printed on this splice are generally discarded.

Tete-Bechs—A pair of stamps printed together so that the images point in opposite vertical directions.

Transit Mark—A mark made by an intermediate post office between the originating and final destination post office.

Typeset Stamp—A stamp printed with regular printer's type, as opposed to engraved, lithographed, etc.

Ungummed—Stamps printed without an adhesive back.

Unhinged—A stamp that has never been mounted with the use of a hinge.

Unperforated—A stamp produced without perforations.

Vignette—The central design portion of a stamp.

Want List—A list of stamps a collector needs to fill gaps in his collection.

Watermark—A mark put into paper by the manufacturer, not readily seen by the naked eye.

Wrapper—A strip of paper with adhesive on one end, used for wrapping bundles of mail. Especially in Britain, it refers to any bit of paper to which a used stamp is still attached.

HOW TO GRADE STAMPS

A person need not be an expert to judge the quality or grade of a stamp. All he needs is a discerning eye, possibly a small linear measuring device, and the grading instructions listed below.

The major catalogs traditionally list stamps simply as "Unused" or "Used." Auction houses, however, will describe the stamps for sale in a more informative manner. The greater the value of the stamp, the more thoroughly it is described.

There is no officially accepted system of grading stamps. What we have done in this book is essentially to set up a system of grading stamps using the suggestions and practices of stamp dealers from all over the country. Total agreement was made to the following categories and grades of stamps that are most frequently traded.

CATEGORIES

Mint—The perfect stamp with superb centering, no faults and usually with original gum (if issued with gum).

Unused—Although unused this stamp may have a hinge mark or may have suffered some change in its gum since it was issued.

Used—Bascially this will be the normal stamp that passed through the government postal system and will bear an appropriate cancellation.

Cancelled to Order—These are stamps that have not passed through the postal system but have been carefully cancelled by the government usually for a commemoration. These are generally considered undesirable by collectors.

Average
Centering

Fine
Centering

Very Fine
Centering

Extra Fine
Centering

Superb
Centering

GRADE—STAMP CENTERING

Average—The perforations cut slightly into the design.

Fine—The perforations do not touch the design at all, but the design will be off center by 50% or more of a superb centered stamp.

Very Fine—The design will be off center by less than 50% of a superb stamp. The off centered design will be visibly noticeable.

Extra Fine—The design will be almost perfectly centered. The margin will be off by less than 25% of a superb stamp.

Superb—This design will be perfectly centered with all four margins exactly the same. On early imperforate issues, superb specimens will have four clear margins that do not touch the design at any point.

GRADE—STAMP GUM

Original Gum—This stamp will have the same gum on it that it had the day it was issued.

Regummed—This stamp will have new gum applied to it as compared to an original gummed stamp. Regummed stamps are worth no more than those with gum missing.

No Gum—This stamp will have had its gum removed or it may have not been issued with gum.

Never Hinged—This stamp has never been hinged so the gum should not have been disturbed in any way.

Lightly Hinged—This stamp has had a hinge applied. A lightly wetted or peelable hinge would do very little damage to the gum when removed.

Heavily Hinged—This stamp has had a hinge applied in such a manner as to secure it to the stamp extremely well. Removal of this hinge usually proves to be disastrous, in most cases, since either part of the hinge remains on the stamp or part of the stamp comes off on the hinge, causing thin spots on the stamp.

GRADE—STAMP FAULTS

Any fault in a stamp such as thin paper, bad perforations, creases, tears, stains, ink marks, pin holes, etc., and depending upon the seriousness of the fault, usually results in grading the stamp to a lower condition.

OTHER STAMP CONSIDERATIONS

CANCELLATIONS

Light Cancel—This stamp has been postally cancelled but the wording and lines are very light and almost unreadable.

Normal Cancel—This stamp has been postally cancelled with just the right amount of pressure. Usually the wording and lines are not distorted and can be made out.

Heavy Cancel—This stamp has been postally cancelled. In the process excessive pressure was used, and the wording and lines are extremely dark and sometimes smeared and in most cases unreadable.

PERFORATIONS

Not to be overlooked in the appearance of a stamp are its perforations. The philatelist might examine these "tear apart" holes with a magnifying glass or microscope to determine the cleanliness of the separations. One must also consider that the different types of paper, upon which the stamp was printed, will sometimes make a difference in the cleanliness of the separations. The term "pulled perf" is used to denote a badly separated stamp in which the perforations are torn or ragged.

COLOR

Other important factors such as color affect the appearance and value of stamps. An expert will have a chart of stamp colors. Chemical changes often occur in inks. Modern printing sometimes uses metallic inks. These "printings" will oxidize upon contact with the natural secretions from animal skin.

The color of certain stamps has been deliberately altered by chemicals to produce a rare shade. Overprints can be eliminated. Postmarks may be eradicated. Replacing gum is a simple process. Some stamps have been found to bear forged watermarks. The back of the paper was cut away and then the stamps rebacked with appropriately watermarked paper.

There are stamp experts who earn a living in the business of stamp repairing. They are craftsmen of the first order. A thin spot on a stamp can be repaired by gluing it on a new layer of paper. Missing perforations can be added. Torn stamps can be put back together. Pieces of stamps may be joined.

In some countries it is accepted practice for an expert, upon examination of a stamp, to certify the authenticity by affixing his signature to the back of the stamp. If the stamp is not genuine, it is his right and duty to so designate on the stamp; but these signatures can also be faked.

REPAIRS, FAKES, AND OTHER UNDESIRABLES

Philately, like most hobbies, is not without its pitfalls. The collector who buys from reputable dealers runs very little risk, as today's stamp pros have high principles and are hard to fool. Buying from auction sales and small dealers, who may not have expert knowledge, is another matter. Here the collector must call into play his own expertise and learn to distinguish the bad from the good.

In the early years of philately, stamps provided a playground for fakers and swindlers. They took advantage of the public's gullibility and the general lack of published information about stamps. Copies were printed of rare stamps, as well as of stamps that never existed in the first place. Cancels were bleached from used specimens to make them appear unused. Fake margins were added to imperforates, to allow ordinary copies to be sold as "superb with jumbo margins." Perforated stamps were reperforated to make them better centered. Thin spots in the paper were filled in, tears closed, missing portions of paper replaced. Stamps were doctored and manipulated in more ways than could be imagined, all in the hope of fooling collectors and making anywhere from a few extra cents to thousands of dollars on them. One of the favorite tricks of fakers was to apply bogus overprints or surcharges. By merely using a rubber handstamp and a pad of ink, they could stamp out a hundred or more "rarities" in a few minutes, turning ordinary British or other issues into varieties not found in any catalog. It was all a great game and proved very profitable, until collectors and the philatelic public at large became wary of such practices. Even though most of these fakes from the hobby's pioneer years have disappeared out of circulation, a few still turn up and must be guarded against.

United States stamps have not been faked nearly so extensively as those of many other nations, notably South America and Japan. Still, the collector should learn to watch for fakes and also repaired specimens.

Total Fake. The counterfeit stamp always varies somewhat from a genuine specimen, though the difference may be very slight. Detection can usually be made if the suspect stamp is examined alongside one known to be genuine. By using a magnifier, the lines of engraving and paper quality can be compared. The ink on a fake is likely to have a fresher appearance and will lie on the surface as a result of being printed at a later date and on less sophisticated equipment; however, this is not always the case. Experts say that when a stamp appears to be a fake, or a reprint, the odds are very good that it is. Some experience is necessary before anyone can get a first glance reaction to a stamp. The presence or absence of a cancel has no bearing on the likelihood of a stamp being a fake, as cancels can be faked too.

Faked Cancel. Faked cancels are very rare on U.S. stamps, as nearly all are worth more unused than used. One notable exception is the 90¢, 1857–1861. These are applied either with a fake handstamp or simply drawn with pen and ink. Skillfully drawn faked cancels can be very deceptive. Faked cancels are *much more numerous* on covers than loose stamps.

Removed Cancels. So-called cleaned copies of used stamps, sold as unused, were once very plentiful and are still encountered from time to time. The faker, of course, chooses lightly cancelled specimens from which the obliteration can be removed without leaving telltale evidence. In the case of imperforates he may trim down the margins to remove part of the cancel. Rarely will he attempt to clean a stamp whose cancel falls across the face or any important portion of the stamp. Holding the stamp to a strong light may reveal the cancel lines. X-ray examination provides positive proof.

Added Margin(s). When margins have been added to an imperforate stamp, the paper fibers are woven together (after moistening) along the back and at the front where the margin extends beyond the stamp's design. They can usually be detected by looking closely for a seam or joint at the point where the design ends and the margin begins. A magnifying glass will be necessary for this. When held against a light, the reverse side will probably show evidence of the weaving operation. Sometimes the added margins are of a slightly different grade of paper.

Reperforated. A stamp that has been reperforated to improve its centering will usually be slightly smaller than a normal specimen, and this can be revealed by placing it atop an untampered copy.

Filled in Thin Spots. If held to a light and examined with a good magnifier, filled in thin spots will normally appear darker than the remainder of the stamp. Such spots are often mistaken for discoloration by beginners. Thin spots are filled in by making a paste of paper pulp and glue and applying it gradually to the injured area. After drying, the stamp is placed in a vise so that no telltale hills or valleys are left. This is not really considered forgery but honest repair work; it becomes forgery only if done with the intent of selling the stamp as undamaged.

Closed Tears. These are almost always visible against a light with a magnifier, even if small. A routine examination of any rare stamp should include a check of its margins for possible closed or open tears.

HOW TO USE THIS BOOK

The main section of this book lists all U.S. stamps with the exception of special issues such as airmail, revenues, etc. Special issues are grouped separately in sections of their own. Please refer to the Table of Contents.

Before pricing your stamps, be sure they are correctly identified. Use the photo section as an aid. In some cases, two or more stamp issues are very similar in appearance and can be distinguished only by minor details. These are always noted in the text. Sometimes the evidence is obvious. If a stamp has perforations, it cannot be earlier than 1857.

Prices are given in columns for used and unused specimens, usually in two grades of condition. You need only refer to the column that applies to your stamp and its condition grade.

Prices shown in this book are actual selling prices, so one should not necessarily expect to receive a discount when buying from dealers.

When a dash (—) appears in place of a price, this indicates that the item is either unavailable in that condition grade or is so seldom available that its price is open to question. It should not be assumed, however, that such items are invariably more valuable than those for which prices are shown.

Prices are given for hinged stamps that have been in collections. In today's stamp market a premium value is placed on stamps that have never been hinged. To determine the premium on any stamp, refer to the premium percentages shown on every page.

The stated values are general guides only and cannot reflect the price of occasional superb specimens, such as imperforates with four wide margins, which may sell considerably higher.

A small box has been provided to the left of each listing for keeping a record of the stamps in your collection.

IMPORTANT

Because of the space limitation on each page we have not been able to include very fine, extra fine, never hinged, or lightly hinged pricing on each stamp. To determine these prices please use the following procedure.

Very Fine Pricing—Prior to 1941: *Double the average price quoted.*

Very Fine Pricing—After 1941; *Add 25% to the fine price.*

Extra Fine Pricing—Prior to 1941: *Triple the average price quoted.*

Never Hinged Pricing—Prior to 1941: *Add the percentage indicated at the right of the issue to any price listed. Example (N-H add 5%).*

Never Hinged Pricing—After 1941: *Add 15% to any price listed.*

Lightly Hinged Pricing—*Add one half of the N-H percentage indicated for each issue to any price listed.*

DEALER BUYING PRICES

Buying pries will vary greatly depending upon condition, rarity, and existing dealers' stock of a particular stamp. With these facts in mind, a dealer can be expected to buy stamps between 40 percent and 50 percent of their quoted prices; but this will depend upon supply and demand.

EQUIPMENT

To collect stamps properly a collector will need some "tools of the trade." These need not be expensive and need not all be bought at the very outset. That might, in fact, be the worst thing to do. Many a beginning collector has spent his budget on equipment, only to have little or nothing left for stamps and then loses interest in the hobby.

It may be economical in the long run to buy the finest quality accessories, but few collectors, just starting out, have a clear idea of what they will and will not be needing. It is just as easy to make impulse purchases of accessories as of stamps and just as unwise. Equipment must be purchased on the basis of what sort of collection is being built *now*, rather than on what the collection may be in the future. There is no shame in working up from an elementary album.

Starter Kits. Starter or beginner outfits are sold in just about every variety shop, drugstore, etc. These come in attractive boxes and contain a juvenile or beginner's album; some stamps, which may be on paper and in need of removal; a packet of gummed hinges; tongs; a pocket stockbook or file; and often other items such as a perforation gauge, booklet on stamp collecting, magnifier, and watermark detector. These kits are specially suited to young collectors and can provide a good philatelic education.

Albums. When the hobby began, more than a century ago, collectors mounted their stamps in whatever albums were at hand. Scrapbooks, school exercise tablets and diaries all were used, as well as homemade albums. Today a number of firms specialize in printing albums of all kinds for philatelists, ranging from softbounds for the cautious type to huge multi-volume sets that cost hundreds of dollars. There are general worldwide albums, country albums, U.N. albums, and albums for mint sheets, covers, and every other conceivable variety of philatelic material. Choose your album according to the specialty you intend to pursue. It is not necessary, however, to buy a printed album at all. Many collectors feel there is not enough room for creativity in a printed album and prefer to use a binder with unprinted sheets. This allows items to be arranged at will on the page, rather than following the publisher's format, and for a personal write-up to be added. Rod-type binders will prove more durable and satisfactory than ring binders for heavy collections. The pages of an album should not be too thin, unless only one side is used. The presence of tiny crisscrossing lines (quadrilled sheets) is intended as an aid to correct alignment. Once items have been mounted and written up, these lines are scarcely visible and do not interfere with the attractiveness of the page.

Hinges. These are small rectangular pieces of lightweight paper, usually clear or semiopaque, gummed and folded. One side is moistened and affixed to the back of the stamp and the other to the album page. Hinges are sold in packets of 1,000 and are very inexpensive. Though by far the most popular device for mounting stamps, the hobbyist has his choice of a number of other products if hinges are not satisfactory to him. These include cello mounts, which encase the stamp in clear sheeting and have a black background to provide a kind of frame. These are self-sticking. Their cost is much higher than hinges. The chief advantage of cello mounts is that they prevent injuries to the stamp and eliminate the moistening necessary in using hinges; however, they add considerably to the weight of each page, making flipping through an album less convenient, and become detached from the page more readily than hinges.

Glassine Interleaving. These are sheets made of thin semitransparent glassine paper, the same used to make envelopes in which stamps are stored. They come punched to fit albums of standard size and are designed to be placed between each set of sheets, to prevent stamps on one page from becoming entangled with those on the facing page. Glassine interleaving is not necessary if cello mounts are used, but any collection mounted with conventional hinges should be interleaved. The cost is small. Glassine interleaving is sold in packets of 100 sheets.

Magnifier. A magnifier is a necessary tool for *most* stamp collectors, excepting those who specialize in first day covers or other items that would not likely require study by magnification. There are numerous types and grades on the market, ranging in price from about $1 to more than $20. The quality of magnifier to buy should be governed by the extent to which it is likely to be used, and the collector's dependence upon it for identification and study. A collector of plate varieties ought to have the best magnifier he can afford and carry it whenever visiting dealers, shows or anywhere that he may wish to examine specimens. A good magnifier is also necessary for a specialist in grilled stamps and for collectors of Civil War and other nineteenth-century covers. Those with built-in illumination are best in these circumstances.

Tongs. Beginners have a habit of picking up stamps with their fingers, which can cause injuries, smudges and grease stains. Efficient handling of tongs is not difficult to learn, and the sooner the better. Do not resort to ordinary tweezers, but get a pair of philatelic tongs which are specially shaped and of sufficiently large size to be easily manipulated.

Perforation Gauge. A very necessary inexpensive article, as the identification of many stamps depends upon a correct measuring of their perforations.

TIPS ON STAMP BUYING

There are many ways to buy stamps: packets, poundage mixtures, approvals, new issue services, auctions and a number of others. To buy wisely, a collector must get to know the language of philately and the techniques used by dealers and auctioneers in selling stamps.

Packets of all different worldwide stamps are sold in graduated sizes from 1,000 up to 50,000. True to their word, they contain no duplicates. The stamps come from all parts of the world and date from the 1800s to the present. Both mint and used are included. When you buy larger quantities of most things, a discount is offered; with stamp packets, it works in reverse. The larger the packet, the higher its price per stamp. This is because the smaller packets are filled almost exclusively with low-grade material.

Packets are suitable only as a collection base. A collector should never count on them to build his entire collection. The contents of one worldwide packet are much like that of another. Country jackets are sold in smaller sizes, but there are certain drawbacks with packets.

1. Most packets contain some cancelled-to-order stamps, which are not very desirable for a collection. These are stamps released with postmarks already on them, and are classified as used but have never gone through the mail. Eastern Europe and Russia are responsible for many C.T.O.'s.

2. The advertised value of packets bears little relation to the actual value. Packet makers call attention to the catalog values of their stamps, based on prices listed in standard reference works. The lowest sum at which a stamp can be listed in these books is 2¢, therefore, a packet of 1,000 automatically has a minimum catalog value of $20. If the retail price is $3 this seems like a terrific buy when, in fact, most of those thousand stamps are so common they are almost worthless.

Poundage mixtures are very different than packets. Here the stamps are all postally used (no C.T.O.'s) and still attached to small fragments of envelopes or parcel wrappings. Rather than sold by count, poundage mixtures are priced by the pound or ounce and quite often by kilos. Price varies depending on the grade, and the grade depends on where the mixture was assembled. Bank mixtures are considered the best, as banks receive a steady flow of foreign registered mail. Mission mixtures are also highly rated. Of course, the mixture should be sealed and unpicked. Unless a mixture is advertised as unpicked, the high values have been removed. The best poundage mixtures are sold only by mail. Those available in shops are of medium or low quality. Whatever the grade, poundage mixtures can be counted on to contain duplicates.

If you want to collect the stamps of a certain country, you can leave a standing order for its new releases with a new issue service. Whenever that government puts out stamps, they will be sent to the collector along with a bill. Usually the service will supply only mint copies. The price charged is not the face value, but the face value with a surcharge added to meet the costs of importing, handling and the like. New issue services are satisfactory only if the collector is positive he wants all the country's stamps, no matter what. Remember that its issues could include semipostals, long and maybe expensive sets, and extra high values.

By far the most popular way to buy stamps is via approvals. There is nothing new about approvals, as they go back to the Victorian era. Not all services are alike, though. Some offer sets, while others sell penny approvals. Then there are remainder approvals, advanced approvals, and seconds on approval. Penny approvals are really a thing of the past, though the term is still used. Before inflation, dealers would send a stockbook containing several thousand stamps, all priced at a penny each. If all the stamps were kept, the collector got a discount plus the book! Today the same sort of service can be found, but instead of 1¢ per stamp, the price is anywhere from 3¢ to 10¢. Remainder approvals are made up from collection remainders. Rather than dismount and sort stamps from incoming collections, the approval merchant saves himself time by sending them out right on the album leaves. The collector receives leaves from someone else's collection with stamps mounted just as he arranged them. Seconds on approval are slightly defective specimens of scarce stamps, which would cost more if perfect. Advanced approvals are designed for specialized collectors who know exactly what they want and have a fairly substantial stamp budget.

In choosing an approval service you should know the ground rules of approval buying and not be unduly influenced by promotional offers. Most approval merchants allow the selections to be kept for ten days to two weeks. The unbought stamps are then returned along with payment for those kept. As soon as the selection is received back, another is mailed. This will go on, regardless of how much or how little is bought, until the company is notified to refrain from sending further selections. The reputable services will always stop when told.

Approval ads range from splashy full pagers in the stamp publications to small three-line classified announcements in magazines and newspapers. Most firms catering to beginners offer loss leaders, or stamps on which they take a loss for the sake of getting new customers. If an approval dealer offers 100 pictorials for a dime, it is obvious he is losing money on that transaction, as 10¢ will not even pay the postage. It is very tempting to order these premiums. Remember that when ordering approvals. What sort of service is it? Will it offer the kind of stamps desired? Will prices be high to pay for the loss leaders? Be careful of confusing advertisements. Sometimes the premium offers seem to promise more than they actually do. A rare, early stamp may be pictured. Of course you do not receive the stamp, but merely a modern commemorative picturing it.

Auction Sales. Stamp auctions are held all over the country and account for millions of dollars in sales annually. Buying at auction is exciting and can be economical. Many sleepers turn up—stamps that can be bought at less than their actual value. To be a good auction buyer, the philatelist must know stamps and their prices pretty well, and know the ropes of auctions. An obvious drawback of auctions is that purchases are not returnable. A dealer will take back a stamp that proves not to be a collector's liking, but an auctioneer will not. Also, auctioneers require immediate payment while a dealer may extend credit.

Stamps sold at auction come from private collections and the stocks of dealers; not necessarily defunct dealers, but those who want to get shelf space. Because they were brought together from a variety of sources, the nature and condition will vary. In catalog descriptions the full book value will be given for each stamp, but of course defective stamps will sell for much less than these figures. A bidder must calculate how much less. Other lots which can be difficult for the bidder to evaluate are those containing more than one stamp. Sometimes a superb specimen will be lotted along with a defective one. Then there are bulk lots which contain odds and ends from collections and such. It is usual in auctioning a collection for the better stamps to be removed and sold separately. The remainder is then offered in a single lot, which may consist of thousands or even tens of thousands of stamps. By all means examine lots before bidding. A period of inspection is always allowed before each sale, usually for several days. There may or may not be an inspection on sale day. If the bidder is not able to make a personal examination but must bid on strength of the catalog description, he should scale his bids for bulk lots much lower than for single stamp lots. He might bid $50 on a single stamp lot with a catalog value of $100, if the condition is listed as top notch, but to bid one-half catalog value on a bulk lot would not be very wise. These lots are not scrutinized very carefully by the auctioneers and some stamps are bound to be disappointing. There may be some heavily canceled, creased, torn, etc. Also, there will very likely be duplication. A bid of one-fifth the catalog value on a bulk lot is considered high. Often a one-tenth bid is successful.

The mechanics of stamp auctions may strike the beginner as complicated. They are run no differently than other auctions. All material to be sold is lotted by the auctioneer; that is, broken down into lots or units and bidding is by lot. Everything in the lot must be bid on, even if just one of the stamps is desired. The motive of bulk lotting is to save time and give each lot a fair sales value.

Before the sale a catalog is published listing all the lots, describing the contents and sometimes picturing the better items. Catalogs are in the mail about 30 days before the sale date. If a bid is to be mailed, it must be sent early. Bids that arrive after the sale are disqualified, even if they would have been successful.

When the bid is received it is entered into a bidbook, along with the bidder's name and address. On sale day each lot opens on the floor at one level above the second highest mail bid. Say the two highest mail bids are $30 and $20. The floor bidding would begin at $25. If the two highest bids are $100 and $500, the opening bid would probably be $150. The larger the amounts involved, the bigger will be the advances. The auctioneer will not accept an advance of $5 on a $500 lot; but on low value lots even dollar advances are sometimes made. Then it becomes a contest of floor versus book. The auctioneer acts as an agent, bidding for the absentee until his limit is reached. If the floor tops him, he has lost. If the floor does not get as high as his bid, he wins the lot at one advance over the highest floor bid.

When a collector buys stamps by mail from a dealer, he should choose one who belongs to the American Stamp Dealers' Association or A.S.D.A. The emblem is carried in their ads.

SELLING YOUR STAMPS

Almost every collector becomes a stamp seller sooner or later. Duplicates are inevitably accumulated, no matter how careful one may be in avoiding them. Then there are the G and VG stamps that have been replaced with F and VF specimens, and have become duplicates by intent. In addition to duplicates, a more advanced collector is likely to have stamps that are not duplicates but for which he has no further use. These will be odds and ends, sometimes quite valuable ones, that once suited the nature of his collection but are now out of place. Collectors' tastes change. The result is a stockpile of stamps that can be converted back to cash.

The alternative to selling the stamps you no longer need or want is trading them with a collector who does want them, and taking his unwanted stamps in return. All stamp clubs hold trading sessions. Larger national stamp societies operate trade-by-mail services for their members. The APS (American Philatelic Society) keeps $8,000,000 worth of stamps constantly circulating in its trading books or "circuit" books. Trading can be an excellent way of disposing of surplus stamps. In most cases it takes a bit longer than selling. Another potential drawback, especially if you are not a club member, is finding the right person with the right stamps.

The nature and value of the material involved may help in deciding whether to sell outright or trade. Also, there are your own personal considerations. If you're not going to continue in the stamp hobby, or need cash for some purpose other than stamp buying, trading is hardly suitable. Likewise, if you have developed an interest in some very exotic group of stamps or other philatelic items it may be impossible to find someone to trade with.

Once you have decided to sell, if indeed you do make that decision, the matter revolves upon how. To a stamp shop? To another collector? Through an auction house? Possibly by running your own advertisements and issuing price lists, if you have enough stamps and spare time to make this worthwhile?

While some individuals have an absolute horror at the prospect of selling anything, stamp collectors tend to enjoy selling. It is difficult to say why. Some enjoy it so much they keep right on selling stamps, as a business, long after their original objective is achieved. Nearly all professional stamp dealers were collectors before entering the trade.

Selling your stamps outright to a dealer, especially a local dealer whom you can personally visit, is not necessarily the most financially rewarding but it is quick and very problem-free. Of course it helps if the dealer knows you and it's even better if he knows some of your stamps. Dealers have no objection to repurchasing stamps they've sold to you. You will find that the dealers encourage their customers to sell to them just as much as they encourage them to buy. The dealers are really anxious to get your stamps if you have good salable material from popular countries. In fact most dealers would prefer buying from the public rather than any other source.

The collector selling stamps to a dealer has to be reasonable in his expectations. A dealer may not be able to use all the stamps you have. It is simply not smart business for a dealer to invest money in something he may not be able to sell. So, if you have esoteric or highly specialized items for sale, it might be necessary to find a specialist who deals in those particular areas rather than selling to a neighborhood stamp shop.

The local stamp shop will almost certainly want to buy anything you can offer in the way of medium to better grade United States stamps of all kinds, including the so-called "back of the book" items. He may not want plate blocks or full sheets of commemoratives issued within the past 20 years. Most dealers are well supplied with material of this nature and have opportunities to buy more of it every day. The same is true of first day covers, with a few exceptions, issued from the 1960s to the present. The dealers either have these items abundantly or can get them from a wholesaler at rock-bottom prices. They would rather buy stamps that are a bit harder to get from the wholesalers, or for which the wholesalers charge higher prices. On the whole you will meet with a favorable reception when offering U.S. stamps to a local dealer. With foreign stamps it becomes another matter: what do you have and how flexible are you in price? Nearly all the stamp shops in this country do stock foreign stamps to one extent or another. They do not, as a rule, attempt to carry comprehensive or specialized stocks of them. In the average shop you will discover that the selection of general foreign consists of a combination of modern mint sets, topicals, souvenir sheets, packets, which come from the wholesaler, and a small sprinkling of older material, usually pre-1900. The price range of this older material will be $5 to $50. Non-specialist collectors of foreign stamps buy this type of item and that is essentially who the local shop caters to. When a local dealer buys rare foreign stamps or a large foreign collection, it is not for himself. He buys with the intent of passing them along to another dealer who has the right customers lined up. He acts only as a middleman or go-between. Therefore the price you receive for better grade foreign stamps tends to be lower than for better grade U.S., which the dealer buys for his own use.

What is a fair price to get for your stamps? This is always difficult to say, as many variable factors are involved. Consider their condition. Think in terms of what the dealer could reasonably hope to charge for them at retail and stand a good chance of selling them. Some of your stamps may have to be discounted because of no gum, poor centering, bent perfs, hinge remnants, repairs, or other problems. But even if your stamps are primarily F or VF, a dealer cannot pay book values for them. If you check his selling prices on his specimens of those same stamps, you can usually count on receiving from 40 to 50 percent of those prices. Considering the discount made from book values by the dealer in pricing his stock, your payment may work out to about 25 percent of book values. For rare United States stamps in top condition you can do better than 25 percent, but on most stamps sold to a dealer this is considered a fair offer. Keep in mind that the difference between a dealer's buying and selling prices is not just "profit margin." Most of the markup goes toward operating costs, for without this markup, there would be no stamp dealers.

THE AMERICAN PHILATELIC SOCIETY

The American Philatelic Society is an internationally recognized association of stamp experts and enthusiasts that offers a number of services and educational opportunities for stamp collectors. The APS is the national representative to the Federation Internationale de Philatelie and is affiliated with more than 700 local stamp clubs (APS Chapters) and almost 200 "specialty groups" (APS Affiliates).

The services that are available with an APS membership include a subscription to *The American Philatelist*, one of the premier stamp magazines in the world, as well as numerous other brochures and publications that are available at a discount to members. The APS Sales Division provides an opportunity for collectors to buy or sell stamps through the mail. Members may request "circuits" of stamps or covers in more than 150 categories of countries and topics. Selections of circuit books are mailed at intervals, and members can choose any items they wish to purchase, and then mail the books on to the next APS member on the circuit. The items are priced by the submitting members, and most range from under $1.00 to $5.00.

The APS also provides an insurance program for members living in the United States and Canada. The insurance policy does not require a detailed inventory, only a general description of a collection and a value estimate, and may be applied for along with a membership application.

The Society also runs the American Philatelic Research Library, with a wide range of resource material including thousands of books, journals, auction catalogs, and other material that are loaned or photocopied and available to members by mail for a nominal fee. The APRL also publishes the *Philatelic Literature Review*, a quarterly journal covering literature of interest to collectors. The magazine is available by separate subscription.

The APS offers, in association with Pennsylvania State University, correspondence courses ranging from "Beginning Collecting" to "Printing Techniques" and week-long summer seminars on philately that feature hands-on instruction by prominent experts. In addition, the APS Education Department produces many brochures and other materials and answers inquiries from beginner and intermediate collectors on various "how-to" aspects of the hobby.

Other APS services include identification of members' stamps by the APS Expert Committee, estate advice, a translation service for international trading, and an annual convention-exhibition stamp show.

THE AMERICAN PHILATELIST

The Society's monthly magazine, which is included in the membership fee, features a monthly column for beginning stamp collectors; regular columns on stamp clubs, exhibitions, topical collecting, and more; articles by experienced philatelists; how-to columns on using the Society's Sales Division; commentary on important issues to collectors from the state of the stamp market to insights on stamp condition and auctions; and detailed listings of all new stamps and postal stationery issued by the U.S. Postal Service.

MEMBERSHIP INFORMATION

The APS offers a variety of memberships including special rates for spouses and children, foreign members, and lifetime memberships. The Society operates on a calendar year, and membership fees are pro-rated on a quarterly basis and include a $3.00 admission fee. The 1991 schedule of membership fees is listed below.

Application received by APS National Headquarters	Admission Fee	Membership Fee	Total		
			U.S.	Canada	Foreign
October, November, December	$3.00	$18.00	$21.00	$24.00	$27.00
January, February, March	3.00	13.50	16.50	18.75	21.00
April, May, June	3.00	9.00	12.00	13.50	15.00
July, August, September	3.00	4.50	7.50	8.25	9.00

For more information, call or write the American Philatelic Society at:

APS
P.O. Box 8000, Dept. HC
State College, PA 16803
(814) 237-3803

IMPORTANT NOTICE: On stamps issued before 1890, prices of unused specimens are for ones without original gum. Specimens with original gum can be expected to command a premium of as much as 50 percent. Beware of regummed specimens.

Scott No.			Fine Unused Each	Ave. Unused Each	Fine Used Each	Ave. Used Each
GENERAL ISSUES						
1847. FIRST ISSUE						
☐1	5¢	Red Brown	—	3000.00	510.00	360.00
☐2	10¢	Black	—	10,000.00	1500.00	900.00
1875. REPRODUCTIONS OF 1847 ISSUE						
☐3	5¢	Red Brown	1000.00	700.00	—	—
☐4	10¢	Black	1200.00	850.00	—	—
1851–1856. REGULAR ISSUE—IMPERFORATE						
☐5A	1¢	Blue (1b)	—	—	3800.00	2100.00
☐6	1¢	Blue (1a)	—	—	5600.00	3200.00
☐7	1¢	Blue (II)	475.00	300.00	90.00	60.00
☐8	1¢	Blue (III)	—	—	1300.00	800.00
☐8A	1¢	Blue (IIIa)	—	1250.00	580.00	350.00
☐9	1¢	Blue (IV)	500.00	200.00	80.00	50.00
☐10	3¢	Orange Brown (I)	—	650.00	42.00	35.00
☐11	3¢	Dull Red (I)	110.00	65.00	7.00	5.00
☐12	5¢	Red Brown (I)	—	—	1000.00	650.00
☐13	10¢	Green (I)	—	—	625.00	365.00
☐14	10¢	Green (II)	—	1000.00	250.00	170.00
☐15	10¢	Green (III)	—	1100.00	250.00	170.00
☐16	10¢	Green (IV)	—	—	1200.00	750.00
☐17	12¢	Black	—	1300.00	250.00	150.00
1857–1861. SAME DESIGNS AS 1851–1856 ISSUE—PERF. 15						
☐18	1¢	Blue (I)	700.00	400.00	350.00	210.00
☐19	1¢	Blue (Ia)	—	—	2200.00	1500.00
☐20	1¢	Blue (II)	400.00	250.00	130.00	80.00
☐21	1¢	Blue (III)	—	2200.00	1150.00	670.00
☐22	1¢	Blue (IIIa)	700.00	380.00	230.00	140.00
☐23	1¢	Blue (IV)	—	1500.00	300.00	175.00
☐24	1¢	Blue (V)	125.00	65.00	28.00	15.00
☐25	3¢	Rose (I)	—	410.00	30.00	18.00
☐26	3¢	Dull Red (II)	45.00	30.00	4.00	2.10
☐26A	3¢	Dull Red (IIa)	105.00	75.00	24.00	14.00
☐27	5¢	Brick Red (I)	—	4300.00	800.00	475.00
☐28	5¢	Red Brown (I)	—	800.00	260.00	150.00
☐28A	5¢	Indian Red (I)	—	—	1750.00	1100.00
☐29	5¢	Brown (I)	740.00	400.00	200.00	115.00
☐30	5¢	Orange Brown (II)	715.00	400.00	875.00	480.00
☐30A	5¢	Brown (II)	400.00	220.00	190.00	110.00
☐31	10¢	Green (I)	—	3000.00	500.00	280.00
☐32	10¢	Green (II)	2000.00	1200.00	170.00	110.00

Scott No.			Fine Unused Each	Ave. Unused Each	Fine Used Each	Ave. Used Each
☐33	10¢	Green (III)	2000.00	1200.00	170.00	110.00
☐34	10¢	Green (IV)	—	1500.00	825.00	
☐35	10¢	Green (IV)	180.00	95.00	52.00	36.00
☐36	12¢	Black (I)	310.00	180.00	75.00	50.00
☐36b	12¢	Black (II)	300.00	160.00	100.00	62.00
☐37	24¢	Gray Lilac	600.00	300.00	200.00	140.00
☐38	30¢	Orange	675.00	410.00	270.00	150.00
☐39	90¢	Blue	1100.00	700.00	—	—

1875. REPRINTS OF 1857–1861 ISSUE

☐40	1¢	Bright Blue	600.00	400.00	—	—
☐41	3¢	Scarlet	3000.00	1900.00	—	—
☐42	5¢	Orange Brown	1000.00	675.00	—	—
☐43	10¢	Blue Green	2300.00	1500.00	—	—
☐44	12¢	Greenish Black	2800.00	1800.00	—	—
☐45	24¢	Blackish Violet	3000.00	1900.00	—	—
☐46	30¢	Yellow Orange	3000.00	1900.00	—	—
☐47	90¢	Deep Blue	4000.00	3000.00	—	—

1861. FIRST DESIGNS—PERF. 12

☐56	3¢	Brown Red	700.00	400.00	—	—
☐62B	10¢	Dark Green	—	—	500.00	280.00

1861–1862. SECOND DESIGNS

☐63	1¢	Blue	120.00	75.00	18.00	12.00
☐63b	1¢	Dark Blue	150.00	88.00	27.00	21.00
☐64	3¢	Pink	—	1900.00	300.00	180.00
☐64b	3¢	Rose Pink	270.00	165.00	46.00	26.00
☐65	3¢	Rose	62.00	36.00	1.80	1.00
☐66	3¢	Lake	—	1000.00	—	—
☐67	5¢	Buff	—	2600.00	380.00	200.00
☐68	10¢	Yellow Green	230.00	140.00	28.00	17.00
☐69	12¢	Black	475.00	290.00	51.00	30.00
☐70	24¢	Red Lilac	600.00	350.00	80.00	42.00
☐70b	24¢	Steel Blue	—	—	280.00	140.00
☐70c	24¢	Violet	—	2100.00	500.00	275.00
☐71	30¢	Orange	465.00	270.00	62.00	38.00
☐72	90¢	Blue	1200.00	650.00	230.00	140.00

1861–1866. NEW VALUES OR NEW COLORS

☐73	2¢	Black	150.00	70.00	23.50	12.00
☐74	3¢	Scarlet	3900.00	2600.00	1800.00	1100.00
☐75	5¢	Red Brown	1250.00	700.00	215.00	125.00
☐76	5¢	Brown	340.00	190.00	50.00	32.00
☐77	15¢	Black	500.00	280.00	60.00	36.00
☐78	24¢	Lilac	265.00	150.00	50.00	30.00

Scott No.		Fine Unused Each	Ave. Unused Each	Fine Used Each	Ave. Used Each
1867. SAME DESIGNS AS 1861–1866 ISSUE					
GRILL WITH POINTS UP					
A. GRILL COVERING ENTIRE STAMP					
□79	3¢ Rose	1800.00	950.00	400.00	200.00
C. GRILL ABOUT 13 x 16 MM.					
□83	3¢ Rose	1800.00	1100.00	370.00	210.00
GRILL WITH POINTS DOWN					
D. GRILL ABOUT 12 x 14 MM.					
□84	2¢ Black	2900.00	2000.00	1000.00	600.00
□85	3¢ Rose	1600.00	900.00	400.00	230.00
Z. GRILL ABOUT 11 x 14 MM.					
□85B	2¢ Black	1500.00	800.00	350.00	190.00
□85C	3¢ Rose	2500.00	2000.00	900.00	500.00
□85E	12¢ Black	2000.00	1200.00	520.00	300.00
E. GRILL ABOUT 11 x 13 MM.					
□86	1¢ Blue	850.00	475.00	240.00	145.00
□87	2¢ Black	360.00	200.00	65.00	36.00
□88	3¢ Rose	280.00	160.00	10.00	6.00
□89	10¢ Green	1400.00	875.00	160.00	96.00
□90	12¢ Black	1700.00	1000.00	180.00	110.00
□91	15¢ Black	3600.00	2000.00	400.00	240.00
F. GRILL ABOUT 9 x 13 MM.					
□92	1¢ Blue	390.00	230.00	95.00	57.00
□93	2¢ Black	140.00	75.00	26.00	16.00
□94	3¢ Red	110.00	58.00	4.00	2.00
□95	5¢ Brown	1100.00	700.00	215.00	120.00
□96	10¢ Yellow Green	700.00	410.00	100.00	58.00
□97	12¢ Black	750.00	400.00	110.00	68.00
□98	15¢ Black	700.00	415.00	120.00	69.00
□99	24¢ Gray Lilac	1500.00	780.00	425.00	250.00
□100	30¢ Orange	2000.00	1100.00	350.00	200.00
□101	90¢ Blue	4100.00	2300.00	850.00	500.00
1875. RE-ISSUE OF 1861–1866 ISSUES					
□102	1¢ Blue	—	370.00	—	500.00
□103	2¢ Black	—	1800.00	—	2600.00
□104	3¢ Brown Red	—	2300.00	—	3100.00
□105	5¢ Light Brown	—	1400.00	—	1800.00
□106	10¢ Green	—	1400.00	—	2400.00
□107	12¢ Black	—	2000.00	—	2800.00
□108	15¢ Black	—	2100.00	—	3100.00
□109	24¢ Deep Violet	—	2600.00	—	3800.00
□110	30¢ Brownish Orange	—	3000.00	—	4300.00
□111	90¢ Blue	—	4000.00	—	11,000.00

Scott No.			Fine Unused Each	Ave. Unused Each	Fine Used Each	Ave. Used Each
1869. PICTORIAL ISSUES						
GRILL ABOUT 9½ x 9½ MM.						
☐112	1¢	Buff	210.00	130.00	60.00	38.00
☐113	2¢	Brown	170.00	100.00	28.00	16.00
☐114	3¢	Ultramarine	150.00	85.00	7.00	4.00
☐115	6¢	Ultramarine	700.00	390.00	90.00	60.00
☐116	10¢	Yellow	750.00	420.00	91.00	52.00
☐117	12¢	Green	780.00	410.00	90.00	52.00
☐118	15¢	Brown & Blue (I)	1000.00	1000.00	280.00	165.00
☐119	15¢	Brown & Blue (II)	825.00	490.00	140.00	82.00
☐120	24¢	Green & Violet	2100.00	1000.00	450.00	280.00
☐121	30¢	Blue & Carmine	2000.00	1100.00	260.00	140.00
☐122	90¢	Carmine & Black	5000.00	3000.00	1100.00	700.00
1875. RE-ISSUE OF 1869 ISSUE, HARD WHITE PAPER—						
WITHOUT GRILL						
☐123	1¢	Buff	310.00	190.00	210.00	120.00
☐124	2¢	Brown	360.00	210.00	300.00	180.00
☐125	3¢	Blue	2800.00	2000.00	1100.00	900.00
☐126	6¢	Blue	—	500.00	—	370.00
☐127	10¢	Yellow	—	810.00	—	800.00
☐128	12¢	Green	—	900.00	—	800.00
☐129	15¢	Brown & Blue (III)	—	900.00	—	400.00
☐130	24¢	Green & Violet	—	700.00	—	360.00
☐131	30¢	Blue & Carmine	—	1000.00	—	700.00
☐132	90¢	Carmine & Black	—	3400.00	—	4200.00
1880. SAME AS ABOVE—SOFT POROUS PAPER						
☐133	1¢	Buff	180.00	115.00	135.00	182.00
1870–1871. PRINTED BY NATIONAL BANK NOTE CO.—GRILLED						
☐134	1¢	Ultramarine	600.00	350.00	52.00	30.00
☐135	2¢	Red Brown	380.00	210.00	32.00	22.00
☐136	3¢	Green	290.00	165.00	10.00	7.00
☐137	6¢	Carmine	1500.00	850.00	250.00	155.00
☐138	7¢	Vermilion	1100.00	550.00	230.00	140.00
☐139	10¢	Brown	1400.00	800.00	380.00	230.00
☐140	12¢	Light Violet	—	—	1600.00	850.00
☐141	15¢	Orange	1800.00	1200.00	660.00	380.00
☐142	24¢	Purple	—	—	—	6000.00
☐143	30¢	Black	—	2400.00	800.00	450.00
☐144	90¢	Carmine	—	3000.00	700.00	400.00
1870–1871. SAME AS ABOVE—WITHOUT GRILL						
☐145	1¢	Ultramarine	160.00	95.00	7.00	4.00
☐146	2¢	Red Brown	78.00	42.00	4.50	3.00
☐147	3¢	Green	120.00	70.00	.70	.40
☐148	6¢	Carmine	240.00	135.00	11.00	6.00
☐149	7¢	Vermilion	315.00	180.00	46.00	27.00
☐150	10¢	Brown	240.00	130.00	11.00	6.50

Scott No.			Fine Unused Each	Ave. Unused Each	Fine Used Each	Ave. Used Each
☐151	12¢	Dull Violet	500.00	280.00	56.00	34.00
☐152	15¢	Bright Orange	490.00	270.00	59.00	34.00
☐153	24¢	Purple	580.00	330.00	73.00	45.00
☐154	30¢	Black	980.00	540.00	90.00	51.00
☐155	90¢	Carmine	1300.00	700.00	168.00	99.00

1873. SAME DESIGNS AS 1870–1871 ISSUE— WITH SECRET MARKS PRINTED BY THE CONTINENTAL BANK NOTE CO. THIN HARD GRAYISH WHITE PAPER

☐156	1¢	Ultramarine	62.00	31.00	1.95	1.50
☐157	2¢	Brown	180.00	90.00	9.00	5.00
☐158	3¢	Green	55.00	28.00	.22	.20
☐159	6¢	Dull Pink	190.00	110.00	9.00	6.00
☐160	7¢	Orange Vermilion	400.00	230.00	52.00	28.00
☐161	10¢	Brown	230.00	130.00	9.10	6.00
☐162	12¢	Black Violet	650.00	360.00	68.00	34.00
☐163	15¢	Yellow Orange	600.00	350.00	58.00	35.00
☐165	30¢	Gray Black	690.00	360.00	58.00	35.00
☐166	90¢	Rose Carmine	1300.00	700.00	180.00	100.00

1875. REGULAR ISSUE

☐178	2¢	Vermilion	175.00	90.00	4.50	3.00
☐179	5¢	Blue	200.00	115.00	9.00	5.00

1879. SAME DESIGNS AS 1870–1875 ISSUES PRINTED BY THE AMERICAN BANK NOTE CO. SOFT POROUS YELLOWISH WHITE PAPER

☐182	1¢	Dark Ultramarine	120.00	68.00	1.40	.90
☐183	2¢	Vermilion	58.00	29.00	1.40	.90
☐184	3¢	Green	46.00	28.00	.25	.20
☐185	5¢	Blue	285.00	120.00	8.00	4.50
☐186	6¢	Pink	450.00	240.00	11.00	7.00
☐187	10¢	Brown (no secret mark)	750.00	390.00	14.00	8.00
☐188	10¢	Brown (secret mark)	500.00	280.00	16.00	9.00
☐188b	10¢	Black Brown	675.00	360.00	70.00	28.00
☐189	15¢	Red Orange	165.00	90.00	16.00	9.00
☐190	30¢	Full Black	475.00	250.00	30.00	17.00
☐191	90¢	Carmine	1000.00	600.00	140.00	85.00

1882. REGULAR ISSUE

☐205	5¢	Yellow Brown	110.00	60.00	4.50	3.00

1881–1882. DESIGNS OF 1873 ISSUE RE-ENGRAVED (N-H ADD 95%)

☐206	1¢	Gray Blue	32.00	18.00	.85	.40
☐207	3¢	Blue Green	38.00	21.00	.28	.19
☐208	6¢	Rose	215.00	115.00	46.00	27.00
☐208a	6¢	Brown Red	200.00	110.00	52.00	31.00

Scott No.			Fine Unused Each	Ave. Unused Each	Fine Used Each	Ave. Used Each
☐209	10¢	Brown	70.00	42.00	2.50	1.50
☐209b	10¢	Black Brown	100.00	55.00	8.00	5.50

1883. REGULAR ISSUE

☐210	2¢	Red Brown	28.00	16.00	.22	.18
☐211	4¢	Blue Green	135.00	75.00	7.50	4.00

1887. REGULAR ISSUE

☐212	1¢	Ultramarine	52.00	30.00	.80	.50
☐213	2¢	Green	21.00	11.00	.16	.14
☐214	3¢	Vermilion	40.00	25.00	33.00	21.00

1888. SAME DESIGNS AS 1870–1883 ISSUES

☐215	4¢	Carmine	140.00	70.00	11.00	6.00
☐216	5¢	Indigo	135.00	75.00	7.00	4.00
☐217	30¢	Orange Brown	290.00	185.00	75.00	42.00
☐218	90¢	Purple	600.00	375.00	125.00	75.00

IMPORTANT NOTICE: From this point onward, values of unused stamps and blocks are for specimens with original gum. Prices given for **blocks** are for blocks of 4, **without** plate number.

Scott No.			Fine Unused Block	Ave. Unused Block	Fine Unused Each	Ave. Unused Each	Fine Used Each	Ave. Used Each
1890–1893. SMALL DESIGN (N-H ADD 95%)								
☐219	1¢	Dull Blue	100.00	80.00	15.00	11.00	.16	.15
☐219D	2¢	Lake	800.00	600.00	125.00	80.00	.48	.28
☐220	2¢	Carmine	90.00	70.00	16.00	9.00	.16	.14
☐220a	2¢	Carmine (Cap on left 2)	150.00	125.00	40.00	30.00	1.10	.85
☐220c	2¢	Carmine (Cap both 2's)	160.00	130.00	110.00	66.00	7.00	5.00
☐221	3¢	Purple	250.00	200.00	50.00	30.00	4.50	3.00
☐222	4¢	Dark Brown	300.00	250.00	48.00	28.00	1.80	1.10
☐223	5¢	Chocolate	280.00	225.00	48.00	29.00	1.80	1.10
☐224	6¢	Brown Red	285.00	250.00	50.00	35.00	14.00	9.00
☐225	8¢	Lilac	275.00	240.00	38.00	25.00	8.00	6.00
☐226	10¢	Green	450.00	400.00	87.00	60.00	2.00	1.10
☐227	15¢	Indigo	700.00	600.00	125.00	85.00	15.00	10.00
☐228	30¢	Black	1000.00	900.00	190.00	110.00	18.00	12.00
☐229	90¢	Orange	1800.00	1600.00	300.00	210.00	90.00	52.00
1893. COLUMBIAN ISSUE (N-H ADD 95%)								
☐230	1¢	Blue	100.00	85.00	20.00	14.00	.40	.30
☐231	2¢	Violet	100.00	85.00	20.00	13.00	.19	.14
☐231c	2¢	"Broken Hat"	250.00	215.00	56.00	40.00	.46	.30
☐232	3¢	Green	275.00	240.00	41.00	28.00	14.00	10.00
☐233	4¢	Ultramarine	400.00	350.00	58.00	40.00	6.00	4.00
☐234	5¢	Chocolate	480.00	350.00	66.00	45.00	6.00	5.00
☐235	6¢	Purple	480.00	350.00	59.00	45.00	18.00	13.00
☐236	8¢	Magenta	360.00	300.00	55.00	36.00	8.00	5.00
☐237	10¢	Black Brown	600.00	450.00	100.00	80.00	7.00	5.00
☐238	15¢	Dark Green	1600.00	900.00	175.00	135.00	60.00	45.00

Scott No.			Fine Unused Block	Ave. Unused Block	Fine Unused Each	Ave. Unused Each	Fine Used Each	Ave. Used Each
☐239	30¢	Orange Brown	2900.00	2000.00	250.00	200.00	82.00	60.00
☐240	50¢	Slate Blue	2900.00	2100.00	375.00	275.00	125.00	85.00
☐241	$1	Salmon	—	—	1100.00	800.00	500.00	375.00
☐242	$2	Brown Red	—	—	1200.00	850.00	450.00	300.00
☐243	$3	Yellow Green	—	—	2100.00	1600.00	900.00	700.00
☐244	$4	Crimson Lake	—	—	2800.00	2000.00	1200.00	900.00
☐245	$5	Black	—	—	4800.00	3400.00	1500.00	1000.00

1894. UNWATERMARKED (N-H ADD 95%)

☐246	1¢	Ultramarine	90.00	80.00	20.00	14.00	2.90	2.00
☐247	1¢	Blue	200.00	175.00	46.00	32.00	1.80	1.10
☐248	2¢	Pink, Type I	100.00	75.00	16.00	10.00	2.00	1.15
☐249	2¢	Carmine Lake, Type I.	550.00	450.00	95.00	70.00	1.35	.85
☐250	2¢	Carmine, Type I	190.00	170.00	18.00	11.00	.26	.16
☐251	2¢	Carmine, Type II	1400.00	1125.00	150.00	95.00	2.80	1.50
☐252	2¢	Carmine, Type III	400.00	300.00	82.00	60.00	3.00	1.75
☐253	3¢	Purple	400.00	300.00	64.00	46.00	6.50	4.00
☐254	4¢	Dark Brown	500.00	400.00	76.00	42.00	3.00	1.80
☐255	5¢	Chocolate	450.00	380.00	64.00	40.00	4.00	2.50
☐256	6¢	Dull Brown	850.00	600.00	120.00	80.00	16.00	10.00
☐257	8¢	Violet Brown	875.00	600.00	90.00	62.00	11.00	7.00
☐258	10¢	Dark Green	1400.00	1000.00	150.00	100.00	5.00	4.00
☐259	15¢	Dark Blue	1800.00	1000.00	210.00	150.00	37.00	26.00
☐260	50¢	Orange	2000.00	1200.00	280.00	170.00	70.00	50.00
☐261	$1	Black (I)	5000.00	4000.00	600.00	400.00	230.00	150.00
☐261A	$1	Black (II)		—	1400.00	800.00	415.00	300.00
☐262	$2	Blue	—	—	1800.00	1200.00	600.00	425.00
☐263	$5	Dark Green	—	—	2600.00	1600.00	1000.00	600.00

1895. DOUBLE LINE WATERMARKED "U.S.P.S." PERF. 12 (N-H ADD 95%)

☐264	1¢	Blue	46.00	30.00	5.00	3.00	.18	16
☐265	2¢	Carmine, Type I	220.00	160.00	18.00	13.00	.74	.50
☐266	2¢	Carmine, Type II	275.00	190.00	17.00	13.00	2.75	1.65
☐267	2¢	Carmine, Type III	50.00	40.00	4.00	3.00	.16	.15
☐268	3¢	Purple	290.00	175.00	29.00	20.00	1.20	.75
☐269	4¢	Dark Brown	300.00	250.00	29.00	20.00	1.35	.80
☐270	5¢	Chocolate	300.00	250.00	30.00	19.00	1.90	1.20
☐271	6¢	Dull Brown	380.00	300.00	50.00	40.00	3.90	2.25
☐272	8¢	Violet Brown	215.00	150.00	40.00	23.00	1.15	.65
☐273	10¢	Dark Green	360.00	250.00	50.00	38.00	1.20	.80
☐274	15¢	Dark Blue	800.00	600.00	130.00	80.00	9.00	6.00
☐275	50¢	Dull Orange	1200.00	1000.00	200.00	140.00	19.00	12.00
☐276	$1	Black (I)	2400.00	1800.00	500.00	300.00	62.00	40.00
☐276A	$1	Black (II)	—	—	1100.00	750.00	115.00	75.00
☐277	$2	Blue	—	—	800.00	500.00	260.00	160.00
☐278	$5	Dark Green	—	—	1600.00	1200.00	400.00	250.00

Scott No.		Fine Unused Block	Ave. Unused Block	Fine Unused Each	Ave. Unused Each	Fine Used Each	Ave. Used Each
1898. REGULAR ISSUE PERF. (N-H ADD 95%)							
☐279	1¢ Deep Green	85.00	50.00	8.50	5.00	.18	.14
☐279B	2¢ Red	85.00	50.00	9.00	5.00	.18	.14
☐279C	2¢ Rose Carmine	690.00	625.00	140.00	82.00	35.00	21.00
☐279D	2¢ Orange Red	80.00	50.00	10.00	8.00	.22	.16
☐280	4¢ Rose Brown	210.00	135.00	26.00	19.00	1.00	.70
☐281	5¢ Dark Blue	210.00	165.00	28.00	19.00	1.00	.62
☐282	6¢ Lake	375.00	250.00	39.00	28.00	2.50	1.40
☐282a	6¢ Purplish Lake	500.00	400.00	52.00	30.00	3.00	1.50
☐282C	10¢ Brown (I)	900.00	675.00	120.00	79.00	2.50	1.50
☐283	10¢ Orange Brown (III)	750.00	500.00	80.00	48.00	2.30	1.25
☐284	15¢ Olive Green	875.00	600.00	115.00	70.00	7.50	4.00
1898. TRANS-MISSISSIPPI EXPOSITION ISSUE (N-H ADD 90%)							
☐285	1¢ Yellow Green	250.00	150.00	24.00	18.00	6.00	4.00
☐286	2¢ Copper Red	250.00	150.00	21.00	16.00	1.80	1.00
☐287	4¢ Orange	910.00	700.00	120.00	90.00	24.00	15.00
☐288	5¢ Dull Blue	910.00	700.00	110.00	80.00	20.00	14.00
☐289	8¢ Violet Brown	1050.00	800.00	150.00	100.00	37.00	24.00
☐290	10¢ Gray Violet	1200.00	1050.00	165.00	115.00	20.00	14.00
☐291	50¢ Sage Green	—	—	575.00	410.00	160.00	100.00
☐292	$1 Black	—	—	1200.00	1000.00	475.00	325.00
☐293	$2 Orange Brown	—	—	2000.00	1600.00	750.00	500.00
1901. PAN-AMERICAN ISSUE (N-H ADD 75%)							
☐294	1¢ Green & Black	220.00	200.00	17.00	9.00	4.00	2.75
☐295	2¢ Carmine & Black	220.00	200.00	15.00	9.00	1.25	.70
☐296	4¢ Chocolate & Black	2000.00	1500.00	82.00	60.00	16.00	12.00
☐297	5¢ Ultramarine & Black	2300.00	1800.00	90.00	60.00	16.00	11.00
☐298	8¢ Brown Violet Black	3000.00	2500.00	116.00	80.00	60.00	50.00
☐299	10¢ Yellow Brown Black	5000.00	4000.00	175.00	110.00	27.00	19.00
1902–1903. PERF. 12 (N-H ADD 80%)							
☐300	1¢ Blue Green	140.00	100.00	8.00	6.00	.16	.14
☐301	2¢ Carmine	140.00	100.00	10.00	7.00	.16	.14
☐302	3¢ Violet	480.00	330.00	40.00	30.00	3.60	2.00
☐303	4¢ Brown	480.00	330.00	40.00	30.00	1.30	.75
☐304	5¢ Blue	650.00	500.00	50.00	40.00	1.10	.70
☐305	6¢ Claret	650.00	500.00	51.00	41.00	2.80	1.50
☐306	8¢ Violet Black	450.00	375.00	32.00	21.00	2.20	1.50
☐307	10¢ Red Brown	750.00	650.00	56.00	45.00	1.70	1.00
☐308	13¢ Purple Black	400.00	300.00	32.00	28.00	9.00	6.00
☐309	15¢ Olive Green	1200.00	800.00	100.00	70.00	7.00	5.00
☐310	50¢ Orange	3900.00	3000.00	400.00	300.00	26.00	15.00
☐311	$1 Black	5400.00	4400.00	600.00	400.00	50.00	36.00
☐312	$2 Dark Blue	—	—	800.00	500.00	170.00	115.00
☐313	$5 Dark Green	—	—	1700.00	1100.00	550.00	400.00

Scott No.			Fine Unused Block	Ave. Unused Block	Fine Unused Each	Ave. Unused Each	Fine Used Each	Ave. Used Each
1906–1908. IMPERFORATED (N-H ADD 70%)								
☐314	1¢	Blue Green	180.00	160.00	24.00	17.00	14.00	11.00
☐315	5¢	Blue	4200.00	3600.00	400.00	300.00	200.00	110.00
1903. PERF. 12 (N-H ADD 50%)								
☐319	2¢	Carmine	80.00	60.00	6.00	4.50	.18	.14
☐319a	2¢	Lake	115.00	90.00	6.00	4.50	.27	.20
1906. IMPERFORATED (N-H ADD 70%)								
☐320	2¢	Carmine	225.00	180.00	21.00	12.00	17.00	10.00
☐320a	2¢	Lake	350.00	300.00	64.00	45.00	39.00	30.00
1904. LOUISIANA PURCHASE ISSUE PERF. 12 (N-H ADD 75%)								
☐323	1¢	Green	185.00	160.00	23.00	15.00	5.00	3.00
☐324	2¢	Carmine	185.00	160.00	21.00	14.00	1.75	.90
☐325	3¢	Violet	800.00	600.00	65.00	45.00	30.00	21.00
☐326	5¢	Dark Blue	900.00	700.00	78.00	60.00	20.00	16.00
☐327	10¢	Red Brown	1600.00	1300.00	140.00	100.00	31.00	20.00
1907. JAMESTOWN EXPOSITION ISSUE (N-H ADD 75%)								
☐328	1¢	Green	240.00	200.00	19.00	12.00	4.00	3.00
☐329	2¢	Carmine	340.00	300.00	22.00	14.00	6.00	4.00
☐330	5¢	Blue	1900.00	1600.00	96.00	65.00	26.00	15.00
1908–1909. DOUBLE LINE WATERMARKED "U.S.P.S." PERF. 12 (N-H ADD 50%)								
☐331	1¢	Green	65.00	45.00	6.00	4.00	.18	.14
☐332	2¢	Carmine	61.00	47.00	6.00	4.50	.18	.14
☐333	3¢	Violet	300.00	260.00	28.00	18.00	3.10	1.90
☐334	4¢	Orange Brown	310.00	260.00	30.00	20.00	1.10	.70
☐335	5¢	Blue	510.00	420.00	39.00	26.00	2.30	1.50
☐336	6¢	Red Orange	425.00	310.00	50.00	30.00	4.75	3.00
☐337	8¢	Olive Green	350.00	225.00	34.00	26.00	3.00	1.90
☐338	10¢	Yellow	600.00	450.00	50.00	35.00	1.50	.90
☐339	13¢	Blue Green	400.00	300.00	34.00	25.00	22.00	12.00
☐340	15¢	Pale Ultramarine	425.00	310.00	42.00	31.00	6.00	3.50
☐341	50¢	Violet	1700.00	1200.00	250.00	145.00	17.00	10.00
☐342	$1	Violet Black	2500.00	1800.00	380.00	240.00	72.00	46.00
IMPERFORATE (N-H ADD 65%)								
☐343	1¢	Green	50.00	42.00	6.00	4.50	4.00	3.00
☐344	2¢	Carmine	95.00	80.00	7.50	6.00	4.50	3.00
☐345	3¢	Deep Violet	190.00	160.00	18.00	11.00	14.00	9.00
☐346	4¢	Orange Brown	300.00	250.00	21.00	17.00	18.00	12.00
☐347	5¢	Blue	450.00	300.00	40.00	29.00	29.00	20.00

Scott No.			Fine Unused Line Pair	Ave. Unused Line Pair	Fine Unused Each	Ave. Unused Each	Fine Used Each	Ave. Used Each
1908–1910. COIL STAMPS								
PERF. 12 HORIZONTALLY (N-H ADD 70%)								
☐348	1¢	Green	150.00	110.00	22.00	14.50	12.00	7.50
☐349	2¢	Carmine	240.00	160.00	36.00	21.00	8.00	4.50
☐350	4¢	Orange Brown	700.00	410.00	85.00	50.00	68.00	40.00
☐351	5¢	Blue	710.00	410.00	100.00	60.00	84.00	51.00
PERF. 12 VERTICALLY (N-H ADD 70%)								
☐352	1¢	Green	275.00	200.00	45.00	30.00	26.00	18.00
☐353	¢	Carmine	265.00	180.00	42.00	24.00	7.50	4.00
☐354	4¢	Orange Brown	675.00	500.00	95.00	65.00	49.00	30.00
☐355	5¢	Blue	750.00	600.00	100.00	75.00	70.00	42.00
☐356	10¢	Yellow	—	—	1300.00	700.00	600.00	375.00

Scott No.			Fine Unused Block	Ave. Unused Block	Fine Unused Each	Ave. Unused Each	Fine Used Each	Ave. Used Each
1909. BLUISH GRAY PAPER								
PERF. 12 (N-H ADD 70%)								
☐357	1¢	Green	700.00	525.00	90.00	65.00	80.00	55.00
☐358	2¢	Carmine	700.00	500.00	80.00	55.00	60.00	40.00
☐359	3¢	Violet	—	—	1400.00	1000.00	—	—
☐360	4¢	Orange Brown	—	—	15,000.00	10,000.00	—	—
☐361	5¢	Blue	—	—	3000.00	2100.00	—	—
☐362	6¢	Orange	—	—	1100.00	700.00	—	—
☐363	8¢	Olive Green	—	—	15,000.00	10,000.00	—	—
☐364	10¢	Yellow	—	—	1100.00	700.00	—	—
☐365	13¢	Blue Green	—	—	1900.00	1300.00	—	—
☐366	15¢	Pale Ultramarine	—	—	900.00	700.00	—	—
1909. LINCOLN MEMORIAL ISSUE (N-H ADD 75%)								
☐367	2¢	Carmine	120.00	80.00	7.00	4.00	2.10	1.50
☐368	2¢	Carmine, Impf.	200.00	150.00	21.00	16.00	17.00	10.00
☐369	2¢	Carmine (On B.G. Paper)	1200.00	1000.00	200.00	120.00	180.00	125.00
1909. ALASKA-YUKON ISSUE (N-H ADD 70%)								
☐370	2¢	Carmine	200.00	150.00	9.00	6.00	2.00	—
☐371	2¢	Carmine, Impf.	225.00	175.00	29.00	20.00	19.00	13.00
1909. HUDSON-FULTON ISSUE (N-H ADD 70%)								
☐372	2¢	Carmine	240.00	180.00	12.00	9.00	4.50	2.50
☐373	2¢	Carmine, Impf.	260.00	200.00	32.00	24.00	22.00	18.00
1910–1911. SINGLE LINE WATERMARKED "U.S.P.S."								
PERF. 12 (N-H ADD 75%)								
☐374	1¢	Green	68.00	50.00	6.00	4.00	.18	.14
☐375	2¢	Carmine	72.00	52.00	7.00	5.00	.18	.14
☐376	3¢	Deep Violet	130.00	100.00	16.00	11.00	1.75	1.10
☐377	4¢	Brown	165.00	115.00	23.00	16.00	.50	.30

Scott No.			Fine Unused Block	Ave. Unused Block	Fine Unused Each	Ave. Unused Each	Fine Used Each	Ave. Used Each
☐378	5¢	Blue	200.00	140.00	25.00	17.00	.50	.28
☐379	6¢	Red Orange	300.00	165.00	29.00	21.00	.85	.50
☐380	8¢	Olive Green	550.00	400.00	92.00	65.00	13.00	8.00
☐381	10¢	Yellow	425.00	360.00	86.00	62.00	4.20	2.50
☐382	15¢	Ultramarine	1200.00	900.00	210.00	150.00	13.50	8.50

IMPERFORATE (N-H ADD 70%)

Scott No.			Fine Unused Block	Ave. Unused Block	Fine Unused Each	Ave. Unused Each	Fine Used Each	Ave. Used Each
☐383	1¢	Green	50.00	40.00	2.60	2.00	2.00	1.30
☐384	2¢	Carmine	120.00	93.00	5.00	2.80	1.60	.80

Scott No.			Fine Unused Line Pair	Ave. Unused Line Pair	Fine Unused Each	Ave. Unused Each	Fine Used Each	Ave. Used Each
1910–1913. COIL STAMPS								
PERF. 12 HORIZONTALLY (N-H ADD 70%)								
☐385	1¢	Green	210.00	140.00	21.00	15.00	13.00	5.00
☐386	2¢	Carmine	410.00	300.00	35.00	21.00	14.00	7.50
PERF. 12 VERTICALLY (N-H ADD 70%)								
☐387	1¢	Green	285.00	210.00	60.00	40.00	28.50	16.00
☐388	2¢	Carmine	2900.00	2400.00	425.00	340.00	130.00	80.00
PERF. 8½ HORIZONTALLY (N-H ADD 70%)								
☐390	1¢	Green	23.00	16.00	4.00	3.00	3.50	2.50
☐391	2¢	Carmine	160.00	120.00	24.00	16.00	8.50	5.00
PERF. 8½ VERTICALLY (N-H ADD 70%)								
☐392	1¢	Green	100.00	70.00	16.00	10.00	15.00	11.00
☐393	2¢	Carmine	160.00	120.00	34.00	24.00	6.00	4.50
☐394	3¢	Violet	235.00	160.00	40.00	26.00	37.00	25.00
☐395	4¢	Brown	235.00	160.00	40.00	26.00	32.00	25.00
☐396	5¢	Blue	235.00	160.00	40.00	26.00	32.00	26.00

Scott No.			Fine Unused Block	Ave. Unused Block	Fine Unused Each	Ave. Unused Each	Fine Used Each	Ave. Used Each
1913–1915. PANAMA-PACIFIC ISSUE								
PERF. 12 (N-H ADD 80%)								
☐397	1¢	Green	120.00	90.00	14.00	8.00	1.90	1.10
☐398	2¢	Carmine	215.00	150.00	15.00	9.00	.80	.50
☐399	5¢	Blue	525.00	410.00	60.00	50.00	10.00	5.00
☐400	10¢	Orange Yellow	810.00	600.00	90.00	65.00	17.00	12.00
☐400A	10¢	Orange	1500.00	1200.00	180.00	125.00	21.00	12.00
PERF. 10 (N-H ADD 80%)								
☐401	1¢	Green	240.00	190.00	19.00	16.00	7.00	5.00
☐402	2¢	Carmine	450.00	300.00	70.00	52.00	2.00	1.50
☐403	5¢	Blue	1500.00	1100.00	175.00	110.00	17.00	12.00
☐404	10¢	Orange	6200.00	4000.00	800.00	500.00	65.00	45.00

Scott No.		Fine Unused Block	Ave. Unused Block	Fine Unused Each	Ave. Unused Each	Fine Used Each	Ave. Used Each
1912–1914. REGULAR ISSUE							
PERF. 12 (N-H ADD 70%)							
☐405	1¢ Green	85.00	65.00	5.00	2.00	.18	.15
☐406	2¢ Carmine	90.00	80.00	5.00	3.50	.18	.15
☐407	7¢ Black	500.00	400.00	72.00	50.00	7.00	4.50
IMPERFORATE (N-H ADD 70%)							
☐408	1¢ Green	19.00	14.00	1.10	.70	.60	.30
☐409	2¢ Carmine	32.00	26.00	1.25	.75	.60	.36

Scott No.		Fine Unused Line Pair	Ave. Unused Line Pair	Fine Unused Each	Ave. Unused Each	Fine Used Each	Ave. Used Each
1912. COIL STAMPS							
PERF. 8½ HORIZONTALLY (N-H ADD 70%)							
☐410	1¢ Green	30.00	20.00	5.00	4.00	3.40	2.00
☐411	2¢ Carmine	36.00	28.00	7.00	4.00	3.00	1.90
PERF. 8½ VERTICALLY (N-H ADD 80%)							
☐412	1¢ Green	78.00	50.00	17.50	11.00	5.00	3.00
☐413	2¢ Carmine	160.00	100.00	27.00	20.00	.72	.50

Scott No.		Fine Unused Block	Ave. Unused Block	Fine Unused Each	Ave. Unused Each	Fine Used Each	Ave. Used Each
1912–1914. SINGLE LINE WATERMARKED "U.S.P.S."							
PERF. 12 (N-H ADD 75%)							
☐414	8¢ Olive Green	300.00	210.00	34.00	22.00	1.35	1.00
☐415	9¢ Salmon Red	400.00	300.00	43.00	30.00	13.00	9.00
☐416	10¢ Orange Yellow	320.00	250.00	31.00	20.00	.45	.26
☐417	12¢ Claret Brown	310.00	210.00	34.00	24.00	4.00	2.75
☐418	15¢ Gray	500.00	310.00	55.00	40.00	3.40	2.25
☐419	20¢ Ultramarine	1000.00	700.00	140.00	90.00	14.00	9.50
☐420	30¢ Orange Red	680.00	500.00	100.00	70.00	14.00	9.50
☐421	50¢ Violet	2500.00	1800.00	375.00	265.00	16.00	10.00
1912. DOUBLE LINE WATERMARKED "U.S.P.S."							
(N-H ADD 75%)							
☐422	50¢ Violet	1400.00	1100.00	190.00	120.00	18.00	9.00
☐423	$1 Violet Black	3100.00	2200.00	425.00	275.00	60.00	42.00
1914–1915. SINGLE LINE WATERMARKED "U.S.P.S."							
PERF. 10 (N-H ADD 55%)							
☐424	1¢ Green	35.00	25.00	2.50	1.40	.16	.14
☐425	2¢ Carmine	25.00	18.00	2.00	1.50	.16	.14
☐426	3¢ Deep Violet	130.00	80.00	11.00	7.00	1.60	.90
☐427	4¢ Brown	230.00	80.00	27.00	20.00	.58	.40
☐428	5¢ Blue	260.00	180.00	23.00	16.00	.58	.40
☐429	6¢ Orange	230.00	150.00	29.00	21.00	1.30	.90

Scott No.			Fine Unused Block	Ave. Unused Block	Fine Unused Each	Ave. Unused Each	Fine Used Each	Ave. Used Each
☐430	7¢	Black	700.00	600.00	70.00	55.00	5.00	4.00
☐431	8¢	Olive Green	310.00	350.00	30.00	20.00	1.60	.90
☐432	9¢	Salmon Red	500.00	400.00	39.00	30.00	10.00	6.50
☐433	12¢	Orange Yellow	500.00	400.00	35.00	26.00	.35	.19
☐434	11¢	Dark Green	180.00	120.00	17.00	12.00	7.50	5.00
☐435	12¢	Claret Brown	220.00	150.00	21.00	15.00	6.00	3.50
☐435a	12¢	Copper Red	250.00	160.00	23.00	14.00	6.00	4.00
☐437	15¢	Gray	700.00	600.00	90.00	65.00	7.00	6.00
☐438	20¢	Ultramarine	1600.00	1100.00	170.00	120.00	4.00	2.50
☐439	30¢	Orange Red	2500.00	1600.00	225.00	160.00	16.00	10.00
☐440	50¢	Violet	8000.00	6000.00	510.00	425.00	17.00	12.00

Scott No.			Fine Unused Line Pair	Ave. Unused Line Pair	Fine Unused Each	Ave. Unused Each	Fine Used Each	Ave. Used Each

1914. COIL STAMPS
PERF. 10 HORIZONTALLY (N-H ADD 75%)

☐441	1¢	Green	7.50	4.50	.90	.80	.85	.60
☐442	2¢	Carmine	45.00	29.00	8.00	6.00	7.00	4.00

PERF. 10 VERTICALLY (N-H ADD 70%)

☐443	1¢	Green	90.00	65.00	18.00	12.00	6.00	4.00
☐444	2¢	Carmine	150.00	100.00	24.00	16.00	1.30	1.00
☐445	3¢	Violet	825.00	700.00	185.00	125.00	100.00	75.00
☐446	4¢	Brown	500.00	400.00	100.00	75.00	33.00	24.00
☐447	5¢	Blue	180.00	150.00	36.00	25.00	20.00	16.00

1914–1916. ROTARY PRESS COIL STAMPS
PERF. 10 HORIZONTALLY (N-H ADD 70%)

☐448	1¢	Green	36.00	25.00	7.00	4.00	2.75	1.80
☐449	2¢	Red (I)	—	—	1700.00	900.00	200.00	140.00
☐450	2¢	Carmine (III)	48.00	36.00	10.00	7.50	3.25	1.80

PERF. 10 VERTICALLY (N-H ADD 70%)

☐452	1¢	Green	62.00	42.00	9.00	6.00	1.50	1.10
☐453	2¢	Red (I)	440.00	350.00	90.00	65.00	4.00	3.00
☐454	2¢	Carmine (II)	400.00	300.00	82.00	64.00	12.00	7.00
☐455	2¢	Carmine (III)	48.00	40.00	7.50	5.00	.90	.45
☐456	3¢	Violet	500.00	400.00	220.00	160.00	90.00	65.00
☐457	4¢	Brown	125.00	90.00	21.00	16.00	17.00	10.00
☐458	5¢	Blue	130.00	90.00	30.00	25.00	17.00	11.00

IMPERFORATE (N-H ADD 60%)

☐459	2¢	Carmine	1300.00	900.00	400.00	300.00	—	—

Scott No.		Fine Unused Block	Ave. Unused Block	Fine Unused Each	Ave. Unused Each	Fine Used Each	Ave. Used Each

1915. DOUBLE LINE WATERMARKED "U.S.P.S."
PERF. 10 (N-H ADD 60%)

| ☐460 | $1 Violet Black | 4000.00 | 3500.00 | 700.00 | 600.00 | 88.00 | 65.00 |

1915. SINGLE LINE WATERMARKED "U.S.P.S."
PERF. 11 (N-H ADD 60%)

| ☐461 | 2¢ Pale Carmine Rose | 300.00 | 185.00 | 100.00 | 65.00 | 90.00 | 45.00 |

1916–1917. UNWATERMARKED
PERF. 10 (N-H ADD 70%)

☐462	1¢ Green	110.00	75.00	8.00	5.00	.38	.20
☐463	2¢ Carmine	98.00	60.00	4.00	2.75	.18	.15
☐464	3¢ Violet	1000.00	800.00	70.00	50.00	13.00	8.50
☐465	4¢ Orange Brown	500.00	400.00	41.00	25.00	2.10	1.25
☐466	5¢ Blue	850.00	650.00	65.00	40.00	2.10	1.50
☐467	5¢ Carmine (error)	—	1000.00	600.00	480.00	—	—
☐468	6¢ Red Orange	600.00	500.00	72.00	50.00	7.10	4.10
☐469	7¢ Black	500.00	400.00	98.00	25.00	14.00	7.00
☐470	58¢ Olive Green	460.00	310.00	46.00	32.00	6.00	3.50
☐471	9¢ Salmon Red	400.00	300.00	48.00	34.00	14.00	9.00
☐472	12¢ Orange Yellow	900.00	700.00	85.00	70.00	1.00	.65
☐473	11¢ Dark Green	230.00	160.00	27.00	20.00	16.00	11.00
☐474	12¢ Claret Brown	450.00	300.00	43.00	30.00	5.75	4.50
☐475	15¢ Gray	900.00	700.00	140.00	90.00	12.00	7.00
☐476	20¢ Ultramarine	2100.00	1800.00	210.00	160.00	12.00	8.00
☐477	50¢ Light Violet	6200.00	5000.00	1000.00	700.00	68.00	43.00
☐478	$1 Violet Black	4000.00	2600.00	650.00	500.00	20.00	12.00

1916–1917. DESIGN OF 1902–1903
PERF. 10 (N-H ADD 70%)

| ☐479 | $2 Dark Blue | 2100.00 | 1600.00 | 350.00 | 280.00 | 41.00 | 30.00 |
| ☐480 | $5 Light Green | 2100.00 | 1600.00 | 300.00 | 210.00 | 46.00 | 30.00 |

IMPERFORATE (N-H ADD 70%)

☐481	1¢ Green	10.00	7.50	.90	.55	.75	.45
☐482	2¢ Carmine	20.00	15.00	1.25	.70	1.10	.90
☐483	3¢ Violet (I)	110.00	85.00	12.00	8.50	8.00	5.00
☐484	3¢ Violet (II)	90.00	62.00	9.00	7.00	4.10	3.00

Scott No.		Fine Unused Line Pair	Ave. Unused Line Pair	Fine Unused Each	Ave. Unused Each	Fine Used Each	Ave. Used Each

1916–1922. ROTARY PRESS COIL STAMPS
PERF. 10 HORIZONTALLY (N-H ADD 60%)

☐486	1¢ Green	4.00	3.00	.75	.60	.28	.16
☐487	2¢ Carmine (II)	100.00	80.00	13.00	9.00	2.75	1.80
☐488	2¢ Carmine (III)	16.00	12.00	3.00	1.60	1.80	1.00
☐489	3¢ Violet	31.00	21.00	4.25	3.00	1.25	.75

Scott No.			Fine Unused Line Pair	Ave. Unused Line Pair	Fine Unused Each	Ave. Unused Each	Fine Used Each	Ave. Used Each
PERF. 10 VERTICALLY (N-H ADD 60%)								
☐490	1¢	Green	4.50	4.00	.65	.42	.24	.16
☐491	2¢	Carmine (II)	—	—	1300.00	750.00	420.00	300.00
☐492	2¢	Carmine (III)	51.00	40.00	9.00	6.00	.18	.14
☐493	3¢	Violet (I)	95.00	70.00	15.00	11.00	3.00	1.75
☐494	3¢	Violet (II)	55.00	48.00	8.50	6.75	.75	.60
☐495	4¢	Orange Brown	65.00	50.00	10.00	6.50	4.00	2.00
☐496	5¢	Blue	26.00	19.00	5.00	3.00	1.00	.60
☐497	10¢	Orange Yellow	98.00	80.00	21.00	16.00	8.00	6.00

Scott No.			Fine Unused Block	Ave. Unused Block	Fine Unused Each	Ave. Unused Each	Fine Used Each	Ave. Used Each
1917–1919. FLAT PLATE PRINTING								
PERF. 11 (N-H ADD 60%)								
☐498	1¢	Green	13.00	11.00	.50	.36	.18	.15
☐499	2¢	Rose (I)	14.00	12.00	.42	.30	.18	.15
☐500	2¢	Deep Rose (Ia)	1300.00	1000.00	210.00	150.00	115.00	70.00
☐501	3¢	Violet (I)	130.00	90.00	11.00	8.00	.24	.20
☐502	3¢	Violet (II)	150.00	110.00	15.00	9.00	.34	.23
☐503	4¢	Brown	140.00	100.00	10.00	5.50	.24	.15
☐504	5¢	Blue	125.00	85.00	8.50	5.50	.18	.15
☐505	5¢	Rose (error)	—	—	400.00	280.00	—	—
☐506	6¢	Red Orange	190.00	125.00	12.00	7.50	.40	.22
☐507	7¢	Black	280.00	200.00	26.00	16.00	1.50	.78
☐508	8¢	Olive Bistre	160.00	110.00	9.00	6.50	1.10	.92
☐509	9¢	Salmon Red	150.00	100.00	14.00	10.00	2.20	1.50
☐510	10¢	Orange Yellow	200.00	150.00	15.00	9.00	.20	.15
☐511	11¢	Light Green	135.00	90.00	8.50	3.20	3.10	2.10
☐512	12¢	Claret Brown	120.00	80.00	8.00	4.50	.60	.50
☐513	13¢	Apple Green	125.00	85.00	10.00	6.50	7.00	5.00
☐514	15¢	Gray	550.00	330.00	37.00	25.00	.90	.66
☐515	20¢	Ultramarine	575.00	410.00	40.00	31.00	.35	.21
☐516	30¢	Orange Red	500.00	350.00	40.00	28.00	1.00	.76
☐517	50¢	Red Violet	900.00	700.00	71.00	50.00	.75	.65
☐518	$1	Violet Brown	850.00	600.00	65.00	42.00	1.80	1.15
☐518b	$1	Deep Brown	2100.00	1700.00	800.00	480.00	450.00	275.00
1917. DOUBLE LINE WATERMARKED "U.S.P.S."								
DESIGN OF 1908–1909								
PERF. 11 (N-H ADD 60%)								
☐519	2¢	Carmine	1800.00	1500.00	225.00	125.00	210.00	100.00
1918. UNWATERMARKED								
PERF. 11 (N-H ADD 55%)								
☐523	$2	Orange Red & Black	7000.00	5500.00	725.00	475.00	210.00	115.00
☐524	$5	Deep Green & Black	3100.00	2100.00	350.00	200.00	25.00	17.00

Scott No.		Fine Unused Block	Ave. Unused Block	Fine Unused Each	Ave. Unused Each	Fine Used Each	Ave. Used Each
1918–1920. OFFSET PRINTING PERF. 11 (N-H ADD 60%)							
☐525	1¢ Gray Green................	15.00	13.00	1.75	.90	.80	.50
☐526	2¢ Carmine (IV).............	165.00	130.00	26.00	13.00	4.00	2.50
☐527	2¢ Carmine (V).............	90.00	70.00	12.00	7.00	1.00	.65
☐528	2¢ Carmine (Va)............	49.00	30.00	7.50	4.00	.22	.15
☐528A	2¢ Carmine (VI)............	250.00	200.00	41.00	27.00	1.00	.75
☐528B	2¢ Carmine (VII)...........	110.00	78.00	15.00	11.00	.18	.15
☐529	3¢ Violet (III)...............	48.00	32.00	2.80	2.25	.18	.15
☐530	3¢ Purple (IV)...............	9.00	5.50	1.00	.60	.18	.15
IMPERFORATE (N-H ADD 60%)							
☐531	1¢ Gray Green................	60.00	55.00	8.00	6.50	7.00	6.00
☐532	2¢ Carmine (IV).............	220.00	185.00	34.00	24.00	29.00	23.00
☐533	2¢ Carmine (V).............	1100.00	800.00	180.00	140.00	59.00	45.00
☐534	2¢ Carmine (Va)...........	85.00	65.00	10.00	7.50	8.00	5.75
☐534A	2¢ Carmine (VI)............	250.00	210.00	30.00	24.00	28.00	20.00
☐534B	2¢ Carmine (VII)...........	—	—	1400.00	900.00	500.00	280.00
☐535	3¢ Violet...................	50.00	40.00	8.00	6.00	6.00	4.50
PERF. 12 ½ (N-H ADD 65%)							
☐536	1¢ Gray Green................	125.00	86.00	11.00	8.00	11.00	7.50

IMPORTANT NOTICE: Beginning here, prices of **blocks** are for blocks of 4 with **plate number attached**. Ordinary blocks of 4 bring lower prices. Plate blocks consisting of more than 4 stamps would sell higher than these sums. Always check the **headings** of price columns to accurately value your stamps.

Scott No.		Fine Unused Plate Blk	Ave. Unused Plate Blk	Fine Unused Each	Ave. Unused Each	Fine Used Each	Ave. Used Each
1919. VICTORY ISSUE (N-H ADD 45%)							
☐537	3¢ Violet	90.00	78.00	8.00	6.00	4.10	2.50
1919–1921. REGULAR ISSUE ROTARY PRESS PRINTING PERF. 11 x 10 (N-H ADD 70%)							
☐538	1¢ Green......................	75.00	49.00	9.00	6.00	8.50	5.00
☐538a	Same Impf. Horiz. Pair ..	—	—	50.00	34.00	—	—
☐539	2¢ Carmine Rose (II)	—	—	2600.00	1300.00	800.00	400.00
☐540	2¢ Carmine Rose (III)	78.00	50.00	9.00	6.00	8.50	6.00
☐530a	Same Impf. Horiz. Pair ..	—	—	42.00	32.00	—	—
☐541	3¢ Violet	300.00	200.00	29.00	21.00	28.50	21.00
PERF. 10 x 11 (N-H ADD 70%)							
☐542	1¢ Green......................	125.00	86.00	9.00	6.00	1.00	.72
PERF. 10 x 10 (N-H ADD 70%)							
☐543	1¢ Green......................	15.00	9.00	.50	.45	.19	.15

Scott No.			Fine Unused Plate Blk	Ave. Unused Plate Blk	Fine Unused Each	Ave. Unused Each	Fine Used Each	Ave. Used Each
PERF. 11 x 11 (N-H ADD 70%)								
☐544	1¢	Green	—	—	—	—	2200.00	1500.00
☐545	1¢	Green	700.00	550.00	120.00	73.00	110.00	75.00
☐546	2¢	Carmine Rose	490.00	400.00	80.00	41.00	78.00	50.00
FLAT PLATE PRINTING								
PERF. 11 (N-H ADD 60%)								
☐547	$2	Carmine & Black	—	—	200.00	170.00	36.00	28.00
1920. PILGRIM ISSUE (N-H ADD 55%)								
☐548	1¢	Green	40.00	32.00	4.10	2.75	2.50	1.75
☐549	2¢	Carmine Rose	58.00	45.00	7.00	3.50	2.00	1.50
☐550	5¢	Deep Blue	400.00	300.00	48.00	30.00	14.00	12.00
1922–1925. PERF. FLAT PLATE PRINTING								
PERF. 11 (N-H ADD 55%)								
☐551	½¢	Olive Brown	7.50	5.50	.26	.16	.18	.14
☐552	1¢	Deep Green	25.00	18.00	1.75	1.15	.18	.13
☐553	1½¢	Yellow Brown	30.00	25.00	2.50	1.90	.35	.23
☐554	2¢	Carmine	21.00	18.00	1.70	1.10	.20	.14
☐555	3¢	Violet	160.00	140.00	16.00	12.00	1.00	.72
☐556	4¢	Yellow Brown	170.00	150.00	18.00	12.00	.35	.20
☐557	5¢	Dark Blue	180.00	165.00	18.00	14.00	.18	.13
☐558	6¢	Red Orange	340.00	300.00	30.00	20.00	.82	.60
☐559	7¢	Black	68.00	60.00	8.00	6.00	.78	.55
☐560	8¢	Olive Green	480.00	400.00	41.00	29.00	.85	.55
☐561	9¢	Rose	150.00	120.00	13.00	7.50	1.20	.90
☐562	10¢	Orange	210.00	190.00	17.00	13.00	.20	.14
☐563	11¢	Blue	30.00	25.00	1.90	1.10	.40	.30
☐564	12¢	Brown Violet	75.00	68.00	7.00	4.50	.18	.14
☐565	14¢	Dark Blue	52.00	42.00	5.00	3.00	1.00	.60
☐566	15¢	Gray	260.00	200.00	24.00	16.00	.18	.14
☐567	20¢	Carmine Rose	215.00	190.00	21.00	15.00	.18	.14
☐568	25¢	Green	200.00	150.00	19.00	13.00	.60	.32
☐569	30¢	Olive Brown	300.00	300.00	45.00	38.00	.45	.32
☐570	50¢	Lilac	1000.00	700.00	56.00	42.00	.18	.16
☐571	$1	Violet Black	450.00	375.00	42.00	33.00	.48	.28
☐572	$2	Deep Blue	1400.00	1100.00	100.00	58.00	10.00	6.50
☐573	$5	Carmine & Blue	8000.00	5000.00	210.00	175.00	14.00	9.00
IMPERFORATE (N-H ADD 45%)								
☐575	1¢	Green	72.00	60.00	8.00	6.00	3.50	2.10
☐576	1½¢	Yellow Brown	21.00	17.00	2.00	.90	1.75	.85
☐577	2¢	Carmine	24.00	17.00	2.10	1.10	1.75	.85
1923–1926. ROTARY PRESS PRINTING								
PERF. 11 x 10 (N-H ADD 55%)								
☐578	1¢	Green	600.00	450.00	60.00	42.00	50.00	35.00
☐579	2¢	Carmine	375.00	240.00	51.00	32.00	45.00	28.00

Scott No.		Fine Unused Plate Blk	Ave. Unused Plate Blk	Fine Unused Each	Ave. Unused Each	Fine Used Each	Ave. Used Each
PERF. 10 (N-H ADD 55%)							
☐581	1¢ Green	95.00	75.00	8.00	4.00	.80	.60
☐582	1½¢ Brown	42.00	30.00	4.00	3.00	.80	.55
☐583	2¢ Carmine	28.00	26.00	2.00	1.10	.18	.15
☐584	3¢ Violet	240.00	180.00	25.00	16.00	2.00	1.15
☐585	4¢ Yellow Brown	165.00	130.00	14.00	9.00	.60	.30
☐586	5¢ Blue	140.00	125.00	14.00	9.00	.32	.19
☐587	6¢ Red Orange	70.00	50.00	6.00	5.50	.60	.36
☐588	7¢ Black	100.00	72.00	9.00	6.00	5.00	3.00
☐589	8¢ Olive Green	210.00	180.00	20.00	14.00	3.15	1.90
☐590	9¢ Rose	46.00	30.00	4.00	3.00	2.10	1.40
☐591	10¢ Orange	600.00	500.00	52.00	40.00	.18	.14
PERF. 11							
☐595	2¢ Carmine	1400.00	1050.00	185.00	100.00	180.00	112.00

Scott No.		Fine Unused Line Pair	Ave. Unused Line Pair	Fine Unused Each	Ave. Unused Each	Fine Used Each	Ave. Used Each
1923–1929. ROTARY PRESS COIL STAMPS							
PERF. 10 VERTICALLY (N-H ADD 55%)							
☐597	1¢ Green	2.00	1.50	.36	.21	.19	.15
☐598	1½¢ Deep Brown	5.00	4.00	.65	.46	.19	.15
☐599	2¢ Carmine (I)	2.00	1.10	.42	.28	.20	.15
☐599A	2¢ Carmine (II)	550.00	360.00	120.00	65.00	14.00	7.50
☐600	3¢ Deep Violet	27.00	21.00	6.50	4.00	.18	.15
☐601	4¢ Yellow Brown	28.00	21.00	4.00	2.60	.50	.29
☐602	5¢ Dark Blue	10.00	6.00	1.75	.90	.25	.16
☐603	10¢ Orange	21.00	15.00	4.00	2.70	.18	.15
PERF. 10 HORIZONTALLY (N-H ADD 55%)							
☐604	1¢ Green	3.00	1.50	.30	.20	.18	.15
☐605	1½¢ Yellow Brown	2.75	1.50	.30	.20	.25	.15
☐606	2¢ Carmine	2.00	1.00	.30	.20	.18	.15

Scott No.		Fine Unused Plate Blk	Ave. Unused Plate Blk	Fine Unused Each	Ave. Unused Each	Fine Used Each	Ave. Used Each
1923. HARDING MEMORIAL ISSUE (N-H ADD 45%)							
☐610	2¢ Black, pf. 11	22.00	16.00	.70	.50	.20	.15
☐611	2¢ Black, imperf.	100.00	75.00	7.50	6.00	5.00	4.00
☐612	2¢ Black, pf. 10 rotary	260.00	200.00	14.00	11.00	2.30	1.75
1924. HUGUENOT-WALLOON ISSUE (N-H ADD 45%)							
☐614	1¢ Green	40.00	26.00	4.00	2.50	3.00	2.50
☐615	2¢ Carmine Rose	72.00	55.00	7.00	4.00	3.00	2.00
☐616	5¢ Dark Blue	340.00	250.00	30.00	25.00	17.00	12.00

Scott No.			Fine Unused Plate Blk	Ave. Unused Plate Blk	Fine Unused Each	Ave. Unused Each	Fine Used Each	Ave. Used Each
1925. LEXINGTON-CONCORD SESQUICENTENNIAL (N-H ADD 45%)								
☐617	1¢	Green	40.00	30.00	4.00	3.00	3.00	1.60
☐618	2¢	Carmine Rose	70.00	52.00	7.00	4.00	3.00	3.00
☐619	5¢	Dark Blue	300.00	210.00	30.00	21.00	15.00	9.00
1925. NORSE-AMERICAN ISSUE (N-H ADD 40%)								
☐620	2¢	Carmine & Black	170.00	120.00	6.00	4.00	5.00	2.10
☐621	5¢	Dark Blue & Black	575.00	410.00	20.00	16.00	14.00	11.00
1925–1926.								
☐622	13¢	Green	140.00	100.00	13.00	10.00	.70	.60
☐623	17¢	Black	180.00	130.00	16.00	13.00	.36	.30
1926–1927. COMMEMORATIVES								
1926. SESQUICENTENNIAL EXPOSITION (N-H ADD 50%)								
☐627	2¢	Carmine Rose	45.00	33.00	3.50	2.00	.60	.40
1926. ERICSSON MEMORIAL ISSUE (N-H ADD 50%)								
☐628	5¢	Gray Lilac	90.00	70.00	6.00	4.00	3.50	2.50
1926. BATTLE OF WHITE PLAINS (N-H ADD 45%)								
☐629	2¢	Carmine Rose	—	38.00	2.50	1.40	2.00	1.10
☐630	2¢	Souv. Sheet of 25	—	—	440.00	340.00	—	—
1926–1928. DESIGNS OF 1922–1925								
ROTARY PRESS PRINTING IMPERFORATE (N-H ADD 40%)								
☐631	1½¢	Brown	58.00	50.00	2.00	1.50	1.70	1.20
PERF. 11 x 10½ (N-H ADD 50%)								
☐632	1¢	Green	2.50	1.60	.23	.20	.18	.14
☐633	1½¢	Yellow Brown	76.00	62.00	2.00	1.50	.18	.13
☐634	2¢	Carmine (I)	1.50	1.00	.24	.20	.18	.14
☐634A	2¢	Carmine (II)	—	—	200.00	150.00	16.00	10.00
☐635	3¢	Violet	8.00	6.00	.42	.30	.18	.14
☐636	4¢	Yellow Brown	78.00	65.00	2.60	2.00	.18	.14
☐637	5¢	Dark Blue	20.00	15.00	2.20	1.50	.18	.14
☐638	6¢	Red Orange	20.00	15.00	2.20	1.50	.18	.14
☐639	7¢	Black	20.00	15.00	2.20	1.50	.18	.14
☐640	8¢	Olive Green	20.00	15.00	2.20	1.50	.18	.14
☐641	9¢	Orange Red	20.00	15.00	2.20	1.50	.18	.14
☐642	10¢	Orange	30.00	21.00	4.50	3.20	.18	14
1927. VERMONT SESQUICENTENNIAL (N-H ADD 45%)								
☐643	2¢	Carmine Rose	43.00	35.00	1.30	.70	1.00	.80
1927. BURGOYNE CAMPAIGN ISSUE (N-H ADD 45%)								
☐644	2¢	Carmine	46.00	40.00	3.50	2.50	2.75	1.75
1928. VALLEY FORGE ISSUE (N-H ADD 45%)								
☐645	2¢	Carmine	34.00	26.00	1.00	.70	.60	.40
1928. BATTLE OF MONMOUTH (N-H ADD 45%)								
☐646	2¢	Carmine	39.00	30.00	1.50	.80	1.00	.72

Scott No.		Fine Unused Plate Blk	Ave. Unused Plate Blk	Fine Unused Each	Ave. Unused Each	Fine Used Each	Ave. Used Each
1928. DISCOVERY OF HAWAII (N-H ADD 40%)							
☐647	2¢ Carmine Rose	125.00	75.00	5.00	2.90	4.00	2.20
☐648	5¢ Blue	250.00	170.00	13.00	9.00	12.00	8.00
1928. AERONAUTICS CONFERENCE (N-H ADD 40%)							
☐649	2¢ Carmine	14.00	10.00	1.25	1.00	.90	.60
☐650	5¢ Blue	67.00	45.00	6.00	4.00	3.90	2.80
1929. GEORGE ROGERS CLARK (N-H ADD 40%)							
☐651	2¢ Carmine & Black	12.00	7.00	.75	.50	.70	.45
1929. DESIGNS OF 1922–1925							
ROTARY PRESS PRINTING—PERF. 11 x 10½ (N-H ADD 40%)							
☐653	½¢ Olive Brown	1.10	.70	.25	.19	.18	.14
1929. EDISON COMMEMORATIVE							
FLAT PLATE PRINTING—PERF. 11 (N-H ADD 40%)							
☐654	2¢ Carmine Rose	30.00	21.00	1.00	.70	.75	.50
ROTARY PRESS PRINTING—PERF. 11 x 10½ (N-H ADD 40%)							
☐655	2¢ Carmine Rose	46.00	31.00	.70	.55	.40	.28

Scott No.		Fine Unused Line Pair	Ave. Unused Line Pair	Fine Unused Each	Ave. Unused Each	Fine Used Each	Ave. Used Each
ROTARY PRESS COIL STAMPS—PERF. 10 VERTICALLY (N-H ADD 40%)							
☐656	2¢ Carmine Rose	61.00	42.00	13.00	9.00	2.00	1.20

Scott No.		Fine Unused Plate Blk	Ave. Unused Plate Blk	Fine Unused Each	Ave. Unused Each	Fine Used Each	Ave. Used Each
1929. SULLIVAN EXPEDITION (N-H ADD 40%)							
☐657	2¢ Carmine Rose	32.00	19.00	.80	.68	.60	.48
1929. 632–42 OVERPRINTED (KANS.) (N-H ADD 45%)							
☐658	1¢ Green	30.00	20.00	2.00	1.50	1.80	1.10
☐659	1½¢ Brown	40.00	30.00	2.40	2.00	2.00	2.10
☐660	2¢ Carmine	35.00	28.00	3.00	2.20	.80	.60
☐661	3¢ Violet	140.00	110.00	15.00	11.00	10.00	5.00
☐662	4¢ Yellow Brown	140.00	110.00	15.00	11.00	8.00	6.00
☐663	5¢ Deep Blue	130.00	90.00	12.00	9.00	8.00	7.00
☐664	6¢ Red Orange	310.00	210.00	24.00	19.00	15.00	11.00
☐665	7¢ Black	310.00	225.00	22.00	18.00	18.00	14.00
☐666	8¢ Olive Green	550.00	410.00	62.00	48.00	60.00	46.00
☐667	9¢ Light Rose	200.00	150.00	11.00	9.00	8.00	7.00
☐668	10¢ct Orange Yellow	300.00	220.00	17.00	13.00	10.00	7.00
1929. 632–42 OVERPRINTED (NEBR.) (N-H ADD 45%)							
☐669	1¢ Green	30.00	22.00	2.00	1.35	1.75	1.00
☐670	1½¢ Brown	40.00	31.00	2.50	1.75	2.00	1.10

Scott No.			Fine Unused Plate Blk	Ave. Unused Plate Blk	Fine Unused Each	Ave. Unused Each	Fine Used Each	Ave. Used Each
□671	2¢	Carmine	29.00	21.00	2.00	1.00	.80	.43
□672	3¢	Violet	140.00	100.00	10.00	7.00	7.50	5.00
□673	4¢	Brown	160.00	100.00	16.00	9.00	9.00	6.00
□674	5¢	Blue	170.00	110.00	13.00	9.00	10.00	7.00
□675	6¢	Orange	400.00	300.00	35.00	21.00	18.00	12.00
□676	7¢	Black	210.00	150.00	20.00	14.00	13.00	7.00
□677	8¢	Olive Green	300.00	220.00	26.00	16.00	18.00	11.00
□678	9¢	Rose	350.00	250.00	30.00	19.00	21.00	14.00
□679	10¢	Orange Yellow	700.00	500.00	90.00	60.00	15.00	9.00

1929. BATTLE OF FALLEN TIMBERS (N-H ADD 35%)

□680	2¢	Carmine Rose	30.00	20.00	.90	.60	.80	.60

1929. OHIO RIVER CANALIZATION (N-H ADD 30%)

□681	2¢	Carmine Rose	21.00	14.00	1.00	.50	.70	.50

1930–1931. COMMEMORATIVES

1930. MASSACHUSETTS BAY COLONY (N-H ADD 35%)

□682	2¢	Carmine Rose	30.00	20.00	.80	.85	.50	.36

1930. CAROLINA-CHARLESTON ISSUE (N-H ADD 35%)

□683	2¢	Carmine Rose	50.00	40.00	1.30	1.00	1.20	1.00

1930. REGULAR ISSUE
ROTARY PRESS PRINTING—PERF. 11 x 10½ (N-H ADD 35%)

□684	1½¢	Brown	3.00	2.00	.35	.30	.18	.14
□685	4¢	Brown	11.00	7.00	.80	.60	.18	.14

Scott No.			Fine Unused Line Pair	Ave. Unused Line Pair	Fine Unused Each	Ave. Unused Each	Fine Used Each	Ave. Used Each

ROTARY PRESS COIL STAMPS
PERF. 10 VERTICALLY (N-H ADD 40%)

□686	1½¢	Brown	8.00	5.00	1.70	1.00	.18	.13
□687	4¢	Brown	14.00	10.00	3.50	2.00	.55	.30

Scott No.			Fine Unused Plate Blk	Ave. Unused Plate Blk	Fine Unused Each	Ave. Unused Each	Fine Used Each	Ave. Used Each

1930. BATTLE OF BRADDOCK'S FIELD (N-H ADD 40%)

□688	2¢	Carmine Rose	42.00	30.00	.90	.75	.80	.65

1930. VON STEUBEN ISSUE (N-H ADD 40%)

□689	2¢	Carmine Rose	24.00	18.00	.55	.50	.45	.38

1931. PULASKI ISSUE (N-H ADD 40%)

□690	2¢	Carmine Rose	15.00	11.00	.26	.22	.21	.15

1931. DESIGNS OF 1922–1926
ROTARY PRESS PRINTING—PERF. 11 x 10½ (N-H ADD 40%)

□692	11¢	Light Blue	15.00	11.00	3.00	1.60	.20	.14
□693	12¢	Brown Violet	25.00	19.00	4.50	3.50	.18	.13

Scott No.			Fine Unused Plate Blk	Ave. Unused Plate Blk	Fine Unused Each	Ave. Unused Each	Fine Used Each	Ave. Used Each
☐694	13¢	Yellow Green	15.00	10.00	2.00	1.60	.24	.16
☐695	14¢	Dark Blue	18.00	12.00	3.00	2.10	.60	.30
☐696	15¢	Gray	40.00	30.00	8.00	6.00	.18	.13

PERF. 10½ x 11 (N-H ADD 40%)

☐697	17¢	Black	25.00	18.00	4.50	2.80	.40	.24
☐698	20¢	Carmine Rose	41.00	26.00	9.50	7.00	.18	.13
☐699	25¢	Blue Green	40.00	24.00	9.00	5.75	.17	.14
☐700	30¢	Brown	70.00	42.00	15.00	9.00	.18	.14
☐701	50¢	Lilac	200.00	100.00	42.00	35.00	.18	.14

1931. RED CROSS ISSUE (N-H ADD 40%)

☐702	2¢	Black & Red	3.00	1.80	.26	.19	.18	.16

1931. SURRENDER OF YORKTOWN (N-H ADD 40%)

☐703	2¢	Carmine Rose & Black	4.00	3.00	.50	.40	.48	.34

1932. WASHINGTON BICENTENNIAL (N-H ADD 40%)

☐704	½¢	Olive Brown	4.00	3.50	.24	.20	.18	.13
☐705	1¢	Green	5.00	4.00	.22	.20	.18	.13
☐706	1½¢	Brown	17.00	13.00	.36	.20	.18	.13
☐707	2¢	Carmine	1.80	1.20	.22	.20	.18	.13
☐708	3¢	Purple	13.00	10.00	.70	.46	.18	.13
☐709	4¢	Light Brown	6.00	5.00	.31	.21	.18	.13
☐710	5¢	Blue	18.00	14.00	1.60	1.10	.18	.13
☐711	6¢	Orange	62.00	50.00	4.00	2.80	.18	.13
☐712	7¢	Black	7.00	5.00	.36	.28	.22	.16
☐713	8¢	Olive Bistre	65.00	46.00	3.50	3.00	.90	.55
☐714	9¢	Pale Red	40.00	30.00	3.00	2.00	.30	.18
☐715	10¢	Orange Yellow	115.00	90.00	12.00	8.50	.16	.14

1932. COMMEMORATIVES

1932. OLYMPIC WINTER GAMES (N-H ADD 30%)

☐716	2¢	Carmine Rose	14.00	10.00	.55	.34	.28	.21

1932. ARBOR DAY ISSUE (N-H ADD 30%)

☐717	2¢	Carmine Rose	9.00	8.00	.24	.19	.17	.14

1932. OLYMPIC SUMMER GAMES (N-H ADD 30%)

☐718	3¢	Purple	16.00	11.00	1.90	1.50	.18	.14
☐719	5¢	Blue	24.00	19.00	3.00	2.10	.29	.21

Scott No.			Fine Unused Line Pair	Ave. Unused Line Pair	Fine Unused Each	Ave. Unused Each	Fine Used Each	Ave. Used Each

1932. ROTARY PRESS COIL STAMPS

☐720	3¢	Deep Violet	2.00	1.50	.24	.19	.18	.14

PERF. 10 VERTICALLY (N-H ADD 30%)

☐721	3¢	Deep Violet	7.00	4.00	3.00	2.00	.18	.14

Scott No.			Fine Unused Line Pair	Ave. Unused Line Pair	Fine Unused Each	Ave. Unused Each	Fine Used Each	Ave. Used Each
PERF. 10 HORIZONTALLY (N-H ADD 30%)								
☐722	3¢	Deep Violet	5.00	4.50	1.80	.90	.75	.60
DESIGN OF 1922–1925—PERF. 10 VERTICALLY (N-H ADD 30%)								
☐723	6¢	Deep Orange..............	50.00	35.00	11.00	7.00	.26	.17

Scott No.			Fine Unused Plate Blk	Ave. Unused Plate Blk	Fine Unused Each	Ave. Unused Each	Fine Used Each	Ave. Used Each
1932. WILLIAM PENN ISSUE (N-H ADD 30%)								
☐724	3¢	Violet	13.00	10.00	.35	.27	.24	.17
1932. DANIEL WEBSTER ISSUE (N-H ADD 30%)								
☐725	3¢	Violet	25.00	19.00	.50	.38	.35	.28
1933. COMMEMORATIVES								
1933. GEORGIA BICENTENNIAL (N-H ADD 30%)								
☐726	3¢	Violet	16.00	12.00	.30	.28	.22	.16
1933. PEACE SESQUICENTENNIAL (N-H ADD 30%)								
☐727	3¢	Violet	7.00	5.00	.24	.19	.17	.14
1933. CENTURY OF PROGRESS EXPOSITION (N-H ADD 30%)								
☐728	1¢	Yellow Green	3.00	2.50	.23	.19	.17	.14
☐729	3¢	Purple........................	4.00	3.00	.23	.19	.17	.14
1933. A.P.S. CONVENTION AND EXHIBITION AT CHICAGO IMPERFORATE—UNGUMMED (N-H ADD 30%)								
☐730	1¢	Yellow Green, sheet of 25	—	—	35.00	30.00	—	—
☐730a	1¢	Yellow Green, sgl......	—	—	.80	.60	.50	.35
☐731	3¢	Violet, sheet of 25......	—	—	32.00	—	29.00	—
☐731a	3¢	Violet, single..............	—	—	.65	.50	.46	.35
1933. N.R.A. ISSUE (N-H ADD 25%)								
☐732	3¢	Violet	2.75	1.80	.22	.19	.18	.14
1933. BYRD ANTARCTIC EXPEDITION (N-H ADD 30%)								
☐733	3¢	Dark Blue...................	17.00	14.00	.65	.50	.60	.50
1933. KOSCIUSZKO ISSUE (N-H ADD 30%)								
☐734	5¢	Blue	38.00	30.00	.70	.50	.40	.24
1934. NATIONAL PHILATELIC EXHIBITION IMPERFORATE—UNGUMMED (N-H ADD 30%)								
☐735	3¢	Dark Blue, sheet of 6 .	—	—	19.00	—	16.00	12.00
☐735a	3¢	Dark Blue, sgl.	—	—	2.50	2.10	2.00	1.60
1934. COMMEMORATIVES								
1934. MARYLAND TERCENTENARY (N-H ADD 30%)								
☐736	3¢	Rose	12.00	9.00	.22	.20	.17	.14

Scott No.		Fine Unused Plate Blk	Ave. Unused Plate Blk	Fine Unused Each	Ave. Unused Each	Fine Used Each	Ave. Used Each
1934. MOTHER'S DAY ISSUE							
ROTARY PRESS PRINTING—PERF. 11 x 10¹/₂ (N-H ADD 30%)							
☐737	3¢ Deep Violet	2.00	1.35	.24	.18	.16	.14
FLAT PRESS PRINTING—PERF. 11 (N-H ADD 30%)							
☐738	3¢ Deep Violet	5.00	4.00	.28	.20	.21	.16
1934. WISCONSIN TERCENTENARY (N-H ADD 30%)							
☐739	3¢ Deep Violet	4.75	3.50	.26	.20	.18	.14
1934. NATIONAL PARKS ISSUE (N-H ADD 25%)							
☐740	1¢ Green	1.80	1.20	.24	.18	.17	.14
☐741	2¢ Red	1.75	1.40	.24	.18	.17	.14
☐742	3¢ Purple	2.50	1.60	.24	.18	.17	.14
☐743	4¢ Brown	9.50	7.00	.46	.30	.42	.30
☐744	5¢ Blue	12.00	9.00	.95	.70	.65	.42
☐745	6¢ Indigo	21.00	15.00	1.20	.90	.80	.65
☐746	7¢ Black	14.00	9.00	.76	.60	.55	.50
☐747	8¢ Green	21.00	15.00	2.00	1.50	1.25	1.00
☐748	9¢ Salmon	20.00	16.00	2.10	1.60	.70	.50
☐749	10¢ Gray Black	31.00	22.00	4.00	3.00	1.00	.70
1934. A.P.S. CONVENTION AND EXHIBITION AT ATLANTIC CITY							
IMPERFORATE SOUVENIR SHEET (N-H ADD 25%)							
☐750	3¢ Purple, sheet of 6	—	—	35.00	—	29.00	21.00
☐750a	3¢ Purple, single	—	—	5.00	4.00	3.00	2.50
1934. TRANS-MISSISSIPPI PHILATELIC EXPOSITION AND							
CONVENTION AT OMAHA							
IMPERFORATE SOUVENIR SHEET (N-H ADD 25%)							
☐751	1¢ Green, sheet of 6	—	—	16.00	—	12.00	9.00
☐751a	1¢ Green, single	—	—	1.80	1.60	1.50	1.10

Scott No.		Plate Block	Block Plain	Mint Each	Used Each
1935. "FARLEY SPECIAL PRINTINGS"					
DESIGNS OF 1933–1934					
PERF. 10¹/₂ x 11—UNGUMMED (N-H ADD 25%)					
☐752	3¢ Violet	15.00	4.50	.16	.14
PERF. 11—GUMMED (N-H ADD 25%)					
☐753	3¢ Dark Blue	20.00	4.00	.58	.50
IMPERFORATE—UNGUMMED (N-H ADD 25%)					
☐754	3¢ Deep Violet	20.00	3.50	.60	.50
☐755	3¢ Deep Violet	20.00	4.75	.65	.60
NATIONAL PARKS					
IMPERFORATE—UNGUMMED (N-H ADD 25%)					
☐756	1¢ Green	6.00	1.50	.20	.14
☐757	2¢ Red	7.00	1.60	.28	.18

Scott No.			Plate Block	Block Plain	Mint Each	Used Each
☐758	3¢	Deep Violet	18.00	10.00	.65	.60
☐759	4¢	Brown	23.00	12.00	1.15	1.00
☐760	5¢	Blue	26.00	17.00	2.20	1.90
☐761	6¢	Dark Blue	48.00	25.00	2.80	2.50
☐762	7¢	Black	40.00	20.00	2.00	1.80
☐763	8¢	Sage Green	45.00	22.00	2.30	1.90
☐764	9¢	Red Orange	50.00	30.00	2.25	2.00
☐765	10¢	Gray Black	60.00	40.00	4.00	3.75

IMPERFORATE—UNGUMMED (N-H ADD 25%)

☐766a	1¢	Yellow Green	—	15.00	.80	.50
☐767a	3¢	Violet	—	15.00	.80	.50
☐768a	3¢	Dark Blue	—	20.00	3.00	2.80
☐769a	1¢	Green	—	12.00	1.85	1.30
☐770a	3¢	Deep Violet	—	27.00	3.50	2.80

DESIGN OF CE 1 (N-H ADD 30%)

☐771	16¢	Dark Blue	90.00	40.00	3.00	2.70

1935–1936. COMMEMORATIVES

Scott No.			Fine Unused Plate Blk	Ave. Unused Plate Blk	Mint Each	Used Each
1935. CONNECTICUT TERCENTENARY (N-H ADD 25%)						
☐772	3¢	Red Violet	2.50	1.75	.21	.16
1935. CALIFORNIA PACIFIC EXPOSITION (N-H ADD 25%)						
☐773	3¢	Purple	2.00	1.60	.21	.16
1935. BOULDER DAM ISSUE (N-H ADD 25%)						
☐774	3¢	Purple	2.50	2.25	.21	.16
1935. MICHIGAN CENTENARY (N-H ADD 25%)						
☐775	3¢	Purple	1.90	1.40	.21	.16
1936. TEXAS CENTENNIAL (N-H ADD 25%)						
☐776	3¢	Purple	2.00	1.60	.21	.16
1936. RHODE ISLAND TERCENTENARY (N-H ADD 25%)						
☐777	3¢	Purple	2.50	1.90	.21	.16

1936. THIRD INTL. PHILATELIC EXHIBITION "TIPEX" IMPERFORATE SOUVENIR SHEET DESIGNS OF 772, 773, 775, 776 (N-H ADD 25%)

☐778	3¢	Red Violet, sheet of 4	—	—	3.00	2.90
☐778a	3¢	Red Violet, single	—	—	.75	.65
☐778b	3¢	Red Violet, single	—	—	.75	.65
☐778c	3¢	Red Violet, single	—	—	.75	.65
☐778d	3¢	Red Violet, single	—	—	.75	.65

1936. ARKANSAS CENTENNIAL (N-H ADD 25%)

☐782	3¢	Purple	2.00	1.60	.21	.16

Scott No.			Fine Unused Plate Blk	Ave. Unused Plate Blk	Fine Unused Each	Ave. Unused Each	Fine Used Each	Ave. Used Each
1936. OREGON TERRITORY CENTENNIAL (N-H ADD 25%)								
☐783	3¢	Purple	2.00	1.50	.20	.17	.16	.14
1936. SUFFRAGE FOR WOMEN ISSUE (N-H ADD 25%)								
☐784	3¢	Dark Violet	1.50	1.00	.20	.17	.16	.14
1936–1937. ARMY AND NAVY ISSUE								
ARMY COMMEMORATIVES (N-H ADD 20%)								
☐785	1¢	Green	1.50	1.20	.21	.18	.16	.14
☐786	2¢	Carmine	1.50	1.20	.21	.18	.16	.14
☐707	3¢	Purple	1.90	1.60	.26	.20	.16	.14
☐788	4¢	Gray	16.00	12.00	.50	.40	.36	.18
☐789	5¢	Ultramarine	18.00	12.50	.85	.60	.40	.18
NAVY COMMEMORATIVES (N-H ADD 25%)								
☐790	1¢	Green	—	1.20	.22	.18	.16	.14
☐791	2¢	Carmaine	1.60	1.25	.22	.20	.16	.14
☐792	3¢	Purple	1.90	1.65	.22	.22	.16	.15
☐793	4¢	Gray	14.00	12.00	.50	.40	.34	.18
☐794	5¢	Ultramarine	19.00	14.00	.85	.60	.38	.22
1937. COMMEMORATIVES								
1937. NORTHWEST ORDINANCE ISSUE (N-H ADD 25%)								
☐795	3¢	Violet	1.90	1.40	.26	.17	.20	.15
1937. VIRGINIA DARE ISSUE (N-H ADD 20%)								
☐796	5¢	Gray Blue	10.00	9.00	.30	.25	.21	.16
1937. S.P.A. CONVENTION ISSUE (N-H ADD 25%)								
DESIGN OF 749 IMPERFORATE SOUVENIR SHEET								
☐797	10¢	Blue Green	—	1.50	—	—	.80	.58
1937. CONSTITUTIONAL SESQUICENTENNIAL (N-H ADD 25%)								
☐798	3¢	Red Violet	2.10	1.80	.22	.20	.18	.14
1937. TERRITORIAL PUBLICITY ISSUE (N-H ADD 25%)								
☐799	3¢	Violet	2.00	1.65	.22	.17	.18	.14
☐800	3¢	Violet	2.00	1.65	.22	.17	.18	.14
☐801	3¢	Bright Violet	2.00	1.65	.22	.17	.18	.14
☐802	3¢	Light Violet	2.00	1.65	.22	.17	.18	.14
1938. PRESIDENTIAL SERIES								
ROTARY PRESS PRINTING—PERF. 11 x 10½ (N-H ADD 25%)								
☐803	½¢	Red Orange	.60	.50	.22	.18	.16	.14
☐804	1¢	Green	.50	.40	.22	.18	.16	.14
☐805	1½¢	Bistre Brown	.50	.40	.22	.18	.16	.14
☐806	2¢	Rose Carmine	.60	.50	.22	.18	.16	.14
☐807	3¢	Deep Violet	.55	.45	.22	.18	.16	.14
☐808	4¢	Red Violet	3.00	2.50	.90	.18	.16	.14
☐809	4½¢	Dark Gray	2.00	1.50	.22	.18	.16	.14

Scott No.			Fine Unused Plate Blk	Ave. Unused Plate Blk	Fine Unused Each	Ave. Unused Each	Fine Used Each	Ave. Used Each
☐810	5¢	Bright Blue	1.50	1.30	.25	.21	.18	.16
☐811	6¢	Red Orange	2.00	1.65	.28	.21	.18	.16
☐812	7¢	Sepia	2.10	1.80	.36	.24	.18	.16
☐813	8¢	Olive Green	2.50	2.20	.38	.26	.18	.16
☐814	9¢	Rose Pink	2.60	2.40	.38	.26	.18	.16
☐815	10¢	Brown Red	2.00	1.80	.35	.24	.18	.16
☐816	11¢	Ultramarine	5.00	4.00	.70	.35	.18	.16
☐817	12¢	Bright Violet	8.00	7.00	1.20	.40	.18	.16
☐818	13¢	Blue Green	10.00	8.00	1.00	.50	.18	.16
☐819	14¢	Blue	7.00	6.00	1.10	.45	.18	.16
☐820	15¢	Blue Gray	3.00	3.00	.60	.35	.18	.16
☐821	16¢	Black	8.00	6.00	1.20	.60	.50	.45
☐822	17¢	Rose Red	7.00	5.50	1.00	.45	.18	.16
☐823	18¢	Brown Carmine	13.00	10.00	2.10	1.40	.18	.16
☐824	19¢	Bright Violet	11.00	9.00	1.90	.90	.60	.50
☐825	20¢	Bright Blue Green	6.00	5.00	1.10	.75	.18	.16
☐826	21¢	Dull Blue	12.00	9.25	2.20	1.35	.18	.16
☐827	22¢	Vermilion	16.00	12.00	1.35	.75	.60	.50
☐828	24¢	Gray Black	24.00	18.00	4.00	2.50	.35	.23
☐829	25¢	Deep Red Lilac	6.00	4.10	1.00	.50	.18	.16
☐830	30¢	Deep Ultramarine	28.00	22.00	5.00	3.50	.18	.16
☐831	50¢	Light Red Violet	42.00	35.00	8.00	5.00	.18	.16

FLAT PLATE PRINTING—PERF. 11 (N-H ADD 20%)

☐832	$1	Purple & Black	50.00	38.00	9.00	6.00	.28	.16
☐832b	$1	Watermarked	—	—	310.00	250.00	70.00	60.00
☐832c	$1	Dry Printing, Thick Paper (1954)	40.00	34.00	8.00	6.50	.26	.15
☐833	$2	Green & Black	160.00	140.00	30.00	21.00	8.00	6.50
☐834	$5	Carmine & Black	600.00	400.00	115.00	100.00	6.00	4.50

1938–1939. COMMEMORATIVES

1938. CONSTITUTION RATIFICATION (N-H ADD 25%)

☐835	3¢	Deep Violet	6.00	5.00	.42	.24	.20	.16

1938. SWEDISH-FINNISH TERCENTENARY (N-H ADD 25%)

☐836	3¢	Red Violet	5.00	3.00	.28	.24	.20	.16

1938. NORTHWEST COLONIZATION (N-H ADD 25%)

☐837	3¢	Bright Violet	13.00	10.00	.25	.24	.20	.16

1938. IOWA TERRITORY CENTENNIAL (N-H ADD 25%)

☐838	3¢	Violet	10.00	7.50	.25	.24	.20	.16

Scott No.			Fine Unused Line Pair	Ave. Unused Line Pair	Fine Unused Each	Ave. Unused Each	Fine Used Each	Ave. Used Each
1939. ROTARY PRESS COIL STAMPS								
PERF. 10 VERTICALLY (N-H ADD 25%)								
☐839	1¢	Green	1.35	1.10	.40	.26	.18	.15
☐840	1½¢	Bistre Brown	1.60	1.40	.45	.26	.18	.15
☐841	2¢	Rose Carmine	2.00	1.60	.40	.30	.20	.15
☐842	3¢	Deep Violet	1.60	1.40	.62	.40	.22	.15
☐843	4¢	Red Violet	26.00	20.00	9.00	7.00	.55	.40
☐844	4½¢	Dark Gray	6.00	4.00	.90	.70	.60	.40
☐845	5¢	Bright Blue	26.00	20.00	7.00	5.00	.50	.35
☐846	6¢	Red Orange	7.00	6.00	2.00	1.10	.20	.15
☐847	10¢	Brown Red	45.00	38.00	15.00	9.00	.70	.50
PERF. 10 HORIZONTALLY (N-H ADD 25%)								
☐848	1¢	Green	2.75	2.25	.90	.70	.21	.15
☐849	1½¢	Bistre Brown	3.50	3.10	1.65	1.25	.55	.45
☐850	2¢	Rose Carmine	6.50	4.50	3.50	2.50	.65	.50
☐851	3¢	Deep Violet	7.00	6.00	3.00	2.30	.55	.48

Scott No.			Fine Unused Plate Blk	Ave. Unused Plate Blk	Fine Unused Each	Ave. Unused Each	Fine Used Each	Ave. Used Each
1939. GOLDEN GATE INTERNATIONAL EXPOSITION (N-H ADD 25%)								
☐852	3¢	Bright Purple	2.00	1.60	.25	.20	.18	.15
1939. NEW YORK WORLD'S FAIR (N-H ADD 20%)								
☐853	3¢	Deep Purple	2.40	1.80	.25	.20	.18	.15
1939. WASHINGTON INAUGURATION SESQUICENTENNIAL (N-H ADD 20%)								
☐854	3¢	Bright Red Violet	5.50	4.00	.60	.35	.20	.15
1939. BASEBALL CENTENNIAL (N-H ADD 20%)								
☐855	3¢	Violet	9.00	7.00	1.80	.60	.22	.16
1939. 25TH ANNIVERSARY PANAMA CANAL (N-H ADD 20%)								
☐856	3¢	Deep Red Violet	4.00	3.50	.26	.21	.17	.15
1939. COLONIAL PRINTING TERCENTENARY (N-H ADD 20%)								
☐857	3¢	Rose Violet	1.80	1.60	.23	.16	.16	.15
1939. 50TH ANNIVERSARY OF STATEHOOD (N-H ADD 20%)								
☐858	3¢	Rose Violet	2.00	1.75	.22	.17	.16	.15
1940. FAMOUS AMERICANS SERIES								
AMERICAN AUTHORS (N-H ADD 20%)								
☐859	1¢	Bright Blue Green	1.70	1.50	.26	.18	.16	.15
☐860	2¢	Rose Carmine	1.70	1.45	.26	.18	.16	.15
☐861	3¢	Bright Red Violet	1.80	1.50	.26	.18	.16	.15
☐862	5¢	Ultramarine	18.00	13.00	.45	.42	.38	.40
☐863	10¢	Dark Brown	58.00	42.00	2.60	2.25	1.90	1.50

Scott No.			Fine Unused Plate Blk	Ave. Unused Plate Blk	Fine Unused Each	Ave. Unused Each	Fine Used Each	Ave. Used Each
AMERICAN POETS (N-H ADD 20%)								
☐864	1¢	Bright Blue Green	2.70	2.40	.26	.24	.19	.14
☐865	2¢	Rose Carmine	2.70	2.50	.26	.24	.19	.14
☐866	3¢	Bright Red Violet........	3.25	2.90	.26	.24	.19	.14
☐867	5¢	Ultramarine...............	16.00	12.00	.50	.45	.38	.30
☐868	10¢	Dark Brown...............	52.00	43.00	2.60	2.30	2.25	2.00
AMERICAN EDUCATORS (N-H ADD 20%)								
☐869	1¢	Bright Blue Green	3.10	2.75	.24	.22	.19	.14
☐870	2¢	Rose Carmine	2.00	1.80	.24	.22	.19	.14
☐871	3¢	Bright Red Violet........	4.00	3.10	.28	.25	.19	.14
☐872	5¢	Ultramarine...............	16.00	13.00	.55	.45	.40	.30
☐873	10¢	Dark Brown...............	41.00	33.00	2.40	2.00	1.90	1.70
AMERICAN SCIENTISTS (N-H ADD 20%)								
☐874	1¢	Bright Blue Green	1.60	1.50	.24	.20	.19	.14
☐875	2¢	Rose Carmine	1.40	1.25	.24	.20	.19	.14
☐876	3¢	Bright Red Violet........	1.75	1.50	.24	.20	.19	.14
☐877	5¢	Ultramarine...............	10.00	8.00	.40	.38	.35	.30
☐878	10¢	Dark Brown...............	33.00	30.00	1.80	1.65	1.60	1.30
AMERICAN COMPOSERS (N-H ADD 20%)								
☐879	1¢	Bright Blue Green	1.75	1.50	.24	.20	.18	.14
☐880	2¢	Rose Carmine	1.80	1.50	.24	.20	.18	.14
☐881	3¢	Bright Red Violet........	1.75	1.60	.24	.20	.18	.15
☐882	5¢	Ultramarine...............	15.00	12.00	.65	.48	.34	.30
☐883	10¢	Dark Brown...............	50.00	41.00	5.00	3.75	1.90	1.75
AMERICAN ARTISTS (N-H ADD 20%)								
☐884	1¢	Bright Blue Green	1.50	1.25	.24	.20	.18	.14
☐885	2¢	Rose Carmine	1.50	1.25	.24	.20	.18	.14
☐886	3¢	Bright Red Violet........	1.50	1.25	.24	.20	.18	.14
☐887	5¢	Ultramarine...............	14.00	11.00	.75	.60	.35	.30
☐888	10¢	Dark Brown...............	41.00	36.00	2.40	1.90	1.70	1.45
AMERICAN INVENTORS (N-H ADD 20%)								
☐889	1¢	Bright Blue Green	3.00	2.50	.24	.20	.18	.14
☐890	2¢	Rose Carmine	1.80	1.50	.24	.20	.18	.14
☐891	3¢	Bright Red Violet........	2.75	2.30	.40	.21	.18	.15
☐892	5¢	Ultramarine...............	21.00	18.00	1.30	.90	.50	.45
☐893	10¢	Dark Brown...............	120.00	90.00	14.00	11.00	3.20	2.60

1940. COMMEMORATIVES

1940. 80TH ANNIVERSARY OF PONY EXPRESS (N-H ADD 20%)

☐894	3¢	Henna Brown.............	5.00	4.00	.30	.26	.21	.16

1940. 50TH ANNIVERSARY OF PAN-AMERICAN UNION (N-H ADD 20%)

☐895	3¢	Light Violet	5.00	4.00	.28	.20	.19	.14

Scott No.		Fine Unused Plate Blk	Ave. Unused Plate Blk	Fine Unused Each	Ave. Unused Each	Fine Used Each	Ave. Used Each
1940. 50TH ANNIVERSARY OF IDAHO (N-H ADD 20%)							
☐896	3¢ Bright Violet.............	3.25	2.60	.24	.19	.16	.14
1940. 50TH ANNIVERSARY OF WYOMING (N-H ADD 20%)							
☐897	3¢ Brown Violet.............	2.50	2.10	.24	.19	.16	.14
1940. 400TH ANNIVERSARY OF COLORADO EXPEDITION (N-H ADD 20%)							
☐898	3¢ Violet	2.50	2.10	.24	.19	.16	.14
1940. NATIONAL DEFENSE ISSUE (N-H ADD 20%)							
☐899	1¢ Bright Blue Green	.70	.60	.24	19	.16	.14
☐900	2¢ Rose Carmine	.70	.60	.24	.19	.16	.14
☐901	3¢ Bright Violet...............	.90	.80	.24	.19	.16	.14
1940. 75TH ANNIVERSARY EMANCIPATION AMENDMENT (N-H ADD 20%)							
☐902	3¢ Deep Violet	5.00	4.00	.26	.23	.21	.15

IMPORTANT NOTICE: Values for mint sheets are provided for the following listings. To command the stated prices, sheets must be complete as issued with the plate number (or numbers) intact.

Scott No.		Mint Sheet	Plate Block	Fine Unused Each	Fine Used Each
1941–1943. COMMEMORATIVES					
1941. VERMONT STATEHOOD					
☐903	3¢ Light Violet	10.50	2.40	.24	.16
1942. KENTUCKY SESQUICENTENNIAL ISSUE					
☐904	3¢ Violet ....,	8.00	1.70	.24	.16
1942. WIN THE WAR ISSUE					
☐905	3¢ Violet	12.00	.75	.24	.16
1942. CHINA ISSUE					
☐906	5¢ Bright Blue................................	20.00	12.00	.30	.28
1943. ALLIED NATIONS ISSUE					
☐907	2¢ Rose Carmine	6.50	.55	.24	.16
1943. FOUR FREEDOMS ISSUE					
☐908	1¢ Green	6.50	.75	.24	.16
1943–1944. OVERRUN COUNTRIES SERIES					
☐909	5¢ (Poland).....................................	16.00	8.00	.24	.18
☐910	5¢ (Czechoslovakia)........................	13.00	4.50	.24	.16
☐911	5¢ (Norway)....................................	8.50	2.00	.24	.16
☐912	5¢ (Luxembourg).............................	8.00	1.85	.24	.16
☐913	5¢ (Netherlands).............................	8.00	1.40	.24	.16
☐914	5¢ (Belgium)...................................	8.00	1.40	.24	.16
☐915	5¢ (France)....................................	8.00	1.40	.24	.16
☐916	5¢ (Greece)....................................	35.00	15.00	.53	.45

*No hinge pricing from 1941 to date is figured at (N-H ADD 15%)

Scott No.			Mint Sheet	Plate Block	Fine Unused Each	Fine Used Each
☐917	5¢	(Yugoslavia)	22.00	8.50	.38	.30
☐918	5¢	(Albania)	18.00	8.50	.28	.22
☐919	5¢	(Austria)	15.00	6.00	.28	.24
☐920	5¢	(Denmark)	20.00	7.00	.30	.28
☐921	5¢	(Korea)	12.00	6.00	.26	.24

1944. COMMEMORATIVES

1944. RAILROAD ISSUE

☐922	3¢ Violet	14.00	1.80	.26	.21

1944. STEAMSHIP ISSUE

☐923	3¢ Violet	7.00	1.80	.26	.16

1944. TELEGRAPH ISSUE

☐924	3¢ Bright Red Violet	6.50	1.25	.26	.16

1944. CORREGIDOR ISSUE

☐925	3¢ Deep Violet	6.50	1.40	.26	.16

1944. MOTION PICTURE ISSUE

☐926	3¢ Deep Violet	8.00	1.40	.26	.16

1945. COMMEMORATIVES

1945. FLORIDA ISSUE

☐927	3¢ Bright Red Violet	6.00	.90	.26	.16

1945. PEACE CONFERENCE ISSUE

☐928	5¢ Ultramarine	6.00	.80	.26	.16

1945. IWO JIMA ISSUE

☐929	3¢ Yellow Green	6.00	.80	.26	.16

1945–1946. ROOSEVELT MEMORIAL ISSUE

☐930	1¢ Blue Green	2.50	.50	.26	.16
☐931	2¢ Carmine Rose	3.00	.55	.26	.16
☐932	3¢ Purple	6.00	.75	.26	.16
☐933	5¢ Bright Blue	6.50	.70	.26	.16

1945. ARMY ISSUE

☐934	3¢ Olive Gray	6.00	.70	.24	.14

1945. NAVY ISSUE

☐935	3¢ Blue	6.00	.70	.24	.14

1945. COAST GUARD ISSUE

☐936	3¢ Bright Blue Green	6.00	.70	.24	.14

1945. ALFRED SMITH ISSUE

☐937	3¢ Purple	12.00	.70	.24	.14

1945. TEXAS CENTENNIAL ISSUE

☐938	3¢ Blue	6.00	.70	.24	.14

*No hinge pricing from 1941 to date is figured at (N-H ADD 15%)

Scott No.	Mint Sheet	Plate Block	Fine Unused Each	Fine Used Each
1946-1947. COMMEMORATIVES				
1946. MERCHANT MARINE ISSUE				
☐939 3¢ Blue Green	5.50	.70	.22	.14
1946. HONORABLE DISCHARGE EMBLEM ISSUE				
☐940 3¢ Dark Violet	12.00	.70	.22	.14
1946. TENNESSEE ISSUE				
☐941 3¢ Dark Violet	6.00	.70	.22	.14
1946. IOWA STATEHOOD ISSUE				
☐942 3¢ Deep Blue	6.00	.70	.22	.14
1946. SMITHSONIAN INSTITUTION ISSUE				
☐943 3¢ Violet Brown	6.00	.70	.22	.14
1946. NEW MEXICO ISSUE				
☐944 3¢ Brown Violet	6.00	.70	.22	.14
1947. EDISON ISSUE				
☐945 3¢ Bright Red Violet	8.00	.70	.22	.14
1947. PULITZER PRIZE				
☐946 3¢ Purple	6.00	.70	.22	.14
1947. U.S. POSTAGE STAMP CENTENARY				
☐947 3¢ Deep Blue	6.00	.70	.22	.14
1947. "CIPEX" SOUVENIR SHEET				
☐948 5¢ & 10¢ Sheet of 2	—	—	.90	.75
☐948a 5¢ Blue, sgl. stp.	—	—	.34	.25
☐948b 10¢ Brown Orange, sgl. stp.	—	—	.52	.34
1947. DOCTORS ISSUE				
☐949 3¢ Brown Violet	6.00	.70	.22	.14
1947. UTAH ISSUE				
☐950 3¢ Dark Violet	6.00	.70	.22	.14
1947. U.S.F. CONSTITUTION ISSUE				
☐951 3¢ Blue Green	6.00	.70	.22	.14
1947. EVERGLADES ISSUE				
☐952 3¢ Bright Green	6.00	.70	.22	.14
1948. COMMEMORATIVES				
1948. CARVER ISSUE				
☐953 3¢ Red Violet	7.50	.70	.22	.14
1948. GOLD RUSH ISSUE				
☐954 3¢ Dark Violet	6.00	.70	.22	.14
1948. MISSISSIPPI TERRITORY ISSUE				
☐955 3¢ Brown Violet	6.00	.70	.22	.14

*No hinge pricing from 1941 to date is figured at (N-H ADD 15%)

Scott No.		Mint Sheet	Plate Block	Fine Unused Each	Fine Used Each
1948. FOUR CHAPLAINS ISSUE					
□956	3¢ Gray Black	6.00	.70	.22	.16
1948. WISCONSIN CENTENNIAL ISSUE					
□957	3¢ Dark Violet	6.00	.70	.22	.16
1948. SWEDISH PIONEER ISSUE					
□958	5¢ Deep Blue	7.00	.70	.22	.16
1948. 100 YEARS PROGRESS OF WOMEN					
□959	3¢ Dark Violet	6.00	.70	.22	.16
1948. WILLIAM ALLEN WHITE ISSUE					
□960	3¢ Red Violet	7.50	.70	.22	.16
1948. U.S.-CANADA FRIENDSHIP					
□961	3¢ Blue	6.00	.70	.22	.16
1948. FRANCIS SCOTT KEY ISSUE					
□962	3¢ Rose Pink	6.00	.70	.22	.16
1948. SALUTE TO YOUTH ISSUE					
□963	3¢ Deep Blue	6.00	.70	.22	.16
1948. OREGON TERRITORY ISSUE					
□964	3¢ Brown Red	6.00	.70	.22	.16
1948. HARLAN FISKE STONE					
□965	3¢ Bright Red Violet	7.00	.70	.22	.16
1948. MT. PALOMAR OBSERVATORY					
□966	3¢ Blue	8.00	.70	.22	.16
1948. CLARA BARTON ISSUE					
□967	3¢ Rose Pink	6.00	.70	.22	.16
1948. POULTRY ISSUE					
□968	3¢ Sepia	6.00	.70	.22	.16
1948. GOLD STAR MOTHERS					
□969	3¢ Orange Yellow	6.00	.70	.22	.16
1948. FORT KEARNY ISSUE					
□970	3¢ Violet	6.00	.70	.22	.16
1948. VOLUNTEER FIREMEN					
□971	3¢ Bright Rose Carmine	6.00	.70	.22	.16
1948. INDIAN CENTENNIAL					
□972	3¢ Dark Brown	6.00	.70	.22	.16
1948. ROUGH RIDERS					
□973	3¢ Violet Brown	6.00	.70	.22	.16
1948. JULIETTE LOW					
□974	3¢ Blue Green	6.00	.70	.22	.16

*No hinge pricing from 1941 to date is figured at (N-H ADD 15%)

Scott No.		Mint Sheet	Plate Block	Fine Unused Each	Fine Used Each
1948. WILL ROGERS					
☐975	3¢ Bright Red Violet	9.00	.70	.22	.16
1948. FORT BLISS					
☐976	3¢ Henna Brown	8.00	.70	.22	.16
1948. MOINA MICHAEL					
☐977	3¢ Rose Pink	7.00	.70	.22	.16
1948. GETTYSBURG ADDRESS					
☐978	3¢ Bright Blue	6.00	.70	.22	.16
1948. AMERICAN TURNERS					
☐979	3¢ Carmine	6.00	.70	.22	.16
1948. JOEL CHANDLER HARRIS					
☐980	3¢ Bright Red Violet	7.50	.70	.22	.16
1949-1950. COMMEMORATIVES					
1949. MINNESOTA CENTENNIAL					
☐981	3¢ Blue Green	5.50	.70	.22	.16
1949. WASHINGTON & LEE UNIVERSITY					
☐982	3¢ Ultramarine	5.50	.70	.22	.16
1949. PUERTO RICO ISSUE					
☐983	3¢ Green	5.50	.70	.22	.16
1949. ANNAPOLIS TERCENTENARY					
☐984	3¢ Aquamarine	5.50	.70	.22	.16
1949. G.A.R. ISSUE					
☐985	3¢ Bright Rose Carmine	5.50	.70	.22	.16
1950. EDGAR ALLAN POE					
☐986	3¢ Bright Red Violet	8.00	.70	.22	.16
1950. BANKERS ASSOCIATION					
☐987	3¢ Yellow Green	5.50	.70	.22	.16
1950. SAMUEL GOMPERS					
☐988	3¢ Bright Red Violet	7.50	.70	.22	.16
1950. WASHINGTON SESQUICENTENNIAL					
☐989	3¢ Bright Blue	6.00	.70	.22	.16
☐990	3¢ Deep Green	6.00	.70	.22	.16
☐991	3¢ Light Violet	6.00	.70	.22	.16
☐992	3¢ Rose Violet	6.00	.70	.22	.16
1950. RAILROAD ENGINEERS					
☐993	3¢ Violet Brown	6.00	.70	.22	.16
1950. KANSAS CITY CENTENARY					
☐994	3¢ Violet	6.00	.70	.22	.16

*No hinge pricing from 1941 to date is figured at (N-H ADD 15%)

Scott No.		Mint Sheet	Plate Block	Fine Unused Each	Fine Used Each
1950. BOY SCOUTS ISSUE					
☐995	3¢ Sepia	6.00	.70	.22	.16
1950. INDIANA SESQUICENTENNIAL					
☐996	3¢ Bright Blue	6.00	.70	.22	.16
1950. CALIFORNIA STATEHOOD					
☐997	3¢ Yellow Orange	6.00	.70	.22	.16
1951-1952. COMMEMORATIVES					
1951. UNITED CONFEDERATE VETERANS					
☐998	3¢ Gray	6.00	.70	.22	.16
1951. NEVADA SETTLEMENT					
☐999	3¢ Light Olive Green	6.00	.70	.22	.16
1951. LANDING OF CADILLAC					
☐1000	3¢ Bright Blue	6.00	.70	.22	.16
1951. COLORADO STATEHOOD					
☐1001	3¢ Violet Blue	6.00	.70	.22	.16
1951. AMERICAN CHEMICAL SOCIETY					
☐1002	3¢ Violet Brown	6.00	.70	.22	.16
1951. BATTLE OF BROOKLYN ISSUE					
☐1003	3¢ Violet	6.00	.70	.22	.16
1952. BETSY ROSS ISSUE					
☐1004	3¢ Carmine Rose	6.00	.70	.22	.16
1952. 4-H CLUB ISSUE					
☐1005	3¢ Blue Green	6.00	.70	.22	.16
1952. BALTIMORE & OHIO RAILROAD					
☐1006	3¢ Bright Blue	6.25	.70	.22	.16
1952. AMERICAN AUTOMOBILE ASSOCIATION (AAA)					
☐1007	3¢ Deep Blue	6.00	.70	.22	.16
1952. NORTH ATLANTIC TREATY ORGANIZATION					
☐1008	3¢ Deep Violet	11.00	.70	.22	.16
1952. GRAND COULEE DAM ISSUE					
☐1009	3¢ Blue Green	6.00	.70	.22	.16
1952. ARRIVAL OF LAFAYETTE					
☐1010	3¢ Ultramarine	6.00	.70	.22	.16
1952. MOUNT RUSHMORE					
☐1011	3¢ Blue Green	6.00	.70	.22	.16
1952. SOCIETY OF CIVIL ENGINEERS					
☐1012	3¢ Violet Blue	6.00	.70	.22	.16

*No hinge pricing from 1941 to date is figured at (N-H ADD 15%)

Scott No.		Mint Sheet	Plate Block	Fine Unused Each	Fine Used Each
1952. WOMEN IN ARMED FORCES					
☐1013	3¢ Deep Blue	6.00	.70	.22	.16
1952. GUTENBERG PRINTING					
☐1014	3¢ Violet	6.00	.70	.22	.16
1952. NEWSPAPERBOYS					
☐1015	3¢ Violet	6.00	.70	.22	.16
1952. INTERNATIONAL RED CROSS					
☐1016	3¢ Deep Blue & Carmine	6.00	.70	.22	.16
1953-1954. COMMEMORATIVES					
1953. NATIONAL GUARD					
☐1017	3¢ Bright Blue	6.00	;70	.22	.16
1953. OHIO STATEHOOD					
☐1018	3¢ Chocolate	8.00	.70	.22	.16
1953. WASHINGTON TERRITORY					
☐1019	3¢ Green	5.75	.70	.22	.16
1953. LOUISIANA PURCHASE					
☐1020	3¢ Violet Brown	5.75	.70	.22	.16
1953. OPENING OF JAPAN					
☐1021	3¢ Green	7.25	.90	.22	.16
1953. AMERICAN BAR ASSOCIATION					
☐1022	3¢ Rose Violet	5.75	.70	.22	.16
1953. SAGAMORE HILL					
☐1023	3¢ Yellow Green	5.75	.70	.22	.16
1953. FUTURE FARMERS					
☐1024	3¢ Deep Blue	5.75	.70	.22	.16
1953. TRUCKING INDUSTRY					
☐1025	3¢ Violet	5.75	.70	.22	.16
1953. GENERAL PATTON					
☐1026	3¢ Blue Violet	6.75	.70	.22	.16
1953. NEW YORK CITY					
☐1027	3¢ Bright Red Violet	5.75	.70	.22	.16
1953. GADSDEN PURCHASE					
☐1028	3¢ Copper Brown	5.75	.70	.22	.16
1954. COLUMBIA UNIVERSITY					
☐1029	3¢ Blue	5.75	.70	.22	.16
1954-1961. LIBERTY SERIES					
☐1030	¹/₂¢ Red Orange	5.75	.70	.22	.16
☐1031	1¢ Dark Green	5.75	.70	.22	.16
☐1031A	1¹/₄¢ Turquoise	5.75	.70	.22	.16

*No hinge pricing from 1941 to date is figured at (N-H ADD 15%)

Scott No.			Mint Sheet	Plate Block	Fine Unused Each	Fine Used Each
☐1032	1¹/₂¢	Brown	7.50	2.10	.22	.16
☐1033	2¢	Rose Carmine	6.00	.65	.22	.16
☐1034	2¹/₂¢	Dark Blue	7.00	.65	.22	.16
☐1035	3¢	Deep Violet	7.00	.65	.22	.16
☐1036	4¢	Red Violet	10.00	.70	.22	.16
☐1037	4¹/₂¢	Green	12.00	.80	.22	.16
☐1038	5¢	Deep Blue	15.00	.70	.22	.16
☐1039	6¢	Orange Red	35.00	1.60	.38	.16
☐1040	7¢	Deep Carmine	38.00	3.10	.36	.16
☐1041	8¢	Dark Violet Blue, Carmine	28.00	3.10	.24	.16
☐1042	8¢	Violet Blue, Carmine (Re-engraved)	28.00	1.40	.26	.14
☐1042A	8¢	Brown	29.00	1.40	.30	.16
☐1043	9¢	Rose Lilac	40.00	2.00	.45	.16
☐1044	10¢	Rose Lake	34.00	1.40	.32	.16
☐1044A	11¢	Carmine, Violet Blue	36.00	1.60	.45	.16
☐1045	12¢	Red	45.00	2.00	.45	.16
☐1046	15¢	Maroon	100.00	4.50	1.10	.16
☐1047	20¢	Ultramarine	80.00	3.00	.60	.16
☐1048	25¢	Green	140.00	7.00	1.50	.16
☐1049	30¢	Black	130.00	5.00	1.35	.16
☐1050	40¢	Brown Carmine	260.00	10.00	2.40	.16
☐1051	50¢	Bright Violet	175.00	8.00	1.85	.16
☐1052	$1	Deep Violet	900.00	30.00	6.50	.22
☐1053	$5	Black	10,000.00	400.00	90.00	8.50

1954-1965. ROTARY PRESS COIL STAMPS
PERF. 10 VERTICALLY OR HORIZONTALLY

Scott No.			Fine Unused Line Pair	Ave. Unused Line Pair	Fine Unused Each	Ave. Unused Each	Fine Used Each	Ave. Used Each
☐1054	1¢	Deep Green	1.10	.90	.28	.24	.21	.16
☐1055	2¢	Rose Carmine	.70	.60	.21	.24	.21	.16
☐1056	2¹/₂¢	Gray Blue	4.00	3.00	.32	.24	.21	.18
☐1057	3¢	Deep Violet	.70	.60	.21	.24	.21	.16
☐1058	4¢	Red Violet	.70	.60	.28	.24	.21	.16
☐1059	4¹/₂¢	Green	16.00	12.00	1.60	1.45	1.25	1.00
☐1059A	25¢	Green	2.00	1.50	.80	.50	.90	.24

Scott No.			Mint Sheet	Plate Block	Fine Unused Each	Fine Used Each
1954. NEBRASKA TERRITORY						
☐1060	3¢	Violet	5.75	.70	.21	.16
1954. KANSAS TERRITORY						
☐1061	3¢	Brown Orange	5.75	.70	.21	.16
1954. GEORGE EASTMAN ISSUE						
☐1062	3¢	Violet Brown	7.75	.70	.21	.16

*No hinge pricing from 1941 to date is figured at (N-H ADD 15%)

Scott No.		Mint Sheet	Plate Block	Fine Unused Each	Fine Used Each
1954. LEWIS & CLARK EXPEDITION					
☐1063	3¢ Dark Brown	5.75	.70	.22	.16
1955. COMMEMORATIVES					
1955. PENNSYLVANIA ACADEMY OF FINE ARTS					
☐1064	3¢ Rose Brown	5.75	.70	.22	.16
1955. LAND GRANT COLLEGES					
☐1065	3¢ Green	5.75	.70	.22	.16
1955. ROTARY INTERNATIONAL ISSUE					
☐1066	8¢ Deep Blue	10.00	1.20	.23	.16
1955. ARMED FORCES RESERVE					
☐1067	3¢ Red Violet	5.75	.70	.22	.16
1955. OLD MAN OF THE MOUNTAINS					
☐1068	3¢ Blue Green	5.75	.70	.22	.16
1955. SOO LOCKS CENTENNIAL					
☐1069	3¢ Blue	5.75	.70	.22	.16
1955. ATOMS FOR PEACE					
☐1070	3¢ Blue	5.75	.70	.22	.16
1955. FORT TICONDEROGA BICENTENNIAL					
☐1071	3¢ Sepia	5.75	.70	.22	.16
1955. ANDREW MELLON ISSUE					
☐1072	3¢ Deep Carmine	6.50	.70	.22	.16
1956. COMMEMORATIVES					
1956. 250TH ANNIVERSARY FRANKLIN'S BIRTH					
☐1073	3¢ Rose Carmine	5.75	.70	.22	.16
1956. BOOKER T. WASHINGTON ISSUE					
☐1074	3¢ Deep Blue	5.75	.70	.22	.16
1956. FIFTH INTL. PHILATELIC EXHIBITION DESIGNS OF 1035 & 1041 IN IMPERF. SOUVENIR SHEET					
☐1075	3¢ & 8¢ Sheet of 2	—	—	3.00	2.00
1956. FIFTH INTL. PHILATELIC EXHIBITION					
☐1076	3¢ Deep Violet	5.75	.70	.22	—
1956. WILDLIFE CONSERVATION ISSUE					
☐1077	3¢ Rose Lake	5.75	.70	.22	.16
☐1078	3¢ Brown	5.75	.70	.22	.16
☐1079	3¢ Green	5.75	.70	.22	.16
1956. PURE FOOD & DRUG ACT					
☐1080	3¢ Dark Blue Green	5.75	.70	.22	.16
1956. HOME OF PRESIDENT BUCHANAN					
☐1081	3¢ Black Brown	5.75	.70	.22	.16

*No hinge pricing from 1941 to date is figured at (N-H ADD 15%)

Scott No.		Mint Sheet	Plate Block	Fine Unused Each	Fine Used Each
1956. LABOR DAY ISSUE					
☐1082	3¢ Deep Blue	5.75	.70	.22	.16
1956. NASSAU HALL—PRINCETON					
☐1083	3¢ Black on Orange	5.75	.70	.22	.16
1956. DEVIL'S TOWER					
☐1084	3¢ Purple	5.75	.70	.22	.16
1956. CHILDREN'S ISSUE					
☐1085	3¢ Dark Blue	5.75	.70	.22	.16
1957. COMMEMORATIVES					
1957. ALEXANDER HAMILTON ISSUE					
☐1086	3¢ Rose Red	5.75	.70	.22	.16
1957. POLIO ISSUE					
☐1087	3¢ Light Purple	5.75	.70	.22	.16
1957. COAST & GEODETIC SURVEY					
☐1088	3¢ Dark Blue	5.75	.70	.22	.16
1957. ARCHITECTS ISSUE					
☐1089	3¢ Red Lilac	5.75	.70	.22	.16
1957. STEEL INDUSTRY CENTENNIAL					
☐1090	3¢ Bright Ultra	5.75	.70	.22	.16
1957. INTERNATIONAL NAVAL REVIEW					
☐1091	3¢ Blue Green	5.75	.70	.22	.16
1957. OKLAHOMA STATEHOOD					
☐1092	3¢ Dark Blue	5.75	.70	.22	.16
1957. SCHOOL TEACHERS					
☐1093	3¢ Rose Lake	5.75	.70	.22	.16
1957. U.S. FLAG ISSUE					
☐1094	4¢ Blue & Red	5.75	.70	.22	.16
1957. 350TH SHIPBUILDING ANNIVERSARY					
☐1095	3¢ Purple	8.00	.70	.22	.16
1957. PHILIPPINES—CHAMPION OF LIBERTY					
☐1096	8¢ Red, Blue & Gold	9.50	1.00	.26	.16
1957. BIRTH OF LAFAYETTE					
☐1097	3¢ Maroon	5.75	.70	.22	.16
1957. WILDLIFE CONSERVATION ISSUE					
☐1098	3¢ Blue, Green & Yellow	5.75	.70	.22	.16
1957. RELIGIOUS FREEDOM					
☐1099	3¢ Black	5.75	.70	.22	.16

*No hinge pricing from 1941 to date is figured at (N-H ADD 15%)

Scott No.		Mint Sheet	Plate Block	Fine Unused Each	Fine Used Each
1958. COMMEMORATIVES					
1958. GARDENING & HORTICULTURE					
☐1100	3¢ Deep Green	5.75	.70	.22	.16
1958. BRUSSELS EXHIBITION					
☐1104	3¢ Deep Claret	5.75	.70	.22	.16
1958. JAMES MONROE BICENTENNIAL					
☐1105	3¢ Purple	8.00	.70	.22	.16
1958. MINNESOTA STATEHOOD					
☐1106	3¢ Green	5.75	.70	.22	.16
1958. INTERNATIONAL GEOPHYSICAL YEAR					
☐1107	3¢ Black & Orange	5.75	.70	.22	.16
1958. GUNSTON HALL BICENTENARY					
☐1108	3¢ Light Green	5.75	.70	.22	.16
1958. MACKINAC BRIDGE ISSUE					
☐1109	3¢ Bluish Green	5.75	.70	.22	.16
1958. SOUTH AMERICA—CHAMPION OF LIBERTY					
☐1110	4¢ Olive Bistre	8.00	.70	.22	.16
☐1111	8¢ Red, Blue & Gold	15.00	2.00	.26	.16
1958. ATLANTIC CABLE CENTENNIAL					
☐1112	4¢ Reddish Purple	6.50	.70	.22	.16
1958-1959. LINCOLN COMMEMORATIVE ISSUE					
☐1113	1¢ Green	3.00	.70	.22	.16
☐1114	3¢ Rust Brown	6.00	.70	.22	.16
☐1115	4¢ Sepia	6.50	.70	.22	.16
☐1116	4¢ Blue	6.50	.70	.22	.16
1958. HUNGARY—CHAMPION OF LIBERTY					
☐1117	4¢ Bluish Green	8.50	.70	.22	.16
☐1118	8¢ Red, Blue & Gold	15.00	1.75	.26	.16
1958. FREEDOM OF THE PRESS					
☐1119	4¢ Black	6.00	.70	.22	.16
1958. OVERLAND MAIL CENTENNIAL					
☐1120	4¢ Crimson Rose	6.00	.70	.22	.16
1958. NOAH WEBSTER					
☐1121	4¢ Dark Carmine Rose	8.50	.70	.22	.16
1958. FOREST CONSERVATION					
☐1122	4¢ Yellow, Brown & Green	6.50	.70	.22	.16
1958. FORT DUQUESNE BICENTENNIAL					
☐1123	4¢ Blue	6.50	.70	.22	.16

*No hinge pricing from 1941 to date is figured at (N-H ADD 15%)

Scott No.		Mint Sheet	Plate Block	Fine Unused Each	Fine Used Each
1959. COMMEMORATIVES					
1959. OREGON STATEHOOD					
☐1124	4¢ Blue Green	6.50	.70	.22	.16
1959. ARGENTINA & CHILE—CHAMPION OF LIBERTY					
☐1125	4¢ Blue	8.50	.70	.22	.16
☐1126	8¢ Red, Blue & Gold	15.00	1.25	.22	.16
1959. 10TH ANNIVERSARY N.A.T.O.					
☐1127	4¢ Blue	8.50	.70	.22	.16
1959. ARCTIC EXPLORATIONS					
☐1128	4¢ Blue	6.50	.70	.22	.16
1959. WORLD PEACE & TRUST					
☐1129	8¢ Maroon	10.00	1.10	.26	.16
1959. SILVER DISCOVERY CENTENNIAL					
☐1130	4¢ Black	6.50	.70	.22	.16
1959. ST. LAWRENCE SEAWAY ISSUE					
☐1131	4¢ Red & Blue	6.50	.70	.22	.16
1959. 49-STAR FLAG ISSUE					
☐1132	4¢ Blue, Red & Yellow	6.50	.70	.22	.16
1959. SOIL CONSERVATION					
☐1133	4¢ Yellow, Green & Blue	6.50	.70	.22	.16
1959. PETROLEUM INDUSTRY CENTENNIAL					
☐1134	4¢ Brown	6.50	.70	.22	.16
1959. DENTAL HEALTH ISSUE					
☐1135	4¢ Green	6.50	.70	.22	.16
1959. GERMANY—CHAMPION OF LIBERTY					
☐1136	4¢ Gray	8.00	.70	.22	.16
☐1137	8¢ Red, Blue & Gold	15.00	1.25	.26	.16
1959. DR. EPHRAIM McDOWELL					
☐1138	4¢ Maroon	8.50	.70	.22	.16
1960-1961. CREDO OF AMERICA SERIES					
☐1139	4¢ Dark Violet, Blue & Carmine	6.50	.70	.22	.16
☐1140	4¢ Olive Bistre & Green	6.50	.70	.22	.16
☐1141	4¢ Gray & Red	6.50	.70	.22	.16
☐1142	4¢ Red & Blue	6.50	.70	.22	.16
☐1143	4¢ Violet & Green	8.50	.70	.22	.16
☐1144	4¢ Green & Brown	8.50	.70	.22	.16
COMMEMORATIVES					
1960. BOY SCOUTS GOLDEN JUBILEE					
☐1145	4¢ Red, Khaki & Blue	6.50	.72	.22	.16

*No hinge pricing from 1941 to date is figured at (N-H ADD 15%)

Scott No.		Mint Sheet	Plate Block	Fine Unused Each	Fine Used Each
1960. WINTER OLYMPIC GAMES					
☐1146	4¢ Blue	6.50	.70	.22	.16
1960. CZECHOSLOVAKIA—CHAMPION OF LIBERTY					
☐1147	4¢ Blue	8.50	.70	.22	.16
☐1148	8¢ Yellow, Blue & Red	14.00	1.30	.26	.16
1960. WORLD REFUGEE YEAR					
☐1149	4¢ Gray Black	6.50	.70	.22	.16
1960. WATER CONSERVATION					
☐1150	4¢ Blue, Green & Orange Brown	6.50	.70	.22	.16
1960. SOUTHEAST ASIA TREATY ORGANIZATION					
☐1151	4¢ Blue	8.50	.70	.22	.16
1960. HONORING AMERICAN WOMEN					
☐1152	4¢ Violet	6.50	.70	.22	.16
1960. 50-STAR FLAG ISSUE					
☐1153	4¢ Red & Blue	6.50	.70	.22	.16
1960. PONY EXPRESS CENTENNIAL					
☐1154	4¢ Sepia	6.50	.70	.22	.16
1960. EMPLOY THE HANDICAPPED					
☐1155	4¢ Blue	6.50	.70	.22	.16
1960. WORLD FORESTRY CONGRESS					
☐1156	4¢ Green	6.50	.70	.22	.16
1960. MEXICAN INDEPENDENCE SESQUICENTENNIAL					
☐1157	4¢ Red & Green	6.50	.70	.22	.16
1960. UNITED STATES—JAPAN TREATY CENTENNIAL					
☐1158	4¢ Blue & Pink	6.50	.70	.22	.16
1960. POLAND—CHAMPION OF LIBERTY					
☐1159	4¢ Blue	8.50	.70	.22	.16
☐1160	8¢ Red, Blue & Gold	14.00	1.25	.26	.16
1960. ROBERT A. TAFT MEMORIAL ISSUE					
☐1161	4¢ Dull Violet	8.50	.70	.22	.16
1960. WHEELS OF FREEDOM					
☐1162	4¢ Dark Blue	6.50	.70	.22	.16
1960. BOYS' CLUBS OF AMERICA					
☐1163	4¢ Indigo, Slate & Red	6.50	.70	.22	.16
1960. FIRST AUTOMATED POST OFFICE					
☐1164	4¢ Dark Blue & Carmine	6.50	.70	.22	.16
1960. FINLAND—CHAMPION OF LIBERTY					
☐1165	4¢ Blue	8.50	.70	.22	.16
☐1166	8¢ Red, Blue & Gold	14.00	1.20	.26	.16

*No hinge pricing from 1941 to date is figured at (N-H ADD 15%)

Scott No.		Mint Sheet	Plate Block	Fine Unused Each	Fine Used Each
1960. CAMP FIRE GIRLS					
☐1167	4¢ Dark Blue & Red	6.50	.70	.22	.16
1960. ITALY—CHAMPION OF LIBERTY					
☐1168	4¢ Green	8.75	.70	.22	.16
☐1169	8¢ Red, Blue & Gold	14.00	1.15	.28	.16
1960. WALTER F. GEORGE MEMORIAL ISSUE					
☐1170	4¢ Dull Violet	8.50	.70	.22	.16
1960. ANDREW CARNEGIE					
☐1171	4¢ Deep Claret	8.50	.70	.22	.16
1960. JOHN FOSTER DULLES MEMORIAL ISSUE					
☐1172	4¢ Dull Violet	8.50	.70	.22	.16
1960. "ECHO I" SATELLITE					
☐1173	4¢ Deep Violet	12.00	.90	.28	.16
1961. COMMEMORATIVES					
1961. INDIA—CHAMPION OF LIBERTY					
☐1174	4¢ Red Orange	8.50	.70	.22	.16
☐1175	8¢ Red, Blue & Gold	14.50	1.25	.28	.16
1961. RANGE CONSERVATION					
☐1176	4¢ Blue, Slate & Brown Orange	6.50	.70	.22	.16
1961. HORACE GREELEY					
☐1177	4¢ Dull Violet	8.00	.70	.22	.16
1961-1965. CIVIL WAR CENTENNIAL SERIES					
1961. FORT SUMTER					
☐1178	4¢ Light Green	10.50	1.00	.28	.16
1962. BATTLE OF SHILOH					
☐1179	4¢ Black on Peach	7.50	.70	.22	.16
1963. BATTLE OF GETTYSBURG					
☐1180	5¢ Blue & Gray	9.50	.90	.22	.16
1964. BATTLE OF THE WILDERNESS					
☐1181	5¢ Dark Red & Black	9.50	.90	.22	.16
1965. APPOMATTOX					
☐1182	5¢ Black & Blue	19.00	1.80	.36	.18
1961. KANSAS STATEHOOD					
☐1183	4¢ Brown, Dark Red & Green on Yellow Paper	6.50	.70	.22	.16
1961. GEORGE W. NORRIS BIRTH CENTENARY					
☐1184	4¢ Blue Green	6.50	.70	.22	.16
1961. NAVAL AVIATION GOLDEN JUBILEE					
☐1185	4¢ Blue	6.50	.70	.22	.16

*No hinge pricing from 1941 to date is figured at (N-H ADD 15%)

Scott No.		Mint Sheet	Plate Block	Fine Unused Each	Fine Used Each
1961. WORKMEN'S COMPENSATION LAW					
☐1186	4¢ Ultramarine	6.50	.70	.22	.16
1961. F. REMINGTON BIRTH CENTENNIAL					
☐1187	4¢ Blue, Red & Yellow	6.50	.70	.22	.16
1961. REPUBLIC OF CHINA ISSUE					
☐1188	4¢ Blue	6.50	.70	.22	.16
1961. DR. J. NAISMITH—BASKETBALL FOUNDER					
☐1189	4¢ Brown	6.50	.70	.22	.16
1961. NURSING PROFESSION					
☐1190	4¢ Blue, Red, Black & Green	6.50	.70	.22	.16
1962. COMMEMORATIVES					
1962. NEW MEXICO STATEHOOD					
☐1191	4¢ Blue, Maroon, Bistre	6.50	.70	.22	.16
1961. ARIZONA STATEHOOD					
☐1192	4¢ Red, Deep Blue, Green	6.50	.70	.22	.16
1962. PROJECT MERCURY					
☐1193	4¢ Dark Blue & Yellow	6.50	.70	.22	.16
1962. MALARIA ERADICATION					
☐1194	4¢ Blue & Bistre	6.50	.70	.22	.16
1962. CHARLES EVANS HUGHES BIRTH CENTENNIAL					
☐1195	4¢ Black on Buff	6.50	.70	.22	.16
1962. SEATTLE WORLD'S FAIR					
☐1196	4¢ Red & Dark Blue	6.50	.70	.22	.16
1962. LOUISIANA STATEHOOD					
☐1197	4¢ Blue, Green, Red	6.50	.70	.22	.16
1962. THE HOMESTEAD ACT					
☐1198	4¢ Slate	6.50	.70	.22	.16
1962. GIRL SCOUTS 50TH ANNIVERSARY					
☐1199	4¢ Red	6.50	.70	.22	.16
1962. BRIEN MCMAHON MEMORIAL ISSUE					
☐1200	4¢ Purple	6.50	.70	.22	.16
1962. NATIONAL APPRENTICESHIP ACT					
☐1201	4¢ Black on Buff	6.50	.70	.22	.16
1962. SAM RAYBURN MEMORIAL ISSUE					
☐1202	4¢ Brown & Blue	6.50	.70	.22	.16
1962. DAG HAMMARSKJOLD MEMORIAL					
☐1203	4¢ Yellow, Brown & Black	6.50	.70	.22	.16
☐1204	4¢ Yellow Color Inverted	6.50	1.60	.24	.16

*No hinge pricing from 1941 to date is figured at (N-H ADD 15%)

Scott No.		Mint Sheet	Plate block	Fine Unused Each	Fine Used Each
1962. CHRISTMAS WREATH					
☐1205	4¢ Green & Red	11.00	.70	.22	.16
1962. HIGHER EDUCATION					
☐1206	4¢ Green & Black	6.50	.70	.22	.16
1962. WINSLOW HOMER					
☐1207	4¢ Brown & Blue	6.50	.70	.22	.16
1963. 50-STAR FLAG					
☐1208	5¢ Red & Blue	14.00	.80	.22	.16
1962-1963. REGULAR ISSUE					
☐1209	1¢ Green	6.50	.70	.22	.16
☐1213	5¢ Dark Blue Gray	13.00	.80	.22	.16

1962-1963. ROTARY PRESS COIL STAMPS PERF. 10 VERTICALLY

Scott No.		Fine Unused Plate Blk	Ave. Unused Plate Blk	Fine Unused Each	Ave. Unused Each	Fine Used Each	Ave. Used Each
☐1225	1¢ Green	2.60	2.00	1.50	.28	.22	.16
☐1229	5¢ Dark Blue Gray	4.00	3.10	1.25	1.00	.22	.16

Scott No.		Mint Sheet	Plate Block	Fine Unused Each	Fine Used Each
1963. COMMEMORATIVES					
1963. CAROLINA CHARTER TERCENTENARY					
☐1230	5¢ Dark Carmine & Brown	6.80	.70	.22	.16
1963. FOOD FOR PEACE—FREEDOM FROM HUNGER					
☐1231	5¢ Green, Buff & Red	6.80	.70	.22	.16
1963. WEST VIRGINIA STATEHOOD					
☐1232	5¢ Green, Red & Black	6.80	.70	.22	.16
1963. EMANCIPATION PROCLAMATION					
☐1233	5¢ Black, Blue & Red	6.80	.70	.22	.16
1963. ALLIANCE FOR PROGRESS					
☐1234	5¢ Bright Blue & Green	6.80	.70	.22	.16
1963. CORDELL HULL					
☐1235	5¢ Blue Green	6.80	.70	.22	.16
1963. ELEANOR ROOSEVELT					
☐1236	5¢ Light Purple	6.80	.70	.22	.16
1963. THE SCIENCES					
☐1237	5¢ Blue & Black	6.80	.70	.22	.16
1963. CITY MAIL DELIVERY					
☐1238	5¢ Red, Blue & Gray	6.80	.70	.22	.16

*No hinge pricing from 1941 to date is figured at (N-H ADD 15%)

Scott No.		Mint Sheet	Plate Block	Fine Unused Each	Fine Used Each
1963. INTERNATIONAL RED CROSS CENTENARY					
☐1239	5¢ Slate & Carmine	7.00	.70	.22	.16
1963. CHRISTMAS ISSUE					
☐1240	5¢ Dark Blue, Blue Black & Red	12.00	.70	.22	.16
1963. JOHN JAMES AUDUBON					
☐1241	5¢ Blue, Brown, Bistre	7.00	.70	.22	.16
1964. COMMEMORATIVES					
1964. SAM HOUSTON					
☐1242	5¢ Black	6.80	.70	.22	.16
1964. CHARLES M. RUSSELL					
☐1243	5¢ Indigo, Red Brown & Olive	6.80	.70	.22	.16
1964. NEW YORK WORLD'S FAIR					
☐1244	5¢ Green	6.80	.70	.22	.16
1964. JOHN MUIR—CONSERVATIONIST					
☐1245	5¢ Brown, Green & Olive	6.80	.70	.22	.16
1964. JOHN F. KENNEDY MEMORIAL					
☐1246	5¢ Blue Gray	6.80	.70	.22	.16
1964. NEW JERSEY TERCENTENARY					
☐1247	5¢ Ultramarine	6.80	.70	.22	.16
1964. NEVADA STATEHOOD					
☐1248	5¢ Red, Yellow & Blue	6.80	.70	.22	.16
1964. REGISTER AND VOTE					
☐1249	5¢ Dark Blue & Red	6.80	.70	.22	.16
1964. WILLIAM SHAKESPEARE					
☐1250	5¢ Brown on Tan	6.80	.70	.22	.16
1964. DOCTORS MAYO					
☐1251	5¢ Green	6.80	.70	.22	.16
1964. AMERICAN MUSIC					
☐1252	5¢ Red, Black & Blue	6.80	.70	.22	.16
1964. AMERICAN HOMEMAKERS					
☐1253	5¢ Multicolored	6.80	.70	.22	.16
1964. CHRISTMAS ISSUE					
☐1254	5¢ Red & Green	—	—	1.35	.16
☐1255	5¢ Red & Green	—	—	1.35	.16
☐1256	5¢ Red & Green	—	—	1.10	.16
☐1257	5¢ Red & Green	—	—	.22	.16
1964. VERRAZANO–NARROWS BRIDGE					
☐1258	5¢ Green	6.80	.70	.22	.16

*No hinge pricing from 1941 to date is figured at (N-H ADD 15%)

Scott No.		Mint Sheet	Plate Block	Fine Unused Each	Fine Used Each
1964. STUART DAVIS—MODERN ART					
☐1259	5¢ Ultramarine, Black & Red	7.00	.70	.22	.16
1964. RADIO AMATEURS					
☐1260	5¢ Red Lilac	7.50	.70	.22	.16
1964. COMMEMORATIVES					
1965. BATTLE OF NEW ORLEANS					
☐1261	5¢ Carmine, Blue & Gray	6.85	.70	.22	.16
1965. PHYSICAL FITNESS—SOKOL CENTENNIAL					
☐1262	5¢ Maroon & Black	6.85	.70	.22	.16
1965. CRUSADE AGAINST CANCER					
☐1263	5¢ Black, Purple, Orange	6.85	.70	.22	.16
1965. SIR WINSTON CHURCHILL MEMORIAL					
☐1264 ·	5¢ Black	6.85	.70	.22	.16
1965. MAGNA CARTA 750TH ANNIVERSARY					
☐1265	5¢ Black, Ochre, Red Lilac	6.85	.70	.22	.16
1965. INTERNATIONAL COOPERATION YEAR					
☐1266	5¢ Dull Blue & Black	6.85	.70	.22	.16
1965. SALVATION ARMY					
☐1267	5¢ Red, Black & Blue	6.85	.70	.22	.16
1965. DANTE ALIGHIERI					
☐1268	5¢ Maroon on Tan	6.85	.70	.22	.16
1965. HERBERT HOOVER					
☐1269	5¢ Red Rose	6.85	.70	.22	.16
1965. ROBERT FULTON BIRTH BICENTENNIAL					
☐1270	5¢ Black & Blue	6.85	.70	.22	.16
1965. FLORIDA SETTLEMENT QUADRICENTENNIAL					
☐1271	5¢ Red, Yellow & Black	6.85	.70	.22	.16
1965. TRAFFIC SAFETY					
☐1272	5¢ Green, Black, Red	6.85	.70	.22	.16
1965. JOHN SINGLETON COPLEY—ARTIST					
☐1273	5¢ Black, Brown, Olive	6.85	.70	.22	.16
1965. INTERNATIONAL TELECOMMUNICATION UNION					
☐1274	11¢ Black, Carmine, Bistre	24.00	8.00	.50	.16
1965. ADLAI E. STEVENSON MEMORIAL					
☐1275	5¢ Light & Dark Blue, Black & Red	6.85	.70	.22	.16
1965. CHRISTMAS ISSUE					
☐1276	5¢ Red, Green & Yellow	12.00	.70	.22	.16

*No hinge pricing from 1941 to date is figured at (N-H ADD 15%)

Scott No.			Mint Sheet	Plate Block	Fine Unused Each	Fine Used Each
1965–1968. PROMINENT AMERICANS SERIES						
☐1278	1¢	Green	6.00	.70	.22	.16
☐1279	1¼¢	Green	20.00	12.00	.22	.16
☐1280	2¢	Slate Blue	6.00	.65	.22	.16
☐1281	3¢	Purple	8.50	.70	.22	.16
☐1282	4¢	Black	11.00	.70	.22	.16
☐1283	5¢	Blue	12.00	.70	.22	.16
☐1283B	5¢	Blue	12.00	.70	.22	.16
☐1284	6¢	Gray Brown	17.00	.80	.22	.16
☐1285	8¢	Violet	23.00	1.10	.30	.16
☐1286	10¢	Lilac	26.00	1.20	.28	.16
☐1286A	12¢	Black	32.00	1.50	.31	.16
☐1287	13¢	Brown	40.00	1.75	.45	.16
☐1288	15¢	Rose Claret	36.00	2.10	.40	.16
☐1288A	15¢	Rose Claret II	34.00	4.50	.36	.16
☐1289	20¢	Olive Green	50.00	2.50	.65	.16
☐1290	25¢	Rose Lake	50.00	2.50	.60	.16
☐1291	30¢	Light Purple	64.00	3.50	.70	.16
☐1292	40¢	Dark Blue	92.00	4.50	1.00	.16
☐1293	50¢	Maroon	100.00	5.00	1.25	.16
☐1294	$1	Purple	210.00	10.00	2.25	.16
☐1295	$5	Gray	800.00	46.00	11.00	2.50

Scott No.			Fine Unused Line Pair	Ave. Unused Line Pair	Fine Unused Each	Ave. Unused Each	Fine Used Each	Ave. Used Each
PERF. 10 HORIZONTALLY								
☐1297	3¢	Purple	.75	.65	.24	.22	.21	.16
☐1298	6¢	Gray Brown	1.60	1.45	.24	.22	.21	.16
PERF. 10 VERTICALLY								
☐1299	1¢	Green	.55	.40	.24	.22	.21	.16
☐1303	4¢	Black	.90	.75	.24	.22	.21	.16
☐1304	5¢	Blue	.60	.55	.24	.22	.21	.16
☐1305	6¢	Gray Brown	.85	.75	.24	.22	.21	.16
☐1305C	$1	Purple	5.00	4.00	2.00	1.90	1.75	1.10

Scott No.			Mint Sheet	Plate Block	Fine Unused Each	Fine Used Each
1966. COMMEMORATIVES						
1966. MIGRATORY BIRD TREATY						
☐1306	5¢	Red, Blue, Black	7.00	.70	.20	.16
1966. HUMANE TREATMENT OF ANIMALS						
☐1307	5¢	Orange Brown & Black	7.00	.70	.20	.16
1966. INDIANA STATEHOOD						
☐1308	5¢	Ochre, Brown & Violet Blue	7.00	.70	.20	.16

*No hinge pricing from 1941 to date is figured at (N-H ADD 15%)

Scott No.		Mint Sheet	Plate Block	Fine Unused Each	Fine Used Each
1966. AMERICAN CIRCUS					
☐1309	5¢ Red, Blue, Pink, Black	7.00	.70	.22	.16
1966. SIXTH INTL. PHILATELIC EXHIBITION "SIPEX"					
☐1310	5¢ Multicolored	7.50	.70	.22	.16
1966. IMPERFORATE SOUVENIR SHEET					
☐1311	5¢ Multicolored	—	.70	.22	.16
1966. BILL OF RIGHTS					
☐1312	5¢ Red, Dark & Light Blue	8.50	.05	.22	.16
1966. POLISH MILLENNIUM					
☐1313	5¢ Red	7.00	.70	.22	.16
1966. NATIONAL PARK SERVICE					
☐1314	5¢ Yellow, Black & Green	7.00	.70	.22	.16
1966. MARINE CORPS RESERVE					
☐1315	5¢ Black, Red, Blue, Olive	7.00	.70	.22	.16
1966. GENERAL FEDERATION OF WOMEN'S CLUBS					
☐1316	5¢ Blue, Pink, Black	7.00	.70	.22	.16
1966. AMERICAN FOLKLORE—JOHNNY APPLESEED					
☐1317	5¢ Red, Black, Green	7.00	.70	.22	.16
1966. BEAUTIFICATION OF AMERICA					
☐1318	5¢ Emerald, Pink, Black	7.00	.70	.22	.16
1966. GREAT RIVER ROAD					
☐1319	5¢ Yellow, Red, Blue, Green	7.00	.70	.22	.16
1966. SERVICEMEN & SAVINGS BONDS					
☐1320	5¢ Red, Light Blue, Dark Blue	7.00	.70	.22	.16
1966. CHRISTMAS ISSUE					
☐1321	5¢ Multicolored	12.00	.70	.22	.16
1966. MARY CASSATT—ARTIST					
☐1322	5¢ Multicolored	9.00	.90	.22	.16
1967. COMMEMORATIVES					
1967. NATIONAL GRANGE CENTENARY					
☐1323	5¢ Orange, Yellow, Black, Brown & Green	8.00	.70	.22	.16
1967. CANADA CENTENNIAL					
☐1324	5¢ Green, Light & Dark Blue, Black	7.00	.70	.22	.16
1967. ERIE CANAL SESQUICENTENNIAL					
☐1325	5¢ Light & Dark Blue, Red & Black	7.00	.70	.22	.16
1967. SEARCH FOR PEACE—LIONS INTL.					
☐1326	5¢ Red, Blue & Black	7.00	.70	.22	.16
1967. HENRY DAVID THOREAU					
☐1327	5¢ Black, Red & Green	7.00	.70	.22	.16

*No hinge pricing from 1941 to date is figured at (N-H ADD 15%)

Scott No.			Mint Sheet	Plate Block	Fine Unused Each	Fine Used Each
1967. NEBRASKA STATEHOOD CENTENNIAL						
☐1328	5¢	Yellow Green & Brown..................................	7.00	.70	.22	.16
1967. VOICE OF AMERICA						
☐1329	5¢	Red, Blue & Black.......................................	7.00	.70	.22	.16
1967. AMERICAN FOLKLORE—DAVY CROCKETT						
☐1330	5¢	Green & Black...	7.00	.70	.22	.16
1967. SPACE ACCOMPLISHMENTS						
☐1331	5¢	Light & Dark Blue, Red, Black...................	—	.70	1.00	.30
☐1332	5¢	Light & Dark Blue, Red, Black...................	—	.70	1.00	.30
1967. URBAN PLANNING						
☐1333	5¢	Blue & Black..	7.50	.70	.22	.16
1967. FINNISH INDEPENDENCE						
☐1334	5¢	Blue...	7.50	.70	.22	.16
1967. THOMAS EAKINS—ARTIST						
☐1335	5¢	Gold & Multicolored....................................	7.50	.70	.22	.16
1967. CHRISTMAS ISSUE						
☐1336	5¢	Multicolored..	7.50	.70	.22	.16
1967. MISSISSIPPI STATEHOOD						
☐1337	5¢	Multicolored..	7.50	.70	.22	.16
1968–1971. REGULAR ISSUES						
1968. FLAG ISSUE						
☐1338	6¢	Red, Blue, Green...	14.00	.70	.22	.16
1968. COMMEMORATIVES						
1968. ILLINOIS STATEHOOD						
☐1339	6¢	Black, Gold, Pink..	7.50	.70	.22	.16
1968. HEMISFAIR '68						
☐1340	6¢	Indigo, Carmine, White...............................	7.50	.70	.22	.16
1968. AIRLIFT TO SERVICEMEN						
☐1341	$1	Multicolored..	140.00	12.00	3.80	2.00
1968. SUPPORT OUR YOUTH (ELKS)						
☐1342	6¢	Blue & Black..	7.50	.70	.22	.16
1968. LAW AND ORDER						
☐1343	6¢	Blue & Black..	7.50	.70	.22	.16
1968. REGISTER & VOTE						
☐1344	6¢	Black & Gold..	7.50	.70	.22	.16
1968. HISTORIC AMERICAN FLAGS						
☐1345	6¢	Dark Blue...	—	—	.50	.40
☐1346	6¢	Red & Dark Blue..	—	—	.45	.38

*No hinge pricing from 1941 to date is figured at (N-H ADD 15%)

Scott No.			Mint Sheet	Plate Block	Fine Unused Each	Fine Used Each
☐1347	6¢	Dark, Blue, Olive Green	—	—	.35	.25
☐1348	6¢	Dark Blue & Red	—	—	.35	.25
☐1349	6¢	Black, Yellow, Red	—	—	.35	.25
☐1350	6¢	Dark Blue & Red	—	—	.35	.25
☐1351	6¢	Blue, Olive Green, Red	—	—	.35	.25
☐1352	6¢	Dark Blue & Red	—	—	.35	.25
☐1353	6¢	Blue, Yellow, Red	—	—	.35	.25
☐1354	6¢	Blue Red, Yellow	—	—	.35	.25

1968. WALT DISNEY
☐1355	6¢	Multicolored	24.00	2.40	.60	.16

1968. FATHER MARQUETTE—EXPLORATIONS
☐1356	6¢	Black, Brown, Green	10.00	1.00	.22	.16

1968. AMERICAN FOLKLORE—DANIEL BOONE
☐1357	6¢	Brown, Yellow, Black, Red	7.50	.70	.22	.16

1968. ARKANSAS RIVER NAVIGATION
☐1358	6¢	Black & Blue	7.50	.70	.21	.16

1968. LEIF ERIKSON
☐1359	6¢	Dark Brown on Brown	7.50	.70	.22	.16

1968. CHEROKEE STRIP LAND RUSH
☐1360	6¢	Brown	7.50	.70	.22	.16

1968. JOHN TRUMBULL PAINTING
☐1361	6¢	Yellow Red, Black	7.50	.70	.22	.16

1968. WILDLIFE CONSERVATION—DUCKS
☐1362	6¢	Multicolored	11.00	1.15	.22	.16

1968. CHRISTMAS ISSUE
☐1363	6¢	Multicolored	8.00	1.75	.22	.16

1968. AMERICAN INDIAN
☐1364	6¢	Multicolored	11.00	1.15	.22	.16

1969. COMMEMORATIVES

1969. BEAUTIFICATION OF AMERICA
☐1365	6¢	Multicolored	—	—	.65	.18
☐1366	6¢	Multicolored	—	—	.65	.18
☐1367	6¢	Multicolored	—	—	.65	.18
☐1368	6¢	Multicolored	—	—	.65	.18

1969. AMERICAN LEGION
☐1369	6¢	Red, Blue, Black	7.50	.70	.22	.16

1969. GRANDMA MOSES PAINTING
☐1370	6¢	Multicolored	7.50	.70	.22	.16

1969. APOLLO 8 MOON ORBIT
☐1371	6¢	Black, Blue, Ochre	11.00	1.15	.22	.16

*No hinge pricing from 1941 to date is figured at (N-H ADD 15%)

Scott No.		Mint Sheet	Plate Block	Fine Unused Each	Fine Used Each
1969. W. C. HANDY—MUSICIAN					
☐1372	6¢ Multicolored	10.00	1.00	.22	.16
1969. SETTLEMENT OF CALIFORNIA					
☐1373	6¢ Multicolored	7.50	.70	.22	.16
1969. MAJOR JOHN WESLEY POWELL—GEOLOGIST					
☐1374	6¢ Multicolored	7.50	.70	.22	.16
1969. ALABAMA STATEHOOD					
☐1375	6¢ Red, Yellow, Brown	7.50	.70	.22	.16
1969. XI INTL. BOTANICAL CONGRESS					
☐1376	6¢ Multicolored	—	—	1.50	.35
☐1377	5¢ Multicolored	—	—	1.50	.35
☐1378	6¢ Multicolored	—	—	1.50	.35
☐1379	6¢ Multicolored	—	—	1.50	.35
1969. DARTMOUTH COLLEGE CASE					
☐1380	6¢ Green	7.50	.80	.22	.16
1969. PROFESSIONAL BASEBALL CENTENARY					
☐1381	6¢ Multicolored	39.00	4.50	.90	.16
1969. INTERCOLLEGIATE FOOTBALL CENTENARY					
☐1382	6¢ Red & Green	13.00	1.50	.40	.16
1969. DWIGHT D. EISENHOWER MEMORIAL					
☐1383	6¢ Blue, Black & Red	5.00	.80	.22	.16
1969. CHRISTMAS ISSUE					
☐1384	6¢ Multicolored	7.50	1.90	.22	.16
1969. HOPE FOR THE CRIPPLED					
☐1385	6¢ Multicolored	7.50	.80	.22	.16
1969. WILLIAM M. HARNETT PAINTING					
☐1386	6¢ Multicolored	5.50	.80	.22	.16
1970. COMMEMORATIVES					
1970. NATURAL HISTORY					
☐1387	6¢ Multicolored	—	—	.30	.16
☐1388	6¢ Multicolored	—	—	.30	.16
☐1389	6¢ Multicolored	—	—	.30	.16
☐1390	6¢ Multicolored	—	—	.30	.16
1970. MAINE STATEHOOD SESQUICENTENNIAL					
☐1391	6¢ Multicolored	7.50	.70	.22	16
1970. WILDLIFE CONSERVATION—BUFFALO					
☐1392	6¢ Black on Tan	7.50	.70	.22	.16
1970–1974. REGULAR ISSUE					
☐1393	6¢ Blue Gray	14.00	.70	.22	.16
☐1393D	7¢ Light Blue	18.00	1.10	.22	.16

*No hinge pricing from 1941 to date is figured at (N-H ADD 15%)

Scott No.			Mint Sheet	Plate Block	Fine Unused Each	Fine Used Each
☐1394	8¢	Black, Blue, Red..........	20.00	1.00	.25	.16
☐1395	8¢	Rose Violet	—		.25	.16
☐1396	8¢	Multicolored	20.00	4.00	.26	.16
☐1397	14¢	Brown	32.00	1.50	.36	.16
☐1398	16¢	Orange Brown	34.00	1.80	.40	.16
☐1399	18¢	Purple	44.00	2.10	.50	.16
☐1400	21¢	Green	46.00	2.15	.50	.35

Scott No.			Fine Unused Line Pair	Ave. Unused Line Pair	Fine Unused Each	Ave. Unused Each	Fine Used Each	Ave. Used Each
1970–1971. ROTARY PRESS COIL STAMPS—PERF. 10 VERTICALLY								
☐1401	6¢	Blue Gray	.70	.60	.24	.22	.21	.16
☐1402	8¢	Rose Violet	.70	.60	.24	.22	.21	.16

Scott No.			Mint Sheet	Plate Block	Fine Unused Each	Fine Used Each
1970. EDGAR LEE MASTERS—POET						
☐1405	6¢	Black & Olive Bistre	7.50	.70	.22	.16
1970. 50TH ANNIVERSARY WOMEN'S SUFFRAGE						
☐1406	6¢	Blue	7.50	.70	.22	.16
1970. SOUTH CAROLINA TERCENTENARY						
☐1407	6¢	Multicolored	7.50	.70	.22	.16
1970. STONE MOUNTAIN MEMORIAL						
☐1408	6¢	Gray Black	7.50	.70	.22	.16
1970. FORT SNELLING						
☐1409	6¢	Multicolored	7.50	.70	.22	.16
1970. ANTI-POLLUTION						
☐1410	6¢	Multicolored	—	—	.35	.16
☐1411	6¢	Multicolored	—	—	.35	.16
☐1412	6¢	Multicolored	—	—	.35	.16
☐1413	6¢	Multicolored	—	—	.35	.16
1970. CHRISTMAS ISSUE						
☐1414	6¢	Multicolored	7.50	1.60	.26	.16
☐1415	6¢	Multicolored	—	—	.46	.16
☐1416	6¢	Multicolored	—	—	.46	.16
☐1417	6¢	Multicolored	—	—	.46	.16
☐1418	6¢	Multicolored	—	—	.46	.16
1970. PRECANCELLED CHRISTMAS ISSUE						
☐1414a	6¢	Multicolored	8.50	3.00	.40	.16
☐1415a	6¢	Multicolored	—	—	.90	.16
☐1416a	6¢	Multicolored	—	—	.90	.16
☐1417a	6¢	Multicolored	—	—	.90	.16
☐1418a	6¢	Multicolored	—	—	.90	.16

*No hinge pricing from 1941 to date is figured at (N-H ADD 15%)

Scott No.		Mint Sheet	Plate Block	Fine Unused Each	Fine Used Each
1970. UNITED NATIONS 25TH ANNIVERSARY					
☐1419	6¢ Black, Red, Blue..	7.50	.70	.22	.16
1970. PILGRIM LANDING 350TH ANNIVERSARY					
☐1420	6¢ Multicolored	7.50	.70	.22	.16
1970. DISABLED AMERICAN VETERANS AND SERVICEMEN ISSUE					
☐1421	6¢ Blue, Black, Red..	—	—	.28	.16
☐1422	6¢ Blue, Black, Red..	—	—	.28	.16
1971. COMMEMORATIVES					
1971. ADVENT OF SHEEP TO AMERICA					
☐1423	6¢ Multicolored	7.50	.70	.22	.16
1971. GENERAL DOUGLAS MacARTHUR					
☐1423	6¢ Red, Blue, Black..	7.50	.70	.22	.16
1971. BLOOD DONORS PROGRAM					
☐1425	6¢ Light Blue, Scarlet, Indigo	7.50	.70	.22	.16
1971. MISSOURI STATEHOOD					
☐1426	8¢ Multicolored	10.00	2.80	.26	.18
1971. WILDLIFE CONSERVATION					
☐1427	8¢ Multicolored	—	—	.26	.16
☐1428	8¢ Multicolored	—	—	.26	.16
☐1429	8¢ Multicolored	—	—	.26	.16
☐1430	8¢ Multicolored	—	—	.26	.16
1971. ANTARCTIC TREATY					
☐1431	8¢ Red & Blue	10.00	1.10	.24	.16
1971. AMERICAN REVOLUTION BICENTENNIAL					
☐1432	8¢ Red, Blue, Black..	11.00	1.25	.24	.16
1971. JOHN SLOAN PAINTING					
☐1433	8¢ Multicolored	10.00	1.10	.24	.16
1971. DECADE OF SPACE ACHIEVEMENTS					
☐1434	8¢ Multicolored	—	—	.26	.16
☐1435	8¢ Multicolored	—	—	.26	.16
1971. EMILY DICKINSON—POET					
☐1436	8¢ Multicolored	9.50	1.00	.26	.16
1971. SAN JUAN 450TH ANNIVERSARY					
☐1437	8¢ Brown, Carmine, Blk.	10.00	1.00	.26	.16
1971. DRUG ADDICTION					
☐1438	8¢ Blue & Black	10.00	1.50	.26	.16
1971. CARE ANNIVERSARY					
☐1439	8¢ Multicolored	10.00	2.00	.26	.16
☐1440	8¢ Dark Brown & Ochre.....................................	—	—	.26	.16

*No hinge pricing from 1941 to date is figured at (N-H ADD 15%)

Scott No.			Mint Sheet	Plate Block	Fine Unused Each	Fine Used Each
☐1441	8¢	Dark Brown & Ochre	—	—	.26	.16
☐1442	8¢	Dark Brown & Ochre	—	—	.26	.16
☐1443	8¢	Dark Brown & Ochre	—	—	.26	.16

1971. CHRISTMAS

☐1444	8¢	Multicolored	9.50	2.75	.22	.16
☐1445	8¢	Multicolored	9.50	2.75	.22	.16

1972. COMMEMORATIVES

1972. SIDNEY LANIER—POET

☐1446	8¢	Multicolored	10.00	1.15	.26	.16

1972. PEACE CORPS

☐1447	8¢	Red & Blue	10.00	1.50	.26	.16

1972. NATIONAL PARKS CENTENNIAL

☐1448	2¢	Multicolored	—	—	.22	.16
☐1449	2¢	Multicolored	—	—	.22	.16
☐1450	2¢	Multicolored	—	—	.22	.16
☐1451	2¢	Multicolored	—	—	.22	.16
☐1452	6¢	Multicolored	7.50	.80	.22	.16
☐1453	8¢	Multicolored	7.50	1.00	.26	.16
☐1454	15¢	Multicolored	17.00	1.75	.40	.35

1972. FAMILY PLANNING

☐1455	8¢	Multicolored	11.00	1.10	.22	.16

1972. AMERICAN REVOLUTION BICENTENNIAL— COLONIAL CRAFTSMEN

☐1456	8¢	Deep Brown, Yellow	—	—	.26	.16
☐1457	8¢	Deep Brown, Yellow	—	—	.26	.16
☐1458	8¢	Deep Brown, Yellow	—	—	.26	.16
☐1459	8¢	Deep Brown, Yellow	—	—	.26	.16

1972. OLYMPIC GAMES

☐1460	6¢	Multicolored	8.50	1.90	.22	.16
☐1461	8¢	Multicolored	10.00	2.60	.22	.16
☐1462	15¢	Multicolored	17.00	4.50	.40	.35

1972. PARENT TEACHER ASSOCIATION

☐1463	8¢	Black & Yellow	10.00	1.00	.22	.16
☐1463a	8¢	Black & Yellow, Reversed Pl. No.	—	1.10	—	—

1972. WILDLIFE CONSERVATION

☐1464	8¢	Multicolored	—	—	.26	.16
☐1465	8¢	Multicolored	—	—	.26	.16
☐1466	8¢	Multicolored	—	—	.26	.16
☐1467	8¢	Multicolored	—	—	.26	.16

1972. MAIL ORDER BUSINESS

☐1468	8¢	Multicolored	10.00	3.00	.26	.16

*No hinge pricing from 1941 to date is figured at (N-H ADD 15%)

Scott No.			Mint Sheet	Plate Block	Fine Unused Each	Fine Used Each
1972. OSTEOPATHIC MEDICINE						
☐1469	8¢	Yellow Orange, Brown	10.00	1.50	.26	.16
1972. TOM SAWYER—AMERICAN FOLKLORE						
☐1470	8¢	Multicolored	10.00	1.10	.26	.16
1972. CHRISTMAS						
☐1471	8¢	Multicolored	10.00	2.75	.26	.16
☐1472	8¢	Multicolored	10.00	2.75	.26	.16
1972. PHARMACY						
☐1473	8¢	Multicolored	12.00	1.20	.26	.16
1972. STAMP COLLECTING						
☐1474	8¢	Multicolored	8.50	1.10	.26	.16
1973. COMMEMORATIVES						
1973. LOVE—"FOR SOMEONE SPECIAL"						
☐1475	8¢	Red, Green, Blue	10.00	1.40	.26	.16
1973. COLONIAL COMMUNICATIONS						
☐1476	8¢	Black, Red, Blue	10.00	1.10	.27	.16
☐1477	8¢	Blue, Red, Brown	10.00	1.10	.27	.16
☐1478	8¢	Multicolored	10.00	1.10	.27	.16
☐1479	8¢	Multicolored	10.00	1.10	.27	.16
1973. BOSTON TEA PARTY						
☐1480	8¢	Multicolored	—	—	.26	.16
☐1481	8¢	Multicolored	—	—	.26	.16
☐1482	8¢	Multicolored	—	—	.26	.16
☐1483	8¢	Multicolored	—	—	.26	.16
1973. GEORGE GERSHWIN—COMPOSER						
☐1484	8¢	Multicolored	10.00	3.50	.26	.16
1973. ROBINSON JEFFERS—POET						
☐1485	8¢	Multicolored	8.50	3.00	.26	.16
1973. HENRY OSSAWA TANNER—ARTIST						
☐1486	6¢	Multicolored	8.50	3.00	.26	.16
1973. WILLA CATHER—NOVELIST						
☐1487	8¢	Multicolored	8.50	3.00	.26	.16
1973. NICOLAUS COPERNICUS						
☐1488	8¢	Black & Orange	10.00	1.00	.26	.16
1973. POSTAL PEOPLE						
☐1489	8¢	Multicolored	—	—	.26	.16
☐1490	8¢	Multicolored	—	—	.26	.16
☐1491	8¢	Multicolored	—	—	.26	.16
☐1492	8¢	Multicolored	—	—	.26	.16
☐1493	8¢	Multicolored	—	—	.26	.16
☐1494	8¢	Multicolored	—	—	.26	.16

*No hinge pricing from 1941 to date is figured at (N-H ADD 15%)

Scott No.			Mint Sheet	Plate Block	Fine Unused Each	Fine Used Each
☐1495	8¢	Multicolored	—	—	.26	.16
☐1496	8¢	Multicolored	—	—	.26	.16
☐1497	8¢	Multicolored	—	—	.26	.16
☐1498	8¢	Multicolored	—	—	.26	.16

1973. HARRY S. TRUMAN MEMORIAL
| ☐1499 | 8¢ | Black, Red, Blue | 7.00 | 1.00 | .26 | .16 |

1973. PROGRESS IN ELECTRONICS
☐1500	6¢	Multicolored	7.50	.72	.26	.16
☐1501	8¢	Multicolored	10.00	1.00	.26	.16
☐1502	15¢	Multicolored	17.00	1.65	.40	.24

1973. LYNDON B. JOHNSON MEMORIAL
| ☐1503 | 8¢ | Multicolored | 7.00 | 2.75 | .26 | .24 |

1973. ANGUS CATTLE—RURAL AMERICA
| ☐1504 | 8¢ | Multicolored | 10.00 | 1.00 | .26 | .24 |

1974. CHAUTAUQUA—RURAL AMERICA
| ☐1505 | 10¢ | Multicolored | 12.00 | 1.20 | .29 | .24 |

1974. WINTER WHEAT—RURAL AMERICA
| ☐1506 | 10¢ | Multicolored | 12.00 | 1.20 | .20 | .24 |

1973. CHRISTMAS
| ☐1507 | 8¢ | Multicolored | 10.00 | 3.00 | .26 | .24 |
| ☐1508 | 8¢ | Multicolored | 10.00 | 3.00 | .26 | .24 |

1973–1974. REGULAR ISSUES
☐1509	10¢	Red & Blue	31.00	7.00	.34	.24
☐1510	10¢	Blue	26.00	1.25	.32	.24
☐1511	10¢	Multicolored	24.00	2.10	.29	.24

Scott No.			Fine Unused Line Pair	Ave. Unused Line Pair	Fine Unused Each	Ave. Unused Each	Fine Used Each	Ave. Used Each

1973–1974. COIL STAMPS—PERF. 10 VERTICALLY
☐1518	63¢	Orange	1.00	.80	.26	.22	.20	.16
☐1519	10¢	Red & Blue	—	—	.28	.25	.24	.16
☐1520	10¢	Blue	1.20	.90	.28	.25	.24	.16

Scott No.			Mint Sheet	Plate Block	Fine Unused Each	Fine Used Each

1974. COMMEMORATIVES
1974. VETERANS OF FOREIGN WARS
| ☐1525 | 10¢ | Carmine & Blue | 12.00 | 1.25 | .30 | .16 |

1974. ROBERT FROST—POET
| ☐1526 | 10¢ | Black | 12.00 | 1.25 | .30 | .16 |

1975. EXPO '74—PRESERVE THE ENVIRONMENT
| ☐1527 | 10¢ | Multicolored | 10.00 | 3.50 | .30 | .16 |

*No hinge pricing from 1941 to date is figured at (N-H ADD 15%)

Scott No.			Mint Sheet	Plate Block	Fine Unused Each	Fine Used Each
1974. HORSE RACING						
☐1528	10¢	Multicolored	12.00	3.40	.30	.16
1975. SKYLAB PROJECT						
☐1529	10¢	Multicolored	12.00	1.25	.30	.16
1974. UNIVERSAL POSTAL UNION CENTENARY						
☐1530	10¢	Multicolored	—	—	.32	.18
☐1531	10¢	Multicolored	—	—	.32	.18
☐1532	10¢	Multicolored	—	—	.32	.18
☐1533	10¢	Multicolored	—	—	.32	.18
☐1534	10¢	Multicolored	—	—	.32	.18
☐1535	10¢	Multicolored	—	—	.32	.18
☐1536	10¢	Multicolored	—	—	.32	.18
☐1537	10¢	Multicolored	—	—	.32	.18
1974. MINERALS HERITAGE ISSUE						
☐1538	10¢	Multicolored	—	—	.30	.16
☐1539	10¢	Multicolored	—	—	.30	.16
☐1540	10¢	Multicolored	—	—	.30	.16
☐1541	10¢	Multicolored	—	—	.30	.16
1974. FORT HARROD BICENTENNIAL						
☐1542	10¢	Multicolored	12.00	1.25	.31	.16
1974. CONTINENTAL CONGRESS						
☐1543	10¢	Red, Blue, Gray	—	—	.30	.16
☐1544	10¢	Red, Blue, Gray	—	—	.30	.16
☐1545	10¢	Red, Blue, Gray	—	—	.30	.16
☐1546	10¢	Red, Blue, Gray	—	—	.30	.16
1974. ENERGY CONSERVATION						
☐1547	10¢	Multicolored	12.00	1.10	.30	.16
1974. LEGEND OF SLEEPY HOLLOW						
☐1548	10¢	Multicolored	12.00	1.10	.30	.16
1974. RETARDED CHILDREN						
☐1549	10¢	Light & Dark Brown	12.00	1.10	.30	.16
1974. CHRISTMAS						
☐1550	10¢	Multicolored	12.00	3.10	.31	.16
☐1551	10¢	Multicolored	12.00	3.20	.31	.16
☐1552	10¢	Multicolored	12.00	3.60	.31	.16
☐1552A	10¢	Multicolored, Plate Block of 12	12.00	4.00	—	—
1975. COMMEMORATIVES—AMERICAN ARTS						
1975. BENJAMIN WEST—ARTIST						
☐1553	10¢	Multicolored	12.00	3.10	.31	.16
1975. PAUL LAURENCE DUNBAR—POET						
☐1554	10¢	Multicolored	12.00	3.10	.31	.16

*No hinge pricing from 1941 to date is figured at (N-H ADD 15%)

Scott No.			Mint Sheet	Plate Block	Fine Unused Each	Fine Used Each
1975. D. W. GRIFFITH—MOTION PICTURES						
☐1555	10¢	Multicolored	14.00	1.30	.32	.16
1975. PIONEER 10 SPACE MISSION						
☐1556	10¢	Multicolored	14.00	1.35	.36	.16
1975. MARINER 10 SPACE MISSION						
☐1557	10¢	Multicolored	14.00	1.35	.36	.16
1975. COLLECTIVE BARGAINING						
☐1558	10¢	Blue, Red, Purple	12.00	2.00	.30	.16
1975. CONTRIBUTORS TO THE CAUSE						
☐1559	8¢	Multicolored	10.00	2.25	.26	.16
☐1560	10¢	Multicolored	12.00	2.40	.32	.16
☐1561	10¢	Multicolored	12.00	2.40	.32	.16
☐1562	18¢	Multicolored	22.00	6.00	.50	.21
1975. LEXINGTON AND CONCORD BATTLES BICENTENNIAL						
☐1563	10¢	Multicolored	8.50	3.25	.30	.16
1975. BATTLE OF BUNKER HILL						
☐1564	10¢	Multicolored	8.50	3.25	.30	.16
1975. CONTINENTAL MILITARY SERVICE UNIFORMS						
☐1565	10¢	Multicolored	—	—	.30	.16
☐1566	10¢	Multicolored	—	—	.30	.16
☐1567	10¢	Multicolored	—	—	.30	.16
☐1568	10¢	Multicolored	—	—	.30	.16
1975. U.S.-SOVIET JOINT SPACE MISSION						
☐1569	10¢	Multicolored	—	—	.30	.16
☐1570	10¢	Multicolored	—	—	.30	.16
1975. INTERNATIONAL WOMEN'S YEAR						
☐1571	10¢	Multicolored	12.00	1.75	.30	.16
1975. U.S. POSTAL SERVICE BICENTENNIAL						
☐1572	10¢	Multicolored	—	—	.30	.16
☐1573	10¢	Multicolored	—	—	.30	.16
☐1574	10¢	Multicolored	—	—	.30	.16
☐1575	10¢	Multicolored	—	—	.30	.16
1975. WORLD PEACE THROUGH LAW						
☐1576	10¢	Blue, Green, Brown	15.00	1.50	.30	.16
1975. BANKING AND COMMERCE						
☐1577	10¢	Multicolored	—	—	.30	.16
☐1578	10¢	Multicolored	—	—	.30	.16
1975. CHRISTMAS						
☐1579	10¢	Multicolored	12.00	3.25	.30	.16
☐1580	10¢	Multicolored	12.00	3.25	.30	.16

*No hinge pricing from 1941 to date is figured at (N-H ADD 15%)

1975–1980. AMERICANA SERIES

Scott No.			Mint Sheet	Plate Block	Fine Unused Each	Fine Used Each
☐1581	1¢	Blue on Green	8.50	.70	.22	.16
☐1582	2¢	Brown on Green	8.50	.70	.22	.16
☐1584	3¢	Olive on Green	9.50	.70	.22	.16
☐1585	4¢	Maroon on Green	11.00	.65	.22	.16
☐1590	9¢	Slate on Green	—	—	.45	.30
☐1591	9¢	Green on Gray	20.00	1.00	.26	.16
☐1592	10¢	Purple	23.00	1.15	.30	.16
☐1593	11¢	Orange on Gray	25.00	1.20	.30	.16
☐1594	12¢	Maroon	26.00	1.00	.30	.16
☐1595	13¢	Brown	—	—	.36	.16
☐1596	13¢	Multicolored	31.00	4.35	.36	.16
☐1597	15¢	Multicolored	36.00	9.00	.42	.16
☐1598	15¢	Multicolored	—	—	.60	.16
☐1599	16¢	Blue & Black	46.00	2.20	.56	.16
☐1603	24¢	Red on Blue	52.00	2.60	.60	.16
☐1604	28¢	Brown & Blue	65.00	3.10	.70	.16
☐1605	29¢	Blue & Blue	62.00	3.35	.80	.16
☐1606	30¢	Green on Blue	62.00	4.00	.80	.16
☐1608	50¢	Black & Orange	100.00	5.00	1.25	.16
☐1610	$1	Multicolored	210.00	11.00	2.50	.16
☐1611	$2	Multicolored	420.00	22.00	5.00	.60
☐1612	$5	Multicolored	1000.00	45.00	10.00	3.25

1975–1978. COIL STAMPS

Scott No.			Fine Line Pair	Ave. Line Pair	Fine Unused Each	Ave. Unused Each	Fine Used Each	Ave. Used Each
☐1613	3.1¢	Brown on Yellow	1.00	.90	.30	.24	.22	.16
☐1614	7.7¢	Gold on Yellow	1.50	1.25	.35	.24	.22	.16
☐1615	7.9¢	Red on Yellow	1.00	.90	.32	.24	.22	.16
☐1615C	8.4¢	Blue on White	2.50	2.10	.32	.24	.22	.16
☐1616	9¢	Green on Gray	1.00	.95	.32	.24	.22	.16
☐1617	10¢	Purple on Gray	1.00	.95	.32	.24	.22	.16
☐1618	13¢	Brown	1.00	.95	.35	.24	.22	.16

1975–1977. REGULAR ISSUES

Scott No.			Mint Sheet	Plate Block	Fine Unused Each	Fine Used Each
☐1622	13¢	Red, Brown, Blue	25.00	7.50	.36	.16
☐1623	13¢	Blue, Red	25.00	8.50	.36	.16
☐1623c	13¢	Blue, Red, pf 10	—	—	2.25	.16

1975. COIL STAMPS

Scott No.			Fine Unused Each	Ave. Unused Each	Fine Used Each	Ave. Used Each
☐1625	13¢	Red, Brown, Blue	.46	.30	.24	.16

*No hinge pricing from 1941 to date is figured at (N-H ADD 15%)

Scott No.			Mint Sheet	Plate Block	Fine Unused Each	Fine Used Each
1976. COMMEMORATIVES—AMERICAN BICENTENNIAL						
1976. SPIRIT OF '76						
☐1629	13¢	Multicolored	—	—	.35	.16
☐1630	13¢	Multicolored	—	—	.35	.16
☐1631	13¢	Multicolored	—	—	.35	.16
1976. INTERPHIL '76						
☐1632	13¢	Dark Blue, Red, Ultramarine	16.00	1.60	.42	.16
1976. STATE FLAGS						
☐	13¢	All 50 States	22.00	6.00	—	—
☐	13¢	Individual States	—	—	.50	.34

☐1633 Delaware	1650 Louisiana		1667 West Virginia
☐1634 Pennsylvania	1651 Indiana		1668 Nevada
☐1635 New Jersey	1652 Mississippi		1669 Nebraska
☐1636 Georgia	1653 Illinois		1670 Colorado
☐1637 Connecticut	1654 Alabama		1671 North Dakota
☐1638 Massachusetts	1655 Maine		1672 South Dakota
☐1639 Maryland	1656 Missouri		1673 Montana
☐1640 South Carolina	1657 Arkansas		1674 Washington
☐1641 New Hampshire	1658 Michigan		1675 Idaho
☐1642 Virginia	1659 Florida		1676 Wyoming
☐1643 New York	1660 Texas		1677 Utah
☐1644 North Carolina	1661 Iowa		1678 Oklahoma
☐1645 Rhode Island	1662 Wisconsin		1679 New Mexico
☐1646 Vermont	1663 California		1680 Arizona
☐1647 Kentucky	1664 Minnesota		1681 Alaska
☐1648 Tennessee	1665 Oregon		1682 Hawaii
☐1949 Ohio	1666 Kansas		

Scott No.			Mint Sheet	Plate Block	Fine Unused Each	Fine Used Each
1976. TELEPHONE CENTENNIAL						
☐1683	13¢	Black, Purple, Red	17.00	1.50	.40	.16
1976. COMMERCIAL AVIATION						
☐1684	13¢	Multicolored	17.00	3.80	.40	.16
1976. CHEMISTRY						
☐1685	13¢	Multicolored	17.00	4.40	.40	.16
1976. BICENTENNIAL SOUVENIR SHEETS						
☐1686	65¢	Sheet of 5	—	—	4.50	3.50
☐1686a	13¢	Multicolored	—	—	.90	.75
☐1686b	13¢	Multicolored	—	—	.90	.75
☐1686c	13¢	Multicolored	—	—	.90	.75
☐1686d	13¢	Multicolored	—	—	.90	.75
☐1686e	13¢	Multicolored	—	—	.90	.75
☐1687	90¢	Sheet of 5	—	—	7.00	6.00
☐1687a	18¢	Multicolored	—	—	1.25	1.10
☐1687b	18¢	Multicolored	—	—	1.25	1.10
☐1687c	18¢	Multicolored	—	—	1.25	1.10
☐1687d	18¢	Multicolored	—	—	1.25	1.10

*No hinge pricing from 1941 to date is figured at (N-H ADD 15%)

Scott No.			Mint Sheet	Plate Block	Fine Unused Each	Fine Used Each
☐1687e	18¢	Multicolored	—	—	1.75	1.40
☐1688	1.20	Sheet of 5	—	—	8.50	8.00
☐1688a	24¢	Multicolored	—	—	2.00	1.50
☐1688b	24¢	Multicolored	—	—	2.00	1.50
☐1688c	24¢	Multicolored	—	—	2.00	1.50
☐1688d	24¢	Multicolored	—	—	2.00	1.50
☐1688e	24¢	Multicolored	—	—	2.00	1.50
☐1689	1.55	Sheet of 5	—	—	10.50	9.50
☐1689a	31¢	Multicolored	—	—	2.10	1.90
☐1689b	31¢	Multicolored	—	—	2.10	1.90
☐1689c	31¢	Multicolored	—	—	2.10	1.90
☐1689d	31¢	Multicolored	—	—	2.10	1.90
☐1689e	31¢	Multicolored	—	—	2.10	1.90

1976. BENJAMIN FRANKLIN

☐1690	13¢	Blue & Multicolored	17.00	1.70	.42	.16

1976. DECLARATION OF INDEPENDENCE

☐1691	13¢	Multicolored	—	—	.40	.16
☐1692	13¢	Multicolored	—	—	.40	.16
☐1693	13¢	Multicolored	—	—	.40	.16
☐1694	13¢	Multicolored	—	—	.40	.16

1976. OLYMPIC GAMES

☐1695	13¢	Multicolored	—	—	.42	.16
☐1696	13¢	Multicolored	—	—	.42	.16
☐1697	13¢	Multicolored	—	—	.42	.16
☐1698	13¢	Multicolored	—	—	.42	.16

1976. CLARA MAASS

☐1699	13¢	Multicolored	13.00	4.75	.42	.16

1976. ADOLPH S. OCHS

☐1700	13¢	Black, Green & White	11.00	1.50	.42	.16

1976. CHRISTMAS

☐1701	13¢	Multicolored	16.00	5.00	.42	.16
☐1702	13¢	Multicolored	16.00	4.00	.42	.16
☐1703	13¢	Multicolored	16.00	7.00	.42	.16

1977. COMMEMORATIVES

1977. WASHINGTON

☐1704	13¢	Multicolored	12.50	3.90	.42	.16

1977. SOUND RECORDING CENTENARY

☐1705	13¢	Multicolored	14.00	1.50	.42	.16

1977. PUEBLO ART

☐1706	13¢	Multicolored	—	—	.38	.16
☐1707	13¢	Multicolored	—	—	.38	.16
☐1708	13¢	Multicolored	—	—	.38	.16
☐1709	13¢	Multicolored	—	—	.38	.16

*No hinge pricing from 1941 to date is figured at (N-H ADD 15%)

Scott No.		Mint Sheet	Plate Block	Fine Unused Each	Fine Used Each
1977. TRANSATLANTIC FLIGHT					
☐1710	13¢ Multicolored	14.00	4.60	.40	.16
1977. COLORADO					
☐1711	13¢ Multicolored	14.00	4.60	.40	.16
1977. BUTTERFLIES					
☐1712	13¢ Multicolored	—	—	.40	.16
☐1713	13¢ Multicolored	—	—	.40	.16
☐1714	13¢ Multicolored	—	—	.40	.16
☐1715	13¢ Multicolored	—	—	.40	.16
1977. LAFAYETTE					
☐1716	13¢ Multicolored	13.00	1.60	.40	.16
1977. SKILLED HANDS					
☐1717	13¢ Multicolored	—	—	.40	.16
☐1718	13¢ Multicolored	—	—	.40	.16
☐1719	13¢ Multicolored	—	—	.40	.16
☐1720	13¢ Multicolored	—	—	.40	.16
1977. PEACE BRIDGE					
☐1721	13¢ Blue & White	16.00	1.60	.40	.16
1977. BATTLE OF ORISKANY					
☐1722	13¢ Multicolored	12.50	3.75	.40	.16
1977. ENERGY CONSERVATION AND DEVELOPMENT					
☐1723	13¢ Multicolored	—	—	.40	.16
☐1724	13¢ Multicolored	—	—	.40	.16
1977. ALTA, CALIFORNIA BICENTENNIAL					
☐1725	13¢ Multicolored	16.00	1.50	.40	.16
1977. ARTICLES OF CONFEDERATION					
☐1726	13¢ Red & Brown on Tan	16.75	1.60	.40	.16
1977. TALKING PICTURES					
☐1727	13¢ Multicolored	17.00	1.60	.40	.16
1977. SURRENDER AT SARATOGA					
☐1728	13¢ Multicolored	13.50	4.15	.40	.16
1977. CHRISTMAS					
☐1729	13¢ Multicolored	34.00	8.00	.38	.16
☐1730	13¢ Multicolored	32.00	4.00	.38	.16
1978. CARL SANDBURG					
☐1731	13¢ Brown, Black, White	18.00	1.50	.36	.16
1978. CAPTAIN COOK ISSUES					
☐1732	13¢ Dark Blue	—	1.55	.36	.16
☐1733	13¢ Green	—	1.50	.36	16

*No hinge pricing from 1941 to date is figured at (N-H ADD 15%)

Scott No.			Mint Sheet	Plate Block	Fine Unused Each	Fine Used Each
1978. INDIAN HEAD PENNY						
☐1734	13¢	Brown & Blue Green	45.00	1.80	.38	.16
1978. NONDENOMINATED "A"						
☐1735	15¢	Orange	32.00	1.80	.38	.16
1978. ROSES						
☐1737	15¢	Multicolored	—	—	.38	.16
1980. WINDMILL—VIRGINIA						
☐1738	15¢	Black	—		.38	.16
1980. WINDMILL—RHODE ISLAND						
☐1739	15¢	Black	—		.38	.16
1980. WINDMILL—MASSACHUSETTS						
☐1740	15¢	Black	—		.38	.16
1980. WINDMILL—ILLINOIS						
☐1741	15¢	Black	—		.38	.16
1980. WINDMILL—TEXAS						
☐1742	15¢	Black	—		.38	.16
1978. HARRIET TUBMAN						
☐1744	13¢	Multicolored	25.00	7.00	.38	.16
1978. AMERICAN FOLK ART ISSUE						
☐1745	13¢	Multicolored	—	—	.38	.16
☐1746	13¢	Multicolored	—	—	.38	.16
☐1747	13¢	Multicolored	—	—	.38	.16
☐1748	13¢	Multicolored	—	—	.38	.16
1978. AMERICAN DANCE ISSUE						
☐1749	13¢	Multicolored	—	—	.38	.16
☐1750	13¢	Multicolored	—		.00	.16
☐1751	13¢	Multicolored	—	—	.38	.16
☐1752	13¢	Multicolored	—	—	.38	.16
1978. FRENCH ALLIANCE						
☐1753	13¢	Blue, Black & Red	12.00	1.50	.38	.16
1978. EARLY CANCER DETECTION						
☐1754	13¢	Brown	16.00	1.60	.38	.16
1978. JIMMIE RODGERS						
☐1755	13¢	Multicolored	17.25	5.00	.38	.16
1978. GEORGE M. COHAN						
☐1756	15¢	Multicolored	21.00	5.50	.46	16
1978. "CAPAX" '78 SOUVENIR SHEET						
☐1757	13¢	Multicolored, set of 6	15.00	—	2.90	2.65
1978. PHOTOGRAPHY						
☐1758	15¢	Multicolored	13.50	5.00	.38	.16

*No hinge pricing from 1941 to date is figured at (N-H ADD 15%)

Scott No.			Mint Sheet	Plate Block	Fine Unused Each	Fine Used Each
1978. VIKING MISSION TO MARS						
☐1759	15¢	Multicolored	20.00	1.85	.45	.16
1978. AMERICAN OWL ISSUE						
☐1760	15¢	Multicolored	—	—	.36	.16
☐1761	15¢	Multicolored	—	—	.36	.16
☐1762	15¢	Multicolored	—	—	.36	.16
☐1763	15¢	Multicolored	—	—	.36	.16
1978. AMERICAN TREES ISSUE						
☐1764	15¢	Multicolored	—	—	.38	.16
☐1765	15¢	Multicolored	—	—	.38	.16
☐1766	15¢	Multicolored	—	—	.38	.16
☐1767	15¢	Multicolored	—	—	.38	.16
1978. CHRISTMAS ISSUES						
☐1768	15¢	Multicolored	34.00	5.00	.38	.16
☐1769	15¢	Multicolored	34.00	5.00	.38	.16
1979. ROBERT F. KENNEDY ISSUE						
☐1770	15¢	Blue	16.25	1.75	.38	.16
1979. MARTIN LUTHER KING ISSUE						
☐1771	15¢	Multicolored	17.00	5.00	.38	.16
1979. INTERNATIONAL YEAR OF THE CHILD						
☐1772	15¢	Light Brown	17.00	1.80	.38	.16
1979. JOHN STEINBECK ISSUE						
☐1773	15¢	Dark Blue	17.00	1.80	.38	.16
1979. ALBERT EINSTEIN ISSUE						
☐1774	15¢	Brown	17.00	1.80	.38	.16
1979. PENNSYLVANIA TOLEWARE ISSUE						
☐1775	15¢	Multicolored	—	—	.38	.16
☐1776	15¢	Multicolored	—	—	.38	.16
☐1777	15¢	Multicolored	—	—	.38	.16
☐1778	15¢	Multicolored	—	—	.38	.16
1979. ARCHITECTURE U.S.A. ISSUE						
☐1779	15¢	Light Blue & Brown	—	—	.38	.16
☐1780	15¢	Light Blue & Brown	—	—	.38	.16
☐1781	15¢	Light Blue & Brown	—	—	.38	.16
☐1782	15¢	Light Blue & Brown	—	—	.38	.16
1979. ENDANGERED FLORA ISSUE						
☐1783	15¢	Multicolored	—	—	.38	.16
☐1784	15¢	Multicolored	—	—	.38	.16
☐1785	15¢	Multicolored	—	—	.38	.16
☐1786	15¢	Multicolored	—	—	.38	.16
1979. SEEING FOR ME ISSUE						
☐1787	15¢	Multicolored	17.00	8.00	.38	.16

*No hinge pricing from 1941 to date is figured at (N-H ADD 15%)

Scott No.		Mint Sheet	Plate Block	Fine Unused Each	Fine Used Each
1979. SPECIAL OLYMPICS					
☐1788	15¢ Multicolored	17.00	4.50	.38	.16
1979. JOHN PAUL JONES					
☐1789	15¢ Multicolored	18.00	4.50	.38	.16
1979. OLYMPIC DECATHALON					
☐1790	10¢ Multicolored	13.00	5.00	.28	.16
1979. OLYMPIC RUNNERS					
☐1791	15¢ Multicolored	—	—	.38	.16
1979. OLYMPIC SWIMMERS					
☐1792	15¢ Multicolored	—	—	.38	.16
1979. OLYMPIC ROWERS					
☐1793	15¢ Multicolored	—	—	.38	.16
1979. OLYMPIC EQUESTRIAN					
☐1794	15¢ Multicolored	—	—	.38	.16
1979. OLYMPIC SKATER					
☐1795	15¢ Multicolored	—	—	.38	.16
1979. OLYMPIC SKIER					
☐1796	15¢ Multicolored	—	—	.38	.16
1979. OLYMPIC SKI JUMPER					
☐1797	15¢ Multicolored	—	—	.38	.16
1979. OLYMPIC GOALTENDER					
☐1798	15¢ Multicolored	—	—	.38	.16
1979. MADONNA					
☐1799	15¢ Multicolored	34.00	5.50	.38	.16
1979. CHRISTMAS					
☐1800	15¢ Multicolored	34.00	5.50	.38	.16
1979. WILL ROGERS					
☐1801	15¢ Multicolored	20.00	5.50	.38	.16
1979. VIETNAM VETERANS					
☐1802	15¢ Multicolored	20.00	5.50	.46	.16
1980. W. C. FIELDS					
☐1803	15¢ Multicolored	20.00	5.50	.46	.16
1980. BENJAMIN BANNEKER					
☐1804	15¢ Multicolored	20.00	5.50	.46	.16
1980. LETTERS PRESERVE MEMORIES					
☐1805	15¢ Violet & Bistre	—	—	.38	.16
1980. PRESERVE MEMORIES—P.S. WRITE SOON					
☐1806	15¢ Violet & Pink	—	—	.38	.16

*No hinge pricing from 1941 to date is figured at (N-H ADD) 15%

Scott No.		Mint Sheet	Plate Block	Fine Unused Each	Fine Used Each
1980. LETTERS LIFT SPIRITS					
☐1807	15¢ Green, Pink & Orange	—	—	.38	.16
1980. LIFT SPIRITS—P.S. WRITE SOON					
☐1808	15¢ Green & Yellow Green	—	—	.38	.16
1980. LETTERS SHAPE OPINIONS					
☐1809	15¢ Scarlet & Blue	—	—	.38	.16
1980. SHAPE OPINIONS—P.S. WRITE SOON					
☐1810	15¢ Scarlet & Blue	—	—	.38	.16
1980. AMERICANA SERIES					
☐1811	1¢ Dark Blue & Green	—	.65	.22	.16
☐1813	3.5¢ Purple & Yellow	—	1.40	.22	.16
☐1816	12¢ Green	—	1.75	.34	.16
1980. NONDENOMINATED "B"					
☐1818	18¢ Purple	—	2.30	.48	.16
1980. FRANCIS PERKINS					
☐1821	15¢ Blue	20.00	1.80	.38	.16
1980. DOLLY MADISON					
☐1822	15¢ Multicolored	49.00	1.80	.38	.16
1980. EMILY BISSELL					
☐1823	15¢ Scarlet & Black	17.00	1.80	.38	.16
1980. HELLEN KELLER—ANNE SULLIVAN					
☐1824	15¢ Multicolored	17.00	1.80	.38	.16
1980. VETERANS ADMINISTRATION					
☐1825	15¢ Carmine & Blue	—	—	.38	.16
1980. GENERAL BERNARDO de GALVEZ					
☐1826	15¢ Multicolored	—	—	.38	.16
1980. CORAL REEFS—VIRGIN ISLANDS					
☐1827	15¢ Multicolored	—	—	.38	.16
1980. CORAL REEFS—FLORIDA					
☐1828	15¢ Multicolored	—	—	.38	.16
1980. CORAL REEFS—AMERICAN SAMOA					
☐1829	15¢ Multicolored	—	—	.38	.16
1980. CORAL REEFS—HAWAII					
☐1830	15¢ Multicolored	—	—	.38	.16
1980. ORGANIZED LABOR					
☐1831	15¢ Multicolored	17.00	5.00	.38	.16
1980. EDITH WHARTON					
☐1832	15¢ Violet	20.00	3.00	.38	.16
1980. EDUCATION					
☐1833	15¢ Multicolored	20.00	3.00	.38	.16

*No hinge pricing from 1941 to date is figured at (N-H ADD 15%)

Scott No.			Mint Sheet	Plate Block	Fine Unused Each	Fine Used Each
1980. INDIAN ARTS						
☐1834	15¢	Multicolored	—	—	.38	.16
☐1835	15¢	Multicolored	—	—	.38	.16
☐1836	15¢	Multicolored	—	—	.38	.16
☐1837	15¢	Multicolored	—	—	.38	.16
1980. ARCHITECTURE						
☐1838	15¢	Black & Red	—	—	.38	.16
☐1839	15¢	Black & Red	—	—	.38	.16
☐1840	15¢	Black & Red	—	—	.38	.16
☐1841	15¢	Black & Red	—	—	.38	.16
1980. CHRISTMAS ISSUE						
☐1842	15¢	Multicolored	17.00	5.50	.38	.16
☐1843	15¢	Multicolored	17.00	8.00	.38	.16
1982. DOROTHEA DIX						
☐1844	1¢	Black	10.00	3.00	.22	.16
1983. IGOR STRAVINSKY						
☐1845	2¢	Brown	9.00	.75	.22	.16
1983. HENRY CLAY						
☐1846	3¢	Green	11.00	.75	.22	.16
1983. CARL SCHURZ						
☐1847	4¢	Purple	12.00	.38	.22	.16
1985. PEARL BUCK						
☐1848	5¢	Reddish Brown	13.00	.38	.22	.16
1985. WALTER LIPPMANN						
☐1849	6¢	Orange	13.00	4.00	.22	.16
1985. ABRAHAM BALDWIN						
☐1850	7¢	Red	14.00	4.00	.22	.16
1985. HENRY KNOX						
☐1851	8¢	Black	21.00	1.10	.26	.16
1985. SYLVANUS THAYER						
☐1852	9¢	Green	21.00	5.00	.26	.16
1984. RICHARD RUSSELL						
☐1853	10¢	Blue	22.00	6.50	.28	.16
1985. ALDEN PARTRIDGE						
☐1854	11¢	Blue	21.00	1.50	.28	.16
1982. CRAZY HORSE						
☐1855	13¢	Brown	32.00	2.00	.38	.16
1985. SINCLAIR LEWIS						
☐1856	14¢	Green	31.00	7.50	.38	.16

*No hinge pricing from 1941 to date is figured at (N-H ADD 15%)

Scott No.		Mint Sheet	Plate Block	Fine Unused Each	Fine Used Each
1981. RACHEL CARSON					
☐1857	17¢ Blue Green	34.00	2.00	.42	.16
1981. GEORGE MASON					
☐1958	18¢ Dark Blue	42.00	3.50	.50	.16
1980. SEQUOYAH					
☐1859	19¢ Light Brown	43.00	3.00	.50	.16
1982. RALPH BUNCHE					
☐1860	20¢ Carmine	48.00	3.50	.65	.16
1983. THOMAS H. GALLAUDET					
☐1861	20¢ Green	48.00	4.00	.55	.16
1984. HARRY S. TRUMAN					
☐1862	20¢ Black & White	46.00	12.00	.60	.16
1985. JOHN J. AUDUBON					
☐1863	22¢ Blue	50.00	11.00	.60	.16
1984. FRANK C. LAUBACH					
☐1864	30¢ Dark Green	64.00	16.00	.70	.16
1981. CHARLES DREW					
☐1865	35¢ Gray	78.00	4.25	.90	.16
1982. ROBERT MILLIKAN					
☐1866	37¢ Blue	80.00	4.50	.80	.16
1985. GRENVILLE CLARK					
☐1867	39¢ Reddish Purple	90.00	20.00	.90	.16
1984. LILLIAN M. GILBRETH					
☐1868	40¢ Green	78.00	19.00	.85	.16
1985. CHESTER W. NIMITZ					
☐1869	50¢ Dark Brown	100.00	6.50	1.10	.16
1981. EVERETT M. DIRKSEN					
☐1874	15¢ Dark Green	17.50	1.80	.38	.16
1981. WHITNEY M. YOUNG					
☐1875	15¢ Multicolored	17.50	1.80	.38	.16
1981. FLOWERS					
☐1876	18¢ Multicolored	—	—	.55	.16
☐1877	18¢ Multicolored	—	—	.55	.16
☐1878	18¢ Multicolored	—	—	.55	.16
☐1879	18¢ Multicolored	—	—	.55	.16
1981. AMERICAN WILDLIFE					
☐1880	18¢ Light Brown	—	—	1.00	.16
☐1881	18¢ Light Brown	—	—	1.00	.16
☐1882	18¢ Light Brown	—	—	1.00	.16
☐1883	18¢ Light Brown	—	—	1.00	.16

*No hinge pricing from 1941 to date is figured at (N-H ADD 15%)

Scott No.			Mint Sheet	Plate Block	Fine Unused Each	Fine Used Each
☐1884	18¢	Light Brown	—	—	1.00	.16
☐1885	18¢	Light Brown	—	—	1.00	.16
☐1886	18¢	Light Brown	—	—	1.00	.16
☐1887	18¢	Light Brown	—	—	1.00	.16
☐1888	18¢	Light Brown	—	—	1.00	.16
☐1889	18¢	Light Brown	—	—	1.00	.16

1981. FLAG—FOR AMBER WAVES OF GRAIN
| ☐1890 | 18¢ | Multicolored | 45.00 | 12.00 | .48 | .16 |

1981. FLAG—FROM SEA TO SHINING SEA
| ☐1891 | 18¢ | Multicolored | —PR. | 7.00 | .48 | .16 |

1981. U.S.A.
| ☐1892 | 6¢ | Carmine & Dark Blue | — | — | .70 | .16 |

1981. FLAG—FOR PURPLE MOUNTAIN MAJESTIES
| ☐1893 | 18¢ | Multicolored | — | — | .48 | .16 |

1982. FLAG OVER SUPREME COURT
| ☐1894 | 20¢ | Carmine & Dark Blue | 48.00 | 11.00 | .52 | .16 |

1983. OMNIBUS
| ☐1897 | 1¢ | Violet | — | — | .23 | .16 |

1982. LOCOMOTIVE
| ☐1897A | 2¢ | Black | — | — | .23 | .16 |

1983. HANDCAR
| ☐1898 | 3¢ | Dark Green | — | — | .23 | .16 |

1982. STAGECOACH
| ☐1898A | 4¢ | Red Brown | — | — | .23 | .16 |

1983. MOTORCYCLE
| ☐1899 | 5¢ | Gray Green | — | — | .23 | .16 |

1983. SLEIGH
| ☐1900 | 5.2¢ | Carmine | — | — | .28 | .16 |

1982. BICYCLE
| ☐1901 | 5.9¢ | Blue | — | — | .28 | .16 |

1984. BABY BUGGY
| ☐1902 | 7.4¢ | Brown | — | — | .28 | .16 |

1982. MAIL WAGON
| ☐1903 | 9.3¢ | Carmine | — | — | .28 | .16 |

1982. HANSOM CAB
| ☐1904 | 10.9¢ | Purple | — | — | .50 | .16 |

1984. RAILROAD CABOOSE
| ☐1905 | 11¢ | Red | — | — | .28 | .16 |

*No hinge pricing from 1941 to date is figured at (N-H ADD 15%)

Scott No.			Mint Sheet	Plate Block	Fine Unused Each	Fine Used Each
1981. ELECTRIC CAR						
☐1906	17¢	Ultramarine	—LP.	5.50	.48	.16
1981. SURREY						
☐1907	18¢	Brown	—LP.	6.00	.38	.16
1982. FIRE PUMPER						
☐1908	20¢	Vermilion	—	—	.55	.16
1981. AMERICAN RED CROSS						
☐1910	18¢	Multicolored	—	2.10	.50	.16
1981. SAVINGS AND LOAN						
☐1911	19¢	Multicolored	—	2.10	.50	.16
1981. SPACE ACHIEVEMENT						
☐1912	18¢	Multicolored	—	—	.60	.16
☐1913	18¢	Multicolored	—	—	.60	.16
☐1914	18¢	Multicolored	—	—	.60	.16
☐1915	18¢	Multicolored	—	—	.60	.16
☐1916	18¢	Multicolored	—	—	.60	.16
☐1917	18¢	Multicolored	—	—	.60	.16
☐1918	18¢	Multicolored	—	—	.60	.16
☐1919	18¢	Multicolored	—	—	.60	.16
1981. PROFESSIONAL MANAGEMENT						
☐1920	18¢	Dark Blue & Black	22.00	2.50	.55	.16
1981. PRESERVATION OF WILDLIFE HABITATS						
☐1921	18¢	Multicolored	—	—	.48	.16
☐1922	18¢	Multicolored	—	—	.48	.16
☐1923	18¢	Multicolored	—	—	.48	.16
☐1924	18¢	Multicolored	—	—	.48	.16
1981. DISABLED PERSONS						
☐1925	18¢	Multicolored	22.00	2.10	.50	.16
1981. EDNA ST. VINCENT MILLAY						
☐1926	18¢	Multicolored	22.00	2.15	.50	.16
1981. ALCOHOLISM						
☐1927	18¢	Dark Blue	55.00	42.00	.80	.16
1981. ARCHITECTURE						
☐1928	18¢	Brown & Black	—	—	.60	.16
☐1929	18¢	Brown & Black	—	—	.60	.16
☐1930	18¢	Brown & Black	—	—	.60	.16
☐1931	18¢	Brown & Black	—	—	.60	.16
1981. BABE ZAHARIAS						
☐1932	18¢	Purple	—	2.30	.50	.16
1981. BOBBY JONES						
☐1933	18¢	Dark Green	—	2.30	.50	.16

*No hinge pricing from 1941 to date is figured at (N-H ADD 15%)

Scott No.		Mint Sheet	Plate Block	Fine Unused Each	Fine Used Each
1981. FREDERIC REMINGTON					
☐1934	18¢ Light Brown & Green	22.00	2.30	.50	.16
1981. JAMES HOBAN					
☐1935	18¢ Multicolored	22.00	2.30	.50	.16
1981. JAMES HOBAN					
☐1936	20¢ Multicolored	24.00	2.60	.55	.16
1981. YORKTOWN MAP					
☐1937	18¢ Multicolored	—	—	.55	.16
1981. VIRGINIA CAPES MAP					
☐1938	18¢ Multicolored	—	—	.55	.16
1981. CHRISTMAS—BOTTICELLI					
☐1939	20¢ Multicolored	47.00	2.40	.55	.16
1981. SEASONS GREETINGS					
☐1940	20¢ Multicolored	25.00	2.40	.55	.16
1981. JOHN HANSON					
☐1941	20¢ Multicolored	26.00	2.60	.55	.16
1981. DESERT PLANTS					
☐1942	20¢ Multicolored	—	—	.55	.16
☐1943	20¢ Multicolored	—	—	.55	.16
☐1944	20¢ Multicolored	—	—	.55	.16
☐1945	20¢ Multicolored	—	—	.55	.16
1981. "C" EAGLE—SINGLE					
☐1946	20¢ Light Brown	48.00	2.60	.55	.16
1981. "C" EAGLE—COIL SINGLE					
☐1947	20¢ Light Brown	—	—	.55	.16
1981. "C" EAGLE—BOOKLET SINGLE					
☐1948	20¢ Light Brown	—	—	.55	.16
1981. BIGHORN SHEEP					
☐1949	20¢ Dark Blue	—	—	.60	.16
1982. FRANKLIN ROOSEVELT					
☐1950	20¢ Dark Blue	29.00	3.00	.60	.16
1982. "LOVE" FLOWERS					
☐1951	20¢ Multicolored	48.00	6.00	1.00	.16
1982. GEORGE WASHINGTON					
☐1952	20¢ Multicolored	28.00	3.00	.60	.16
1982. STATE BIRDS AND FLOWERS					
☐1953–2002	20¢ Multicolored	32.00	—	.50	.16

*No hinge pricing from 1941 to date is figured at (N-H ADD 15%)

Scott No.			Mint Sheet	Plate Block	Fine Unused Each	Fine Used Each

1982. THE NETHERLANDS
| ☐2003 | 20¢ | Dark Blue & Red | 31.00 | 2.75 | .55 | .16 |

1982. LIBRARY OF CONGRESS
| ☐2004 | 20¢ | Rose & Dark Gray | 25.00 | 2.60 | .58 | .16 |

1982. CONSUMER EDUCATION
| ☐2005 | 20¢ | Light Blue & Dark Blue | — | 10.00 | 1.15 | .16 |

1982. KNOXVILLE WORLD'S FAIR
☐2006	20¢	Multicolored	32.00	3.50	.65	.16
☐2007	20¢	Multicolored	32.00	3.50	.65	.16
☐2008	20¢	Multicolored	32.00	3.50	.65	.16
☐2009	20¢	Multicolored	32.00	3.50	.65	.16

1982. HORATIO ALGER
| ☐2010 | 20¢ | Carmine & Black | 25.00 | 2.50 | .55 | .16 |

1982. AGING TOGETHER
| ☐2011 | 20¢ | Light Rose | 25.00 | 2.50 | .55 | .16 |

1982. THE BARRYMORES
| ☐2012 | 20¢ | Multicolored | 28.00 | 2.80 | .60 | .16 |

1982. DR. MARY WALKER
| ☐2013 | 20¢ | Multicolored | 25.00 | 2.60 | .55 | .16 |

1982. INTERNATIONAL PEACE GARDEN
| ☐2014 | 20¢ | Multicolored | 25.00 | 2.40 | .58 | .16 |

1982. AMERICA'S LIBRARIES
| ☐2015 | 20¢ | Orange-Red & Black | 25.00 | 2.40 | .58 | .16 |

1982. JACKIE ROBINSON
| ☐2016 | 20¢ | Multicolored | 60.00 | 10.00 | 2.00 | .16 |

1982. TOURO SYNAGOGUE
| ☐2017 | 20¢ | Multicolored | 36.00 | 19.00 | 1.00 | .16 |

1982. WOLF TRAP FARM PARK
| ☐2018 | 20¢ | Multicolored | 24.00 | 2.40 | .60 | .16 |

1982. ARCHITECTURE—WRIGHT
| ☐2019 | 20¢ | Black and Brown | — | — | .60 | .16 |

1982. ARCHITECTURE—VAN DER ROHE
| ☐2020 | 20¢ | Black and Brown | — | — | .60 | .16 |

1982. ARCHITECTURE—GROPIUS
| ☐2021 | 20¢ | Black and Brown | — | — | .60 | .16 |

1982. ARCHITECTURE—SAARINEN
| ☐2022 | 20¢ | Black and Brown | — | — | .60 | .16 |
| ☐Architecture, above four attached | | | 38.00 | 4.50 | .60 | .16 |

*No hinge pricing from 1941 to date is figured at (N-H ADD 15%)

Scott No.		Mint Sheet	Plate Block	Fine Unused Each	Fine Used Each
1982. FRANCIS OF ASSISI					
☐2023	20¢ Multicolored	28.00	3.00	.60	.16
1982. PONCE DE LEON					
☐2024	20¢ Multicolored	38.00	20.00	.95	16
1982. CHRISTMAS ISSUE, CAT AND DOG					
☐2025	13¢ Multicolored	15.00	2.00	.40	.16
1982. CHRISTMAS ISSUE, TIEPOLO'S "MADONNA AND CHILD"					
☐2026	20¢ Multicolored	28.00	15.00	.60	.16
1982. SEASON'S GREETINGS, SLEDDING					
☐2027	20¢ Multicolored		—	.75	.16
1982. SEASON'S GREETINGS, BUILDING SNOWMAN					
☐2028	20¢ Multicolored	—		.75	.16
1982. SEASON'S GREETINGS, ICE SKATING					
☐2029	20¢ Multicolored		—	.75	.16
1982. SEASON'S GREETINGS, TRIMMING TREE					
☐2030	20¢ Multicolored		—	.75	.16
☐Season's Greetings, above four attached		42.00	5.00	.75	.16
1982. SCIENCE AND INDUSTRY					
☐2031	20¢ Multicolored	26.00	2.50	.55	.16
1983. BALLOONING					
☐2032	20¢ Multicolored	—	—	.55	.16
1982. BALLOONING					
☐2033	20¢ Multicolored		—	.55	.16
1982. BALLOONING					
☐2034	20¢ Multicolored		—	.55	.16
1982. BALLOONING					
☐2035	20¢ Multicolored	—	—	.55	.16
☐Ballooning, above four attached		25.00	2.75	.55	.16
1983. TREATY OF AMITY					
☐2036	20¢ Blue and Black	24.00	2.50	.62	.16
1983. CIVILIAN CONSERVATION CORPS					
☐2037	20¢ Multicolored	24.00	2.50	.62	.16
1983. JOSEPH PRIESTLEY					
☐2038	20¢ Rust Brown	24.00	2.50	.62	.16
1983. VOLUNTEER					
☐2039	20¢ Black and Red	42.00	17.50	.62	.16
1983. CONCORD					
☐2040	20¢ Beige	24.00	2.60	.62	.16

*No hinge pricing from 1941 to date is figured at (N-H ADD 15%)

Scott No.		Mint Sheet	Plate Block	Fine Unused Each	Fine Used Each
1983. BROOKLYN BRIDGE					
☐2041	20¢ Blue	28.00	2.60	.60	.16
1983. TENNESSEE VALLEY AUTHORITY					
☐2042	20¢ Multicolored	38.00	16.00	.90	.16
1983. PHYSICAL FITNESS					
☐2043	20¢ Multicolored	38.00	16.00	.62	.16
1982. SCOTT JOPLIN					
☐2044	20¢ Multicolored	29.00	2.50	.68	.16
1983. MEDAL OF HONOR					
☐2045	20¢ Multicolored	27.00	3.00	.68	.16
1983. BABE RUTH					
☐2046	20¢ Blue	78.00	6.50	1.25	.16
1983. NATHANIEL HAWTHORNE					
☐2047	20¢ Multicolored	25.00	2.60	.62	.16
1983. SUMMER OLYMPICS 1984					
☐2048	13¢ Multicolored	—	—	.42	.16
1983. SUMMER OLYMPICS 1984					
☐2049	13¢ Multicolored	—	—	.42	.16
1983. SUMMER OLYMPICS 1984					
☐2050	13¢ Multicolored	—	—	.42	.16
1983. SUMMER OLYMPICS 1984					
☐2051	13¢ Multicolored	—	—	.42	.16
1983. TREATY OF PARIS					
☐2052	20¢ Multicolored	22.00	2.60	.60	.16
1983. CIVIL SERVICE					
☐2053	20¢ Multicolored	36.00	2.60	.60	.16
1983. METROPOLITAN OPERA					
☐2054	20¢ Yellow & Brown.........................	24.00	2.60	.60	.16
1983. INVENTORS					
☐2055	20¢ Multicolored	36.00	4.00	.65	.16
1983. INVENTORS					
☐2056	20¢ Multicolored	36.00	4.00	.65	.16
1983. INVENTORS					
☐2057	20¢ Multicolored	36.00	4.00	.65	.16
1983. INVENTORS					
☐2058	20¢ Multicolored	36.00	4.00	.65	.16
1983. STREETCARS					
☐2059	20¢ Multicolored	30.00	2.75	.65	.16

*No hinge pricing from 1941 to date is figured at (N-H ADD 15%)

Scott No.		Mint Sheet	Plate Block	Fine Unused Each	Fine Used Each
1983. STREETCARS					
☐2060	20¢ Multicolored	26.00	2.75	.60	.16
1983. STREETCARS					
☐2061	20¢ Multicolored	26.00	2.75	.60	.16
1983. STREETCARS					
☐2062	20¢ Multicolored	26.00	2.75	.60	.16
1983. CHRISTMAS, MADONNA					
☐2063	20¢ Multicolored	25.00	2.50	.60	.16
1983. CHRISTMAS, SEASON'S GREETINGS					
☐2064	20¢ Multicolored	32.00	2.50	.60	.16
1983. MARTIN LUTHER					
☐2065	20¢ Multicolored	25.00	2.50	.60	.16
1984. ALASKA STATEHOOD					
☐2066	20¢ Multicolored	25.00	2.60	.60	.16
1984. WINTER OLYMPICS 1984					
☐2067	20¢ Multicolored	30.00	3.60	.60	.16
1984. WINTER OLYMPICS 1984					
☐2068	20¢ Multicolored	30.00	3.60	.60	.16
1984. WINTER OLYMPICS 1984					
☐2069	20¢ Multicolored	30.00	3.60	.60	.16
1984. WINTER OLYMPICS 1984					
☐2070	20¢ Multicolored	30.00	3.60	.60	.16
1984. FEDERAL DEPOSIT INSURANCE CORPORATION					
☐2071	20¢ Red & Yellow	25.00	2.40	.60	.16
1984. LOVE					
☐2072	20¢ Multicolored	32.00	2.40	.60	.16
1984. CARTER G. WOODSON					
☐2073	20¢ Multicolored	25.00	2.40	.58	.16
1984. SOIL AND WATER CONSERVATION					
☐2074	20¢ Multicolored	25.00	2.40	.58	.16
1984. CREDIT UNION					
☐2075	20¢ Multicolored	25.00	2.40	.58	.16
1984. ORCHIDS					
☐2076	20¢ Multicolored	32.00	3.60	.65	.16
1984. ORCHIDS					
☐2077	20¢ Multicolored	32.00	3.60	.65	.16
1984. ORCHIDS					
☐2078	20¢ Multicolored	32.00	3.60	.65	.16

*No hinge pricing from 1941 to date is figured at (N-H ADD 15%)

Scott No.		Mint Sheet	Plate Block	Fine Unused Each	Fine Used Each
1984. ORCHIDS					
☐2079	20¢ Multicolored	32.00	3.00	.65	.16
1984. HAWAII STATEHOOD					
☐2080	20¢ Blue & Yellow	28.00	2.40	.58	.16
1984. NATIONAL ARCHIVES					
☐2081	20¢ Brown & Black	32.00	2.40	.58	.16
1984. SUMMER OLYMPICS 1984					
☐2082	20¢ Multicolored	41.00	4.50	1.00	.16
1984. SUMMER OLYMPICS 1984					
☐2083	20¢ Multicolored	41.00	4.50	1.00	.16
1984. SUMMER OLYMPICS 1984					
☐2084	20¢ Multicolored	41.00	4.50	1.00	.16
1984. SUMMER OLYMPICS 1984					
☐2085	20¢ Multicolored	41.00	4.50	1.00	.16
1984. LOUISIANA WORLD'S FAIR					
☐2086	20¢ Multicolored	20.00	2.40	.58	.16
1984. HEALTH RESEARCH					
☐2087	20¢ Multicolored	28.00	2.40	.58	.16
1984. DOUGLAS FAIRBANKS					
☐2088	20¢ Black & White	34.00	17.00	.58	.16
1984. JIM THORPE					
☐2089	20¢ Black & White	29.00	3.00	.62	.16
1984. JOHN McCORMACK					
☐2090	20¢ Multicolored	27.00	2.50	.58	.16
1984. ST. LAWRENCE SEAWAY					
☐2091	20¢ Multicolored	27.00	2.80	.58	.16
1984. WATERFOWL PRESERVATION					
☐2092	20¢ Multicolored	36.00	2.60	.80	.16
1984. ROANOKE VOYAGES 1584					
☐2093	20¢ Multicolored	28.00	2.60	.58	.16
1984. HERMAN MELVILLE					
☐2094	20¢ Green	25.00	2.60	.58	.16
1984. HORACE MOSES					
☐2095	20¢ Orange & Brown	56.00	16.00	.58	.16
1984. SMOKEY THE BEAR					
☐2096	20¢ Multicolored	24.00	3.00	.58	.16
1984. ROBERTO CLEMENTE					
☐2097	20¢ Multicolored	85.00	10.00	2.00	.16

*No hinge pricing from 1941 to date is figured at (N-H ADD 15%)

Scott No.			Mint Sheet	Plate Block	Fine Unused Each	Fine Used Each
1984. DOGS: BEAGLE						
☐2098	20¢	Multicolored	30.00	4.00	.65	.16
1984. DOGS: RETRIEVER						
☐2099	20¢	Multicolored	30.00	4.00	.65	.16
1984. DOGS: MALAMUTE						
☐2100	20¢	Multicolored	30.00	4.00	.65	.16
1984. DOGS: COONHOUND						
☐2101	20¢	Multicolored	30.00	4.00	.65	.16
1984. CRIME PREVENTION						
☐2102	20¢	Multicolored	25.00	2.50	.60	.16
1984. HISPANIC AMERICANS						
☐2103	20¢	Multicolored	20.00	2.50	.60	.16
1984. FAMILY UNITY						
☐2104	20¢	Multicolored	42.00	18.00	.60	.16
1984. ELEANOR ROOSEVELT						
☐2105	20¢	Blue	24.00	2.50	.60	.16
1984. NATION OF READERS						
☐2106	20¢	Brown & Maroon	24.00	2.50	.60	.16
1984. MADONNA AND CHILD						
☐2107	20¢	Multicolored	24.00	2.50	.60	.16
1984. SANTA CLAUS						
☐2108	20¢	Multicolored	26.00	2.50	.60	.16
1984. VIETNAM MEMORIAL						
☐2109	20¢	Multicolored	23.00	3.40	.60	.16
1985. JEROME KERN						
☐2110	22¢	Multicolored	28.00	3.00	.65	.16
1985. "D" NON-DENOMINATIONAL						
☐2111	22¢	Green	88.00	34.00	.75	.16
1985. "D" NON-DENOMINATIONAL COIL						
☐2112	22¢	Green	—	7.50	.65	.16
1985. "D" NON-DENOMINATIONAL BOOKLET						
☐2113	22¢	Green	—	—	.70	.16
1985. FLAG OVER DOME						
☐2114	22¢	Multicolored	42.00	2.60	.60	.16
1985. FLAG OVER DOME COIL						
☐2115	22¢	Multicolored	—	—	.60	.16
1985. FLAG OVER DOME BOOKLET						
☐2116	22¢	Multicolored	—	—	.60	.16

*No hinge pricing from 1941 to date is figured at (N-H ADD 15%)

Scott No.		Mint Sheet	Plate Block	Fine Unused Each	Fine Used Each
1985. SEASHELLS: DOGWINKLE					
□2117	22¢ Brown	—	—	.60	.16
1985. SEASHELLS: HELMET					
□2118	22¢ Brown	—	—	.60	.16
1985. SEASHELLS: NEPTUNE					
□2119	22¢ Brown	—	—	.60	.16
1985. SEASHELLS: SCALLOP					
□2120	22¢ Pink	—	—	.60	.16
1985. SEASHELLS: WHELK					
□2121	22¢ Brown	—	—	.60	.16
1985. EXPRESS MAIL U.S.A.					
□2122	$10.75 Multicolored	—	—	24.00	11.00
1985. SCHOOL BUS					
□2123	3.4¢ Dark Brown	—	—	.23	.16
1985. BUCKBOARD					
□2124	4.9¢ Dark Brown	—	—	.23	.16
1986. STAR ROUTE TRUCK					
□2125	5.5¢ Carmine	—	—	.23	.16
1985. TRICYCLE 1880s					
□2126	6¢ Red	—	—	.23	.16
1985. TRACTOR					
□2127	7.1¢ Lake	—	—	.23	.14
1985. AMBULANCE					
□2128	8.3¢ Green	—	—	.23	.14
1985. TOW TRUCK					
□2129	8.5¢ Dark Green	—	—	.23	.14
1985. OIL WAGON 1890s					
□2130	10.1¢ Black	—	—	.26	.14
1985. STUTZ AUTO					
□2131	11¢ Blue	—	—	.23	.14
1985. STANLEY STEAMER 1909					
□2132	12¢ Blue	—	—	.26	.14
1985. PUSHCART 1880s					
□2133	12.5¢ Black	—	—	.32	.14
1985. ICEBOAT 1880s					
□2134	14¢ Blue	—	—	.32	.14
1986. DOG SLED 1920s					
□2135	17¢ Blue	—	—	.32	.14

*No hinge pricing from 1941 to date is figured at (N-H ADD 15%)

HOW TO FIND YOUR STAMP

This new stamp catalog takes the confusion out of finding and identifying individual stamps. A complete, new FULL-COLOR FAST-FIND PHOTO INDEX is illustrated on the following pages. All of the stamp photographs are arranged in Scott numerical order and date of issue. Below each stamp picture is the Scott number and the page number on which the stamp listing appears.

GENERAL ISSUE—SCOTT NO. 1–116 (1847–1869)

1, 39, 48a
PG 21

2, 4, 948b
PG 21

5, 9, 18–24, 40
PG 21

10, 11, 25, 26
41–PG 21

12, 27–30A
42–PG 21

13–16, 31–35,
43–PG 21

17, 36, 44
PG 21

37, 45
PG 22

38, 46
PG 22

39, 47
PG 22

56, 63, 85, 86
92, 102–PG 22

64–66, 74, 79, 88
94, 104–PG 22

57–67, 75, 76, 80
95, 195–PG 22

58–62B, 68, 85D,
89, 96, 106–PG 22

59, 69, 85E, 90
97, 107–PG 22

60, 70, 78, 99
109–PG 22

61, 71, 81, 100,
110–PG 22

62, 72, 101,
111–PG 22

73, 84, 85B, 87,
93, 103–PG 22

77, 85F, 91, 98,
108–PG 22

112, 123, 133
PG 24

113, 124
PG 24

114, 125
PG 24

115, 126
PG 24

116, 127
PG 24

A-1

117, 128
PG 24

118, 119, 129
PG 24

120, 130
PG 24

121, 131
PG 24

122, 132
PG 24

134, 156, 167
182, 206–PG 24

135, 157, 168
203–PG 24

136, 158, 169,
214–PG 24

137, 148, 159,
195, 208–PG 24

138, 149, 160,
171, 196–PG 24

139, 150, 161,
197, 209–PG 24

140–151, 162,
173, 198–PG 24

141, 152, 163,
189, 199–PG 24

142, 153, 164,
175, 200–PG 24

143, 154, 165
190, 201, 217–PG 24

144, 155, 166,
202, 218–PG 24

179, 181, 185,
204–PG 25

205, 205C, 216
PG 25

210, 211B, 213,
PG 26

211, 211D, 215
PG 26

212–RG 26

219–PG 26

219D, 220–PG 26

221–PG 26

222–PG 26

GENERAL ISSUE—SCOTT NO. 1026–1050 (1953–1955)

1026–PG 56

1027–PG 56

1028–PG 56

1029–PG 56

1030–PG 56

1031, 1054–PG 56

1031A, 1054A–PG 56

1032–PG 57

1033, 1055–PG 57

1034, 1056–PG 57

1035–1075–PG 57

1036–1058–PG 57

1037, 1059–PG 57

1038–PG 57

1039–PG 57

1040–PG 57

1041, 1075B–PG 57

1042A–PG 57

1043–PG 57

1044A–PG 57

1044–PG 57

1045–PG 57

1046–PG 57

1047–PG 57

1048–PG 57

1049–PG 57

1050–PG 57

GENERAL ISSUE—SCOTT NO. 1051–1072 (1955)

1051–PG 57

1052–PG 57

1053–PG 57

1060–PG 57

1061–PG 57

1062–PG 57

1063–PG 58

1064–PG 58

1065–PG 58

1066–PG 58

1067–PG 58

1068–PG 58

1069–PG 58

1070–PG 58

1071–PG 58

1072–PG 58

1073–PG 58

1074–PG 58

1075–PG 58

1076–PG 58

1077–PG 58

1078–PG 58

1079–PG 58

GENERAL ISSUE—SCOTT NO. 1080-1093 (1956-1957)

1080-PG 58

1081-PG 58

1082-PG 59

1083-PG 59

1084-PG 59

1085-PG 59

1086-PG 59

1087-PG 59

1088-PG 59

1089-PG 59

1090-PG 59

1091-PG 59

1092-PG 59

1093-PG 59

1094–PG 59

1095–PG 59

1096–PG 59

1097–PG 59

1098–PG 59

1099–PG 59

1100–PG 60

1104–PG 60

1105–PG 60

1106–PG 60

1107–PG 60

1108–PG 60

1109–PG 60

1110–PG 60

1111–PG 60

GENERAL ISSUE—SCOTT NO. 1112–1127 (1958–1959)

1112–PG 60

1113–PG 60

1114–PG 60

1115–PG 60

1116–PG 60

1117–PG 60

1118–PG 60

1119–PG 60

1120–PG 60

1121–PG 60

1122–PG 60

1123–PG 60

1124–PG 61

1125–PG 61

1126–PG 61

1127–PG 61

GENERAL ISSUE—SCOTT NO. 1128–1143 (1959–1960)

1128–PG 61

1129–PG 61

1130–PG 61

1131–PG 61

1132–PG 61

1133–PG 61

1134–PG 61

1135–PG 61

1136–PG 61

1137–PG 61

1138–PG 61

1139–PG 61

1140–PG 61

1141–PG 61

1142–PG 61

1143–PG 61

GENERAL ISSUE—SCOTT NO. 1144–1160 (1960–1961)

1144–PG 61

1145–PG 61

1146–PG 62

1147–PG 62

1148–PG 62

1149–PG 62

1150–PG 62

1151–PG 62

1152–PG 62

1153–PG 62

1154–PG 62

1155–PG 62

1156–PG 62

1157–PG 62

1158–PG 62

1159–PG 62

1160–PG 62

A-32

GENERAL ISSUE—SCOTT NO. 1161–1180 (1960–1963)

1161–PG 62

1162–PG 62

1163–PG 62

1164–PG 62

1165–PG 62

1166–PG 62

1167–PG 63

1168–PG 63

1169–PG 63

1170–PG 63

1171–PG 63

1172–PG 63

1173–PG 63

1174–PG 63

1175–PG 63

1176–PG 63

1177–PG 63

1178–PG 63

1179–PG 63

1180–PG 63

1181–PG 63

1182–PG 63

1183–PG 63

1184–PG 63

1185–PG 63

1186–PG 64

1187–PG 64

1188–PG 64

1189–PG 64

1190–PG 64

1191–PG 64

1192–PG 64

1193–PG 64

1194–PG 64

1195–PG 64

1196-PG 64

1197-PG 64

1198-PG 64

1199-PG 64

1200-PG 64

1201-PG 64

1202-PG 64

1203-PG 64

1204-PG 64

1206-PG 65

1205-PG 65

1207-PG 65

1208-PG 65

1209, 1225-PG 65

1213-PG 65

1230-PG 65

GENERAL ISSUE—SCOTT NO. 1231–1244 (1963–1964)

1231–PG 65

1232–PG 65

1233–PG 65

1234–PG 65

1235–PG 65

1236–PG 65

1237–PG 65   1238–PG 65

1239–PG 66

1240–PG 66

1241–PG 66

1242–PG 66

1243–PG 66

1244–PG 66

GENERAL ISSUE—SCOTT NO. 1245–1261 (1964–1965)

1245–PG 66   1246–PG 66   1247–PG 66   1248–PG 66

1249–PG 66   1250–PG 66   1251–PG 66   1252–PG 66

1253–PG 66   1254–PG 66   1255–PG 66   1256–PG 66   1257–PG 66

1258–PG 66   1259–PG 67   1260–PG 67   1261–PG 67

GENERAL ISSUE—SCOTT NO. 1262–1278 (1965)

1262–PG 67 1263–PG 67 1264–PG 67 1265–PG 67

1266–PG 67 1267–PG 67 1268–PG 67 1269–PG 67

1270–PG 67 1271–PG 67 1272–PG 67 1273–PG 67

1274–PG 67 1275–PG 67 1276–PG 67 1278–PG 68

1279—PG 68

1280—PG 68

1281, 1297—PG 68

1282, 1303—PG 68

1283, 1304—PG 68

1283B—PG 68

1284, 1298—PG 68

1285—PG 68

1286—PG 68

1286A—PG 68

1287—PG 68

1288—PG 68

1289—PG 68

1290—PG 68

1291—PG 68

1292—PG 68

1293—PG 68

1294, 1305C—PG 68

1295—PG 68

1305—PG 68

1306—PG 68

1307—PG 68

1308—PG 68

1309—PG 69

1311-PG 69

1310-PG 69

1312-PG 69

1313-PG 69

1314-PG 69

1315-PG 69

1316-PG 69

1317-PG 69

1318-PG 69

1319–PG 69   1320–PG 69   1321–PG 69   1322–PG 69   1323–PG 69

1324–PG 69   1325–PG 69   1326–PG 69

1327–PG 69   1328–PG 70   1329–PG 70   1330–PG 70

1331–PG 70   1332–PG 70   1333–PG 70   1334–PG 70

GENERAL ISSUE—SCOTT NO. 1335–1356 (1967–1968)

1335–PG 70

1336–PG 70

1337–PG 70

1338, 1338A
PG 70

1338F, G–PG 70

1339–PG 70

1340–PG 70

1341–PG 70

1342–PG 70

1343–PG 70

1344–PG 70

1345–PG 70

1354–PG 71

1355–PG 71

1356–PG 71

GENERAL ISSUE—SCOTT NO. 1357–1371 (1968–1969)

1357–PG 71

1358–PG 71

1359–PG 71

1360–PG 71

1361–PG 71

1362–PG 71

1363–PG 71

1364–PG 71

1365–1368–PG 71

1369–PG 71

1370–PG 71

1371–PG 71

1372–PG 72

1373–PG 72

1374–PG 72

1375–PG 72

1376–1379–PG 72

1380–PG 72

1381–PG 72

1382–PG 72

1383–PG 72

1384–PG 72

HOPE
FOR THE CRIPPLED

1385–PG 72

SIX CENTS
UNITED STATES POSTAGE
AMERICAN PAINTING
WILLIAM M. HARNETT

1386–PG 72

AMERICAN BALD EAGLE | AFRICAN ELEPHANT HERD
HAIDA CEREMONIAL CANOE | THE AGE OF REPTILES

1387–1390–PG 72

MAINE STATEHOOD 1820–1970

1391–PG 72

WILDLIFE CONSERVATION

1392–PG 72

EISENHOWER·USA

1393–PG 72

1393D–PG 72

EISENHOWER USA 8¢

1394–PG 73

EISENHOWER·USA 8¢

1395–PG 73

UNITED STATES POSTAL SERVICE
U.S. MAIL
8 cents

1396–PG 73

LaGuardia 14¢

1397–PG 73

Ernie Pyle
Journalist

1398–PG 73

ELIZABETH BLACKWELL FIRST WOMAN PHYSICIAN
US POSTAGE 18¢

1399–PG 73

GIANNINI
AMADEO P.
USA 21¢
BANKER

1400–PG 73

EDGAR LEE MASTERS
AMERICAN POET
UNITED STATES 6¢

1405–PG 73

WOMAN SUFFRAGE
1920–1970
50TH ANNIVERSARY 6¢

1406–PG 73

GENERAL ISSUE—SCOTT NO. 1407–1424 (1970–1971)

1407–PG 73

1408–PG 73

1409–PG 73

1410–1413–PG 73

1414–PG 73

1415–1418–PG 73

1419–PG 74

1420–PG 74

1421–PG 74   1422–PG 74

1423–PG 74

1424–PG 74

GENERAL ISSUE—SCOTT NO. 1425–1439 (1971)

1425–PG 74

1426–PG 74

1427–1430–PG 74

1431–PG 74

1432–PG 74

1433–PG 74

1434–PG 74   1435–PG 74

1436–PG 74

1437–PG 74

1438–PG 74

1439–PG 74

GENERAL ISSUE—SCOTT NO. 1440–1455 (1971–1972)

1440–1443–PG 74

1444–PG 75

1445–PG 75

1446–PG 75

1447–PG 75

1448–1451–PG 75

1452–PG 75

1453–PG 75

1454–PG 75

1455–PG 75

1460–PG 75

1461–PG 75

1456–1459–PG 75

1462–PG 75

1463–PG 75

1464–1467–PG 75

1468–PG 75

1469–PG 76

1470–PG 76

1471–PG 76

1472–PG 76

1473–PG 76

1474–PG 76

1475–PG 76

1476–PG 76

1477–PG 76

1478–PG 76

1479–PG 76

1480–1483–PG 76

1484–PG 76

1485–PG 76

1486–PG 76

1487–PG 76

1488–PG 76

1489–PG 76

1490–PG 76

1491–PG 76

1492–PG 76

1493–PG 76

1494–PG 76

1495–PG 77

1496–PG 77

1497–PG 77

1498–PG 77

1499–PG 77

1500–PG 77

1501–PG 77

1502–PG 77

GENERAL ISSUE—SCOTT NO. 1503–1529 (1973–1974)

1503–PG 77

1504–PG 77

1505–PG 77

1506F–PG 77

1507–PG 77

1508–PG 77

1509, 1519–PG 77

1510–PG 77

1511–PG 77

1518–PG 77

1525–PG 77

1526–PG 77

1527–PG 77

1528–PG 78

1529–PG 78

GENERAL ISSUE—SCOTT NO. 1530–1546 (1974)

Letters
mingle souls
10c US

1530–PG 78

Universal
Postal Union
1874–1974
10c US

1531–PG 78

Letters
mingle souls
10c US

1532–PG 78

Universal
Postal Union
1874–1974
10c US

1533–PG 78

Letters
mingle souls
10c US

1534–PG 78

Universal
Postal Union
1874–1974
10c US

1535–PG 78

Letters
mingle souls
10c US

1536–PG 78

1538–1539–PG 78
1540–1541–PG 78

Universal
Postal Union
1874–1974
10c US

1537–PG 78

1543–1546–PG 78

FIRST KENTUCKY
SETTLEMENT
FORT HARROD
1774   1974

1542–PG 78

GENERAL ISSUE—SCOTT NO. 1547–1562 (1974–1975)

1547–PG 78

1548–PG 78

1549–PG 70

1550–PG 78

1551–PG 78

1552–PG 78

1553–PG 78

1554–PG 78

1555–PG 79

1556–PG 79

1557–PG 79

1558–PG 79

1559–PG 79

1560–PG 79

1561–PG 79

1562–PG 79

GENERAL ISSUE—SCOTT NO. 1563–1574 (1975)

1563–PG 79

1564–PG 79

1565–PG 79

1566–PG 79

1567–PG 79

1568–PG 79

1569–PG 79

1570–PG 79

1571–PG 79

1572–PG 79

1573–PG 79

1574–PG 79

1575–PG 79

1577–1578–PG 79

1576–PG 79

1581–PG 80

1582–PG 80

1584–PG 80

1585–PG 80

1579–PG 79

1580–PG 79

1590–PG 80

1592–PG 80

1593–PG 80

1594–PG 80

1595–PG 80

1596–PG 80

1597–1598–PG 80

1599–PG 80

1603–PG 80

1604–PG 80

1605–PG 80

1606–PG 80

1608–PG 80

GENERAL ISSUE—SCOTT NO. 1610–1687 (1975–1976)

1610–PG 80

1611–PG 80

1612–PG 80

1613–PG 80

1614–PG 80

1615–PG 80

1615C–PG 80

1629–1630–1631–PG 81

1622–PG 80

1623–PG 80

1632–PG 81

1633–1682–PG 81

1683–PG 81

1684–PG 81

1685–PG 81

1686–PG 81

1687–PG 81

GENERAL ISSUE—SCOTT NO. 1688–1703 (1976)

1688–PG 82

1689–PG 82

1690–PG 82

1691–1692–1693–1694–PG 82

1695–PG 82   1696–PG 82

1697–PG 82   1698–PG 82   1699–PG 82

1700–PG 82

1701–PG 82

1702–1703–PG 82

GENERAL ISSUE—SCOTT NO. 1704-1718 (1977)

1704–PG 82

1705–PG 82

1706–PG 82

1707–PG 82

1708–PG 82

1709–PG 82

1710–PG 83

1711–PG 83

1712–PG 83

1713–PG 83

1714–PG 83

1715–PG 83

1716–PG 83

1717–PG 83

1718–PG 83

A-59

1719–PG 83

1720–PG 83

1721–PG 83

1722–PG 83

1723–PG 83

1724–PG 83

1725–PG 83

1726–PG 83

1727–PG 83

1728–PG 83

1729–PG 83

1730–PG 83

1731–PG 83

1732–PG 83

1733–PG 83

1734–PG 84

1735–PG 84

GENERAL ISSUE—SCOTT NO. 1737-1755 (1978)

1737–PG 84

1738–1739–1740–1741–1742–PG 84

1744–PG 84

1745–PG 84

1746–PG 84

1747–PG 84

1748–PG 84

1749–PG 84

1750–PG 84

1751–PG 84

1752–PG 84

1753–PG 84

1754–PG 84

1755–PG 84

1756–PG 84

1757–PG 84

1758–PG 84

1759–PG 85

1760–PG 85

1761–PG 85

1762–PG 85

1763–PG 85

1764–PG 85

1765–PG 85

GENERAL ISSUE—SCOTT NO. 1766–1781 (1978–1979)

1766–PG 85

1767–PG 85

1768–PG 85

1769–PG 85

1770–PG 85

1771–PG 85

1772–PG 85

1773–PG 85

1774–PG 85

1775–PG 85

1776–PG 85

1777–PG 85

1778–PG 85

1779–PG 85

1780–PG 85

1781–PG 85

GENERAL ISSUE—SCOTT NO. 1782-1800 (1979)

1782–PG 85

Endangered Flora

1783–PG 85

1784–PG 85

1785–PG 85

1786–PG 85

1787–PG 85

1788–PG 86

1789–PG 86

1790–PG 86

1791–PG 86

1792–PG 86

1793–PG 86

1794–PG 86

1795–PG 86

1796–PG 86

1797–PG 86

1798–PG 86

1799–PG 86

1800–PG 86

GENERAL ISSUE—SCOTT NO. 1801-1824 (1979-1980)

1801-PG 86

1802-PG 86

1803-PG 86

1804-PG 86

1805-1806
PG 86

1807-1808
PG 87

1809-1810
PG 87

1811-PG 87

1813-PG 87

1818-PG 87

1821-PG 87

1822
PG 87

1823-PG 87

1824-PG 87

GENERAL ISSUE—SCOTT NO. 1825-1840 (1980)

1825–PG 87   1826–PG 87   1827–PG 87   1828–PG 87   1829–PG 87

1830–PG 87   1831–PG 87   1832–PG 87   1833–PG 87

1834–PG 88   1835–PG 88   1836–PG 88   1837–PG 88

1838–PG 88   1839–PG 88   1840–PG 88

1841–PG 88

1842–PG 88

1843–PG 88

1844–PG 88

1845–PG 88

1846–PG 88

1847–PG 88

1848–PG 88

1849–PG 88

1850–PG 88

1851–PG 88

1852–PG 88

1853–PG 88

1854–PG 88

1855–PG 88

1856–PG 88

1857–PG 89

1858–PG 89

1859–PG 89

GENERAL ISSUE—SCOTT NO. 1860-1891 (1982-1985)

1860–PG 89

1861–PG 89

1862–PG 89

1863–PG 89

1864–PG 89

1865–PG 89

1866–PG 89

1867–PG 89

1868–PG 89

1869–PG 89

1874–PG 89

1875–PG 89

1876–PG 89

1877–PG 89

1878–PG 89

1879–PG 89

1880–PG 89

1881–PG 89

1882–PG 89

1886–PG 90

1887–PG 90

1883–PG 89

1884–PG 90

1888–PG 90

1889–PG 90

1885–PG 90

1890–PG 90

1891–PG 90

A-68

GENERAL ISSUE—SCOTT NO. 1892–1920 (1981–1984)

1892-PG 90

1893-PG 90

1894-PG 90

1903-PG 90

1905-PG 90

1906-PG 91

1907-PG 91

1908-PG 91

1910-PG 91

1911-PG 91

1920-PG 91

1912–1919-PG 91

1921-PG 91

1922-PG 91

1923-PG 91

1924-PG 91

1925-PG 91

1926-PG 91

1927-PG 91

1928-PG 91

1929-PG 91

1930-PG 91

1931-PG 91

1932-PG 91

1933-PG 91

1934-PG 92

1935-PG 92

1936-PG 92

1937–1938-PG 92

1939-PG 92

1949-PG 92

1940-PG 92

1941-PG 92

1946–1948-PG 92

1950-PG 92

1942–1945-PG 92

1951-PG 92

2004-PG 93

1952-PG 92

2003-PG 93

2005-PG 93

1953–2002-PG 92

2006–2009-PG 93

2010-PG 93

2011-PG 93

2012-PG 93

2013-PG 93

2014-PG 93

2015-PG 93

2016-PG 93

2017-PG 93

2018-PG 93

2023-PG 94

2019–2022-PG 93

2024-PG 94

2025-PG 94

2026-PG 94

2027–2030-PG 94

2031-PG 94

2032–2035-PG 94

2036-PG 94

2037-PG 94

2038-PG 94

2039-PG 94

2040-PG 94

2041-PG 95

2042-PG 95

2043-PG 95

2044-PG 95

2045-PG 95

2046-PG 95

2048–2051-PG 95

2047-PG 95

2052-PG 95

2053-PG 95

2054-PG 95

2055-PG 95

2056-PG 95

2057-PG 95

2058-PG 95

2059-PG 95

2060-PG 96

2061-PG 96

2062-PG 96

2063-PG 96

2065-PG 96

2064-PG 96

2066-PG 96

2067–2070-PG 96

2071-PG 96

2072-PG 96

2073-PG 96

2074-PG 96

GENERAL ISSUE—SCOTT NO. 2075–2092 (1984)

2075-PG 96

2080-PG 97

2082–2085-PG 97

2076–2079-PG 96–97

2081-PG 97

2086-PG 97

2088-PG 97

2089-PG 97

2090-PG 97

2087-PG 97

2091-PG 97

2092-PG 97

2093-PG 97

2094-PG 97

2095-PG 97

2096-PG 97

2097-PG 97

2098-PG 98

2099-PG 98

2100-PG 98

2101-PG 98

2102-PG 98

2104-PG 98

Hispanic Americans
A Proud Heritage USA 20
2103-PG 98

2105-PG 98

2106-PG 98

2107-PG 98

2108-PG 98

GENERAL ISSUE—SCOTT NO. 2109–2136 (1984–1986)

Vietnam Veterans Memorial USA 20c

2109-PG 98

2110-PG 98

Domestic Mail US Postage

2111–2113
PG 98

2114–2116-PG 9

USA $10.75

2122-PG 99

School Bus 1920s
3.4 USA

2123-PG 99

Buckboard 1880s
USA 4.9

2124-PG 99

Star Route Truck
5.5 USA 1910s

2125-PG 99

2117–2121
PG 99

Tricycle 1880s
6 USA

2126-PG 99

Ambulance 1860s
8.3 USA

2128-PG 99

Oil Wagon 1890s
10.1 USA

2130-PG 99

Stutz Bearcat 1933
11 USA

2131-PG 99

Stanley Steamer 1909
USA 12

2132-PG 99

Pushcart 1880s
12.5 USA

2133-PG 99

Iceboat 1880s
USA 14

2134-PG 99

Dog Sled 1920s
17 USA

2135-PG 99

Bread Wagon 1880s
25 USA

2136-PG 101

2137-PG 101

2138–2141-PG 101

2143-PG 101

2144-PG 101

2145-PG 101

2142-PG 101

2146-PG 101

2147-PG 101

2149-PG 101

2150-PG 101

2152-PG 101

2153-PG 101

2154-PG 101

2155–2158-PG 101–102

2159-PG 102

2160–2163-PG 102

2164-PG 102

Season's Greetings USA22

2166-PG 102

2165-PG 102

2167-PG 102

2168-PG 102

2169-PG 102

2170-PG 102

2171-PG 102

2172-PG 102

2177-PG 102

2179-PG 103

2183-PG 103

2191-PG 103

2194-PG 103

2195-PG 103

2196-PG 103

2198–2201-PG 103–104

2202-PG 104

2203-PG 104

2204-PG 104

2210-PG 104

2211-PG 104

2205–2209-PG 104

2216-PG 104

2217-PG 104

2218-PG 104

2219-PG 104

2220–2223-PG 104–105

2224-PG 105

2239-PG 105

2235–2238-PG 105

2240–2243-PG 105

2244-PG 105

2245-PG 105

2246-PG 105

2247-PG 105

2248-PG 105

2249-PG 105

2250-PG 105

2251-PG 106

2275-PG 106

2276-PG 106

2286–2335-PG 107

2336-PG 107

2337-PG 107

2338-PG 107

2349-PG 107

2350-PG 107

2351–2354-PG 107

2355–2359-PG 107–108

2360-PG 108

2361-PG 108

2367-PG 108

2368-PG 108

2369-PG 108

2370-PG 108

2371-PG 108

2372–2375-PG 108

2376-PG 108

2377-PG 108

2378-PG 108

2379-PG 108

2380-PG 108

GENERAL ISSUE—SCOTT NO. 2381–2399 (1988)

2381–2385-PG 108–109

2386–2389-PG 109

2394-PG 109

2395-PG 109

2390–2393-PG 109

2396-PG 109

2397-PG 109

2398-PG 109

2399-PG 109

A-89

2400-PG 109

2401-PG 110

2402-PG 110

2403-PG 110

2404-PG 110

2410-PG 110

2411-PG 110

2405–2409-PG 110

2412-PG 110

2413-PG 110

2414-PG 110

2416-PG 110

2417-PG 110

2418-PG 110

2419-PG 110

2420-PG 110

2421-PG 111

2422–2425-PG 111

2426-PG 111

2427-PG 111

2428-PG 111

2434–2437-PG 111

2439-PG 111

2440-PG 111

2442-PG 111

2443-PG 111

2444-PG 111

2452-PG 112

2445–2448-PG 111–112

2449-PG 112

2470–2474-PG 112

2508–2511-PG 113

2496–2500
PG 112–113

2501–2505-PG 113

2506–2507-PG 113

GENERAL ISSUE—SCOTT NO. 2512–2539 (1990–1991)

2512-PG 113

2513-PG 113

2514-PG 113

2515-PG 113

2517-PG 113

2521-PG 113

2523-PG 113

2524-PG 113

2528-PG 114

2530-PG 114

2531-PG 114

2532-PG 114

2533-PG 114

2534-PG 114

2535-PG 114

2537-PG 114

2538-PG 114

2539-PG 114

A-94

2540-PG 114

2541-PG 114

2542-PG 114

2545–2549
PG 114

2550-PG 114

Honoring
Those Who Served

2551-PG 114

2558-PG 115

2553–2557-PG 114–115

2560-PG 115

2561-PG 115

2562–2566-PG 115

GENERAL ISSUE—SCOTT NO. 2567–2615 (1991–1992)

2568–2577-PG 115

2567-PG 115

2578-PG 115

2579-PG 115

2582-PG 115

2583-PG 115

2584-PG 115

2585-PG 115

2604-PG 115

2607-PG 115

2608-PG 115

2609-PG 115

2611–2615-PG 116

A-96

2616-PG 116

2618-PG 116

2620–2623-PG 116

2630-PG 116

2631–2634-PG 116

2635-PG 116

2636-PG 116

2637–2641-PG 116

2642–2646-PG 116–117

2647–2696-PG 117

2697-PG 117

2698-PG 117

2699-PG 117

2700–2703-PG 117

2704-PG 117

2705–2709-PG 117

2710-PG 118

2711-PG 118

2712-PG 118

2713-PG 118

2714-PG 118

2719-PG 118

2721-PG 118

2722-PG 118

2723-PG 118

2724-PG 118

2725-PG 118

2726-PG 118

2727-PG 118

2728-PG 118

2729-PG 118

2730-PG 118

A-100

2741–
2745-
PG 118

2746-PG 119

2747-PG 119

2748-PG 119

2749-PG 119

2750—2753-PG 119

2754-PG 119

2755-PG 119

2756—
2759-
PG 119

2760—
2764-
PG 119

2765-
PG 119

2766-PG 119

2767–
2770–
PG 119

2779–2782-PG 119–120

2804-PG 120

2805-PG 120

A-102

2806-PG 120

Scott No.		Mint Sheet	Plate Block	Fine Unused Each	Fine Used Each
1986. BREAD WAGON 1880s					
☐2136	25¢ Brown	—	—	.55	.13
1985. MARY McCLEOD BETHUNE					
☐2137	22¢ Multicolored	29.00	3.00	.62	.14
1985. DUCKS: BROADBILL					
☐2138	22¢ Multicolored	42.00	5.00	.90	.14
1985. DUCKS: MALLARD					
☐2139	22¢ Multicolored	42.00	5.00	.90	.14
1985. DUCKS: CANVASBACK					
☐2140	22¢ Multicolored	42.00	5.00	.90	.14
1985. DUCKS: REDHEAD					
☐2141	22¢ Multicolored	42.00	5.00	.90	.14
1985. WINTER SPECIAL OLYMPICS					
☐2142	22¢ Multicolored	21.00	3.00	.60	.14
1985. LOVE					
☐2143	22¢ Multicolored	28.00	3.00	.60	.14
1985. RURAL ELECTRIFICATION ADMINISTRATION					
☐2144	22¢ Multicolored	52.00	2.50	.80	.14
1985. AMERIPEX SHOW					
☐2145	22¢ Multicolored	24.00	2.50	.60	.14
1985. ABIGAIL ADAMS					
☐2146	22¢ Multicolored	25.00	2.50	.60	.14
1985. BARTHOLDI, STATUE OF LIBERTY					
☐2147	22¢ Multicolored	25.00	2.50	.60	.14
1985. GEORGE WASHINGTON					
☐2149	18¢ Multicolored	—	—	.42	.14
1985. ENVELOPES					
☐2150	2.1¢ Multicolored	—	—	.45	.14
1985. KOREAN VETERANS					
☐2152	22¢ Red & Green...............................	30.00	3.10	.65	.14
1985. SOCIAL SECURITY					
☐2153	22¢ Blue..	25.00	2.90	.60	.14
1985. WORLD WAR I VETERANS					
☐2154	22¢ Red & Green...............................	30.00	4.00	.65	.14
1985. HORSES: QUARTER HORSE					
☐2155	22¢ Multicolored	42.00	5.00	.80	.14
1985. HORSES: MORGAN					
☐2156	22¢ Multicolored	42.00	5.00	.80	.14

*No hinge pricing from 1941 to date is figured at (N-H ADD 15%)

Scott No.		Mint Sheet	Plate Block	Fine Unused Each	Fine Used Each
1985. HORSES: SADDLEBRED					
☐2157	22¢ Multicolored	42.00	5.00	1.00	.14
1985. HORSES: APPALOOSA					
☐2158	22¢ Multicolored	42.00	5.00	1.00	.14
1985. PUBLIC EDUCATION					
☐2159	22¢ Multicolored	50.00	6.00	1.10	.14
1985. YOUTH YEAR: Y.M.C.A.					
☐2160	22¢ Multicolored	46.00	5.00	.85	.14
1985. YOUTH YEAR: BOY SCOUTS					
☐2161	22¢ Multicolored	46.00	5.00	.85	.14
1985. YOUTH YEAR: BIG BROTHERS					
☐2162	22¢ Multicolored	46.00	5.00	.85	14
1985. YOUTH YEAR: CAMPFIRE					
☐2163	22¢ Multicolored	46.00	5.00	.85	.14
1985. HELP END HUNGER					
☐2164	22¢ Multicolored	29.00	2.80	.65	.14
1985. MADONNA					
☐2165	22¢ Multicolored	20.00	2.60	.65	.14
1985. POINSETTIA					
☐2166	22¢ Multicolored	26.00	2.60	.65	.14
1986. ARKANSAS					
☐2167	22¢ Multicolored	26.00	2.60	.65	.14
1986. MARGARET MITCHELL					
☐2168	1¢ Brown	6.00	—	.23	.14
1987. MARY LYON					
☐2169	2¢ Blue	6.00	—	.23	.14
1986. PAUL DUDLEY WHITE M.D.					
☐2170	3¢ Blue	9.00	—	.23	.14
1986. FATHER FLANAGAN					
☐2171	4¢ Blue	9.00	—	.23	.14
1986. HUGO L. BLACK					
☐2172	5¢ Olive Green	11.00	.75	.23	.14
1990. LUIS MUNOZ MARIN					
☐2173	5¢ Carmine	11.00	—	.23	.14
1988. RED CLOUD					
☐2176	10¢ Lake	22.00	—	.23	.14
1987. JULIA WARD HOWE					
☐2177	14¢ Red	26.00	2.00	.32	.14

*No hinge pricing from 1941 to date is figured at (N-H ADD 15%)

Scott No.	Mint Sheet	Plate Block	Fine Unused Each	Fine Used Each
1988. BUFFALO BILL CODY				
☐2178 15¢ Claret	40.00	—	.42	.14
1986. BELVA ANN LOCKWOOD				
☐2179 17¢ Blue Green	32.00	2.50	.40	.14
1988. CHESTER CARLSON				
☐2180 21¢ Blue Violet	40.00	—	.55	.14
1988. MARY CASSATT				
☐2182 23¢ Purple	42.00	—	.55	.14
1986. JACK LONDON				
☐2183 25¢ Blue	44.00	3.00	.58	.14
1989. SITTING BULL				
☐2184 28¢ Myrtle Green	50.00	—	.60	.14
1992. EARL WARREN				
☐2184A 29¢ Blue	60.00	—	.70	.20
1986. DENNIS CHAVEZ				
☐2185 35¢ Black	68.00	—	.70	.20
1990. CLAIRE CHENAULT				
☐2186 40¢ Dark Blue	82.00	—	.85	.20
1988. DR. HARVEY CUSHING				
☐2188 45¢ Blue	80.00	—	.90	.20
1987. HUBERT HUMPHREY				
☐2190 52¢ Purple	92.00	—	1.10	.20
1986. JOHN HARVARD				
☐2191 56¢ Brown	110.00	—	1.15	.14
1988. H.H. ARNOLD				
☐2192 65¢ Scarlet	110.00	—	1.50	.40
1987. WENDELL WILLKIE				
☐2193 75¢ Magenta	145.00	—	1.65	.40
1986. BERNARD REVEL				
☐2194 $1.00 Green	190.00	—	2.40	.13
1988. JOHNS HOPKINS				
☐2194A $1.00 Dark Green	45.00	—	2.00	.40
1986. WILLIAM JENNINGS BRYAN				
☐2195 $2.00 Violet	360.00	—	4.10	.50
1987. BRET HARTE				
☐2196 $5.00 Brown	170.00	—	9.00	1.10
1986. STAMP COLLECTING: AMERICAN PHILATELIC ASSOC.				
☐2198 22¢ Multicolored	—	—	.78	.13

*No hinge from 1941 to date is figured at (N-H ADD 15%)

Scott No.		Mint Sheet	Plate Block	Fine Unused Each	Fine Used Each
1986. STAMP COLLECTING: LITTLE BOY					
☐2199	22¢ Multicolored	—	—	.60	.14
1986. STAMP COLLECTING: MAGNIFIER					
☐2200	22¢ Multicolored	—	—	.60	.14
1986. STAMP COLLECTING: RUBBER STAMP					
☐2201	22¢ Multicolored	—	—	.60	.14
1986. LOVE					
☐2202	22¢ Multicolored	26.00	2.90	.60	.14
1986. SOJOURNER TRUTH					
☐2203	22¢ Multicolored	29.00	2.90	.65	.14
1986. TEXAS—SAN JACINTO 1836					
☐2204	22¢ Multicolored	29.00	2.90	.65	.14
1986. FISH: MUSKELLUNGE					
☐2205	22¢ Multicolored	—	—	.72	.14
1986. FISH: ATLANTIC COD					
☐2206	22¢ Multicolored	—	—	.70	.14
1986. FISH: LARGEMOUTH BASS					
☐2207	22¢ Multicolored	—	—	.70	.14
1986. FISH: BLUEFIN TUNA					
☐2208	22¢ Multicolored	—	—	.70	.14
1986. FISH: CATFISH					
☐2209	22¢ Multicolored	—	—	.70	.13
1986. PUBLIC HOSPITALS					
☐2210	22¢ Multicolored	25.00	3.15	.60	.14
1986. DUKE ELLINGTON					
☐2211	22¢ Multicolored	32.00	3.15	.60	.14
1986. AMERIPEX '86-PRESIDENTS I					
☐2216	22¢ Brown & Black			.50	.14
1986. AMERIPEX '86-PRESIDENTS II					
☐2217	22¢ Brown & Black			.50	.14
1986. AMERIPEX '86-PRESIDENTS III					
☐2218	22¢ Brown & Black			.50	.14
1986. AMERIPEX '86-PRESIDENTS IV					
☐2219	22¢ Brown & Black			.50	.14
1986. POLAR EXPLORERS: KANE					
☐2220	22¢ Multicolored	—	—	1.00	.14
1986. POLAR EXPLORERS: GREELY					
☐2221	22¢ Multicolored	—	—	1.00	.14

*No hinge pricing from 1941 to date is figured at (N-H ADD 15%)

Scott No.		Mint Sheet	Plate Block	Fine Unused Each	Fine Used Each
1986. POLAR EXPLORERS: STEFANSSON					
☐2222	22¢ Multicolored	—	—	1.00	.14
1986. POLAR EXPLORERS: HENSON					
☐2223	22¢ Multicolored	—	—	1.00	.14
1986. LIBERTY					
☐2224	22¢ Carmine & Blue	25.00	3.10	.60	.14
1986. NAVAJO ART					
☐2235	22¢ Multicolored	25.00	3.25	.62	.14
1986. NAVAJO ART					
☐2236	22¢ Multicolored	—	—	.62	.14
1986. NAVAJO ART					
☐2237	22¢ Multicolored	—	—	.62	.14
1986. NAVAJO ART					
☐2238	22¢ Multicolored	—	—	.62	.14
1986. T.S. ELIOT					
☐2239	22¢ Brown	—	—	.60	.14
1986. FOLK ART: HIGHLANDER					
☐2240	22¢ Multicolored	36.00	3.50	.62	.14
1986. FOLK ART: SHIP					
☐2241	22¢ Multicolored	—	—	.62	.14
1986. FOLK ART: NAUTICAL					
☐2242	22¢ Multicolored	—	—	.62	.14
1986. FOLK ART: CIGAR STORE					
☐2243	22¢ Multicolored	—	—	.62	.14
1986. CHRISTMAS: PEROGINO GALLERY					
☐2244	22¢ Multicolored	46.00	2.50	.60	.14
1986. CHRISTMAS: GREETINGS					
☐2245	22¢ Multicolored	46.00	2.50	.60	.14
1987. MICHIGAN STATEHOOD					
☐2246	22¢ Multicolored	27.00	2.50	.60	.14
1987. PAN AMERICAN GAMES					
☐2247	22¢ Multicolored	25.00	2.50	.60	.14
1987. LOVE					
☐2248	22¢ Multicolored	—	—	.60	.14
1987. JEAN BAPTISTE POINTE DU SABLE					
☐2249	22¢ Multicolored	24.00	3.00	.60	.14
1987. ENRICO CARUSO					
☐2250	22¢ Multicolored	28.00	2.50	.60	.14

*No hinge pricing from 1941 to date is figured at (N-H ADD 15%)

Scott No.		Mint Sheet	Plate Block	Fine Unused Each	Fine Used Each
1987. GIRL SCOUTS					
☐2251	22¢ Multicolored	25.00	2.50	.60	.14
1988. CONESTOGA WAGON					
☐2252	3¢ Claret	—	—	.23	.14
1988. MILK WAGON					
☐2253	5¢ Black	—	—	.23	.14
1988. ELEVATOR					
☐2254	5.3¢ Black	—	—	.23	.14
1988. CARRETA					
☐2255	7.6¢ Brown	—	—	.23	.14
1988. WHEELCHAIR					
☐2256	8.4¢ Claret	—	—	.23	.14
1988. CANAL BOAT					
☐2257	10¢ Sky Blue	—	—	.28	.14
1988. POLICE WAGON					
☐2258	13¢ Black	—	—	.28	.14
1988. RAILROAD COALCAR					
☐2259	13.2¢ Slate Green	—	—	.38	.14
1988. TUG BOAT					
☐2260	15¢ Violet	—	—	.38	.14
1988. POPCORN WAGON					
☐2261	16.7¢ Rose	—	—	.38	.14
1988. RACING CAR					
☐2262	17.5¢ Violet	—	—	.40	.14
1988. CABLE CAR					
☐2263	20¢ Blue Violet	—	—	.40	.14
1988. FIRE ENGINE					
☐2264	20.5¢ Rose	—	—	.55	.14
1988. RAILROAD MAILCAR					
☐2265	21¢ Green	—	—	.55	.14
1988. TANDEM BICYCLE					
☐2266	24.1¢ Ultramarine	—	—	.55	.14
1987. SPECIAL OCCASIONS					
☐2267– 2274	22¢ Multicolored	—	—	.65	.14
1987. UNITED WAY UNITING COMMUNITIES					
☐2275	22¢ Multicolored	25.00	3.00	.60	.14
1987. AMERICAN FLAG					
☐2276	22¢ Multicolored	—	—	.60	.14

*No hinge pricing from 1941 to date is figured at (N-H ADD 15%)

Scott No.		Mint Sheet	Plate Block	Fine Unused Each	Fine Used Each
1987. "E" EARTH					
☐2277	25¢ Multicolored	55.00	3.00	.60	.15
1987. FLAG ON CLOUDS					
☐2278	25¢ Multicolored	55.00	3.00	.60	.15
1987. FLAG YOSEMITE					
☐2280	25¢ Multicolored	—	—	.60	.15
1987. HONEY BEE					
☐2281	25¢ Multicolored	—	—	.60	.15
1987. PHEASANT					
☐2283	25¢ Multicolored	—	—	.60	.15
1987. GROSBEAK					
☐2284	25¢ Multicolored	—	—	.60	.15
1987. OWL					
☐2285	25¢ Multicolored	—	—	.60	.15
1987. AMERICAN WILDLIFE					
☐2286–2335	22¢ Multicolored	44.00	—	.70	.14
1987. DELAWARE					
☐2336	22¢ Multicolored	28.00	3.00	.60	.14
1987. PENNSYLVANIA					
☐2337	22¢ Multicolored	36.00	3.75	.80	.14
1987. NEW JERSEY					
☐2338	22¢ Multicolored	32.00	3.40	.70	.14
1987. FRIENDSHIP WITH MOROCCO					
☐2349	22¢ Multicolored	27.00	2.90	.60	.14
1987. WILLIAM FAULKNER					
☐2350	22¢ Green................................	26.00	2.90	.60	.14
1987. LACEMAKING					
☐2351–2354	22¢ Blue	36.00	4.00	.60	.14
1987. CONSTITUTION (BICENTENNIAL)					
☐2355	22¢ Multicolored	—	—	.50	.14
1987. CONSTITUTION (WE THE PEOPLE)					
☐2356	22¢ Multicolored	—	—	.50	.14
1987. CONSTITUTION (ESTABLISH JUSTICE)					
☐2357	22¢ Multicolored	—	—	.50	.14
1987. CONSTITUTION (AND SECURE)					
☐2358	22¢ Multicolored	—	—	.50	.14

*No hinge pricing from 1941 to date is figured at (N-H ADD 15%)

Scott No.		Mint Sheet	Plate Block	Fine Unused Each	Fine Used Each
1987. CONSTITUTION (DO ORDAIN)					
☐2359	22¢ Multicolored	—	—	.50	.14
1987. U.S. CONSTITUTION					
☐2360	22¢ Multicolored	29.00	3.40	.65	.14
1987. C.P.A. CERTIFIED PUBLIC ACCOUNTANTS					
☐2361	22¢ multicolored	26.00	3.40	.65	.14
1987. LOCOMOTIVES					
☐2362–2366	22¢ Multicolored	—	—	.50	.15
1987. CHRISTMAS: MARONI, NATIONAL GALLERY					
☐2367	22¢ Multicolored	42.00	3.00	.58	.14
1987. GREETINGS					
☐2368	22¢ Multicolored	42.00	3.00	.58	.14
1988. OLYMPICS (WINTER)					
☐2369	22¢ Multicolored	24.00	3.00	.58	.14
1988. AUSTRALIA BICENTENNIAL					
☐2370	22¢ Multicolored	21.00	3.00	.58	.14
1988. J.W. JOHNSON					
☐2371	22¢ Multicolored	25.00	3.00	.58	.14
1988. CATS (SHORT HAIR)					
☐2372	22¢ Multicolored	26.00	4.50	.62	.14
1988. CATS (HIMALAYAN)					
☐2373	22¢ Multicolored	—	—	.62	.14
1988. CATS (BURMESE)					
☐2374	22¢ Multicolored	—	—	.62	.14
1988. CATS (PERSIAN)					
☐2375	22¢ Multicolored	—	—	.62	.14
1988. KNUTE ROCKNE					
☐2376	22¢ Multicolored	28.00	3.50	.62	.14
1988. FRANCIS OUIMET					
☐2377	25¢ Multicolored	40.00	3.50	.62	.14
1988. LOVE					
☐2378	25¢ Multicolored	50.00	3.00	.62	.14
1988. LOVE					
☐2379	45¢ Multicolored	40.00	5.00	.62	.14
1988. OLYMPICS (SUMMER)					
☐2380	25¢ Multicolored	28.00	3.00	.62	.14
1988. CARS (LOCOMOBILE)					
☐2381	25¢ Multicolored	—	—	.62	.14

*No hinge pricing from 1941 to date is figured at (N-H ADD 15%)

Scott No.		Mint Sheet	Plate Block	Fine Unused Each	Fine Used Each
1988. CARS (PIERCE-ARROW)					
☐2382	25¢ Multicolored	—	—	.65	.14
1988. CARS (CORD)					
☐2383	25¢ Multicolored	—	—	.65	.14
1988. CARS (PACKARD)					
☐2384	25¢ Multicolored	—	—	.65	.14
1988. CARS (DUESENBERG)					
☐2385	25¢ Multicolored	—	—	.65	.14
1988. ANTARCTIC: NATHANIEL PALMER					
☐2386	25¢ Multicolored	48.00	4.50	.65	.14
1988. ANTARCTIC: LT. CHARLES WILKES					
☐2387	25¢ Multicolored	48.00	4.50	.65	.14
1988. ANTARCTIC: RICHARD E. BYRD					
☐2388	25¢ Multicolored	48.00	4.50	.65	.14
1988. ANTARCTIC: LINCOLN ELLSWORTH					
☐2389	25¢ Multicolored	48.00	4.50	.65	.14
1988. CAROUSEL: DEER					
☐2390	25¢ Multicolored	48.00	4.80	.65	.14
1988. CAROUSEL: HORSE					
☐2391	25¢ Multicolored	50.00	4.80	.65	.14
1988. CAROUSEL: CAMEL					
☐2392	25¢ Multicolored	50.00	4.80	.65	.14
1988. CAROUSEL: GOAT					
☐2393	25¢ Multicolored	50.00	4.80	.65	.14
1988. EXPRESS MAIL					
☐2394	$8.75 Multicolored	—	72.00	18.00	8.00
1988. OCCASIONS: HAPPY BIRTHDAY					
☐2395	25¢ Multicolored	—	—	.65	.14
1988. OCCASIONS: BEST WISHES					
☐2396	25¢ Multicolored	—	—	.65	.14
1988. OCCASIONS: THINKING OF YOU					
☐2397	25¢ Multicolored	—	—	.65	.14
1988. OCCASIONS: LOVE YOU					
☐2398	25¢ Multicolored	—	—	.65	.14
1988. CHRISTMAS (BOTTICELLI)					
☐2399	25¢ Multicolored	27.00	3.00	.62	.12
1988. GREETINGS (CHRISTMAS)					
☐2400	25¢ Multicolored	28.00	3.00	.62	.12

*No hinge pricing from 1941 to date is figured at (N-H ADD 15%)

Scott No.		Mint Sheet	Plate Block	Fine Unused Each	Fine Used Each
1988. MONTANA					
☐2401	25¢ Multicolored	28.00	3.00	.65	.13
1988. A. PHILIPP RANDOLPH					
☐2402	25¢ Multicolored	28.00	3.00	.65	.13
1988. NORTH DAKOTA					
☐2403	25¢ Multicolored	28.00	3.00	.65	.13
1988. WASHINGTON					
☐2404	25¢ Multicolored	28.00	3.00	.65	.13
1988. STEAMBOATS: EXPERIMENT					
☐2405	25¢ Multicolored	—	—	.65	14
1988. STEAMBOATS: PHOENIX					
☐2406	25¢ Multicolored	—	—	.65	.14
1988. STEAMBOATS: NEW ORLEANS					
☐2407	25¢ Multicolored	—	—	.65	.14
1988. STEAMBOATS: WASHINGTON					
☐2408	25¢ Multicolored	—	—	.65	.14
1988. STEAMBOATS: WALK IN THE WATER					
☐2409	25¢ Multicolored	—	—	.65	.14
1988. WORLD STAMP EXPO '89					
☐2410	25¢ Black & Carmine	24.00	2.50	.55	.14
1988. ARTURO TOSCANINI					
☐2411	25¢ Multicolored	24.00	2.50	.55	.14
1988. BICENTENNIAL: HOUSE OF REPRESENTATIVES					
☐2412	25¢ Multicolored	24.00	3.75	.80	.14
1988. BICENTENNIAL: UNITED STATES SENATE					
☐2413	25¢ Multicolored	35.00	3.60	.80	.14
1988. BICENTENNIAL: EXECUTIVE BRANCH					
☐2414	25¢ Multicolored	35.00	4.00	1.00	.14
1988. SOUTH DAKOTA 1889: STATEHOOD					
☐2416	25¢ Multicolored	24.00	3.00	.55	.14
1988. LOU GEHRIG					
☐2417	25¢ Multicolored	30.00	3.15	.65	.14
1989. ERNEST HEMINGWAY					
☐2418	25¢ Multicolored	26.00	3.00	.60	.14
1989. MOON LANDING					
☐2419	$2.40 Multicolored	100.00	21.00	5.00	3.50
1989. LETTER CARRIERS					
☐2420	25¢ Multicolored	20.00	3.00	.60	.14

*No hinge pricing from 1941 to date is figured at (N-H ADD 15%)

Scott No.	Mint Sheet	Plate Block	Fine Unused Each	Fine Used Each
1989. BILL OF RIGHTS				
☐2421 25¢ Multicolored	45.00	6.00	1.40	.14
1989. DINOSAURS: TYRANNOSAURUS				
☐2422 25¢ Multicolored	35.00	6.50	.70	.14
1989. DINOSAURS: PTERANODON				
☐2423 25¢ Multicolored	35.00	6.50	.70	.14
1989. DINOSAURS: STEGOSAURUS				
☐2424 25¢ Multicolored	35.00	6.50	.70	.14
1989. DINOSAURS: BRONTOSAURUS				
☐2425 25¢ Multicolored	35.00	6.50	.70	.14
1989. COLUMBIAN ARTIFACTS				
☐2426 25¢ Multicolored	28.00	3.00	.60	.14
1989. CHRISTMAS: MADONNA				
☐2427 25¢ Multicolored	27.00	3.00	.60	.14
1989. CHRISTMAS: SLEIGH				
☐2428 25¢ Multicolored	27.00	3.00	.60	.14
1989. MAIL DELIVERY: STAGECOACH				
☐2434 25¢ Multicolored	34.00	4.00	.60	.14
1989. MAIL DELIVERY: PADDLEWHEEL				
☐2435 25¢ Multicolored	34.00	4.00	.60	.14
1989. MAIL DELIVERY: BIPLANE				
☐2436 25¢ Multicolored	34.00	4.00	.60	.14
1989. MAIL DELIVERY: AUTOMOBILE				
☐2437 25¢ Multicolored	34.00	4.00	.60	.14
1990. IDAHO CENTENARY: BLUEBIRD				
☐2439 25¢ Multicolored	26.00	3.00	.60	.14
1990. LOVE				
☐2440 25¢ Multicolored	26.00	3.00	.62	.14
1990. BLACK HERITAGE. IDA B. WELLS				
☐2442 25¢ Multicolored	26.00	3.00	.62	.14
1990. BEACH UMBRELLA				
☐2443 25¢ Multicolored	—	3.50	.40	.14
1990. WYOMING CENTENARY—MOUNTAIN				
☐2444 25¢ Multicolored	26.00	6.00	1.00	.14
1990. CLASSIC FILMS: WIZARD OF OZ				
☐2445 25¢ Multicolored	60.00	6.00	1.00	.14
1990. CLASSIC FILMS: GONE WITH THE WIND				
☐2446 25¢ Multicolored	60.00	6.00	1.00	.14

*No hinge pricing from 1941 to date is figured at (N-H ADD 15%)

Scott No.		Mint Sheet	Plate Block	Fine Unused Each	Fine Used Each
1990. CLASSIC FILMS: BEAU GESTE					
☐2447	25¢ Multicolored	60.00	6.00	1.00	.14
1990. CLASSIC FILMS: STAGECOACH					
☐2448	25¢ Multicolored	60.00	6.00	1.00	.14
1990. LITERARY ARTS: MARIANNE MOORE					
☐2449	25¢ Multicolored	26.00	3.00	.60	.14
1990. TRANSPORTATION					
☐2451– 2464	4¢, 5¢, 10¢, 23¢ Multicolored	—	2.75	.35	.14
1990. LIGHTHOUSES: ADMIRALTY HEAD					
☐2470	25¢ Multicolored	—	—	.35	.14
1990. LIGHTHOUSES: CAPE HATTERAS					
☐2471	25¢ Multicolored	—	—	.35	.14
1990. LIGHTHOUSES: WEST QUODDY HEAD					
☐2472	25¢ Multicolored	—	—	.35	.14
1990. LIGHTHOUSES: AMERICAN SHOALS					
☐2473	25¢ Multicolored	—	—	.35	.14
1990. LIGHTHOUSES: SANDY HOOK					
☐2474	25¢ Multicolored	—	—	.35	.14
1990. BOBCAT					
☐2476	$2.00 Multicolored	90.00	20.00	4.50	.70
1990. KESTRAL					
☐2481	1¢ Multicolored	8.00	1.00	.25	.15
1990. BLUEBIRD					
☐2482	2¢ Multicolored	9.00	1.00	.25	.15
1990. FAWN					
☐2487	19¢ Multicolored	45.00	3.00	.45	.15
1990. CARDINAL					
☐2489	30¢ Multicolored	56.00	3.00	.42	.15
1990. WOOD DUCK					
☐2493	29¢ Black & Multicolored	—	—	.60	.15
1990. OLYMPIANS: JESSE OWENS					
☐2496	25¢ Multicolored	32.00	5.00	.75	.18
1990. OLYMPIANS: RAY EWRY					
☐2497	25¢ Multicolored	32.00	5.00	.75	.18
1990. OLYMPIANS: HAZEL WIGHTMAN					
☐2498	25¢ Multicolored	32.00	5.00	.75	.18
1990. OLYMPIANS: EDDIE EAGAN					
☐2499	25¢ Multicolored	32.00	5.00	.75	.18

*No hinge pricing from 1941 to date is figured at (N-H ADD 15%)

Scott No.	Mint Sheet	Plate Block	Fine Unused Each	Fine Used Each
1990. OLYMPIANS: HELENE MADISON				
☐2500　25¢ Multicolored	32.00	5.00	.75	.18
1990. INDIAN: ASSINIBOINE				
☐2501　25¢ Multicolored	—	—	—	.18
1990. INDIAN: CHEYENNE				
☐2502　25¢ Multicolored	—	—	—	.18
1990. INDIAN: COMANCHE				
☐2503　25¢ Multicolored	—	—	—	.18
1990. INDIAN: FLATHEAD				
☐2505　25¢ Multicolored	—	—	.72	.18
1990. INDIAN: SHOSHONE				
☐2505　25¢ Multicolored	—	—	.72	.18
1990. MICRONESIA				
☐2506　25¢ Multicolored	30.00	3.15	.60	.14
1990. MARSHALL ISLANDS				
☐2507　25¢ Multicolored	30.00	3.15	.60	.14
1990. SEA CREATURES: KILLER WHALE				
☐2508　25¢ Multicolored	30.00	3.15	.60	.14
1990. SEA CREATURES: NORTHERN SEA LION				
☐2509　25¢ Multicolored	30.00	3.15	.60	.14
1990. SEA CREATURES: SEA OTTER				
☐2510　25¢ Multicolored	30.00	3.15	.60	.14
1990. SEA CREATURES: DOLPHIN				
☐2511　25¢ Multicolored	30.00	3.15	.60	.14
1990. GRAND CANYON				
☐2512　25¢ Multicolored	26.00	3.00	.60	.14
1990. DWIGHT D. EISENHOWER				
☐2513　25¢ Multicolored	26.00	3.00	.60	.14
1990. CHRISTMAS: MADONNA				
☐2514　25¢ Multicolored	26.00	3.00	.60	.14
1990. CHRISTMAS: CHRISTMAS TREE				
☐2515　25¢ Multicolored	26.00	3.00	.60	.14
1991. "F" FLOWER: TULIP				
☐2517　29¢ Multicolored	58.00	4.00	.65	.14
1991. "F" STAMP RATE: EXTRA POSTAGE				
☐2521　4¢ Multicolored	9.00	.80	.35	.14
1991. FLAG: MT. RUSHMORE				
☐2523　29¢ Multicolored	—	6.00	.68	.14
1991. FLOWER: TULIP				
☐2524　29¢ Multicolored	50.00	4.00	.66	.14

*No hinge pricing from 1941 to date is figured at (N-H ADD 15%)

Scott No.		Mint Sheet	Plate Block	Fine Unused Each	Fine Used Each
1991. FLAG: OLYMPIC RINGS					
☐2528	29¢ Multicolored	—	—	.65	.14
1991. FISHING BOAT					
☐2529	19¢ Multicolored	—	—	.45	.14
1991. BALLOONING					
☐2530	19¢ Multicolored	—	—	.45	.14
1991. FLAGS: ON PARADE					
☐2531	29¢ Multicolored	52.00	3.00	.65	.15
1991. SWITZERLAND: 700TH ANNIVERSARY					
☐2532	50¢ Multicolored	38.00	5.00	1.15	.18
1991. VERMONT: BICENTENNIAL					
☐2533	29¢ Multicolored	30.00	3.00	.65	.14
1991. SAVINGS BONDS: 50TH ANNIVERSARY					
☐2534	29¢ Multicolored	30.00	3.00	.65	.14
1991. LOVE: HEART					
☐2535	29¢ Multicolored	30.00	3.00	.65	.14
1991. LOVE: LOVE BIRDS					
☐2537	52¢ Multicolored	50.00	5.00	1.15	.14
1991. LITERARY ARTS: WILLIAM SAROYAN					
☐2538	29¢ Multicolored	29.00	3.00	.65	.14
1991. USPS: OLYMPIC RINGS					
☐2539	$1.00 Multicolored	41.00	9.00	2.15	.30
1991. EAGLE: OLYMPIC RINGS					
☐2540	$2.90 Multicolored	90.00	25.00	6.20	1.50
1991. DOMESTIC: EXPRESS MAIL					
☐2541	9.95 Multicolored	300.00	80.00	19.00	5.50
1991. INTERNATIONAL: EXPRESS MAIL					
☐2542	$14.00 Multicolored	410.00	90.00	26.00	12.00
1991. FISHING FLIES					
☐2545	29¢ Multicolored	—	—	.75	.14
☐2546	29¢ Multicolored	—	—	.75	.14
☐2547	29¢ Multicolored	—	—	.75	.14
☐2548	29¢ Multicolored	—	—	.75	.14
☐2549	29¢ Multicolored	—	—	.75	.14
1991. PERFORMING ARTS: COLE PORTER					
☐2550	29¢ Multicolored	30.00	3.00	.65	.14
1991. DESERT STORM: SOUTHWEST ASIA					
☐2551	29¢ Multicolored	30.00	3.00	.65	.14
1991. 1992 SUMMER OLYMPICS: BARCELONA					
☐2553	29¢ Multicolored	28.00	8.50	.65	.14
☐2554	29¢ Multicolored	28.00	8.50	.65	.14

*No hinge pricing from 1941 to date is figured at (N-H ADD 15%)

Scott No.			Mint Sheet	Plate Block	Fine Unused Each	Fine Used Each
☐2555	29¢	Multicolored	28.00	8.50	.65	.14
☐2556	29¢	Multicolored	28.00	8.50	.65	.14
☐2557	29¢	Multicolored	28.00	8.50	.65	.14

1991. NUMISMATICS: COINS AND NOTES

☐2558	29¢	Multicolored	—	3.00	.65	.14

1991. WORLD WAR II

☐2559	29¢	Multicolored	—	8.00	.90	.60

1991. BASKETBALL: 100TH ANNIVERSARY

☐2560	29¢	Multicolored	30.00	3.00	.65	.14

1991. DISTRICT OF COLUMBIA: BICENTENNIAL

☐2561	29¢	Multicolored	30.00	3.00	.65	.14

1991. COMEDIANS

☐2562	29¢	Multicolored	—	—	.65	.13
☐2563	29¢	Multicolored	—	—	.65	.13
☐2564	29¢	Multicolored	—	—	.65	.13
☐2565	29¢	Multicolored	—	—	.65	.13
☐2566	29¢	Multicolored	—	—	.65	.13

1991. BLACK HERITAGE

☐2567	29¢	Multicolored	30.00	3.00	.65	.13

1991. SPACE EXPLORATION

☐2568	29¢	Multicolored	—	—	.65	.13
☐2569	29¢	Multicolored	—	—	.65	.13
☐2570	29¢	Multicolored	—	—	.65	.13
☐2571	29¢	Multicolored	—	—	.65	.13
☐2572	29¢	Multicolored	—	—	.65	.13
☐2573	29¢	Multicolored	—	—	.65	.13
☐2574	29¢	Multicolored	—	—	.65	.13
☐2575	29¢	Multicolored	—	—	.65	.13
☐2576	29¢	Multicolored	—	—	.65	.13
☐2577	29¢	Multicolored	—	—	.65	.13

1991. CHRISTMAS

☐2578	29¢	Multicolored	27.00	3.00	.65	.13
☐2579	29¢	Multicolored	27.00	3.00	.65	.13
☐2582	29¢	Multicolored	—	—	.65	.13
☐2583	29¢	Multicolored	—	—	.65	.13
☐2584	29¢	Multicolored	—	—	.65	.13
☐2585	29¢	Multicolored	—	—	.65	.13

1992. BULK RATE

☐2604	10¢	Multicolored	—	—	.26	.13
☐2607	23¢	Multicolored	—	—	.60	.13
☐2608	23¢	Multicolored	—	—	.60	.13
☐2609	29¢	Multicolored	—	—	.60	.13

*No hinge pricing from 1941 to date is figured at (N-H ADD 15%)

Scott No.			Mint Sheet	Plate Block	Fine Unused Each	Fine Used Each
1992. WINTER OLYMPICS						
☐2611	29¢	Multicolored	26.00	8.00	.70	.13
☐2612	29¢	Multicolored	26.00	8.00	.70	.13
☐2613	29¢	Multicolored	26.00	8.00	.70	.13
☐2613	29¢	Multicolored	26.00	8.00	.70	.13
☐2614	29¢	Multicolored	26.00	8.00	.70	.13
☐2615	29¢	Multicolored	26.00	8.00	.70	.13
1992. WORLD COLUMBIAN STAMP EXPO						
☐2616	29¢	Multicolored	30.00	2.90	.65	.13
1992. BLACK HERITAGE						
☐2617	29¢	Multicolored	30.00	2.90	.65	.13
1992. LOVE						
☐2618	29¢	Multicolored	30.00	2.90	.65	.13
1992. OLYMPIC BASEBALL						
☐2619	29¢	Multicolored	40.00	5.00	.90	.13
1992. VOYAGES OF COLUMBUS						
☐2620	29¢	Multicolored	30.00	4.00	.65	.13
☐2621	29¢	Multicolored	30.00	4.00	.65	.13
☐2622	29¢	Multicolored	30.00	4.00	.65	.13
☐2623	29¢	Multicolored	30.00	4.00	.65	.13
1992. NEW YORK STOCK EXCHANGE BICENTENNIAL						
☐2630	29¢	Green, Red & Black	26.00	3.00	.65	.13
1992. SPACE ACCOMPLISHMENTS						
☐2631	29¢	Multicolored	38.00	3.00	.65	.13
☐2632	29¢	Multicolored	38.00	3.00	.65	.13
☐2633	29¢	Multicolored	38.00	3.00	.65	.13
☐2634	29¢	Multicolored	38.00	3.00	.65	.13
1992. ALASKA HIGHWAY—50TH ANNIVERSARY						
☐2635	29¢	Multicolored	30.00	2.90	.60	.13
1992. KENTUCKY STATEHOOD BICENTENNIAL						
☐2636	29¢	Multicolored	30.00	2.90	.60	.13
1992. SUMMER OLYMPICS						
☐2637	29¢	Multicolored	30.00	8.50	.60	.13
☐2638	29¢	Multicolored	30.00	8.50	.60	.13
☐2639	29¢	Multicolored	30.00	8.50	.60	.13
☐2640	29¢	Multicolored	30.00	8.50	.60	.13
☐2641	29¢	Multicolored	30.00	8.50	.60	.13
1992. HUMMINGBIRDS						
☐2642	29¢	Multicolored	—	—	.65	.13
☐2643	29¢	Multicolored	—	—	.65	.13
☐2644	29¢	Multicolored	—	—	.65	.13
☐2645	29¢	Multicolored	—	—	.65	.13

*No hinge pricing from 1941 to date is figured at (N-H ADD 15%)

Scott No.			Mint Sheet	Plate Block	Fine Unused Each	Fine Used Each
☐2646	29¢	Multicolored	—	—	.65	.13
☐2646A		Five Above Attached	—	—	4.50	—

1992. WILD FLOWERS

☐	29¢	Multicolored, 50 Vari. Attached	32.00	—	—	—
☐	29¢	Multicolored, Individual Flowers...............	—	—	.65	.13

☐2647 Indian Paintbrush
☐2648 Fragrant Water Lily
☐2649 Meadow Beauty
☐2650 Jack-in-the-Pulpit
☐2651 California Poppy
☐2652 Large Flower Trillium
☐2653 Tickseed
☐2654 Shooting Star
☐2655 Stream Violet
☐2656 Bluets
☐2657 Herb Robert
☐2658 Marsh Marigold
☐2659 Sweet White Violet
☐2660 Claret Cup Cactus
☐2661 White Mountain Avens
☐2662 Sessile Bellwort
☐2663 Blue Flag

☐2664 Harlequin Lupine
☐2665 Twin Flower
☐2666 Common Sunflower
☐2667 Sego Lily
☐2668 Virginia Bluebells
☐2669 Ohi'a Lehua
☐2670 Rosebud Orchid
☐2671 Showy Evening Primrose
☐2672 Fringed Gentian
☐2673 Yellow Lady's Slipper
☐2674 Passion Flower
☐2675 Bunch Berry
☐2676 Pasque Flower
☐2677 Round-Lobed Hepatica
☐2678 Wild Columbine
☐2679 Firewood

☐2680 Indian Pond Lily
☐2681 Turk's Cap Lily
☐2682 Dutchman's Breeches
☐2683 Trumpet Honeysuckle
☐2684 Jacob's Ladder
☐2685 Plains Prickly Pear
☐2686 Mots Campion
☐2687 Bearberry
☐2688 Mexican Hat
☐2689 Harebell
☐2690 Desert Five Spot
☐2691 Smooth Solomon's Seal
☐2692 Red Maids
☐2693 Yellow Skunk Cabbage
☐2694 Rue Anemone
☐2695 Standing Cypress
☐2696 Wild Flax

1992. WORLD WAR II

☐2697		Souvenir Sheet Multicolored.....................	12.00	—	7.00	.14
	29¢	Single Stamps	—	—	.62	.14

1992. LITERARY ART SERIES

☐2698	29¢	Multicolored	30.00	3.10	.62	.14

1992. THEODORE VON KÁRMÁN

☐2699	29¢	Multicolored	30.00	3.10	.62	.14

1992. MINERALS

☐2700	29¢	Multicolored	30.00	3.65	.62	.14
☐2701	29¢	Multicolored	30.00	3.65	.62	.14
☐2702	29¢	Multicolored	30.00	3.65	.62	.14
☐2703	29¢	Multicolored	30.00	3.65	.62	.14

1992. JUAN RODRÍGUEZ CABRILLO

☐2704	29¢	Multicolored	30.00	3.25	.62	.14

1992. WILD ANIMALS

☐2705	29¢	Multicolored	—	—	.62	.14
☐2706	29¢	Multicolored	—	—	.62	.14
☐2707	29¢	Multicolored	—	—	.62	.14
☐2708	29¢	Multicolored	—	—	.62	.14
☐2709	29¢	Multicolored	—	—	.62	.14
☐2709A	29¢	Multicolored Five Above Attached.............	—	—	3.50	.14

*No hinge pricing from 1941 to date is figured at (N-H ADD 15%)

Scott No.		Mint Sheet	Plate Block	Fine Unused Each	Fine Used Each
1992. MADONNA AND CHILD					
☐2710	29¢ Multicolored	30.00	3.00	.65	.14
1992. HORSE AND RIDER					
☐2711	29¢ Multicolored	—	3.00	.65	.14
1992. TOY LOCOMOTIVE					
☐2712	29¢ Multicolored	—	3.00	.65	.14
1992. TOY FIRE PUMPER					
☐2713	29¢ Multicolored	—	3.00	.65	.14
1992. RIVERBOAT ON WHEELS					
☐2714	29¢ Multicolored	—	3.00	.65	.14
1992. HAPPY NEW YEAR					
☐2719	29¢ Multicolored	20.00	3.00	.65	.14
1993. ELVIS					
☐2721	29¢ Multicolored	28.00	3.00	.65	.14
1993. OKLAHOMA					
☐2722	29¢ Multicolored	28.00	3.00	.65	.14
1993. HANK WILLIAMS					
☐2723	29¢ Multicolored	28.00	3.00	.65	.14
1993. AMERICAN MUSIC—ELVIS PRESLEY					
☐2724	29¢ Multicolored	28.00	3.00	.65	.14
1993. AMERICAN MUSIC—BILL HALEY					
☐2725	29¢ Multicolored	28.00	3.00	.65	.14
1993. AMERICAN MUSIC—CLYDE McPHATTER					
☐2726	29¢ Multicolored	28.00	3.00	.65	.14
1993. AMERICAN MUSIC—RITCHIE VALENS					
☐2727	29¢ Multicolored	28.00	3.00	.65	.14
1993. AMERICAN MUSIC—OTIS REDDING					
☐2728	29¢ Multicolored	28.00	3.00	.65	.14
1993. AMERICAN MUSIC—BUDDY HOLLY					
☐2729	29¢ Multicolored	28.00	3.00	.65	.14
1993. AMERICAN MUSIC—DINAH WASHINGTON					
☐2730	29¢ Multicolored	28.00	3.00	.65	.14
1993. SPACE FANTASY					
☐2741	29¢ Multicolored	—	—	.65	.14
☐2742	29¢ Multicolored	—	—	.65	.14
☐2743	29¢ Multicolored	—	—	.65	.14
☐2744	29¢ Multicolored	—	—	.65	.14
☐2745	29¢ Multicolored	—	—	.65	.14

* No hinge pricing from 1941 to date is figured at (N-H ADD 15%)

		Mint Sheet	Plate Block	Fine Unused Each	Fine Used Each
1993. PERCY LAVON JULIAN					
□2746	29¢ Multicolored	28.00	3.00	.65	.14
1993. OREGON TRAIL					
□2747	29¢ Multicolored	28.00	3.00	.65	.14
1993. WORLD UNIVERSITY GAMES					
□2748	29¢ Multicolored	28.00	3.00	.65	.14
1993. GRACE KELLY					
□2749	29¢ Multicolored	28.00	3.00	.65	.14
1993. CIRCUS					
□2750	29¢ Multicolored	28.00	3.00	.65	.14
□2751	29¢ Multicolored	28.00	3.00	.65	.14
□2752	29¢ Multicolored	28.00	3.00	.65	.14
□2753	29¢ Multicolored	28.00	3.00	.65	.14
1993. CHEROKEE STRIP LAND RUN					
□2754	29¢ Multicolored	28.00	3.00	.65	.14
1993. DEAN ACHESON					
□2755	29¢ Multicolored	28.00	3.00	.65	.14
1993. SPORTING HORSES					
□2756	29¢ Multicolored	28.00	3.00	.65	.14
□2757	29¢ Multicolored	28.00	3.00	.65	.14
□2758	29¢ Multicolored	28.00	3.00	.65	.14
□2759	29¢ Multicolored	28.00	3.00	.65	.14
1993. GARDEN FLOWERS					
□2760	29¢ Multicolored	28.00	3.00	.65	.14
□2761	29¢ Multicolored	28.00	3.00	.65	.14
□2762	29¢ Multicolored	28.00	3.00	.65	.14
□2763	29¢ Multicolored	28.00	3.00	.65	.14
□2764	29¢ Multicolored	28.00	3.00	.65	.14
1993. WORLD WAR II 1943					
□2765	29¢ Multicolored	—	7.50	.65	.14
1993. JOE LOUIS					
□2766	Multicolored	28.00	3.00	.65	.14
1993. BROADWAY MUSICALS					
□2767	29¢ Multicolored	28.00	3.00	.65	.14
□2768	29¢ Multicolored	28.00	3.00	.65	.14
□2769	29¢ Multicolored	28.00	3.00	.65	.14
□2770	29¢ Multicolored	28.00	3.00	.65	.14
1993. NATIONAL POSTAL MUSEUM					
□2779	29¢ Multicolored	28.00	3.00	.65	.14
□2780	29¢ Multicolored	28.00	3.00	.65	.14
□2781	29¢ Multicolored	28.00	3.00	.65	.14
□2782	29¢ Multicolored	28.00	3.00	.65	.14

* No hinge pricing from 1941 to date is figured at (N-H ADD 15%)

			Mint Sheet	Plate Block	Fine Unused Each	Fine Used Each
1993. MARIANA ISLANDS						
☐2804	29¢	Multicolored	28.00	3.00	.65	.14
1993. COLUMBUS LANDING						
☐2805	29¢	Multicolored	28.00	3.00	.65	.14
1993. AIDS AWARENESS						
☐2806	29¢	Multicolored	28.00	3.00	.65	.14

Scott No.			Fine Unused Plate Blk	Ave. Unused Plate Blk	Fine Unused Each	Ave. Unused Each	Fine Used Each	Ave. Used Each
AIRMAIL STAMPS								
1918. FIRST ISSUE—(N-H ADD 45%)								
☐C1	6¢	Orange	700.00	600.00	70.00	50.00	36.00	21.00
☐C2	16¢	Green	1250.00	1080.00	100.00	80.00	38.00	27.00
☐C3	24¢	Carmine & Blue	1500.00	1300.00	100.00	80.00	42.00	27.00
1923. SECOND ISSUE—(N-H ADD 35%)								
☐C4	8¢	Dark Green	350.00	300.00	30.00	24.00	15.00	10.00
☐C5	16¢	Dark Blue	1900.00	1600.00	100.00	80.00	40.00	32.00
☐C6	24¢	Carmine	2500.00	2100.00	110.00	90.00	32.00	27.00
1926–1927. LONG MAP (N-H ADD 35%)								
☐C7	10¢	Dark Blue	40.00	30.00	3.25	2.50	.45	.30
☐C8	15¢	Olive Brown	48.00	36.00	4.00	3.00	2.40	1.90
☐C9	20¢	Yellow Green	150.00	90.00	9.50	7.50	2.00	1.60
1927. LINDBERGH TRIBUTE ISSUE (N-H ADD 25%)								
☐C10	10¢	Dark Blue	170.00	120.00	8.50	6.00	2.30	1.40
1928. BEACON (N-H ADD 20%)								
☐C11	5¢	Carmine & Blue	48.00	36.00	4.00	3.00	.55	.30
1930. WINGED GLOBE—FLAT PRESS (N-H ADD 35%)								
☐C12	5¢	Violet	190.00	120.00	9.50	8.00	.40	.30
1930. GRAF ZEPPELIN ISSUE (N-H ADD 20%)								
☐C13	65¢	Green	2250.00	2000.00	280.00	225.00	215.00	175.00
☐C14	$1.30	Brown	5400.00	4800.00	800.00	600.00	525.00	400.00
☐C15	$2.60	Blue	8500.00	7000.00	1100.00	850.00	650.00	500.00
1931–1932.								
WINGED GLOBE—ROTARY PRESS (N-H ADD 25%)								
☐C16	5¢	Violet	95.00	80.00	7.00	3.80	.45	.30

*No hinge pricing from 1941 to date is figured at (N-H ADD 15%)

Scott No.			Fine Unused Plate Blk	Ave. Unused Plate Blk	Fine Unused Each	Ave. Unused Each	Fine Used Each	Ave. Used Each
☐C17	8¢	Olive Bistre	32.00	26.00	2.50	1.80	.32	.22

1933. CENTURY OF PROGRESS ISSUE (N-H ADD 25%)
| ☐C18 | 50¢ | Green........................ | 675.00 | 600.00 | 90.00 | 80.00 | 78.00 | 55.00 |

1934. DESIGN OF 1930 (N-H ADD 25%)
| ☐C19 | 6¢ | Orange..................... | 28.00 | 23.00 | 3.00 | 2.10 | .21 | .15 |

1935–1937. TRANSPACIFIC ISSUE (N-H ADD 10%)
☐C20	25¢	Blue	24.00	20.00	1.30	1.00	.90	.75
☐C21	20¢	Green........................	125.00	100.00	8.50	7.00	1.80	1.10
☐C22	50¢	Carmine	125.00	100.00	8.50	7.50	5.00	3.20

1938. EAGLE (N-H ADD 20%)
| ☐C23 | 6¢ | Blue & Carmine......... | 8.00 | 6.50 | .50 | .36 | .22 | .15 |

1939. TRANSATLANTIC (N-H ADD 20%)
| ☐C24 | 30¢ | Dull Blue .... | 165.00 | 135.00 | 8.50 | 7.00 | 1.50 | .90 |

1941–1944. TRANSPORT PLANE (N-H ADD 20%)
☐C25	6¢	Carmine	1.05	.90	.25	.20	.18	.14
☐C26	8¢	Olive Green	2.00	1.65	.25	.20	.18	.14
☐C27	10¢	Violet	9.50	8.00	1.40	1.00	.21	.14
☐C28	15¢	Brown Carmine..........	12.00	10.00	2.75	2.30	.36	.28
☐C29	20¢	Bright Green	12.00	9.00	2.75	2.00	.36	.28
☐C30	30¢	Blue	12.50	8.50	2.80	2.00	.41	.28
☐C31	50¢	Orange.....................	90.00	78.00	12.00	9.00	4.00	3.00

Scott No.			Mint Sheet	Plate Block	Fine Unused Each	Fine Used Each

1946–1947. DC-4 SKYMASTER
| ☐C32 | 5¢ | Carmine .... | 7.00 | .75 | .22 | .12 |
| ☐C33 | 5¢ | Carmine .... | 13.00 | .75 | .22 | .12 |

1947. REGULAR ISSUE
☐C34	10¢	Black........................	11.00	1.50	.30	.12
☐C35	15¢	Bright Blue Green	20.00	2.00	.41	.12
☐C36	25¢	Blue	50.00	5.00	1.00	.12

Scott No.			Fine Unused Line Pair	Ave. Unused Line Pair	Fine Unused Each	Ave. Unused Each	Fine Used Each	Ave. Used Each

1948. DESIGN OF 1947
| ☐C37 | 5¢ | Carmine .... | 9.00 | 8.00 | 1.00 | .85 | .78 | .30 |

* No hinge pricing from 1941 to date is figured at (N-H ADD 15%)

Scott No.			Mint Sheet	Plate Block	Fine Unused Each	Fine Used Each
1948. NEW YORK CITY JUBILEE ISSUE						
☐C38	5¢	Red	16.00	5.00	.22	.16
1949. DESIGN OF 1947						
☐C39	6¢	Carmine	13.00	.40	.22	.16
1949. ALEXANDRIA BICENTENNIAL						
☐C40	6¢	Carmine	8.00	.40	.22	.16

Scott No.			Fine Unused Line Pair	Ave. Unused Line Pair	Fine Unused Each	Ave. Unused Each	Fine Used Each	Ave. Used Each
1949. DESIGN OF 1947								
☐C41	6¢	Carmine	13.50	12.00	3.25	2.80	.20	.14

Scott No.			Mint Sheet	Plate Block	Fine Unused Each	Fine Used Each
1949. U.P.U.—UNIVERSAL POSTAL UNION ISSUE						
☐C42	10¢	Purple	13.00	1.80	.35	.30
☐C43	15¢	Ultramarine	16.50	1.50	.40	.35
☐C44	25¢	Carmine	32.00	7.00	.60	.48
1949. WRIGHT BROTHERS ISSUE						
☐C45	6¢	Magenta	10.00	.85	.25	.16
1952. HAWAII—DIAMOND HEAD						
☐C46	80¢	Bright Red Violet	325.00	31.00	7.00	1.40
1953. 50TH ANNIVERSARY POWERED FLIGHT						
☐C47	6¢	Carmine	7.50	.75	.22	.16
1954. EAGLE IN FLIGHT						
☐C48	4¢	Bright Blue	12.50	2.00	.22	.16
1957. 50TH ANNIVERSARY AIR FORCE						
☐C49	6¢	Blue	7.25	.75	.22	.16
1958. DESIGN OF 1954						
☐C50	5¢	Red	13.00	1.80	.22	.16
1958. JETLINER SILHOUETTE						
☐C51	7¢	Blue	16.00	.75	.22	.16

Scott No.			Fine Unused Line Pair	Ave. Unused Line Pair	Fine Unused Each	Ave. Unused Each	Fine Used Each	Ave. Used Each
☐C52	7¢	Blue	16.00	14.00	2.25	1.75	.21	.15

*No hinge pricing from 1941 to date is figured at (N-H ADD 15%)

Scott No.			Mint Sheet	Plate Block	Fine Unused Each	Fine Used Each

1959. COMMEMORATIVES
1959. ALASKA STATEHOOD

☐C53	7¢	Dark Blue	7.50	.72	.22	.14

1959. BALLOON JUPITER FLIGHT

☐C54	7¢	Dark Blue & Red	7.50	.72	.22	.14

1959. HAWAII STATEHOOD

☐C55	7¢	Rose Red	7.50	.72	.22	.14

1959. PAN AMERICAN GAMES

☐C56	10¢	Red & Blue	11.00	1.60	.26	.16

1959–1961. REGULAR ISSUE

☐C57	10¢	Black & Green	70.00	7.75	1.25	.85
☐C58	15¢	Black & Orange	21.00	2.00	.46	.14
☐C59	25¢	Black & Maroon	26.00	2.80	.58	.14

1960. DESIGN OF 1958

☐C60	7¢	Carmine	15.75	.70	.22	.14

Scott No.			Fine Unused Line Pair	Ave. Unused Line Pair	Fine Unused Each	Ave. Unused Each	Fine Used Each	Ave. Used Each
☐C61	7¢	Carmine	40.00	36.00	4.75	3.75	.34	.24

Scott No.			Mint Sheet	Plate Block	Fine Unused Each	Fine Used Each

1961. DESIGNS OF 1959–1960

☐C62	13¢	Black & Red	21.00	2.00	.40	.14
☐C63	15¢	Black & Orange	17.00	1.60	.37	.14

1962. JETLINER OVER CAPITOL

☐C64	8¢	Carmine	20.00	.90	.25	.14

Scott No.			Fine Unused Line Pair	Ave. Unused Line Pair	Fine Unused Each	Ave. Unused Each	Fine Used Each	Ave. Used Each
☐C65	8¢	Carmine	6.00	5.10	.45	.34	.20	.14

Scott No.			Mint Sheet	Plate Block	Fine Unused Each	Fine Used Each

1963. FIRST INTERNATIONAL POSTAL CONFERENCE CENTENARY

☐C66	15¢	Dull Red, Dark Brown & Blue	29.00	3.75	.75	.58

1963. POSTAL CARD RATE

☐C67	6¢	Red	16.50	2.10	.24	.14

1963. AMELIA EARHART

☐C68	8¢	Carmine & Maroon	10.00	1.20	.26	.16

*No hinge pricing from 1941 to date is figured at (N-H ADD 15%)

Scott No.			Mint Sheet	Plate Block	Fine Unused Each	Fine Used Each
1964. DR. ROBERT H. GODDARD						
☐C69	8¢	Blue, Red, Bistre	22.00	2.10	.55	.18
1967–1969.						
1967. ALASKA PURCHASE CENTENARY						
☐C70	8¢	Dark Brown	12.50	1.90	.35	.18
1967.						
☐C71	20¢	Blue, Brown, Bistre	41.00	4.25	1.00	.15
1968.						
☐C72	10¢	Carmine	23.00	1.10	.28	.15

Scott No.			Fine Unused Line Pair	Ave. Unused Line Pair	Fine Unused Each	Ave. Unused Each	Fine Used Each	Ave. Used Each
☐C73	10¢	Carmine	2.25	2.00	.35	.30	.18	.15

Scott No.			Mint Sheet	Plate Block	Fine Unused Each	Fine Used Each
1968. 50TH ANNIVERSARY AIRMAIL SERVICE						
☐C74	10¢	Black, Blue, Red	14.00	3.00	.32	.14
1968.						
☐C75	20¢	Red, Blue, Black	24.00	2.10	.55	.16
1969. FIRST MAN ON THE MOON						
☐C76	10¢	Red, Blue, Brown	10.50	1.70	.35	.16
1971–1973.						
☐C77	9¢	Red	20.00	1.10	.28	.26
☐C78	11¢	Carmine	21.00	1.00	.28	.16
☐C79	13¢	Carmine	30.00	1.60	.38	.16
☐C80	17¢	Green, Blue, Red	22.00	2.10	.48	.16
☐C81	21¢	Blue, Red, Black	21.00	2.00	.45	.16

Scott No.			Fine Unused Line Pair	Ave. Unused Line Pair	Fine Unused Each	Ave. Unused Each	Fine Used Each	Ave. Used Each
☐C82	11¢	Carmine	1.00	.95	.40	.32	.18	.14
☐C83	13¢	Carmine	1.10	1.00	.40	.35	.18	.14

Scott No.			Mint Sheet	Plate Block	Fine Unused Each	Fine Used Each
1972. NATIONAL PARKS CENTENNIAL						
☐C84	11¢	Multicolored	10.00	1.10	.33	.16
1972. OLYMPIC GAMES						
☐C85	11¢	Multicolored	12.00	3.00	.33	.16
1973. PROGRESS IN ELECTRONICS						
☐C86	11¢	Multicolored	12.00	1.10	.33	.16

*No hinge pricing from 1941 to date is figured at (N-H ADD 15%)

Scott No.			Mint Sheet	Plate Block	Fine Unused Each	Fine Used Each
1974.						
☐C87	18¢	Red, Blue, Black................................	21.00	2.20	.48	.36
☐C88	26¢	Red, Blue, Black................................	28.00	2.50	.62	.15
1976.						
☐C89	25¢	Red, Blue, Black................................	27.00	2.75	.62	.15
☐C90	31¢	Red, Blue, Black................................	29.00	3.00	.70	.15
1979.						
☐C91	31¢	Blue, Brown, Red................................	79.00	4.00	.95	.30
☐C92	31¢	Blue, Brown, Red................................	82.00	4.75	.95	.30
1979.						
☐C93	21¢	Blue, Brown, Red................................	90.00	5.00	.60	.28
☐C94	21¢	Blue, Brown, Red................................	90.00	5.00	.60	.28
1980.						
☐C95	25¢	Multicolored	160.00	11.00	1.10	.24
☐C96	25¢	Multicolored	160.00	11.00	1.10	.24
☐C97	31¢	Multicolored	38.00	12.00	.75	.34
1981.						
☐C98	40¢	Multicolored	40.00	10.00	.90	.16
☐C99	28¢	Multicolored	30.00	8.50	.65	.19
☐C100	35¢	Multicolored	32.00	10.00	.80	.19
1983.						
☐C101	28¢	Multicolored	48.00	6.00	1.50	.26
☐C102	28¢	Multicolored	48.00	6.00	1.50	.26
☐C103	28¢	Multicolored	48.00	6.00	1.50	.26
☐C104	28¢	Multicolored	48.00	6.00	1.50	.26
☐C105	40¢	Multicolored	62.00	7.00	1.30	.30
☐C106	40¢	Multicolored	62.00	7.00	1.30	.30
☐C107	40¢	Multicolored	62.00	7.00	1.30	.30
☐C108	40¢	Multicolored	62.00	7.00	1.30	.30
☐C109	35¢	Multicolored	55.00	8.50	1.20	.32
☐C110	35¢	Multicolored	55.00	8.50	1.20	.32
☐C111	35¢	Multicolored	55.00	8.50	1.20	.32
☐C112	35¢	Multicolored	55.00	8.50	1.20	.32
1985.						
☐C113	33¢	Multicolored	34.00	3.50	.75	.26
☐C114	39¢	Multicolored	40.00	4.00	.85	.26
☐C115	44¢	Multicolored	44.00	4.50	1.00	.26
☐C116	44¢	Multicolored	60.00	7.50	1.25	.26
1988.						
☐C117	44¢	Multicolored	49.00	7.10	1.10	.26
☐C118	45¢	Multicolored	49.00	5.00	1.10	.26
☐C119	36¢	Multicolored	39.00	4.00	.90	.26

*No hinge pricing from 1941 to date is figured at (N-H ADD 15%)

Scott No.			Mint Sheet	Plate Block	Fine Unused Each	Fine Used Each
1989.						
☐C120	45¢	Multicolored	31.00	4.50	1.10	.26
☐C121	45¢	Multicolored	47.00	4.50	1.10	.26
☐C122	45¢	Multicolored	66.00	6.50	1.25	.26
☐C123	45¢	Multicolored	66.00	6.50	1.25	.26
☐C124	45¢	Multicolored	66.00	6.50	1.25	.26
☐C125	45¢	Multicolored	66.00	6.50	1.25	.26
☐C126	45¢	Multicolored	66.00	6.50	4.25	.26
1990.						
☐C127	45¢	Multicolored	48.00	6.00	1.00	.26
☐C128	50¢	Multicolored	54.00	4.50	1.00	.26
☐C129	40¢	Multicolored	40.00	5.00	1.00	.26
☐C130	50¢	Multicolored	53.00	5.00	1.00	.26
1991.						
☐C131	50¢	Multicolored	54.00	5.00	1.15	.26

Scott No.			Fine Unused Plate Blk	Ave. Unused Plate Blk	Fine Unused Each	Ave. Unused Each	Fine Used Each	Ave. Used Each
AIRMAIL SPECIAL DELIVERY								
☐CE1	16¢	Dark Blue	19.00	16.00	.90	.75	.65	.55
☐CE2	16¢	Red & Blue	9.00	7.00	.50	.45	.41	.16
SPECIAL DELIVERY STAMPS								
1885.								
☐E1	10¢	Blue	—	—	225.00	128.00	31.00	16.50
1888.								
☐E2	10¢	Blue	—	—	230.00	124.00	8.00	5.00
1893. (N-H ADD 80%)								
☐E3	10¢	Orange	—	—	130.00	85.00	12.50	8.00
1894. (N-H ADD 80%)								
☐E4	10¢	Blue	—	—	550.00	325.00	19.00	9.00
1895. (N-H ADD 80%)								
☐E5	10¢	Blue	—	—	105.00	68.00	2.40	1.50
1902. (N-H ADD 55%)								
☐E6	10¢	Ultramarine	—	—	65.00	55.00	2.60	1.50
1908. (N-H ADD 55%)								
☐E7	10¢	Green	—	—	40.00	36.00	28.00	16.00
1911. (N-H ADD 40%)								
☐E8	10¢	Ultramarine	—	—	61.00	50.00	4.00	2.50
1914. (N-H ADD 40%)								
☐E9	10¢	Ultramarine	—	—	115.00	90.00	6.00	3.00

*No hinge pricing from 1941 to date is figured at (N-H ADD 15%)

Scott No.		Fine Unused Plate Blk	Ave. Unused Plate Blk	Fine Unused Each	Ave. Unused Each	Fine Used Each	Ave. Used Each
1916. (N-H ADD 40%)							
☐E10	10¢ Pale Ultramarine	—	—	215.00	175.00	17.00	12.00
1917. (N-H ADD 40%)							
☐E11	10¢ Ultramarine..............	—	—	13.50	9.00	.50	.36
1922–1925. (N-H ADD 30%)							
☐E12	10¢ Deep Ultramarine......	300.00	200.00	19.00	14.00	.24	.16
☐E13	10¢ Deep Orange.............	210.00	140.00	19.50	16.00	1.10	.50
☐E14	20¢ Black.........................	52.00	34.00	2.75	2.25	1.50	.60
1927–1951. (N-H ADD 30%)							
☐E15	10¢ Gray Violet................	7.00	5.50	.72	.60	.21	.16
☐E16	15¢ Orange......................	5.00	4.00	.85	.64	.21	.16
☐E17	13¢ Blue	4.50	3.00	.65	.45	.21	.16
☐E18	17¢ Yellow......................	30.00	26.00	3.10	2.50	1.60	1.40
☐E19	20¢ Black.........................	9.00	7.50	1.75	1.25	.21	.14

Scott No.		Mint Sheet	Plate Block	Fine Unused Each	Fine Used Each
1954.					
☐E20	20¢ Blue	24.00	2.60	.55	.14
1957.					
☐E21	30¢ Maroon	30.00	2.70	.62	.14
1969.					
☐E22	45¢ Red & Blue	60.00	7.50	1.30	.14
1971.					
☐E23	60¢ Blue & Red	54.00	5.00	1.00	.14

Scott No.		Fine Unused Plate Blk	Ave. Unused Plate Blk	Fine Unused Each	Ave. Unused Each	Fine Used Each	Ave. Used Each
1911. REGISTRATION STAMPS (N-H ADD 30%)							
☐F1	10¢ Ultramarine...............	1200.00	900.00	54.00	40.00	4.00	2.75

Scott No.		Mint Sheet	Plate Block	Fine Unused Each	Fine Used Each
☐FA1	15¢ Postman	19.00	4.00	.35	.22

Scott No.		Name Block 6	Name Block 4	Plain Block 4	Unused Each	Used Each
UNITED NATIONS						
1951.						
☐1	1¢ Magenta	.90	.65	.40	.23	.16
☐2	1½¢ Blue Green	.90	.65	.40	.23	.16

*No hinge pricing from 1941 to date is figured at (N-H ADD 15%)

Scott No.			Name Block 6	Name Block 4	Plain Block 4	Unused Each	Used Each
☐2a	1½¢	Precancelled....................	—	—	—	—	28.00
☐3	2¢	Purple	1.00	.60	.55	.22	.16
☐4	3¢	Magenta & Blue	.90	.65	.55	.22	.16
☐5	5¢	Blue	1.10	.85	.65	.22	.16
☐6	10¢	Chocolate	3.00	2.00	1.30	.28	.21
☐7	15¢	Violet & Blue	3.00	1.90	1.35	.32	.21
☐8	20¢	Dark Brown	11.00	7.00	4.00	.72	.48
☐9	25¢	Olive Gray & Blue	13.00	10.00	4.00	.65	.48
☐10	50¢	Indigo	70.00	40.00	24.00	6.00	3.50
☐11	$1	Red	26.00	18.00	10.00	2.10	1.15
☐1–11		First Postage Set Complete........	—	90.00	50.00	8.50	6.00
1952.							
☐12	5¢	War Memorial Bldg.	7.00	5.00	2.00	.60	.25
☐13–14	3¢, 5¢	Fourth H.R. Day	18.00	10.00	5.00	.80	.45
1953.							
☐15–16	3¢, 5¢	Refugees	20.00	12.00	7.00	1.00	.85
☐17–18	3¢, 5¢	U.P.U.	22.00	17.00	8.00	1.80	1.25
☐19–20	3¢, 5¢	Technical Assist	16.50	10.00	6.00	1.10	.90
☐21–22	3¢, 5¢	Human Rights	23.00	18.50	12.00	2.50	1.10
1954.							
☐23–24	3¢, 8¢	FAO (Agriculture)	15.00	13.00	8.00	1.90	1.00
☐25–26	3¢, 8¢	OIT (Labor Org.)	36.00	21.00	16.00	3.00	1.30
☐27–28	3¢, 8¢	UN Day	42.00	30.00	20.00	4.50	2.50
☐29–30	3¢, 8¢	H.R. Day	95.00	80.00	55.00	16.00	4.00
1955.							
☐31–32	3¢, 8¢	I.C.A.O	42.00	32.00	22.00	6.00	2.50
☐33–34	3¢, 8¢	UNESCO	19.00	10.00	6.00	1.25	.90
☐35–37	3¢, 4¢, 8¢	UN Day	38.00	31.00	16.00	5.00	1.50
☐38	3¢, 4¢, 8¢	UN Day Sheet	—	—	—	190.00	55.00
☐39–40	3¢, 8¢	Human Rights	15.00	13.00	8.25	1.60	.90
1956.							
☐41–42	3¢, 8¢	Telecommunication	14.00	10.00	6.50	1.25	.90
☐43–44	3¢, 8¢	World Health	14.00	10.00	6.50	1.25	.90
☐45–46	3¢, 8¢	UN Day	3.00	1.50	1.25	.36	.28
☐47–48	3¢, 8¢	Human Rights	2.60	1.50	1.25	.38	.31
1957.							
☐49–50	3¢, 8¢	W.M.O. Meteorological	2.25	1.80	1.40	.34	.24
☐51–52	3¢, 8¢	U.N.E.F. 1st Printing	2.25	1.80	1.40	.34	.24
☐53–54	3¢, 8¢	U.N.E.F. 2nd Printing	3.10	1.90	1.50	.36	.25
☐55–56	3¢, 8¢	Security Council	2.00	1.80	1.50	.34	.24
☐57–58	3¢, 8¢	Human Rights	2.00	1.80	1.50	.34	.24
1958.							
☐59–60	3¢, 8¢	Atomic Energy	2.00	1.80	1.50	.36	.24
☐61–62	3¢, 8¢	General Assembly	2.00	1.80	1.50	.36	.24

Scott No.		Name Block 6	Name Block 4	Plain Block 4	Unused Each	Used Each
☐63–64	4¢, 8¢ Regular Issues	2.00	1.75	1.50	.36	.24
☐65–66	4¢, 8¢ Economic Council	2.00	1.75	1.50	.36	.24
☐67–68	4¢, 8¢ Human Rights	2.00	1.75	1.50	.36	.24
☐69–70	4¢, 8¢ Flushing Meadows	2.00	1.90	1.50	.36	.24
☐71–72	4¢, 8¢ E.C.E.	2.00	1.90	1.50	.36	.26
☐73–74	4¢, 8¢ Trusteeship	2.10	1.90	1.60	.36	.24
☐75–76	4¢, 8¢ World Refugee Year	2.10	1.90	1.60	.36	.24
1960.						
☐77–78	4¢, 8¢ Palais de Chaillot	2.10	1.75	1.50	.36	.24
☐79–80	4¢, 8¢ Forestry Congress	2.10	1.75	1.50	.36	.24
☐83–84	4¢, 8¢ 15th Anniversary	2.10	1.75	1.50	.36	.24
☐85	4¢, 8¢ 15th Ann. Souv. Sheet	2.10	1.75	—	2.50	1.65
☐86–87	4¢, 8¢ International	2.10	1.75	1.50	.36	.24
1961.						
☐88–89	4¢, 8¢ Court of Justice	2.10	1.80	1.50	.38	.30
☐90–91	4¢, 7¢ Monetary Fund	2.10	1.80	1.50	.38	.30
☐92	30¢ Regular Issue	5.00	4.00	2.50	.60	.32
☐93–94	4¢, 11¢ E.C. for Latin Am.	5.00	4.00	2.65	.60	.32
☐95–96	4¢, 11¢ E.C. for Africa	3.10	2.25	1.80	.38	.30
☐97–99	3¢, 4¢,13¢ Children's Fund	4.10	3.50	2.80	.60	.30
1962.						
☐100–01	4¢ 7¢ Housing	3.10	2.50	1.75	.38	.26
☐102–03	4¢ 11¢ Malaria	4.10	3.00	2.75	.50	.32
☐104–07	1¢, 3¢, 5¢, 11¢ Reg. Issue	5.00	4.00	3.00	.55	.36
☐108–09	5¢, 15¢ Hammarskjold	9.50	7.50	4.50	.70	.50
☐110–11	4¢, 11¢ U.N. Congo	7.50	6.50	3.80	.70	.50
☐112–13	4¢, 11¢ Peaceful Space Use	4.00	2.75	2.25	.46	.30
1963.						
☐114–15	5¢, 11¢ Econ. Development	3.40	2.60	2.00	.45	.32
☐116–17	5¢, 11¢ Freedom—Hunger	3.40	2.60	2.00	.45	.32
☐118	25¢ UNTEA W. Irian	4.50	3.50	3.00	.62	.38
☐119–20	5¢, 11¢, 10th Hdqrs. Anniv.	3.40	2.60	2.00	.42	.32
☐121–22	5¢, 11¢, 15th Anniv. H. Rights	3.40	2.60	2.00	.42	.32
1964.						
☐123–24	5¢, 11¢ Maritime	3.10	2.25	2.10	.45	.32
☐125–27	2¢, 7¢, 10¢ Reg. Issue	3.10	2.25	2.10	.45	.32
☐128	50¢ New Regular	7.50	6.00	4.00	.80	.70
☐129–30	5¢, 11¢ Trade & Develop	3.00	2.25	2.00	.40	.32
☐131–32	5¢, 11¢ Narcotics Control	3.00	2.25	2.00	.40	.34
☐133	5¢ Nuclear Tests End	1.25	.90	.80	.26	.22
☐134–36	4¢, 5¢, 11¢ Education	2.30	2.15	2.00	.45	.38
1965.						
☐137–38	5¢, 11¢ Special Fund	2.65	2.15	1.85	.38	.28
☐139–40	5¢, 11¢ U.N. in Cyprus	2.65	2.15	1.85	.38	.28
☐141–42	5¢, 11¢ I.T.U. (Satellite)	2.65	2.15	1.85	.38	.28
☐143–44	5¢, 15¢ Co-operation	2.90	2.30	1.85	.40	.40

Scott No.			Name Block 6	Name Block 4	Plain Block 4	Unused Each	Used Each
☐145	5¢,	15¢ Min. Sheet	—	—	—	.90	.65
☐146–49	1¢,	15¢, 20¢, 25¢ Regular	17.00	11.00	7.50	1.90	1.10
☐150	$1	Regular Issue (1966)	21.00	14.00	10.00	2.25	2.00
☐151–53	4¢,	5¢, 11¢ Population Trends	3.15	2.50	2.15	.50	.50
1966.							
☐154–55	5¢,	15¢ World Federation	3.00	2.10	1.80	.38	.28
☐156–57	5¢,	11¢ W.H.O. Building	3.00	2.15	1.80	.38	.28
☐158–59	5¢,	11¢ Coffee Agreement	3.00	2.15	1.80	.38	.28
☐160	15¢	Peacekeeping	2.90	2.00	1.85	.40	.27
☐161–63	4¢,	5¢, 11¢ UNICEF Anniv.	3.00	2.50	2.00	.50	.30
1967.							
☐164–65	5¢,	11¢ Development	3.00	2.00	1.65	.36	.29
☐166–67	1½¢,	5¢ Regular Issue	2.50	1.85	1.40	.36	.29
☐168–69	5¢,	11¢ Independence	3.00	2.00	1.65	.36	.29
1967.							
☐170–74	4¢,	5¢, 8¢, 10¢, 15¢ EXPO	9.00	6.50	5.00	1.10	.90
☐175–76	5¢,	15¢ Intl. Tourist Year	2.85	2.20	2.00	.36	.30
☐177–78	6¢,	13¢ Toward Disarm	3.25	2.75	2.10	.40	.36
☐179	6¢	Chagall Sheet of Six	—	—	—	.65	.60
☐180	6¢	Chagall Window	1.50	1.00	.80	.26	.20
1968.							
☐181–82	6¢,	13¢, Secretariat	3.25	2.70	2.00	.45	.36
☐183–84	6¢,	75¢ Starcke Statue	21.00	18.00	11.00	2.00	1.75
☐185–86	6¢,	13¢ ONUDI	3.00	2.30	1.90	.36	.32
☐187	6¢	Regular Issue	1.75	1.00	.85	.26	.20
☐188–89	6¢,	20¢ Weather Watch	4.15	3.00	2.50	.45	.40
☐190–91	6¢,	13¢ Int'l. Year Human Rts.	3.75	3.10	2.50	.45	.40
1969.							
☐192–93	6¢,	13¢ UNITAR	3.00	2.40	2.00	.43	.36
☐194–95	6¢,	15¢ ECLA Bldg	3.25	2.65	2.25	.48	.40
☐196	13¢,	Regular Issue	2.75	2.00	1.80	.34	.26
☐197–98	6¢,	13¢ Peace thru Law	3.00	2.35	2.15	.45	.36
☐199–00	6¢,	20¢ Labor & Devl	4.00	3.10	2.75	.48	.45
☐201–02	6¢,	13¢ Art Series	3.75	2.70	2.25	.46	.34
☐203–04	6¢,	25¢ Japan Peace Bell	4.25	3.50	2.75	.50	.52
☐205–06	6¢,	13¢ Mekong Basin	3.75	2.50	2.00	.45	.33
☐207–08	6¢,	13¢ Cancer	3.10	2.40	2.00	.40	.33
☐209–11	6¢,	13¢, 25¢ 25th U.V. Anniv.	8.00	6.50	5.00	1.35	.87
☐212		Same, Souvenir Sheet	—	—	—	1.35	1.15
☐213–14	6¢,	13¢ Peace, Just. Prog.	3.10	2.50	2.00	.45	.35
1971.							
☐215	6¢	Sea Bed	1.75	1.00	.80	.25	.18
☐216–17	6¢,	13¢ Refugees	3.40	2.60	2.00	.35	.32
☐218	13¢	World Food Prog.	2.60	2.00	1.40	.30	.24
☐219	20¢	U.P.U. Building	3.50	2.50	1.85	.34	.36

Scott No.			Name Block 6	Name Block 4	Plain Block 4	Unused Each	Used Each
☐220–21	3¢,	13¢ Anti-Discrim.	3.80	3.00	2.00	.42	.36
☐222–23	8¢,	60¢ Regular Issue	10.00	7.00	6.00	1.40	1.25
☐224–25	8¢,	21¢ Intl. Schools	6.00	4.25	3.10	.70	.60
1972.							
☐226	95¢	Regular Issue	12.00	11.00	9.00	2.10	1.50
☐227	8¢,	Non-Proliferation	2.00	1.60	.90	.22	.20
☐228	15¢	World Health	3.00	2.25	1.60	.34	.28
☐229–30	8¢,	15¢ Environment	4.00	3.00	2.25	.46	.42
☐231	21¢	E.C. Europe	4.00	3.15	2.25	.45	.40
☐232–33	8¢,	15¢ U.N. Art Sert.	4.15	3.25	2.25	.46	.40
1973.							
☐234–35	8¢,	15¢ Disarmament	4.50	3.00	2.40	.50	.40
☐236–37	8¢,	15¢ Drug Abuse	4.50	3.50	2.75	.60	.52
☐238–39	8¢,	21¢ U.N. Volunteers	5.00	4.00	2.90	.62	.58
☐240–41	8¢,	15¢ Namibia	5.00	3.40	2.80	.60	.50
☐242–43	8¢,	21¢ Human Rights	5.00	3.80	2.80	.68	.55
1974.							
☐244–45	10¢,	21¢ ILO Hdqr.	6.50	5.00	4.00	.76	.67
☐246	10¢	UPU Centenary	2.25	1.75	1.00	.24	.20
☐247–48	10¢,	18¢ Brazil Mural	4.75	3.80	3.00	.65	.55
☐249–51	2¢,	10¢, 18¢ Regular	5.00	4.00	3.00	.65	.56
☐252–53	10¢,	18¢ Population	5.50	4.00	3.00	.58	.50
☐254–55	10¢,	26¢ Law of Sea	6.50	5.00	3.75	1.90	.70
1975.							
☐256–57	10¢,	26¢ Space Usage	7.50	4.50	3.90	.90	.70
☐258–59	10¢,	18¢ Women's Year	4.50	4.00	3.00	.75	.55
☐260–61	10¢,	26¢ UN 30th Anniv.	7.50	6.00	3.10	.75	.62
☐262	36¢	Same Souv. Sheet	—	—	—	1.00	.82
☐263–64	10¢,	18¢ Namibia	5.50	4.00	2.90	.60	.50
☐265–66	13¢,	26¢ Peacekeeping	8.00	5.00	4.00	.90	.70
1976.							
☐267–71	3¢,	4¢, 9¢, 30¢, 50¢ Regular	15.00	10.00	7.00	1.80	1.45
☐272–73	13¢,	26¢ WFUNA	7.50	6.00	4.50	.80	.70
☐274–75	13¢,	31¢ UNCTAD	8.00	6.00	5.00	.85	.80
☐276–77	13¢,	25¢ HABITAT	7.50	6.00	5.00	.85	.75
☐278–79	13¢,	31¢ 25th Postal Anniv.	34.00	28.00	20.00	4.00	2.25
☐280	13¢	Food Council	3.00	2.15	1.75	.38	.26
1977.							
☐281–82	13¢,	31¢ WIPO	8.10	6.50	4.10	1.10	.82
☐283–84	13¢,	25¢ Water Conf.	8.40	6.10	4.00	.90	.75
☐285–86	13¢,	31¢ Security Council	7.50	6.50	4.50	.75	.65
☐287–88	13¢,	25¢ Combat Racism	6.50	5.00	3.50	.78	.80
☐289–90	13¢,	18¢ Atomic Energy	6.00	5.00	3.60	.75	.60

Scott No.		Name Block 6	Name Block 4	Plain Block 4	Unused Each	Used Each
1978.						
☐291–93	1¢, 25¢, $1 Regular	20.00	15.00	11.00	2.80	2.00
☐294–95	13¢, 31¢ Small Pox	9.00	7.50	5.00	1.00	.85
☐296–97	13¢, 18¢ Namibia	6.50	5.00	3.00	.75	.60
☐298–99	13¢, 25¢ ICAO-Air Safety	7.40	6.10	4.50	.80	.70
☐300–01	13¢, 18¢ General Assembly	6.50	4.50	3.00	.67	.56
☐302–03	13¢, 31¢ Technical Cooperation	10.00	8.00	6.00	1.15	.80
1979.						
☐304–07	5¢, 14¢, 15¢, 20¢ Regular Issues	9.00	7.00	5.00	1.25	.90
☐308–09	15¢, 20¢ UNDRO	7.00	5.50	4.00	.80	.70
☐310–11	15¢, 31¢ Intl. Year of Child	9.00	7.50	5.50	1.10	1.00
☐312–13	15¢, 31¢ Namibia	8.00	6.00	4.50	1.00	.80
☐314–15	15¢, 31¢ Court of Justice	7.50	5.50	4.00	.75	.65
1980.						
☐316–17	15¢, 31¢ Economic Order	8.00	6.50	4.50	.95	.78
☐318–19	15¢, 20¢, Women's Decade	6.50	5.50	4.00	.80	.65
☐320–21	15¢, 31¢ Peacekeeping	8.50	7.00	5.00	1.00	1.00
☐322–23	15¢, 31¢ 35th Anniversary	8.50	7.00	5.00	.90	.86
☐324	15¢ Same, Souvenir Sheet	—	—	—	1.00	.95
☐325–40	15¢ World Flags	—	19.00	—	4.50	4.00
☐325–28	15¢ World Flags	—	6.00	—	1.10	1.10
☐329–32	15¢ World Flags	—	6.00	—	1.10	1.10
☐333–36	15¢ World Flags	—	6.00	—	1.10	1.10
☐337–40	15¢ World Flags	—	6.00	—	1.10	1.10
☐341–42	15¢, 20¢ Economic and Social Council.	6.50	5.50	4.00	.90	.85
1981.						
☐343	15¢ Palestinian People	3.60	2.50	1.90	.40	.30
☐344–45	20¢, 35¢ Disabled Persons	10.00	7.50	6.00	1.50	.95
☐346–47	20¢, 31¢ Fresco	—	7.50	6.00	1.50	.90
☐348–49	20¢, 40¢ Sources of Energy	12.00	9.00	7.00	1.60	1.00
☐350–65	1981 World Flags	—	30.00	—	7.00	4.50
☐350–53	20¢ World Flags	—	10.00	—	2.00	1.00
☐358–61	20¢ World Flags	—	10.00	—	2.00	1.00
☐354–57	15¢ 20¢ World Flags	—	10.00	—	2.00	1.00
☐362–65	20¢ World Flags	—	10.00	—	2.00	1.00
☐366–67	18¢ 28¢ Volunteers Program	—	8.50	7.00	1.40	.90
1982.						
☐368–70	17¢, 28¢, 40¢ Definitives	12.00	9.00	7.50	2.10	1.50
☐371–72	20¢, 40¢ Human Environment	11.00	8.00	7.00	1.60	1.10
☐373	20¢ Space Exploration	4.50	4.00	3.00	.70	.40
☐374–89	World Flags	36.00	26.00	21.00	6.50	6.00
☐390–91	20¢, 28¢ Nature Conservation	10.00	6.50	5.00	1.50	.85
1983.						
☐392–93	20¢, 40¢ Communication	11.00	8.00	6.50	1.50	1.15
☐394–95	20¢, 37¢ Safety at Sea	11.00	7.00	6.50	1.50	1.15

Scott No.			Name Block 6	Name Block 4	Plain Block 4	Unused Each	Used Each
☐396	20¢	World Food	6.25	5.00	4.00	.90	.45
☐397–98	20¢,	28¢ Trade	10.00	8.00	6.50	1.75	.90
☐399–14		World Flags	35.00	26.00	19.00	7.00	5.50
☐415–16	20¢,	40¢ Human Rights	16.00	11.00	7.50	3.00	1.45
1984.							
☐417–18	20¢,	40¢ Population Conference	10.00	7.00	3.00	2.40	1.10
☐419–20	20¢,	40¢ World Food Day	10.00	7.00	3.00	2.40	1.10
☐421–22	20¢,	50¢ Heritage	10.00	7.00	3.40	2.50	1.20
☐423–24	20¢,	50¢ Refugees	10.00	7.00	3.10	2.60	1.20
☐425–40		World Flags	30.00	26.00	17.00	15.00	2.00
☐441–42	20¢,	35¢ Youth Year	29.00	7.00	3.10	3.00	1.10
1985.							
☐443	23¢	Turin Centre	10.00	6.50	4.00	.80	.45
☐444	50¢	U.N. University	14.00	11.00	6.50	1.30	.90
☐445–46	22¢,	$3.00 People of the World	23.00	14.00	7.00	6.50	1.25
☐447–48	22¢,	45¢ 40th U.N. Anniversary	18.00	10.00	7.00	1.50	1.25
☐449	22¢,	45¢ 40th Anniversary Souvenir Sheet	—	—	—	2.00	1.50
☐450–65	22¢	World Flags	—	—	7.00	3.00	1.50
☐466–67	22¢,	33¢ UNICEF	9.50	8.50	6.50	1.30	1.00
1986.							
☐468	22¢	Africa in Crisis	7.00	6.50	5.50	.60	.38
☐469–72	22¢	U.N. Resources	9.00	6.50	5.50	—	1.80
☐473–74	22¢,	44¢ Philately	7.50	6.50	6.00	1.70	.90
☐475–76	22¢,	33¢ Peace Year	7.00	6.50	6.00	1.80	.95
☐477–92	22¢	World Flags	11.00	10.00	9.00	2.75	1.60
☐493	22¢,	44¢ WFUNA Souvenir Sheet	—	—	—	6.00	4.50
1987.							
☐494	22¢	Trygve H. Lie	8.00	6.00	4.00	.78	.38
☐495–96	22¢,	44¢ Shelter Homeless	9.00	7.00	6.00	1.50	1.00
☐497–98	22¢,	33¢ Fight Drugs	9.00	7.00	6.00	1.60	1.00
☐499–514	22¢	World Flags	8.00	7.00	6.00	1.80	1.25
☐515–16	22¢,	39¢ United Nations Day	8.50	7.00	6.00	1.55	1.00
☐516–18	22¢,	44¢ Child Immunizations	8.00	7.00	5.50	1.50	1.00
1988.							
☐519–20	22¢,	33¢ World Hunger	7.50	6.50	5.50	1.10	.85
☐521	3¢	U.N. A Better World	5.50	4.00	3.00	.26	.18
☐522–23	25¢,	44¢ Forest Survival	6.00	4.00	3.00	1.75	1.30
☐524–25	25¢,	50¢ Int. Volunteers	8.00	6.00	3.50	1.75	1.10
☐526–27	25¢,	38¢ Health Sports	8.00	6.00	3.50	1.30	1.00
☐528–43	25¢	World Flags	8.00	6.00	4.00	3.10	2.00
☐544	25¢	Human Rights	—	—	—	—	—
☐545	25¢	Human Rights Souvenir Sheet	—	—	—	3.50	1.65

Scott No.			Name Block 6	Name Block 4	Plain Block 4	Unused Each	Used Each
1989.							
☐546–47	25¢,	45¢ World Bank	9.50	7.50	6.50	1.80	.85
☐548	25¢	Nobel Peace Prize	7.50	5.50	3.00	1.00	.20
☐549	45¢	U.N. Building	7.50	5.50	2.75	1.10	.20
☐550–51	25¢,	36¢ World Weather	7.50	6.50	5.00	1.50	.60
☐552–53	25¢,	90¢ U.N. Vienna	12.00	9.00	7.00	3.00	1.10
☐554–69		World Flags	12.00	9.00	7.00	2.50	1.10
☐570–71		Human Rights	13.00	12.50	10.00	4.00	.60
1990.							
☐572	25¢	Int'l Trade Center	5.50	4.50	3.50	.60	.20
☐573–74	25¢	40¢ AIDS	7.00	6.00	4.00	1.00	.55
☐575–76	25¢	90¢ Medicinal Plants	12.50	9.00	7.00	1.75	1.15
☐577–78	25¢,	45¢ U.N. 45th Anniversary	9.50	8.50	6.00	1.25	.60
☐579	25¢,	45¢ U.N. 45th Anniversary Souvenir Sheet	7.50	5.00	3.50	1.50	1.00
☐580–81	25¢,	36¢ Crime Prevention	7.50	5.50	3.50	1.00	.60
☐582–83	25¢,	45¢ Human Rights	9.00	7.50	6.00	1.40	.70
1991.							
☐584–87	30¢	Economic Comm. Europe	9.00	6.00	4.10	2.10	1.20
☐588–89	30¢,	36¢ Namibia	9.50	7.50	6.00	1.50	.80
☐590–91	30¢,	50¢ U.N. Golden Rule	9.50	7.50	6.00	1.50	.80
☐592	$2.00	U.N. Building	10.00	8.50	7.00	2.50	1.60
☐593–94	30¢,	70¢ Children's Rights	10.00	8.50	7.00	2.00	1.25
☐595–96	30¢,	90¢ Banning Chem. Weapons	10.00	8.50	7.00	1.60	1.15
☐597–98	30¢,	40¢ UNPA 40th Anniversary	9.50	8.00	7.00	1.50	.80
☐599–600	30¢,	50¢ Human Rights	11.50	10.00	8.50	2.30	1.00
1992.							
☐601–02	29¢,	50¢ UNESCO Heritage	10.00	9.50	7.50	1.50	.80
☐603–04	29¢	Clean Oceans	7.50	6.50	5.00	1.10	.65
☐605–08	29¢	UNICEF Summit	7.50	6.50	5.00	1.25	1.00
☐609–10	29¢	Mission to Earth	7.50	6.00	5.00	1.30	1.10
☐611–12	29¢,	59¢ Science and Technology	7.50	6.00	5.00	1.00	.80
☐613–15	4¢,	40¢ Definitives	9.00	7.50	6.00	1.10	.75
☐616–17	29¢,	50¢ Human Rights	8.00	6.00	5.00	1.35	.90

UNITED NATIONS AIRMAILS

1951–1957.							
☐C1	6¢	Airmail (1951)	21.00	18.00	12.00	2.10	1.80
☐C2	10¢	Airmail	21.00	18.00	12.00	2.10	1.80
☐C3	15¢	Airmail	21.00	18.00	12.00	2.10	1.80
☐C4	25¢	Airmail	21.00	18.00	12.00	2.10	1.80
☐C1–4		First Issue Airmails	68.00	60.00	50.00	8.00	1.80
☐C5–7	4¢,	5¢, 7¢ Airmail (1957)	4.00	3.50	2.40	.60	.50

Scott No.		Name Block 6	Name Block 4	Plain Block 4	Unused Each	Used Each
1963–1964.						
☐C8–10	6¢, 8¢, 13¢ Airmail (1963)	18.00	12.00	6.00	.90	.50
☐C11–12	15¢, 25¢ Airmail (1964)	18.00	13.00	6.00	2.00	.85
1968–1972.						
☐C13	20¢ Airmail (1968)	6.00	4.00	3.50	.75	.40
☐C14	10¢ Airmail (1969)	6.00	4.00	3.50	.75	.40
☐C15–18	9¢, 11¢, 17¢, 21¢ (1972)	10.00	7.00	5.00	.85	.90
1974–1977.						
☐C19–21	13¢, 18¢, 26¢ (1974)	9.00	7.00	5.50	1.10	.90
☐C22–23	25¢, 31¢ (1977)	9.50	7.50	5.50	1.10	.95

		Unused Each	Used Each
UNITED NATIONS SOUVENIR CARDS			
☐1	WHO, First Printing	6.00	—
☐1a	WHO, Second Printing	4.50	—
☐2	Art at U.N.	3.50	—
☐3	Disarmament	3.50	—
☐4	Human Rights	5.00	—
☐5	Universal Postal Union	5.00	—
☐6	World Population	20.00	—
☐7	Outer Space	8.00	—
☐8	Peacekeeping	10.00	—
☐9	World Federation of U.N.	10.00	—
☐10	World Food Council	6.50	—
☐11	World Intellectual Property	4.00	—
☐12	Combat Racism	4.00	—
☐13	Namibia	4.00	—
☐14	ICAO-Air Safety	4.00	—
☐15	International Year of the Child	4.50	—
☐16	Court of Justice	4.50	—
☐17	Women's Decade	20.00	—
☐18	Economic and Social Council	6.00	—
☐19	Disabled Persons	4.50	—
☐20	Energy Sources	5.00	—

Scott No.		Name Block 6	Name Block 4	Plain Block 4	Unused Each	Used Each
UNITED NATIONS—GENEVA, SWITZERLAND, iSSUES						
DENOMINATIONS ARE GIVEN IN SWISS CURRENCY						
DESIGNS ARE SIMILAR TO U.N. NEW YORK ISSUES						
1969–1970.						
☐1–14	5¢ to 10 franc	140.00	100.00	50.00	12.00	10.00
1971.						
☐15	30¢ Sea Bed	2.00	1.75	1.35	.36	.30
☐16	50¢ Refugees	4.00	3.00	2.10	.50	.40

Scott No.			Name Block 6	Name Block 4	Plain Block 4	Unused Each	Used Each
☐17	50¢	World Food Prog.	5.00	4.00	2.10	.50	.50
☐18	75¢	U.P.U. Building	10.00	8.50	5.00	.90	.80
☐19–20	30¢,	50¢ Anti-Discrim.	9.50	8.00	5.00	1.00	.60
☐21	1.10 fr.	Intl. Schools	14.00	10.00	7.00	1.50	1.10
1972.							
☐22	40¢	Regular Issue	3.80	3.00	2.10	.45	.36
☐23	40¢	Non-Proliferation	9.50	7.00	4.00	.75	.45
☐24	80¢	World Health	9.50	7.00	5.00	.80	.90
☐25–26	40¢,	80¢ Environment	15.00	9.00	7.00	1.50	1.30
☐27	1.10 fr.	E.C. Europe	15.00	10.00	7.50	1.40	1.30
☐28–29	40¢,	80¢ U.N. Art-Sert	14.00	11.00	7.50	1.50	1.65
1973.							
☐30–31	60¢,	1.10 fr. Disarm	15.00	13.00	10.00	2.00	1.60
☐32	60¢	Drug Abuse	8.00	7.00	5.50	.90	.60
☐33	80¢	U.N. Volunteers	8.50	7.00	5.50	.95	.80
☐34	60¢	Namibia	8.50	7.00	5.50	1.00	.70
☐35–36	40¢,	80¢ Human Rights	10.00	8.00	6.50	1.20	.90
1974.							
☐37–38	60¢,	80¢ ILO Hdqrs.	11.00	8.50	6.50	1.60	1.20
☐39–40	30¢,	60¢ UPU Centenary	8.00	7.50	5.00	1.25	.85
☐41–42	60¢,	1 fr. Brazil Mural	11.00	10.00	7.50	2.00	1.60
☐43–44	60¢,	80¢ Population	11.00	9.00	7.50	1.60	1.10
☐45	1.30 fr.	Law of Sea	11.00	9.00	7.50	1.60	1.20
1975.							
☐46–47	60¢,	80¢ Space Usage	15.00	9.00	7.50	1.40	1.25
☐48–49	60¢,	90¢ Women's Year	14.00	8.00	7.00	1.75	1.65
☐50–51	60¢,	90¢ U.N. Anniv.	14.00	9.00	7.00	1.50	1.30
☐52	1.50 fr.	Same, Souv. Sheet	—	—	—	1.50	1.40
☐53–54	50¢,	1.30 fr. Namibia	14.00	9.00	7.00	1.60	1.45
☐55–56	60¢,	70¢ Peacekeeping	14.00	9.00	7.00	1.40	1.25
1976.							
☐57	90¢	WFUNA	9.50	6.50	4.50	1.10	.90
☐58	1.10 fr.	UNCTAD	9.00	6.50	4.50	1.15	1.10
☐59–60	40¢	1.50 fr. HABITAT	15.00	9.00	7.00	1.60	1.45
☐61–62	80¢,	1.10 fr. U.N. Postal Anniv.	55.00	42.00	32.00	7.50	5.00
☐63	70¢	World Food Council	8.00	5.50	4.00	.85	.70
1977.							
☐64	80¢	WIPO	7.50	6.00	4.50	.95	.75
☐65–66	80¢	1.10 fr. Water Conf.	12.00	10.00	8.00	1.60	1.40
☐67–68	80¢,	1.10 fr. Security Council	12.00	10.00	8.00	1.60	1.40
☐69–70	40¢,	1.10 fr. Combat Racism	12.00	10.00	8.00	1.50	1.25
☐71–72	80¢,	1.10 fr. Atomic Energy	14.00	11.00	9.00	1.75	1.40
☐73	35¢	Doves	8.00	4.00	3.00	.50	.40
☐74–75	80¢,	1.10 fr. Smallpox	13.00	10.00	8.00	1.65	1.30
☐76	80¢	Namibia	8.00	7.00	6.00	.95	.80

Scott No.			Name Block 6	Name Block 4	Plain Block 4	Unused Each	Used Each
☐77–78	70¢,	80¢ ICAO-Air Safety	11.00	8.50	7.50	1.40	1.15
☐79–80	70¢,	1.10 Fr. General Assembly	11.00	8.50	7.50	1.65	1.20
☐81	80¢	Technical Cooperation	8.50	6.00	4.00	.85	.70
1979.							
☐82–83	80¢,	1.50 UNDRO	16.00	13.00	10.00	2.10	1.85
☐84–85	80¢,	1.10 Intl. Year of the Child	18.00	15.00	10.00	1.75	1.35
☐86	1.10 fr.	Namibia	11.00	8.50	5.00	1.00	.90
☐87–88	80¢,	1.10 Court of Justice	15.00	12.00	8.00	1.75	1.50
1980.							
☐89	80¢	Economic Order	9.00	7.50	4.00	.85	.70
☐90–91	40¢,	70¢ Women's Decade	11.00	8.50	5.00	1.10	1.00
☐92	1.10 fr.	Peacekeeping	10.00	8.00	5.00	1.10	1.00
☐93–94	40¢,	70¢, 35th Anniversary	10.00	8.00	5.00	1.10	1.00
☐95	40¢,	70¢ Sheet	—	—	—	1.40	1.25
96–97	40¢,	70¢ Economic and Social Council.	10.00	8.00	5.00	1.10	1.00
1981.							
☐98	80¢	Palestinian People	7.50	6.00	4.00	.85	.70
☐99–100	40¢,	1.50 fr. Disabled Persons	15.00	10.00	7.00	1.65	1.30
☐101	80¢	Bulgarian Mural	8.00	6.00	5.00	.90	.70
☐102	1.10 fr.	Energy Sources	10.00	7.50	5.50	1.10	.95
☐103–04	40¢,	70¢ Volunteers	10.00	7.50	5.50	1.10	.95
1982.							
☐105–06	1 fr.,	Definitives	11.00	8.50	7.00	1.40	1.25
☐107–08	40¢,	1.20 fr., Human Environment	11.00	8.50	7.00	1.40	1.35

Scott No.		Fine	Ave.

UNUSED BOOKLET PANES

Scott No.		Fine	Ave.
☐319g	2¢ Carmine	125.00	74.00
☐331a	1¢ Green	140.00	95.00
☐332a	2¢ Carmine	110.00	85.00
☐374a	1¢ Green	120.00	80.00
☐375a	2¢ Carmine	95.00	75.00
☐405b	1¢ Green	50.00	39.00
☐406a	2¢ Carmine	60.00	34.00
☐424d	1¢ Green	5.00	4.00
☐425e	2¢ Carmine	12.00	10.00
☐462a	1¢ Green	11.00	7.00
☐463a	2¢ Carmine	68.00	46.00
☐498e	1¢ Green	2.75	2.00
☐499e	2¢ Rose	3.00	2.00
☐501b	3¢ Violet I	50.00	32.00
☐502b	3¢ Violet II	46.00	35.00
☐552b	1¢ Dark Green	6.50	4.00
☐554c	2¢ Carmine	7.00	5.00
☐583a	2¢ Carmine	50.00	42.00
☐632a	1¢ Green	5.00	3.75
☐634d	2¢ Carmine	1.80	1.25
☐720b	3¢ Dark Violet	30.00	20.00
☐804b	1¢ Green	10.00	3.00
☐806a	2¢ Red Carmine	7.00	4.00
☐807a	3¢ Dark Violet	10.00	7.00
☐1035a	3¢ Dark Violet	5.00	3.00
☐1036a	4¢ Red Violet	4.00	3.00
☐1213a	5¢ "ZIP"	3.00	2.50
☐1213x	5¢ Mailman	6.50	4.00
☐1213y	5¢ Zone No	8.50	5.00
☐1278a	1¢ Jeff. (8)	2.00	1.00
☐1278ae	1¢ Gum (8)	2.50	1.50
☐1278b	1¢ Green (4)	.90	.50
☐1280a	2¢ Blue Gray (5)	1.50	.90
☐1280c	2¢ Blue Gray (6)	1.10	.65
☐1284b	6¢ F.D.R. (8)	2.00	1.65
☐1284c	6¢ F.D.R. (5)	2.00	1.50
☐1393a	6¢ Ike (8)	2.10	1.50
☐1393ae	6¢ T. Gum (8)	3.00	1.70
☐1393b	6¢ Ike (5)	1.50	.90
☐1395a	8¢ Ike (8)	2.10	1.65
☐1395b	8¢ Ike (6)	1.85	1.40
☐1395c	8¢ Ike (4)	2.00	1.50
☐1395d	8¢ Ike (7)	2.10	1.70

Scott No.		Fine	Ave.
☐1510b	10¢ Mem'l (5)	1.80	1.25
☐1510c	10¢ Mem'l (8)	2.00	1.40
☐1510d	10¢ Mem'l (6)	6.00	2.75
☐1595a	13¢ Bell (6)	2.10	1.60
☐1595b	13¢ Bell (7)	3.00	1.80
☐1595c	13¢ Bell (8)	2.10	1.60
☐1595d	13¢ Bell (6)	2.10	1.60
☐1623a	13¢ (7), 9¢ (1)	4.00	3.00
☐1623c	Same, Perf. 10	35.00	26.00
☐1736a	"A" Eagle (no denomination)	3.50	2.75
☐1737a	15¢ Multicolored	4.00	3.00
☐1742a	15¢ Multicolored	4.00	3.00
☐C10a	10¢ Lindbergh	100.00	80.00
☐C25a	6¢ Carmine	12.00	4.00
☐C39a	6¢ Small	11.00	6.00
☐C51a	7¢ Blue	12.00	7.00
☐C60a	7¢ Carmine	16.00	8.00
☐C64c	8¢ Carmine "Zip"	2.00	1.50
☐C64bx	8¢ Mailman	10.00	6.00
☐C64by	8¢ Zone No	50.00	28.00
☐C72b	10¢ Carmine (8)	4.00	3.50
☐C72c	10¢ Carmine (5)	6.00	3.50
☐C78a	11¢ Carmine (4)	1.80	1.25
☐C79a	13¢ Letter (5)	2.10	1.50

Scott No.		Fine

SOUVENIR CARDS

		Fine
☐1	Truck w/gum	70.00
	Truck w/o gum	11.00
☐2	Barcelona	400.00
☐3	SIPEX Scenes	180.00
☐3a	SIPEX Miner	12.00
☐4	EFIMEX	3.50
☐5	SANDIPEX	70.00
☐	Ana '69	70.00
☐	FRESNO	450.00
☐6	ASDA '69	22.00
☐7	INTERPEX '70	62.00
☐8	COMPEX '70	15.00
☐	ANA 1970	100.00
☐9	PHILYMPIA	2.50
☐10	HAPEX	16.00

Scott No.		Fine
☐11	INTERPEX '71	2.50
☐12	WESTPEX	2.50
☐13	NAPEX '71	2.75
☐	ANA 1971	4.00
☐14	TEXANEX	3.00
☐15	EXFILIMA	2.10
☐16	ASDA '71	2.50
☐17	ANPHILEX	1.50
☐18	INTERPEX '72	1.60
☐19	NOPEX	1.50
☐20	BELGICA	1.60
☐	ANA 1972	4.00
☐21	Olympia Phil. Munchen	1.60
☐22	EXFILBRA	1.60
☐23	Postal Forum	1.60
☐24	SEPAD '72	1.60
☐25	ASDA '72	1.40
☐26	Stamp Expo '75	2.10
☐27	INTERPEX '73	1.80
☐28	IBRA	2.40
☐29	COMPEX '73	2.00
☐30	APEX	2.40
☐	ANA 1973	7.00
☐31	PLOSKA	2.50
☐32	NAPEX '73	2.30
☐33	ASDA '73	1.80
☐34	Stamps Expo '73	2.40
☐35	Hobby Show Chicago	3.75
☐36	MILCOPEX '72	3.00
☐37	INTERNABA 1974	2.75
☐	ANA 1974	9.00
☐38	STOCKHOLMIA '74	3.25
☐39	EXFILMEX '74	3.00
☐40	ESPANA '75	2.50
☐41	NAPEX '75	9.50
☐42	ARPHILA '75	2.50
☐43	Women's Year	26.00
☐	ANA 1975	12.00
☐44	ASDA '75	40.00
☐45	WERABA '76	4.00
☐46	INTERPHIL '76	8.00

Scott No.		Fine
☐	INTERPHIL Program with BEP Card	9.00
☐47	Science BEP	8.50
☐48	Science U.S.P.S.	7.00
☐49	Stamp Expo '76	8.00
☐50	Colorado Statehood	3.50
☐51	HAFNIA '76	3.50
☐	ANA 1976	8.00
☐52	ITALIA '76	3.50
☐53	NORDPOSTA '76	4.10
☐54	MILCOPEX '77	2.75
☐55	ROMPEX '77	3.00
☐56	AMPHILEX '77	3.75
☐	ANA 1977	4.00
☐57	SAN MARCO	4.10
☐58	Puripex	2.75
☐59	ASDA '77	3.50
☐60	ROPEX '78	4.50
☐	Paper Money Show	4.50
☐61	NAPOSTA '78	3.15
☐62	CENTEX '78	3.50
☐63	BRASILIANA '79	5.00
☐64	JAPEX '79	5.00
☐	ANA '80	20.00
☐65	LONDON '80	5.00
☐	Money Show '80	12.00
☐66	NORWEX '80	5.00
☐67	NAPEX '80	12.50
☐	Visitor Center	9.00
☐68	ASDA STAMP FESTIVAL '80	15.00
☐69	ESSEN '80	6.00
☐70	STAMP EXPO '81	20.00
☐	Visitor Center	9.00
☐71	WIPA '81	5.00
☐	Paper Money	18.00
☐	ANA '81	14.00
☐72	STAMP COLLECTORS MONTH	5.00
☐73	PHILATOKYO '81	5.00
☐74	NORD POSKTA '81	4.75

Scott No.		Fine Unused Each	Ave. Unused Each	Fine Used Each	Ave. Used Each
POSTAGE DUE STAMPS					
1879. PERFORATED 12 (N-H ADD 80%)					
☐J1	1¢ Brown	26.00	16.00	6.00	3.00
☐J2	2¢ Brown	170.00	110.00	5.00	2.40
☐J3	3¢ Brown	21.00	13.00	3.00	1.50
☐J4	5¢ Brown	250.00	160.00	32.00	14.50
☐J5	10¢ Brown	315.00	190.00	12.00	7.00
☐J6	30¢ Brown	160.00	95.00	30.00	15.00
☐J7	50¢ Brown	200.00	120.00	38.00	19.00
1884–1889. SAME DESIGN—PERF. 12 (N-H ADD 80%)					
☐J15	1¢ Red Brown	30.00	15.00	3.00	1.80
☐J16	2¢ Red Brown	38.00	19.00	3.00	1.80
☐J17	3¢ Red Brown	420.00	140.00	92.00	46.00
☐J18	5¢ Red Brown	210.00	115.00	11.00	7.00
☐J19	10¢ Red Brown	200.00	115.00	9.00	5.00
☐J20	30¢ Red Brown	95.00	54.00	28.00	15.00
☐J21	50¢ Red Brown	900.00	510.00	115.00	62.00
1891–1893. SAME DESIGN—PERF. 12 (N-H ADD 80%)					
☐J22	1¢ Bright Claret	12.00	6.50	.62	.40
☐J23	2¢ Bright Claret	10.00	7.10	.54	.34
☐J24	3¢ Bright Claret	30.00	16.00	3.50	2.10
☐J25	5¢ Bright Claret	32.00	18.00	3.50	2.10
☐J26	10¢ Bright Claret	60.00	32.00	9.00	6.50
☐J27	30¢ Bright Claret	210.00	120.00	90.00	48.00
☐J28	50¢ Bright Claret	240.00	140.00	90.00	48.00
1894. NEW SMALL DESIGN—NO WTMK.—PERF. 12 (N-H ADD 55%)					
☐J29	1¢ Vermilion	500.00	400.00	150.00	75.00
☐J30	2¢ Vermilion	240.00	200.00	50.00	35.00
☐J31	1¢ Claret	20.00	15.00	9.00	3.50
☐J32	2¢ Claret	16.00	8.50	2.50	1.50
☐J33	3¢ Claret	70.00	35.00	19.00	10.00
☐J34	5¢ Claret	85.00	45.00	25.00	15.00
☐J35	10¢ Claret	86.00	45.00	16.00	9.00
☐J36	30¢ Claret (Shades)	200.00	150.00	60.00	35.00
☐J37	50¢ Claret (Shades)	475.00	270.00	160.00	90.00
1895. SAME NEW SMALL DESIGN—D.L. WTMK.—PERF. 12 (N-H ADD 80%)					
☐J38	1¢ Claret	7.00	4.00	.42	.27
☐J39	2¢ Claret	7.00	3.00	.28	.20
☐J40	3¢ Claret	30.00	16.00	1.20	.65
☐J41	5¢ Claret	32.00	16.00	1.20	.65
☐J42	10¢ Claret	34.00	19.00	2.60	1.50
☐J43	30¢ Claret	260.00	150.00	28.00	14.00
☐J44	50¢ Claret	170.00	98.00	23.00	14.00

Scott No.			Fine Unused Each	Ave. Unused Each	Fine Used Each	Ave. Used Each
1910–1912. SMALL DESIGN—S.L. WTMK.—PERF. 12 (N-H ADD 80%)						
☐J45	1¢	Claret	17.00	10.50	2.25	1.30
☐J46	2¢	Claret	17.00	10.50	.30	.16
☐J47	3¢	Claret	300.00	175.00	19.00	12.00
☐J48	5¢	Claret	50.00	32.00	4.00	2.10
☐J49	10¢	Claret	64.00	45.00	9.00	4.75
☐J50	50¢	Claret	510.00	285.00	76.00	40.00
1914–1916. SAME SMALL DESIGN—S.L. WTMK. PERF. 10. (N-H ADD 80%)						
☐J52	1¢	Carmine	36.00	20.00	8.00	4.00
☐J53	2¢	Carmine	36.00	15.00	.28	.16
☐J54	3¢	Carmine	400.00	210.00	20.00	11.00
☐J55	5¢	Carmine	21.00	10.00	1.90	1.00
☐J56	10¢	Carmine	34.00	19.00	1.10	.60
☐J57	30¢	Carmine	130.00	80.00	15.00	8.50
☐J58	50¢	Carmine	4900.00	2500.00	380.00	220.00
☐J59	1¢	Rose (No Wtmk.)	1000.00	600.00	190.00	100.00
☐J60	2¢	Rose (No Wtmk.)	76.00	42.00	11.00	7.00

Scott No.			Fine Unused Plate Blk	Ave. Unused Plate Blk	Fine Unused Each	Ave. Unused Each	Fine Used Each	Ave. Used Each
1917–1926. SAME SMALL DESIGN—NO WTMK.—PERF. 11 (N-H ADD 40%)								
☐J61	1¢	Carmine Rose	39.00	26.00	1.60	1.00	.21	.16
☐J62	2¢	Carmine Rose	30.00	26.00	1.50	1.00	.21	.15
☐J63	3¢	Carmine Rose	96.00	72.00	7.50	5.00	.21	.15
☐J64	5¢	Carmine Rose	96.00	70.00	7.50	5.00	.21	.15
☐J65	10¢	Carmine Rose	110.00	95.00	11.00	6.50	.21	.15
☐J66	30¢	Carmine Rose	400.00	300.00	52.00	32.00	.60	.31
☐J67	50¢	Carmine Rose	600.00	480.00	63.00	40.00	.21	.15
☐J68	1/2¢	Dull Red	12.00	9.00	.60	.41	.21	.15
1930–1931. NEW DESIGN FLAT PRESS—PERF. 11 x 11 (N-H ADD 30%)								
☐J69	1/2¢	Carmine	30.00	25.00	2.40	1.80	.80	.50
☐J70	1¢	Carmine	28.00	20.00	2.00	1.65	.21	.16
☐J71	2¢	Carmine	35.00	30.00	3.10	2.50	.21	.16
☐J72	3¢	Carmine	200.00	185.00	21.00	15.00	1.10	.75
☐J73	5¢	Carmine	210.00	190.00	18.00	12.00	1.65	1.10
☐J74	10¢	Carmine	385.00	320.00	36.00	25.00	.75	.40
☐J75	30¢	Carmine	1200.00	900.00	90.00	72.00	1.10	.80
☐J76	50¢	Carmine	1300.00	100.00	110.00	80.00	.41	.26
☐J77	$1	Carmine	250.00	200.00	21.00	18.00	.21	.16
☐J78	$5	Carmine	350.00	275.00	30.00	21.00	.21	.16

Scott No.			Fine Unused Plate Blk	Ave. Unused Plate Blk	Fine Unused Each	Ave. Unused Each	Fine Used Each	Ave. Used Each
1931–1956. SAME DESIGN—ROTARY PRESS—PERF. 10 x 10¹/₂ (N-H ADD 20%)								
☐J79	¹/₂¢	Carmine	19.00	13.00	1.10	.60	.18	.13
☐J80	1¢	Carmine	2.00	1.50	.22	.16	.18	.13
☐J81	2¢	Carmine	2.00	1.50	.22	.16	.18	.13
☐J82	3¢	Carmine	2.80	1.60	.26	.22	.18	.13
☐J83	5¢	Carmine	4.00	2.10	.36	.26	.18	.13
☐J84	10¢	Carmine	8.00	5.0	1.25	.72	.18	.13
☐J85	30¢	Carmine	42.00	25.00	9.00	5.00	.18	.13
☐J86	50¢	Carmine	50.00	32.00	9.00	5.00	.18	.13
☐J87	$1	Red (10¹/₂ x 11)	210.00	200.00	40.00	28.00	.19	.14

Scott No.			Mint Sheet	Plate Block	Fine Unused Each	Fine Used Each
1959. NEW SERIES—NEW DESIGN—ROTARY PRESS—PERF. 11 x 10¹/₂ (N-H ADD 20%)						
☐J88	¹/₂¢	Red & Black	400.00	170.00	1.60	1.50
☐J89	1¢	Red & Black	3.00	.40	.18	.14
☐J90	2¢	Red & Black	4.00	.42	.18	.14
☐J91	3¢	Red & Black	6.00	.46	.18	.14
☐J92	4¢	Red & Black	7.50	.80	.18	.14
☐J93	5¢	Red & Black	9.00	.75	.18	.14
☐J94	6¢	Red & Black	11.00	1.10	.19	.14
☐J95	7¢	Red & Black	13.00	1.25	.18	.14
☐J96	8¢	Red & Black	15.00	1.50	.18	.14
☐J97	10¢	Red & Black	18.00	1.65	.18	.14
☐J98	30¢	Red & Black	52.00	4.50	.60	.14
☐J99	50¢	Red & Black	85.00	5.00	.95	.20
☐J100	$1	Red & Black	180.00	9.50	2.00	.20
☐J101	$5	Red & Black	810.00	42.00	10.00	.21
1978. SAME DESIGN, NEW VALUES						
☐J102	11¢	Red & Black	21.00	4.00	.31	.21
☐J103	13¢	Red & Black	24.00	3.00	.36	.26
1985. SAME DESIGN, NEW VALUES						
☐J104	17¢	Red & Black	65.00	30.00	.42	.36

Scott No.		Fine
U.S. UNUSED ZIP CODE BLOCKS OF FOUR		
☐1181	5¢ Battle-Wilderness	.90
☐1182	5¢ Appomattox	1.80
☐1242	5¢ Sam Houston	.70
☐1243	5¢ Chas. M. Russell	.70
☐1244	5¢ N.Y. World's Fair	.70
☐1247	5¢ N.J. Tercentenary	.70
☐1248	5¢ Nevada Statehood	.70
☐1249	5¢ Register & Vote	.70
☐1250	5¢ Wm. Shakespeare	.70
☐1251	5¢ Mayo Brothers	.70
☐1252	5¢ American Music	.70
☐1253	5¢ Homemakers	.70
☐1254–57	5¢ Christmas, 1964	1.35
☐1258	5¢ Verr.-Narr. Bridge	.70
☐1259	5¢ Modern Art	.70
☐1260	5¢ Radio Amateurs	.70
☐1261	5¢ Battle—N. Orleans	.70
☐1262	5¢ Physical Fitness	.70
☐1263	5¢ Cancer Crusade	.70
☐1264	5¢ Churchill Mem'l	.70
☐1265	5¢ Magna Carta	.70
☐1266	5¢ Intl. Co-op Year	.70
☐1267	5¢ Salvation Army	.70
☐1268	5¢ Dante Alighieri	.70
☐1269	5¢ Herbert Hoover	.70
☐1270	5¢ Robert Fulton	.70
☐1272	5¢ Traffic Safety	.70
☐1273	5¢ John S. Copley	.70
☐1274	11¢ Intl. Telecom. Un.	8.00
☐1276	5¢ Christmas, 1965	.70
☐1278	1¢ Thomas Jefferson	.70
☐1280	2¢ F. Lloyd Wright	.65
☐1281	3¢ Francis Parkman	.70
☐1284	6¢ F.D. Roosevelt	.80
☐1285	8¢ Albert Einstein	1.10
☐1286	10¢ Andrew Jackson	1.20
☐1286A	12¢ Henry Ford	1.50
☐1288	15¢ O.W. Holmes	2.10
☐1289	20¢ Geo. C. Marshall	2.50
☐1290	25¢ F. Douglass	2.50
☐1291	30¢ John Dewey	3.50
☐1292	40¢ Thomas Paine	4.50
☐1293	50¢ Lucy Stone	5.00
☐1294	$1 Eugene O'Neill	10.00
☐1306	5¢ Migr. Bird Treaty	.70
☐1307	5¢ Humane to Animals	.70

Scott No.		Fine
☐1308	5¢ Indiana Statehood	.70
☐1309	5¢ American Circus	.70
☐1310	5¢ 6th Intl. Phil. Exh.	.70
☐1312	5¢ Bill of Rights	.85
☐1313	5¢ Polish Millennium	.70
☐1314	5¢ Natl. Park Service	.70
☐1315	5¢ Marine Reserves	.70
☐1316	5¢ Women's Clubs	.70
☐1317	5¢ Johnny Appleseed	.70
☐1318	5¢ Beautify America	.70
☐1319	5¢ Great River Road	.70
☐1320	5¢ Servicemen-Bonds	.70
☐1321	5¢ Christmas, 1966	.70
☐1322	5¢ Mary Cassatt	.90
☐1323	5¢ National Grange	1.00
☐1324	5¢ Canada Centennial	.70
☐1325	5¢ Erie Canal	.70
☐1326	5¢ Search for Peace	.70
☐1327	5¢ Henry D. Thoreau	.70
☐1328	5¢ Nebraska Statehood	.70
☐1329	5¢ Voice of America	.70
☐1330	5¢ Davy Crockett	.70
☐1331–32	5¢ Twin Space	5.00
☐1333	5¢ Urban Planning	.70
☐1334	5¢ Finnish Independ.	.70
☐1336	5¢ Christmas, 1967	.70
☐1337	5¢ Miss. Statehood	.70
☐1338	6¢ American Flag	.70
☐1339	6¢ Illinois Statehood	.70
☐1341	$1 Airlift	12.00
☐1342	6¢ Support Our Youth	.70
☐1343	6¢ Law & Order	.70
☐1344	6¢ Register & Vote	.70
☐1353–54	6¢ Historic Flags	2.00
☐1355	6¢ Walt Disney	2.40
☐1356	6¢ Fr. Marquette	1.00
☐1357	6¢ Daniel Boone	.70
☐1358	6¢ Arkansas River	.70
☐1359	6¢ Leif Erikson	.70
☐1360	6¢ Cherokee Strip	.70
☐1361	6¢ Trumbull Painting	.70
☐1362	6¢ Wildlife Conserv.	1.15
☐1364	6¢ American Indian	1.15
☐1365–68	6¢ Beautify America	4.00
☐1369	6¢ American Legion	.70
☐1370	6¢ Grandma Moses	.70
☐1371	6¢ Apollo 8	1.15
☐1372	6¢ W.C. Handy	1.00
☐1373	6¢ California	.70

Scott No.		Fine
☐1374	6¢ J.W. Powell	.70
☐1375	6¢ Alabama	.70
☐1376–79	6¢ Botanical	6.00
☐1380	6¢ Dartmouth Case	.80
☐1381	6¢ Baseball	4.50
☐1382	6¢ Football	1.50
☐1383	6¢ Eisenhower	.80
☐1385	6¢ Rehabilitation	.80
☐1386	6¢ Wm. M. Harnett	.80
☐1387–90	6¢ Natural History	1.10
☐1391	6¢ Maine Statehood	.70
☐1392	6¢ Buffalo	.70
☐1393	6¢ Eisenhower-Reg.	.70
☐1393D	7¢ Franklin	1.10
☐1394	8¢ Eisenhower	1.00
☐1396	8¢ Postal Service	4.00
☐1397	14¢ F. LaGuardia	1.50
☐1398	16¢ Ernie Pyle	1.80
☐1399	18¢ Dr. E. Blackwell	2.10
☐1400	21¢ A.P. Giannini	2.15
☐1405	6¢ E.L. Masters	.70
☐1406	6¢ Women's Suffrage	.70
☐1407	6¢ So. Carolina	.70
☐1408	6¢ Stone Mountain	.70
☐1409	6¢ Fort Snelling	.70
☐1410–13	6¢ Anti-Pollution	1.90
☐1414	6¢ Nativity	1.60
☐1414a	6¢ Precancelled	1.60
☐1415–18	6¢ Christmas Toys	3.00
☐1415–18a	6¢ Precancelled	10.00
☐1419	6¢ United Nations	.70
☐1420	6¢ Pilgrim Landing	.70
☐1421–22	6¢ D.A.V & P.O.W.	1.60
☐1423	6¢ Sheep	.70
☐1424	6¢ D. MacArthur	.70
☐1425	6¢ Blood Donors	.70
☐1426	8¢ Mo. Statehood	2.80
☐1427–30	8¢ Wildlife Cons.	1.15
☐1431	8¢ Antarctic Treaty	1.10
☐1432	8¢ Amer. Revolution	1.25
☐1433	8¢ John Sloan	1.10
☐1434–35	8¢ Space Achievement	1.25
☐1436	8¢ Emily Dickinson	1.00
☐1437	8¢ San Juan	1.00
☐1438	8¢ Drug Addiction	1.50
☐1439	8¢ CARE	2.00
☐1440–43	8¢ Historic Pres.	2.00
☐1444	8¢ Nativity	2.75
☐1445	8¢ Partridge	2.75

Scott No.		Fine
☐1446	8¢ Sidney Lanier	1.15
☐1447	8¢ Peace Corps	1.50
☐1448–51	2¢ Cape Hatteras	.75
☐1452	6¢ Wolf Trap Farm	.80
☐1453	8¢ Yellowstone	1.00
☐1454	15¢ Mt. McKinley	1.75
☐1455	8¢ Family Planning	1.10
☐1456–59	8¢ Colonial Crafts	1.10
☐1460	6¢ Olympic Games	1.90
☐1461	8¢ Olympic Games	2.60
☐1462	15¢ Olympic Games	4.50
☐1463	8¢ P.T.A.	1.00
☐1464	8¢ Wildlife	1.10
☐1468	8¢ Mail Order	3.00
☐1469	8¢ Osteopathic	1.50
☐1470	8¢ Tom Sawyer	1.10
☐1471	8¢ Xmas-Religious	2.75
☐1472	8¢ Xmas-Santa Claus	2.75
☐1473	8¢ Pharmacy	1.20
☐1474	8¢ Stamp Collectors	1.10
☐1475	8¢ Love	1.40
☐1476	8¢ Pamphlet Printing	1.10
☐1477	8¢ Posting Broadside	1.10
☐1478	8¢ Post Rider	1.10
☐1479	8¢ Drummer	1.10
☐1480–83	8¢ Bost. Tea Party	1.20
☐1484	8¢ George Gershwin	3.50
☐1485	8¢ Robinson Jeffers	3.00
☐1486	8¢ Tanner	3.00
☐1487	8¢ Willa Cather	3.00
☐1488	8¢ N. Copernicus	3.00
☐1500	6¢ Electronics	.72
☐1501	8¢ Electronics	1.00
☐1502	15¢ Electronics	1.65
☐1504	8¢ Angus Cattle	1.00
☐1505	10¢ Chautauqua	1.15
☐1506	10¢ Winter Wheat	1.20
☐1507	8¢ Xmas-Religious	3.00
☐1508	8¢ Xmas-Tree	3.00
☐1510	10¢ Jefferson Mem'l	1.25
☐1511	10¢ Zip Code	2.10
☐1525	10¢ V.F.W.	1.25
☐1526	10¢ Robert Frost	1.25
☐1527	10¢ EXPO''74—Envir.	3.50
☐1528	10¢ Horse Racing	3.40
☐1529	10¢ Skylab Project	1.25
☐1538–41	10¢ Minerals	1.20
☐1542	10¢ Fort Harrod	1.25
☐1543–46	10¢ Cont. Congress	1.25

Scott No.			**Fine**
☐1547	10¢	Energy Conserv.	1.10
☐1548	10¢	Sleepy Hollow	1.10
☐1549	10¢	Retarded Children	1.10
☐1550	10¢	Xmas-Religious	3.10
☐1551	10¢	Xmas-Sleigh	3.20
☐1553	10¢	B. West	3.10
☐1554	10¢	P. Dunbar	3.10
☐1555	10¢	D.W. Griffith	1.30
☐1556	10¢	Pioneer-Jupiter	1.35
☐1557	10¢	Mariner 10	1.35
☐1558	10¢	Collective Barg	2.00
☐1559	8¢	Sybil Ludington	2.25
☐1560	10¢	Salem Poor	2.40
☐1561	10¢	Haym Solomon	2.40
☐1562	18¢	Peter Francisco	6.00
☐1563	10¢	Lex.-Concord	3.25
☐1564	10¢	Bunker Hill	3.25
☐1565–68	10¢	Uniforms	1.35
☐1569–70	10¢	Apollo-Soyuz	1.15
☐1571	10¢	Women's Year	1.75
☐1572–75	10¢	Postal Service	1.20
☐1576	10¢	World Peace	1.50
☐1577–78	10¢	Banking & Com.	1.15
☐1579	10¢	Xmas-Religious	3.25
☐1580	10¢	Xmas-Post Card	3.25
☐1581	1¢	Ability to Write	.70
☐1582	2¢	Freedom to Speak	.70
☐1585	4¢	Public that Reads	.65
☐1591	9¢	Freedom to Assemble	1.00
☐1592	10¢	Justice	1.15
☐1593	11¢	Freedom of Press	1.20
☐1596	13¢	Eagle & Shield	4.35
☐1603	24¢	Old North Church	2.60
☐1629–31	13¢	Spirit of '76	3.00
☐1632	13¢	Interphil '76	1.60
☐1633–82	13¢	State Flags	1.50
☐1683	13¢	Telephone	1.50
☐1684	13¢	Aviation	3.80
☐1685	13¢	Chemistry	4.40
☐1690	13¢	Ben Franklin	1.70
☐1691–94	13¢	Dec. of Indep.	2.00
☐1695–98	13¢	Olympic Games	1.75
☐1699	13¢	Clara Maass	4.75
☐1700	13¢	Adolph Ochs	1.50
☐1701	13¢	Nativity	5.00
☐1702	13¢	Winter Pastime	4.00
☐1704	13¢	Wash. at Princeton	3.90
☐1705	13¢	Sound Recording	1.50
☐1706–09	13¢	Pueblo Art (6)	2.00

Scott No.			**Fine**
☐1710	13¢	Transatlantic Flight	4.60
☐1711	13¢	Colorado	4.60
☐1712	13¢	Butterflies	1.50
☐1716	13¢	Lafayette	1.60
☐1717–20	20¢	,13¢ Skilled Hands	1.85
☐1721	13¢	Peace Bridge	1.60
☐1722	13¢	Herkimer	3.75
☐1723–24	24¢	,13¢ Energy	1.60
☐1725	13¢	Alta	1.50
☐1726	13¢	Confederation	1.60
☐1727	13¢	Pictures	1.60
☐1728	13¢	Saratoga	4.15
☐1730	13¢	Mailbox	4.00
☐1731	13¢	Sandburg	1.50
☐1732	13¢	Capt. Cook	1.55
☐1733	13¢	Capt. Cook R&S	1.50
☐1734	13¢	Indian Cent	1.80
☐1735	15¢	No Value "A" Eagle	7.00
☐1744	13¢	Harriet Tubman	1.90
☐1745–48	13¢	Quilts	1.90
☐1749–52	13¢	Dance	2.00
☐1753	13¢	French Alliance	1.50
☐1754	13¢	Papanicolau	1.60
☐1755	13¢	Jimmie Rodgers	5.00
☐1756	15¢	George M. Cohan	5.50
☐1757	13¢	Capex SS	2.90
☐1758	15¢	Photography	5.00
☐1759	15¢	Viking	1.85
☐1760–63	15¢	Owls	1.80
☐1764–67	15¢	Trees	1.90
☐1768	15¢	Madonna	5.00
☐1769	15¢	Xmas Hobby Horse	5.00
☐1770	15¢	R.F. Kennedy	1.75
☐1771	15¢	M.L. King	5.00
☐1772	15¢	Intl. Year of Child	1.80
☐1773	15¢	Steinbeck	1.80
☐1774	15¢	Einstein	1.80
☐1775–78	15¢	Toleware	2.75
☐1779–82	15¢	Architecture	2.00
☐1783–86	15¢	Endangered Flora	2.00
☐1788	15¢	Special Olympics	4.50
☐1789	15¢	John Paul Jones	4.50
☐1790	15¢	Olympics	5.00
☐1791–94	15¢	Summer Olympics	1.80
☐1795–98	15¢	Winter Olympics	2.25
☐1799	15¢	Madonna	5.50
☐1800	15¢	Xmas Santa	5.50
☐1801	15¢	Will Rogers	5.50
☐1802	15¢	Vietnam Veterans	5.50

Scott No.		Fine
☐1803	15¢ Fields	5.50
☐1804	15¢ Banneker	5.50
☐1805–10	15¢ Letter Writing	6.00
☐1811	15¢ Perkins	.65
☐1822	15¢ Madison	1.80
☐1823	15¢ Bissell	1.80
☐1824	15¢ Keller/Sullivan	1.80
☐1825	15¢ Vets. Admin.	1.65
☐1826	15¢ De Galvez	1.65
☐1827–30	15¢ Coral Reefs	2.25
☐1831	15¢ Org. Labor	5.00
☐1832	15¢ Wharton	3.00
☐1833	15¢ Education	3.00
☐1834–37	15¢ Indian Masks	2.40
☐1838–41	15¢ Architecture	2.10
☐1842	15¢ Christmas Madonna	5.50
☐1849	17¢ Rachel Carson	4.00
☐1850	18¢ Geo. Mason	4.00
☐1851	19¢ Sequoyah	1.10
☐1859	35¢ Dr. Charles Drew	3.00
☐1874	15¢ Everett Dirksen	1.80
☐1875	15¢ Whitney Young	1.80
☐1876–79	18¢ Flowers	2.30
☐1910	18¢ Red Cross	2.10
☐1911	18¢ Savings & Loan	2.10
☐1912–19	18¢ Space Achievement	6.00
☐1920	18¢ Management	2.50
☐1921–24	18¢ Habitats	2.15
☐1925	18¢ Disabled	2.10
☐1926	18¢ Edna St. Vincent Millay	2.15
☐1928–31	18¢ Architecture	2.50
☐1932	18¢ Babe Zaharias	2.30
☐1933	18¢ Bobby Jones	2.30
☐1934	18¢ Remington	2.30
☐1935	18¢ James Hoban	2.30
☐1936	20¢ James Hoban	2.60
☐1937–38	18¢ Yorktown, Virginia	2.40
☐1939	20¢ Christmas Madonna	2.40
☐1940	20¢ Christmas Child Art	2.40
☐1941	20¢ John Hanson	2.60
☐1942–45	20¢ Desert Plants	2.60
☐C69	8¢ Robert H. Goddard	2.10
☐C70	8¢ Alaska Purchase	1.90
☐C71	20¢ Columbia Jays	4.25
☐C72	10¢ Stars	1.10
☐C74	10¢ 50 Years Airmail	3.00
☐C75	20¢ U.S.A. & Jet	2.10
☐C76	10¢ Moon Landing	1.70
☐C77	9¢ Delta Plane	1.10

Scott No.		Fine
☐C78	11¢ Plane Silhouette	1.00
☐C79	13¢ Letter	1.60
☐C80	17¢ Liberty Head	2.10
☐C81	21¢ "USA"	2.00
☐C84	11¢ City of Refuge	1.10
☐C85	11¢ Olympic Games	3.00
☐C86	11¢ Electronics	1.10
☐C87	18¢ Statue of Liberty	2.20
☐C88	26¢ Mount Rushmore	2.50
☐C89	5¢ Plane & Globes	2.75
☐C90	31¢ Plane, Flag & Globes	3.00
☐C91–92	31¢ Wright Bros.	4.00
☐C93–94	21¢ Chanute	5.00
☐C95–96	25¢ Wiley Post	11.00
☐C97	31¢ Olympics	12.00
☐C98	40¢ Mazzel	10.00
☐C99	28¢ Scott	8.50
☐C100	35¢ Curtiss	10.00
☐E22	45¢ Special Delivery	9.00
☐E23	60¢ Special Delivery	6.00

U.S. UNUSED MAIL EARLY INSCRIPTION BLOCKS

Scott No.		Fine
☐1278	1¢ T. Jefferson	.70
☐1280	2¢ F.L. Wright	.65
☐1281	3¢ Parkman	.70
☐1284	6¢ F.D. Roosevelt	.80
☐1285	8¢ A. Einstein	1.10
☐1286	10¢ A. Jackson	1.20
☐1286A	12¢ Henry Ford	1.50
☐1288	15¢ O.W. Holmes	2.10
☐1289	20¢ G.C. Marshall	2.50
☐1290	25¢ F. Douglass	2.50
☐1291	30¢ John Dewey	3.50
☐1292	40¢ T. Paine	4.50
☐1293	50¢ Lucy Stone	5.00
☐1294	$1 E. O'Neill	10.00
☐1338	6¢ American Flag	.70
☐1340	6¢ Hemis Fair '68	.70
☐1341	$1 Airlift	12.00
☐1342	6¢ Support Our Youth	.70
☐1343	6¢ Law & Order	.70
☐1344	6¢ Register & Vote	.70
☐1347–49	6¢ Historic Flags	.70
☐1355	6¢ Walt Disney	2.40
☐1356	6¢ Fr. Marquette	1.00
☐1357	6¢ Daniel Boone	.70
☐1358	6¢ Arkansas River	.70
☐1359	6¢ Leif Erikson	.70

Scott No.			Fine
☐1360	6¢	Cherokee Strip	.70
☐1361	6¢	Trumbull Painting	.70
☐1362	6¢	Wildlife Conserv.	1.15
☐1364	6¢	American Indian	1.15
☐1365–68	6¢	Beautify America	5.00
☐1369	6¢	American Legion	.70
☐1370	6¢	Grandma Moses	.70
☐1371	6¢	Apollo 8	1.15
☐1372	6¢	W.C. Handy	1.00
☐1373	6¢	California	.70
☐1374	6¢	J.W. Powell	.70
☐1375	6¢	Alabama	.70
☐1376–79	6¢	Botanical	7.00
☐1380	6¢	Dartmouth Case	.80
☐1381	6¢	Baseball	4.50
☐1382	6¢	Football	1.50
☐1383	6¢	Eisenhower	.80
☐1385	6¢	Rehabilitation	.80
☐1386	6¢	W.M. Harnett	.80
☐1387–90	6¢	Nat. History	1.25
☐1391	6¢	Maine	.70
☐1392	6¢	Buffalo	.70
☐1393	6¢	Eisenhower	.70
☐1393D	7¢	B. Franklin	1.10
☐1394	8¢	Eisenhower	1.00
☐1396	8¢	Postal Service (4)	4.00
☐1397	14¢	F. LaGuardia	1.50
☐1398	16¢	Ernie Pyle	1.80
☐1399	18¢	Dr. E. Blackwell	2.10
☐1400	21¢	A.P. Giannini	2.15
☐1405	6¢	E.L. Masters	.70
☐1406	6¢	Women's Suffrage	.70
☐1407	6¢	South Carolina	.70
☐1408	6¢	Stone Mountain	.70
☐1409	6¢	Fort Snelling	.70
☐1410–13	6¢	Anti-Pollution	2.60
☐1414	6¢	Nativity	1.60
☐1414a	6¢	Precancelled	1.50
☐1415–18	6¢	Christmas Toys	5.00
☐1415a–18a	6¢	Precancelled	16.00
☐1419	6¢	United Nations	.70
☐1420	6¢	Pilgrim Landing	.70
☐1421–22	6¢	D.A. & P.O.W.	1.80
☐1423	6¢	Sheep	.70
☐1424	6¢	Gen. MacArthur	.70
☐1425	6¢	Blood Donors	.70
☐1426	6¢	Missouri (4)	2.80
☐1427–30	8¢	Wildlife	1.75
☐1431	8¢	Antarctic	1.10

Scott No.			Fine
☐1432	8¢	Bicentennial	1.25
☐1433	8¢	J. Sloan Painting	1.10
☐1434–35	8¢	Space Accomp.	1.60
☐1436	8¢	Emily Dickinson	1.00
☐1437	8¢	San Juan	1.00
☐1438	8¢	Drug Addiction	1.50
☐1439	8¢	CARE	2.00
☐1440–43	8¢	Historic Press	1.25
☐1444	8¢	Nativity (4)	2.75
☐1445	8¢	Partridge (4)	2.75
☐1446	8¢	Sidney Lanier	1.15
☐1447	8¢	Peace Corps	1.50
☐1448–51	2¢	Hatteras (8)	1.50
☐1452	8¢	Wolf Trap Farm	.80
☐1453	8¢	Yellowstone	1.00
☐1454	15¢	Mt. McKinley	1.75
☐1455	8¢	Family Planning	1.10
☐1456–59	8¢	Craftman	1.35
☐1460	6¢	Olympic Games	1.90
☐1461	8¢	Olympic Games	2.60
☐1462	15¢	Olympic Games	2.75
☐1463	8¢	P.T.A.	4.50
☐1464–67	8¢	Wildlife	1.50
☐1468	8¢	Mail Order (4)	3.00
☐1469	8¢	Osteopathic	1.50
☐1470	8¢	Tom Sawyer	1.10
☐1471	8¢	Religious	2.75
☐1472	8¢	Santa Claus	2.75
☐1473	8¢	Pharmacy	1.20
☐1474	8¢	Stamp Collector	1.10
☐1475	8¢	Love	1.40
☐1476	8¢	Pamphlet Printing	1.10
☐1477	8¢	Posting Broadside	1.10
☐1478	8¢	Post Rider	1.10
☐1479	8¢	Drummer	1.10
☐1480–83	8¢	Bost. Tea Party	1.70
☐1488	8¢	Copernicus	1.00
☐1500	6¢	Electronics	.72
☐1501	8¢	Electronics	1.00
☐1502	15¢	Electronics	1.65
☐1504	8¢	Angus Cattle	1.00
☐1505	10¢	Chautauqua	1.20
☐1506	10¢	Winter Wheat	1.20
☐1507	8¢	Religious (4)	3.00
☐1508	8¢	Xmas Tree (4)	3.00
☐1510	10¢	Jefferson Mem'l	1.25
☐1511	10¢	Zip Code	2.10
☐1525	10¢	V.F.W.	1.25
☐1526	10¢	Robert Frost	1.25

Scott No.			Fine
☐1528	10¢	Horse Racing (4)	3.40
☐1529	10¢	Skylab Project	1.25
☐1538–41	10¢	Minerals	1.65
☐1542	10¢	Fort Harrod	1.25
☐1543–46	10¢	Cont. Cong.	1.65
☐1547	10¢	Energy Cons.	1.10
☐1548	10¢	Sleepy Hollow	1.10
☐1549	10¢	Retarded Children	1.10
☐1550	10¢	Xmas-Religious	3.10
☐1551	10¢	Xmas-Sleigh (4)	3.20
☐1553	10¢	Benjamin West	3.10
☐1554	10¢	Paul Dunbar	3.10
☐1555	10¢	D.W. Griffith	1.30
☐1556	10¢	Pioneer-Jupiter	1.35
☐1557	10¢	Mariner 10	1.35
☐1558	10¢	Coll. Bargaining	2.00
☐1559	8¢	Sybil Ludington	2.25
☐1560	10¢	Salem Poor	2.40
☐1561	10¢	Haym Salomon	2.40
☐1562	10¢	Peter Francisco	6.00
☐1565–68	10¢	Uniforms (4)	1.50
☐1571	10¢	Women's Year	1.75
☐1572–75	10¢	Postal Service (4)	1.20
☐1576	10¢	World Peace	1.50
☐1577–78	10¢	Banking & Comm.	1.65
☐1579	10¢	Xmas-Religious	3.25
☐1580	10¢	Xmas Post Card (4)	3.25
☐1581	1¢	Ability Write	.70
☐1582	2¢	Freedom to Speak	.70
☐1584	3¢	Cast A Ballot	.70
☐1585	4¢	Public that Reads	.65
☐1591	9¢	Freedom to Assemble	1.00
☐1593	11¢	Freedom of Press	1.15
☐1596	13¢	Eagle & Shield	1.20
☐1603	24¢	Old North Church	2.60
☐1632	13¢	Interphil '76	1.60
☐1633–82	13¢	State Flags	6.00
☐1683	13¢	Telephone	1.50
☐1684	13¢	Aviation	3.80
☐1685	13¢	Chemistry	4.40
☐1690	13¢	Ben. Franklin	1.70
☐1691–94	13¢	Independence	3.50
☐1695–98	13¢	Olympic Games	1.80
☐1700	13¢	Adolph Ochs	1.50
☐1701	13¢	"Nativity" (4)	5.00
☐1702	13¢	"Winter Pastime"	4.00
☐1705	13¢	Sound Recording	7.00
☐1710	13¢	Transatlantic	4.60
☐1711	13¢	Colorado	4.60

Scott No.			Fine
☐1712–15	13¢	Butterflies	1.65
☐1716	13¢	Lafayette	1.60
☐1717–20	13¢	Skilled Hands (4)	1.80
☐1721	13¢	Peace Bridge	1.60
☐1725	13¢	California	1.50
☐1726	13¢	Articles of Conf.	1.60
☐1727	13¢	Talking Pictures	1.60
☐1730	13¢	Mailbox	4.00
☐1735	15¢	Eagle Issue "A"	1.80
☐1818	18¢	Eagle Issue "B"	2.30
☐C72	10¢	Stars	1.10
☐C74	10¢	Airmail 50th Ann.	3.00
☐C75	20¢	U.S.A. Airmail	2.10
☐C76	10¢	Moon Landing	1.70
☐C77	9¢	Delta Wing	1.10
☐C78	1¢	Silhouette	1.00
☐C79	13¢	Letter	1.00
☐C80	17¢	Liberty Head	2.10
☐C81	21¢	U.S.A. Airmail	2.00
☐C84	11¢	City of Refuge	1.10
☐C85	11¢	Olympic Games	3.00
☐C86	11¢	Electronics	1.10
☐C87	18¢	Liberty	2.20
☐C88	26¢	Mt. Rushmore	2.50
☐C89	25¢	Plane & Globes	2.75
☐C90	31¢	Plane/Flag/Globes	3.00
☐E22	45¢	Arrows	7.50
☐E23	60¢	Arrows	5.00

Scott No.			Fine Ctr Line Blk of 4	Fine Arrow Blk of 4

U.S. UNUSED CENTER LINE AND ARROW BLOCKS

Scott No.			Fine Ctr Line Blk of 4	Fine Arrow Blk of 4
☐314	1¢	Imperforate	190.00	110.00
☐320	2¢	Imperforate	190.00	115.00
☐343	1¢	Imperforate	60.00	35.00
☐344	2¢	Imperforate	70.00	45.00
☐345	3¢	Imperforate	125.00	85.00
☐346	4¢	Imperforate	250.00	185.00
☐347	5¢	Imperforate	310.00	210.00
☐368	2¢	Lincoln, Imp.	175.00	115.00
☐371	2¢	Alaska-Yukon, Imperf.	240.00	160.00
☐373	2¢	Hudson-Fulton, Imperf.	250.00	165.00
☐383	1¢	Imperforate	35.00	16.00
☐384	2¢	Imperforate	45.00	22.00
☐408	1¢	Imperforate	12.00	7.00

Scott No.		Fine Ctr Line Blk of 4	Fine Arrow Blk of 4
□409	2¢ Imperforate	16.00	8.50
□481	1¢ Imperforate	10.00	4.00
□482	2¢ Imperforate	12.00	9.00
□484	3¢ Imperforate Type II	210.00	60.00
□524	5¢ Green & Blk	900.00	700.00
□531	1¢ Offset, Imperf.	60.00	40.00
□532	2¢ Offset, Imperf. Type IV	210.00	160.00
□534	2¢ Offset, Imperf. Type Va	70.00	50.00
□534A	2¢ Offset, Imp. Type VI	180.00	150.00
□535	3¢ Offset, Imperf.	42.00	40.00
□573	$5 Carm. & Blk	900.00	800.00
□575	1¢ Imperforate	60.00	45.00
□576	1½¢ Imperforate	19.00	9.00
□577	2¢ Imperforate	20.00	10.00
□611	2¢ Harding Imperf.	80.00	35.00
□620	2¢ Norse-Amer'n	38.00	28.00
□621	5¢ Norse-Amer'n	90.00	60.00
□631	1½¢ Harding, Rotary Imperf.	20.00	12.00
□703	2¢ Yorktown	3.50	2.60
□832	$1 Purple & Blk	45.00	38.00
□833	$2 Yel./Gm./Blk	120.00	100.00
□834	$5 Red & Blk	510.00	425.00
□C1	6¢ Airmail	350.00	280.00
□C2	16¢ Airmail	450.00	410.00
□C3	24¢ Airmail	500.00	410.00
□C23	36¢ Airmail	3.00	2.50
□CE2	16¢ Spec. Del. Airmail	3.00	2.50

Scott No.		Fine

1927–1940. MINT SHEETS

□643	2¢ Vermont	290.00
□644	2¢ Burgoyne	300.00
□645	2¢ Valley Forge	180.00
□646	2¢ Molly Pitcher	190.00
□647	2¢ Hawaii	650.00
□648	5¢ Hawaii	1800.00
□649	2¢ Aeronautics	90.00
□650	5¢ Aeronautics	415.00
□651	2¢ George R. Clark	44.00
□654	2¢ Edison-Flat	120.00

Scott No.		Fine
□655	2¢ Edison-Rotary	135.00
□657	2¢ Sullivan	140.00
□680	2¢ Fallen Timbers	150.00
□681	2¢ Ohio River Canal	125.00
□682	2¢ Mass. Bay	100.00
□683	2¢ Carolina-Charleston	190.00
□688	2¢ Braddock	145.00
□689	2¢ Von Steuben	80.00
□690	2¢ Pulaski	50.00
□702	2¢ Red Cross	21.00
□703	2¢ Yorktopwn	27.00
□704	½¢ Wash. Bicent'l	18.00
□705	1¢ Wash. Bicent'l	20.00
□706	1½¢ Wash. Bicent'l	70.00
□707	2¢ Wash. Bicent'l	13.00
□708	3¢ Wash. Bicent'l	91.00
□709	4¢ Wash. Bicent'l	42.00
□710	5¢ Wash. Bicent'l	215.00
□711	6¢ Wash. Bicent'l	500.00
□712	7¢ Wash. Bicent'l	42.00
□713	8¢ Wash. Bicent'l	550.00
□714	9¢ Wash. Bicent'l	415.00
□715	10¢ Wash. Bicent'l	1700.00
□716	2¢ Lake Placid	70.00
□717	2¢ Arbor Day	28.00
□718	2¢ Olympics	190.00
□719	5¢ Olympics	300.00
□724	3¢ Penn	52.00
□725	3¢ Webster	80.00
□726	3¢ Oglethorpe	52.00
□727	3¢ Newburgh	24.00
□728	1¢ Chicago	16.00
□729	3¢ Chicago	23.00
□732	3¢ N.R.A.	15.00
□733	3¢ Byrd	45.00
□734	5¢ Kosciuszko	100.00
□736	3¢ Maryland	32.00
□737	3¢ Mother's Day (R)	11.00
□738	3¢ Mother's Day (F)	14.00
□739	3¢ Wisconsin	15.00
□740	1¢ Natl. Parks	7.00
□741	2¢ Natl. Parks	10.00
□742	3¢ Natl. Parks	12.00
□743	4¢ Natl. Parks	30.00
□744	5¢ Natl. Parks	52.00
□745	6¢ Natl. Parks	80.00
□746	7¢ Natl. Parks	45.00

Scott No.		Fine
☐747	8¢ Natl. Parks	110.00
☐748	9¢ Natl. Parks	120.00
☐749	10¢ Natl. Parks	200.00
☐772	3¢ Connecticut	10.00
☐773	3¢ San Diego	7.00
☐774	3¢ Boulder Dam	8.00
☐775	3¢ Michigan	7.00
☐776	3¢ Texas	8.00
☐777	3¢ Rhode Island	10.00
☐782	3¢ Arkansas	8.00
☐783	3¢ Oregon	8.00
☐784	3¢ Susan B. Anthony	12.00
☐785	1¢ Army	6.00
☐786	2¢ Army	7.00
☐787	3¢ Army	12.00
☐788	4¢ Army	32.00
☐789	5¢ Army	47.00
☐790	1¢ Navy	5.00
☐791	2¢ Navy	7.00
☐792	3¢ Navy	9.00
☐793	4¢ Navy	32.00
☐794	5¢ Navy	47.00
☐795	3¢ N.W. Territory	7.50
☐796	5¢ Virginia Dare	15.00
☐798	3¢ Constitution	9.00
☐799	3¢ Hawaii	8.00
☐800	3¢ Alaska	8.00
☐801	3¢ Puerto Rico	8.00
☐802	3¢ Virgin Islands	8.00
☐835	3¢ Ratification	18.00
☐836	3¢ Swede-Finn	9.00
☐837	3¢ N.W. Territory	21.00
☐838	3¢ Iowa	15.00
☐852	3¢ Golden Gate	8.00
☐853	3¢ N.Y. Fair	9.00
☐854	3¢ Inauguration	26.00
☐855	3¢ Baseball	75.00
☐856	3¢ Canal Zone	12.00
☐857	3¢ Printing	7.00
☐858	3¢ Four States	7.00
☐859	1¢ Irving	6.00
☐860	2¢ Cooper	7.00

Scott No.		Fine
☐861	3¢ Emerson	7.00
☐862	5¢ Alcott	29.00
☐863	10¢ Clemens	135.00
☐864	1¢ Longfellow	7.50
☐865	2¢ Whittier	8.00
☐866	3¢ Lowell	10.00
☐867	5¢ Whitman	38.00
☐868	10¢ Riley	165.00
☐869	1¢ Mann	7.00
☐870	2¢ Hopkins	7.50
☐871	3¢ Elliot	15.00
☐872	5¢ Willard	42.00
☐873	10¢ B.T. Washington	170.00
☐874	1¢ Audubon	6.00
☐875	2¢ Long	7.00
☐876	3¢ Burbank	9.00
☐877	5¢ Reed	20.00
☐878	10¢ Addams	110.00
☐879	1¢ Fosters	5.00
☐880	2¢ Sousa	9.00
☐881	3¢ Herbert	9.00
☐882	5¢ MacDowell	36.00
☐883	10¢ Nevin	300.00
☐884	1¢ Sturat	4.50
☐885	2¢ Whistler	7.00
☐886	3¢ St. Gaudens	8.00
☐887	5¢ French	40.00
☐888	10¢ Remington	155.00
☐889	1¢ Whitney	8.00
☐890	2¢ Morse	8.00
☐891	3¢ McCormick	24.00
☐892	5¢ Howe	80.00
☐893	10¢ Bell	850.00
☐894	3¢ Pony Express	16.00
☐895	3¢ Pan American	16.00
☐896	3¢ Idaho	11.00
☐897	3¢ Wyoming	9.00
☐898	3¢ Coronado	10.00
☐899	1¢ Defense	7.00
☐900	2¢ Defense	8.00
☐901	3¢ Defense	10.00
☐902	3¢ Emancipation	14.00

Scott No.			Fine Unused Each	Ave. Unused Each	Fine Used Each	Ave. Used Each
OFFICIAL STAMPS						
1873. CONTINENTAL PRINTING (N-H ADD 70%)						
☐O1	1¢	Agricultural Department.........................	70.00	35.00	42.00	25.00
☐O2	2¢		50.00	28.00	18.00	12.00
☐O3	3¢		50.00	25.00	4.00	2.70
☐O4	4¢		58.00	29.00	14.00	8.00
☐O5	10¢		115.00	58.00	50.00	30.00
☐O6	12¢		170.00	80.00	70.00	42.00
☐O7	15¢		115.00	50.00	48.00	28.00
☐O8	24¢		135.00	70.00	60.00	35.00
☐O9	30¢		185.00	90.00	90.00	52.00
☐O10	1¢	Executive Department............................	280.00	150.00	90.00	51.00
☐O11	2¢		180.00	95.00	75.00	42.00
☐O12	3¢		220.00	120.00	65.00	40.00
☐O13	6¢		320.00	180.00	210.00	130.00
☐O14	10¢		300.00	160.00	200.00	110.00
☐O15	1¢	Interior Department	18.00	10.00	4.50	2.10
☐O16	2¢		18.00	10.00	2.40	1.25
☐O17	3¢		24.00	14.00	3.00	1.25
☐O18	6¢		18.00	10.00	3.00	1.25
☐O19	10¢		18.00	10.00	7.00	3.40
☐O20	12¢		30.00	17.00	4.50	2.50
☐O21	15¢		42.00	24.00	11.00	6.00
☐O22	24¢		34.00	19.00	8.00	4.00
☐O23	30¢		45.00	24.00	9.00	6.00
☐O24	90¢		80.00	50.00	17.00	10.00
☐O25	1¢	Justice Department................................	55.00	28.00	24.00	14.00
☐O26	2¢		80.00	45.00	25.00	15.00
☐O27	3¢		75.00	40.00	9.00	6.00
☐O28	6¢		75.00	40.00	13.00	7.00
☐O29	10¢		82.00	45.00	27.00	15.00
☐O30	12¢		60.00	35.00	16.00	9.00
☐O31	15¢		140.00	70.00	50.00	26.00
☐O32	24¢		325.00	200.00	130.00	72.00
☐O33	30¢		350.00	180.00	90.00	48.00
☐O34	90¢		450.00	250.00	180.00	105.00
☐O35	1¢	Navy Department..................................	36.00	20.00	11.00	7.00
☐O36	2¢		32.00	18.00	10.00	6.00
☐O37	3¢		32.00	17.00	4.50	2.50
☐O38	6¢		32.00	17.00	7.00	4.00
☐O39	7¢		180.00	100.00	70.00	40.00
☐O40	10¢		42.00	24.00	14.00	8.00
☐O41	12¢		52.00	30.00	11.00	7.00
☐O42	15¢		82.00	45.00	29.00	16.00
☐O43	24¢		82.00	45.00	34.00	20.00
☐O44	30¢		72.00	40.00	16.00	10.00
☐O45	90¢		310.00	170.00	90.00	55.00
☐O47	1¢	Post Office Department..........................	8.00	4.50	4.00	1.90

Scott No.			Fine Unused Each	Ave. Unused Each	Fine Used Each	Ave. Used Each
☐048	2¢		9.00	5.00	3.00	1.70
☐049	3¢		2.50	1.15	.95	.60
☐050	6¢		8.00	4.00	2.00	1.25
☐051	10¢		30.00	20.00	19.00	11.00
☐052	12¢		21.00	11.00	5.00	3.00
☐053	15¢		25.00	13.00	10.00	5.00
☐054	24¢		31.00	17.00	11.00	7.00
☐055	30¢		32.00	18.00	10.00	6.00
☐056	90¢		48.00	26.00	14.00	8.00
☐057	1¢	State Department	50.00	29.00	14.00	8.00
☐058	2¢		105.00	60.00	30.00	18.00
☐059	3¢		40.00	22.00	10.00	6.00
☐060	6¢		38.00	21.00	10.00	6.00
☐061	7¢		75.00	40.00	20.00	12.00
☐062	10¢		70.00	36.00	18.00	10.00
☐063	12¢		80.00	48.00	27.00	18.00
☐064	15¢		85.00	48.00	20.00	13.00
☐065	24¢		180.00	100.00	75.00	40.00
☐066	30¢		190.00	90.00	50.00	32.00
☐067	90¢		360.00	200.00	125.00	65.00
☐068	$2		500.00	290.00	300.00	150.00
☐072	1¢	Treasury Department	18.00	10.00	2.10	1.15
☐073	2¢		21.00	12.00	2.10	1.15
☐074	3¢		13.00	8.00	1.50	.72
☐075	6¢		19.00	11.00	1.50	.72
☐076	7¢		45.00	24.00	13.00	7.00
☐077	10¢		52.00	26.00	5.00	3.40
☐078	12¢		52.00	27.00	3.50	2.00
☐079	15¢		41.00	23.00	5.00	3.00
☐080	24¢		200.00	105.00	48.00	26.00
☐081	30¢		72.00	36.00	6.00	3.10
☐082	90¢		74.00	40.00	6.00	3.10
☐083	1¢	War Department	70.00	36.00	4.80	2.80
☐084	2¢		62.00	32.00	7.00	3.20
☐085	3¢		56.00	30.00	2.00	1.00
☐086	6¢		235.00	125.00	4.50	2.40
☐087	7¢		56.00	30.00	32.00	20.00
☐088	10¢		21.00	12.00	4.00	3.00
☐089	12¢		60.00	34.00	4.50	2.60
☐090	15¢		19.00	10.00	3.00	2.00
☐091	24¢		19.00	10.00	4.00	2.00
☐092	30¢		21.00	12.00	4.00	1.80
☐093	90¢		42.00	24.00	12.00	8.00

1879. AMERICAN PRINTING—SOFT POROUS PAPER (N-H ADD 80%)

☐094	1¢	Agricultural Department	1300.00	750.00	—	—
☐095	3¢		180.00	100.00	34.00	21.00

Scott No.			Fine Unused Each	Ave. Unused Each	Fine Used Each	Ave. Used Each
☐096	1¢	Interior Department	130.00	70.00	65.00	36.00
☐097	2¢		2.60	1.25	1.00	.52
☐098	3¢		2.00	1.00	.90	.45
☐099	6¢		3.00	1.40	1.15	.60
☐0100	10¢		32.00	18.00	20.00	13.00
☐0101	12¢		70.00	36.00	36.00	22.00
☐0102	15¢		150.00	90.00	70.00	41.00
☐0103	24¢		1200.00	700.00	—	—
☐0106	3¢	Justice Department	50.00	26.00	22.00	14.00
☐0107	6¢		100.00	60.00	70.00	40.00
☐0108	3¢	Post Office Department	9.00	5.00	1.50	1.00
☐0109	3¢	Treasury Department	26.00	14.00	4.10	2.10
☐0110	6¢		50.00	26.00	18.00	10.00
☐0111	10¢		65.00	34.00	15.00	9.00
☐0112	30¢		710.00	380.00	140.00	75.00
☐0113	90¢		715.00	400.00	140.00	75.00
☐0114	1¢	War Department	2.40	1.15	1.00	.62
☐0115	2¢		3.00	1.80	1.15	.50
☐0116	3¢		3.00	1.50	.80	.50
☐0117	6¢		3.10	1.70	.85	.50
☐0118	10¢		21.00	11.00	10.00	7.00
☐0119	12¢		17.00	9.00	3.10	1.80
☐0120	30¢		48.00	24.00	26.00	14.00

1910–1911. POSTAL SAVINGS STAMPS (N-H ADD 70%)

Scott No.			Fine Unused Each	Ave. Unused Each	Fine Used Each	Ave. Used Each
☐0121	2¢	Black, D.L. Wmk	10.00	5.00	1.30	.86
☐0122	50¢	Dark Green, D.L. Wmk	105.00	60.00	32.00	18.00
☐0123	$1	Ultramarine, D.L. Wmk	100.00	55.00	10.00	6.00
☐0124	1¢	Dark Violet, S.L. Wmk	4.00	3.00	1.40	.80
☐0125	2¢	Black, S.L. Wmk	30.00	16.00	4.00	2.60
☐0126	10¢	Carmine, S.L. Wmk	8.00	5.00	1.25	.75

Scott No.			Fine Unused Block	Ave. Unused Block	Fine Unused Each	Ave. Unused Each	Fine Used Each	Ave. Used Each
1912. PARCEL POST DUE STAMPS (N-H ADD 45%)								
☐JQ1	1¢	Dark Green	275.00	210.00	7.50	6.00	4.00	2.50
☐JQ2	2¢	Dark Green	410.00	300.00	60.00	45.00	14.00	9.00
☐JQ3	5¢	Dark Green	100.00	60.00	9.00	7.00	4.00	3.00
☐JQ4	10¢	Dark Green	1100.00	900.00	140.00	100.00	38.00	24.00
☐JQ5	25¢	Dark Green	550.00	400.00	80.00	41.00	4.50	2.50
1912–1913. PARCEL POST STAMPS (N-H ADD 45%)								
☐Q1	1¢	P.O. Clerk	65.00	40.00	3.50	2.40	1.30	.80
☐Q2	2¢	City Carrier	75.00	45.00	4.00	2.60	1.00	.70
☐Q3	3¢	Railway Clerk	130.00	95.00	7.00	6.00	4.50	3.40
☐Q4	4¢	Rural Carrier	500.00	400.00	20.00	16.00	2.60	1.80
☐Q5	5¢	Mail Train	500.00	390.00	20.00	15.00	1.90	1.25
☐Q6	10¢	Steamship	300.00	170.00	32.00	21.00	2.00	1.60

Scott No.			Fine Unused Block	Ave. Unused Block	Fine Unused Each	Ave. Unused Each	Fine Used Each	Ave. Used Each
□Q7	15¢	Mail Truck	375.00	250.00	40.00	28.00	9.00	6.00
□Q8	20¢	Airplane	500.00	375.00	90.00	60.00	18.00	12.00
□Q9	25¢	Manufacturing	400.00	300.00	45.00	30.00	6.00	4.50
□Q10	50¢	Dairying	1400.00	1100.00	180.00	140.00	30.00	26.00
□Q11	75¢	Harvesting	550.00	400.00	60.00	40.00	24.00	18.00
□Q12	$1	Fruit Growing	1800.00	1200	260.00	180.00	20.00	15.00

1925–1929 SPECIAL HANDLING STAMPS (N-H ADD 35%)

□QE1	10¢	Yellow Green	24.00	16.00	1.75	1.00	1.00	.70
□QE2	15¢	Yellow Green	30.00	24.00	1.50	1.00	.90	.70
□QE3	20¢	Yellow Green	40.00	24.00	2.00	2.00	2.00	1.10
□QE4	25¢	Yellow Green	250.00	175.00	20.00	15.00	8.00	4.50
□QE4A	25¢	Deep Green	300.00	190.00	25.00	18.00	5.00	3.50

1919–1922 U.S. OFFICES IN CHINA ISSUES (N-H ADD 60%)
SHANGHAI 2¢ CHINA

□K1	2¢	on 1¢	100.00	72.00	20.00	12.00	21.00	13.00
□K2	4¢	on 2¢	100.00	72.00	20.00	12.00	21.00	13.00
□K3	6¢	on 3¢	200.00	140.00	35.00	23.00	46.00	28.00
□K4	8¢	on 4¢	225.00	165.00	40.00	24.00	46.00	28.00
□K5	10¢	on 2¢	300.00	210.00	45.00	30.00	50.00	32.00
□K6	12¢	on 6¢	275.00	200.00	56.00	36.00	65.00	40.00
□K7	14¢	on 7¢	300.00	210.00	56.00	36.00	80.00	45.00
□K8	16¢	on 8¢ Olive Bistre	280.00	200.00	45.00	28.00	54.00	32.00
□K8a	16¢	on 8¢ Olive Green	290.00	200.00	44.00	28.00	46.00	32.00
□K9	18¢	on 9¢	290.00	190.00	45.00	30.00	56.00	36.00
□K10	20¢	on 10¢	290.00	190.00	42.00	28.00	52.00	32.00
□K11	24¢	on 12¢ Br. Car.	290.00	190.00	46.00	32.00	60.00	37.00
□K11a	24¢	on 12¢ Cl. Br.	310.00	260.00	67.00	44.00	76.00	50.00
□K12	30¢	on 15¢	310.00	225.00	58.00	38.00	75.00	45.00
□K13	40¢	on 20¢	400.00	310.00	85.00	55.00	110.00	68.00
□K14	60¢	on 30¢	400.00	310.00	80.00	50.00	100.00	65.00
□K15	$1	on 50¢	2500.00	1500.00	375.00	280.00	425.00	300.00
□K16	$2	on $1	2000.00	1400.00	310.00	250.00	250.00	270.00
□K17	2¢	on 1¢ Loc. Sur.	370.00	300.00	85.00	44.00	70.00	45.00
□K18	4¢	on 2¢ Loc. Sur.	350.00	250.00	70.00	46.00	65.00	48.00

Scott No.			Imperforated (a)		Part Perforated (b)		Perforated (c)	
			Fine	Ave.	Fine	Ave.	Fine	Ave.

1862–1971. U.S. REVENUE STAMPS

□R1	1¢	Express	50.00	28.00	34.00	18.00	1.00	.52
□R2	1¢	Play Cards	750.00	410.00	400.00	250.00	91.00	48.00
□R3	1¢	Proprietary	500.00	265.00	92.00	52.00	.38	.26
□R4	1¢	Telegraph	400.00	190.00	—	—	7.25	4.00
□R5	2¢	Bank Ck., Blue	.80	.48	1.00	.58	.20	.16
□R6	2¢	Bank Ck., Orange	—	—	70.00	40.00	.20	.16
□R7	2¢	Certif., Blue	10.00	5.25	—	—	27.00	12.00
□R8	2¢	Certif., Orange	—	—	—	—	23.00	12.00

*No hinge pricing from 1941 to date is figured at (N-H ADD 15%)

Scott No.			Imperforated (a) Fine	Ave.	Part Perforated (b) Fine	Ave.	Perforated (c) Fine	Ave.
☐R9	2¢	Express, Blue	10.00	5.00	14.00	7.50	.31	.16
☐R10	2¢	Express, Orange	—	—	—	—	5.50	3.10
☐R11	2¢	Ply. Cds., Blue	—	—	100.00	58.00	2.60	1.50
☐R12	2¢	Ply. Cds., Orange	—	—	—	—	23.00	13.00
☐R13	2¢	Proprietary, Blue	—	—	90.00	50.00	.32	.21
☐R14	2¢	Proprietary, Orange	—	—	—	—	32.00	17.00
☐R15	2¢	U.S.I.R.	—	—	—	—	.20	.15
☐R16	3¢	Foreign Ex.	—	—	140.00	80.00	2.25	1.00
☐R17	3¢	Playing Cds.	—	—	—	—	95.00	50.00
☐R18	3¢	Proprietary	—	—	180.00	100.00	1.80	.80
☐R19	3¢	Telegraph	40.00	21.00	12.50	7.50	2.80	1.25
☐R20	4¢	Inland Exch.	—	—	—	—	1.60	.90
☐R21	4¢	Playing Cards	—	—	—	—	340.00	180.00
☐R22	4¢	Proprietary	—	—	170.00	100.00	4.00	3.10
☐R23	5¢	Agreement	—	—	—	—	.31	.16
☐R24	5¢	Certificate	2.40	1.30	8.00	4.80	.21	.16
☐R25	5¢	Express	3.50	2.00	4.50	2.80	.34	.20
☐R26	5¢	Foreign Ex.	—	—	—	—	.34	.21
☐R27	5¢	Inland Exch.	3.50	2.00	3.50	2.00	.26	.16
☐R28	5¢	Playing Cds.	—	—	—	—	12.00	6.00
☐R29	5¢	Proprietary	—	—	—	—	18.00	8.00
☐R30	6¢	Inland Exch.	—	—	—	—	.95	.50
☐R32	10¢	Bill of Ldg.	42.00	23.00	140.00	74.00	.80	.41
☐R33	10¢	Certificate	80.00	40.00	110.00	61.00	.31	.18
☐R34	10¢	Contract Bill	—	—	92.00	52.00	.32	.18
☐R35	10¢	For Ex. Bill	—	—	—	—	5.00	3.00
☐R36	10¢	Inland Exch.	100.00	60.00	2.90	1.75	.24	.16
☐R37	10¢	Power of Aty.	300.00	160.00	18.00	10.00	.36	.22
☐R38	10¢	Proprietary	—	—	—	—	13.00	6.00
☐R39	15¢	Foreign Exch.	—	—	—	—	12.00	6.00
☐R40	15¢	Inland Exch.	24.00	13.00	10.00	6.00	1.00	.50
☐R41	20¢	Foreign Exch.	40.00	22.00	—	—	28.00	14.50
☐R42	20¢	Inland Exch.	12.00	7.00	15.00	9.00	.41	.24
☐R43	25¢	Bond	91.00	50.00	6.00	3.40	1.70	.90
☐R44	25¢	Certificate	6.00	3.00	6.00	3.00	.20	.16
☐R45	25¢	Entry of Gds.	15.00	9.00	31.00	19.00	.60	.28
☐R46	25¢	Insurance	9.00	6.00	10.00	6.00	.28	.16
☐R47	25¢	Life Insr.	30.00	18.00	90.00	52.00	5.50	3.50
☐R48	25¢	Power of Atty.	5.00	3.50	15.00	10.00	.28	.16
☐R49	25¢	Protest	21.00	11.00	140.00	72.00	6.00	3.00
☐R50	25¢	Warehouse Rct.	34.00	20.00	130.00	75.00	20.00	10.00
☐R51	30¢	Foreign Exch.	60.00	30.00	410.00	250.00	36.00	16.00
☐R52	30¢	Inland Exch.	36.00	20.00	40.00	21.00	2.50	1.30
☐R53	40¢	Inland Exch.	410.00	230.00	4.00	2.40	2.40	1.30
☐R54	50¢	Convey, Blue	10.00	6.00	1.10	.75	.21	.16
☐R55	50¢	Entry of Gds.	—	—	10.00	5.80	.31	.16
☐R56	50¢	Foreign Exch.	35.00	20.00	30.00	17.00	4.00	2.10
☐R57	50¢	Lease	21.00	12.00	50.00	30.00	5.00	2.65

*No hinge pricing from 1941 to date is figured at (N-H ADD 15%)

Scott No.			Imperforated (a)		Part Perforated (b)		Perforated (c)	
			Fine	Ave.	Fine	Ave.	Fine	Ave.
☐R58	50¢	Life Insur.	26.00	15.00	50.00	28.00	.80	.45
☐R59	50¢	Mortgage	9.00	5.00	1.50	1.00	.42	.26
☐R60	50¢	Orig. Process	2.40	1.50	—	—	.36	.21
☐R61	50¢	Passage Tkt.	65.00	34.00	100.00	52.00	.54	.30
☐R62	50¢	Prob. of Will	30.00	17.00	41.00	24.00	16.00	8.75
☐R63	50¢	Sty. Bond, Bl.	105.00	59.00	2.75	1.40	.31	.16
☐R64	60¢	Inland Exch.	75.00	42.00	43.00	24.00	4.85	2.85
☐R65	70¢	Foreign Exch.	280.00	160.00	80.00	45.00	4.85	2.75
☐R66	$1	Conveyance	10.00	6.00	240.00	136.00	2.40	1.15
☐R67	$1	Entry of Gds.	24.00	12.50	—	—	1.50	.85
☐R68	$1	Foreign Exch.	48.00	25.00	—	—	.70	.40
☐R69	$1	Inland Exch.	10.00	6.00	210.00	105.00	.52	.30
☐R70	$1	Lease	31.00	17.00	—	—	1.35	.80
☐R71	$1	Life Insur.	135.00	76.00	—	—	4.60	2.40
☐R72	$1	Manifest	45.00	25.00	—	—	20.00	11.50
☐R73	$1	Mortgage	15.50	9.00	—	—	120.00	65.00
☐R74	$1	Passage Tkt.	148.00	87.00	—	—	130.00	65.00
☐R75	$1	Power of Atty.	56.00	30.00	—	—	1.75	.95
☐R76	$1	Prob. of Will	52.00	29.00	—	—	32.00	17.50
☐R77	$1.30	Foreign Exch.	1300.00	1000.00	—	—	43.00	24.00
☐R78	$1.50	Inland Exch.	20.00	11.00	—	—	3.00	1.50
☐R79	$1.60	Foreign Exch.	600.00	350.00	—	—	85.00	45.00
☐R80	$1.90	Foreign Exch.	1800.00	1200	—	—	54.00	29.00
☐R81	$2	Conveyance	85.00	50.00	600.00	400.00	2.00	.95
☐R82	$2	Mortgage	74.00	41.00	—	—	2.40	1.35
☐R83	$2	Prob. of Will	1800.00	1300.00	—	—	40.00	21.00
☐R84	$2.50	Inland Exch.	910.00	500.00	—	—	3.00	1.60
☐R85	$3	Chart. Pty.	90.00	50.00	—	—	3.75	1.95
☐R86	$3	Manifest	85.00	48.00	—	—	20.00	11.00
☐R87	$3.50	Inland Exch.	1000.00	700.00	—	—	43.00	24.00
☐R88	$5	Chtr. Party	200.00	115.00	—	—	4.50	2.65
☐R89	$5	Conveyance	30.00	16.00	—	—	4.50	2.65
☐R90	$5	Manifest	80.00	42.00	—	—	80.00	44.00
☐R91	$5	Mortgage	78.00	45.00	—	—	16.00	9.00
☐R92	$5	Prob. of Will	365.00	200.00	—	—	16.00	9.00
☐R93	$10	Chrt. Party	400.00	220.00	—	—	20.00	10.00
☐R94	$10	Conveyance	72.00	42.00	—	—	52.00	30.00
☐R95	$10	Mortgage	300.00	160.00	—	—	20.00	11.00
☐R96	$10	Prob. of Will	800.00	400.00	—	—	20.00	11.00
☐R97	$15	Mortgage	750.00	460.00	—	—	85.00	48.00
☐R98	$20	Conveyance	56.00	31.00	—	—	30.00	18.00
☐R99	$20	Prob. of Will	810.00	450.00	—	—	760.00	450.00
☐R100	$25	Mortgage	675.00	380.00	—	—	80.00	45.00
☐R101	$50	U.S.I.R.	150.00	90.00	—	—	76.00	43.00
☐R102	$200	U.S.I.R.	950.00	510.00	—	—	500.00	300.00

*No hinge pricing from 1941 to date is figured at (N-H ADD 15%)

Scott No.		Fine Used Each	Ave. Used Each
1871. SECOND ISSUE R103 THROUGH R131 HAVE BLUE FRAMES AND A BLACK CENTER			
☐R103	1¢	24.00	13.00
☐R104	2¢	1.00	.60
☐R105	3¢	12.00	6.25
☐R106	4¢	40.00	23.00
☐R107	5¢	1.00	.62
☐R108	6¢	64.00	35.00
☐R109	10¢	86	.48
☐R110	15¢	19.00	10.00
☐R111	20¢	4.50	2.40
☐R112	25¢	65	.36
☐R113	30¢	48.00	26.00
☐R114	40¢	26.00	16.00
☐R115	50¢	62	.38
☐R116	60¢	56.00	30.00
☐R117	70¢	24.00	12.00
☐R118	$1	3.00	1.60
☐R119	$1.30	225.00	120.00
☐R120	$1.50	10.00	6.00
☐R121	$1.60	265.00	150.00
☐R122	$1.90	125.00	65.00
☐R123	$2	10.00	5.50
☐R124	$2.50	19.00	10.00
☐R125	$3	30.00	17.00
☐R126	$3.50	110.00	54.00
☐R127	$5	16.00	9.00
☐R128	$10	80.00	48.00
☐R129	$20	260.00	140.00
☐R130	$25	260.00	140.00
☐R131	$50	275.00	160.00

Scott No.		Fine Used Each	Ave. Used Each
1871-1872. THIRD ISSUE SAME DESIGNS AS SECOND ISSUE			
☐R134	1¢ Claret & Blk.	22.00	12.00
☐R135	2¢ Org. & Blk.	21	.16
☐R136	4¢ Bm. & Blk.	26.00	14.00
☐R137	5¢ Org. & Blk.	31	.16
☐R138	6¢ Rog. & Blk.	27.00	15.00
☐R139	15¢ Bm. & Blk.	10.00	5.00
☐R140	30¢ Org. & Blk.	10.00	6.00
☐R141	40¢ Bm. & Blk.	21.00	12.00
☐R142	60¢ Org. & Blk.	45.00	25.00
☐R143	70¢ Gm. & Blk.	30.00	16.00
☐R144	$1 Gm. & Blk.	1.25	.70
☐R145	$2 Verm'n & Blk.	19.00	10.00
☐R146	$2.50 Claret & Blk.	29.00	15.00
☐R147	$3 Gm. & Blk.	30.00	17.00
☐R148	$5 Verm'n & Blk.	17.00	8.00
☐R149	$10 Gm. & Blk.	62.00	34.00
☐R150	$20 Org. & Blk.	360.00	210.00
1874. FOURTH ISSUE			
☐R151	2¢ Org. & Blk, Gm. Paper	21	.16
1875. ISSUE			
☐R152a	2¢ Blue, Silk Paper	21	.16
☐R152b	2¢ Blue, Watermarked	21	.16
☐R152c	2¢ Blue, Rouletted	26.00	13.00

Scott No.			Fine Un-cancelled Each	Ave. Un-cancelled Each	Fine Used Each	Ave. Used Each
1898. POSTAGE AND NEWSPAPER STAMPS SURCHARGED I.R.						
☐R153	1¢	Green, Small I.R.	1.40	.70	1.10	.40
☐R154	1¢	Green, Large I.R.	.26	.21	.21	.16
☐R154a	1¢	Green Inverted Surch.	8.00	4.00	5.00	2.80
☐R155	2¢	Carmine, Large I.R.	.25	.21	.60	.31
☐R155a	2¢	Carmine, Inverted Surch.	1.20	.75	.90	.72
☐R159	$5	Blue, Surch. down	185.00	100.00	120.00	70.00
☐R160	$5	Blue, Surch. up	85.00	48.00	58.00	36.00
1898. DOCUMENTARY "BATTLESHIP" DESIGN						
☐R161	½¢	Orange	3.50	2.00	6.00	3.60
☐R162	½¢	Dark Gray	.26	.21	.20	.16
☐R163	1¢	Pale Blue	.26	.21	.20	.16
☐R164	2¢	Carmine	.26	.21	.20	.16
☐R165	3¢	Dark Blue	.86	.48	.20	.16
☐R166	4¢	Pale Rose	.38	.26	—	.16
☐R167	5¢	Lilac	.26	.21	.16	.16
☐R168	10¢	Dark Brown	.50	.30	.16	.16
☐R169	25¢	Purple Brown	.50	.30	.16	.16
☐R170	40¢	Blue Lilac (cut .25)	60.00	30.00	1.15	.90
☐R171	50¢	Slate Violet	7.00	3.50	.18	.16
☐R172	80¢	Bistre (cut .15)	26.00	14.00	.41	.26
1898–1899. DOCUMENTARY STAMPS						
☐R173	$1	Dark Green	4.50	3.10	.20	.16
☐R174	$3	Dark Brown (cut .18)	9.00	6.00	.46	.31
☐R175	$5	Orange (cut .25)	—	—	1.00	.60
☐R176	$10	Black (cut .75)	—	—	1.00	.60
☐R177	$30	Red (cut 25.00)	—	—	2.70	1.60
☐R178	$50	Gray Brown (cut 1.50)	—	—	70.00	42.00
☐R179	$100	Brown & Black (cut 12.00)	—	—	3.80	2.65
☐R180	$500	Lake & Black (cut 180.00)	—	—	26.00	14.00
☐R181	$100	Green & Black (cut 100.00)	—	—	410.00	260.00
					310.00	260.00
1900. DOCUMENTARY STAMPS						
☐R182	$1	Carmine (cut .15)	9.00	4.50	.52	.32
☐R183	$3	Green (cut 8.00)	60.00	40.00	38.00	23.00
1900–1902. SURCHARGED LARGE BLACK NUMERALS						
☐R184	$1	Gray (cut .09)	4.50	3.50	.21	.16
☐R185	$2	Gray (cut .09)	4.00	3.25	.21	.16
☐R186	$3	Gray (cut 1.15)	38.00	19.00	10.00	6.10
☐R187	$5	Gray (cut .40)	21.00	13.00	5.00	3.10
☐R188	$10	Gray (cut 3.25)	40.00	26.00	11.00	5.50
☐R189	$50	Gray (cut 80.00)	540.00	290.00	330.00	190.00
☐R190	$1	Green (cut .35)	9.00	4.00	2.50	1.60
☐R191	$2	Green (cut .30)	8.50	4.00	1.00	.65
☐R192	$5	Green (cut 1.60)	49.00	30.00	17.00	11.00
☐R193	$10	Green (cut 27.50)	225.00	130.00	140.00	75.00
☐R194	$50	Green (cut 220.00)	900.00	500.00	600.00	375.00

Scott No.			Fine Un-cancelled Each	Ave. Un-cancelled Each	Fine Used Each	Ave. Used Each
1914. DOCUMENTARY SINGLE LINE WATERMARK						
☐R195	½¢	Rose	4.60	2.65	2.40	1.60
☐R196	1¢	Rose	1.15	.62	.21	.16
☐R197	2¢	Rose	1.15	.62	.21	.16
☐R198	3¢	Rose	27.00	16.00	21.00	11.00
☐R199	4¢	Rose	8.50	4.00	1.00	.50
☐R200	5¢	Rose	2.75	1.25	.21	.16
☐R201	10¢	Rose	2.10	1.15	.21	.16
☐R202	25¢	Rose	15.00	9.00	.50	.31
☐R203	40¢	Rose	11.00	5.00	.52	.36
☐R204	50¢	Rose	3.50	1.80	.21	.16
☐R205	80¢	Rose	42.00	26.00	6.50	4.00
1914. DOCUMENTARY DOUBLE LINE WATERMARK						
☐R206	½¢	Rose	1.00	.50	.52	.35
☐R207	1¢	Rose	.23	.21	.21	.16
☐R208	2¢	Rose	.23	.21	.21	.16
☐R209	3¢	Rose	1.10	.55	.26	.20
☐R210	4¢	Rose	1.85	1.00	.34	.21
☐R211	5¢	Rose	1.00	.51	.21	.16
☐R212	10¢	Rose	.42	.24	.21	.16
☐R213	25¢	Rose	3.50	2.10	.82	.48
☐R214	40¢	Rose (cut .60)	40.00	23.00	7.50	4.00
☐R215	50¢	Rose	7.50	4.50	.21	.16
☐R216	80¢	Rose (cut 1.10)	48.00	24.00	9.00	5.00
☐R217	$1	Green (cut .06)	13.00	7.50	.21	.16
☐R218	$2	Carmine (cut .10)	24.00	16.00	.21	.16
☐R219	$2	Carmine (cut .25)	40.00	21.00	1.00	.60
☐R220	$5	Blue (cut .65)	31.00	18.00	2.00	1.00
☐R221	$10	Orange (cut 1.10)	70.00	40.00	4.50	3.00
☐R222	$30	Vermilion (cut 2.35)	140.00	85.00	9.00	6.00
☐R223	$50	Violet (cut 200.00)	815.00	450.00	610.00	335.00
☐R224	$60	Brown (cut 47.50)	—	—	105.00	62.00
☐R225	$100	Green (cut 14.50)	—	—	40.00	21.00
1917–1933. TENTH ISSUE DOCUMENTARY STAMPS—PERF. 11						
☐R228	1¢	Rose	.24	.21	.20	.16
☐R229	2¢	Rose	.24	.22	.20	.16
☐R230	3¢	Rose	.60	.30	.24	.16
☐R231	4¢	Rose	.35	.22	.20	.16
☐R232	5¢	Rose	.30	.22	.20	.16
☐R233	8¢	Rose	1.25	.85	.20	.16
☐R234	10¢	Rose	.26	.21	.20	.16
☐R235	20¢	Rose	.90	.50	.20	.16
☐R236	25¢	Rose	.90	.50	.20	.16
☐R237	40¢	Rose	.90	.50	.20	.16
☐R238	50¢	Rose	1.10	.65	.20	.16
☐R239	80¢	Rose	3.00	1.80	.20	.16

Scott No.			Fine Un-cancelled Each	Ave. Un-cancelled Each	Fine Used Each	Ave. Used Each
☐R240	$1	Green	4.00	3.00	.22	.16
☐R241	$2	Rose	7.50	5.00	.22	.16
☐R242	$3	Violet (cut .15)	22.00	14.00	.46	.30
☐R243	$4	Brown (cut .20)	15.00	8.50	1.00	.64
☐R244	$5	Blue (cut .13)	9.00	5.00	.26	.16
☐R245	$10	Orange (cut .20)	19.00	13.00	.64	.40

1917. DOCUMENTARY STAMPS—PERF. 12

Scott No.			Fine Un-cancelled Each	Ave. Un-cancelled Each	Fine Used Each	Ave. Used Each
☐R246	$30	Vermilion (cut .80)	27.00	16.00	2.10	1.40
☐R247	$60	Brown (cut 1.00)	38.00	24.00	7.00	4.00
☐R248	$100	Green (cut .45)	24.00	14.00	1.00	.52
☐R249	$500	Blue (cut 9.50)	—	—	32.00	18.00
☐R250	$1000	Orange (cut 3.50)	90.00	50.00	40.00	30.00

1928–1929. DOCUMENTARY STAMPS—PERF. 10

Scott No.			Fine Un-cancelled Each	Ave. Un-cancelled Each	Fine Used Each	Ave. Used Each
☐R251	1¢	Carmine Rose	1.70	1.10	.90	.60
☐R252	2¢	Carmine Rose	.52	.36	.21	.16
☐R253	4¢	Carmine Rose	5.00	2.50	3.10	1.90
☐R254	5¢	Carmine Rose	1.15	.50	.32	.21
☐R255	10¢	Carmine Rose	1.60	.95	.90	.58
☐R256	20¢	Carmine Rose	5.00	3.00	4.15	2.65
☐R257	$1¢	Green (cut 1.90)	55.00	36.00	27.00	16.00
☐R258	$2	Rose	17.00	8.50	1.60	.95
☐R259	$10	Orange (cut 8.00)	90.00	55.00	30.00	20.00

1929–1930. DOCUMENTARY STAMPS—PERF. 11 x 10

Scott No.			Fine Un-cancelled Each	Ave. Un-cancelled Each	Fine Used Each	Ave. Used Each
☐R260	2¢	Carmine Rose	2.40	1.50	1.75	1.00
☐R261	5¢	Carmine Rose	1.90	1.10	1.00	.70
☐R262	10¢	Carmine Rose	7.00	4.00	6.00	3.75
☐R263	20¢	Carmine Rose	13.00	7.75	7.00	5.00

Scott No.			Fine Used Each	Ave. Used Each	Fine Used Each	Ave. Used Each
			Violet Paper (a)		Green Paper (b)	

1871–1874. PROPRIETARY STAMPS—ALL USED

Scott No.			Fine Used Each Violet Paper (a)	Ave. Used Each	Fine Used Each Green Paper (b)	Ave. Used Each
☐RB1	1¢	Green & Black	3.50	2.00	5.00	3.00
☐RB2	2¢	Green & Black	4.00	2.40	11.00	7.00
☐RB3	3¢	Green & Black	10.00	6.00	34.00	19.00
☐RB4	4¢	Green & Black	6.50	4.00	12.00	6.75
☐RB5	4¢	Green & Black	100.00	55.00	100.00	67.00
☐RB6	6¢	Green & Black	26.00	15.00	80.00	44.00
☐RB7	10¢	Green & Black	140.00	80.00	33.00	18.00
☐RB8	50¢	Green & Black	600.00	350.00	800.00	485.00

Scott No.			Silk Paper (a) Fine	Ave.	Watermarked (b) Fine	Ave.	Rouletted (c) Fine	Ave.

1875–1881. PROPRIETARY STAMPS—ALL USED

Scott No.			Silk Paper (a) Fine	Ave.	Watermarked (b) Fine	Ave.	Rouletted (c) Fine	Ave.
☐RB11	1¢	Green	2.00	1.00	.38	.21	43.00	21.00
☐RB12	2¢	Brown	2.10	1.10	1.10	.75	50.00	30.00

Scott No.			Silk Paper (a)		Watermarked (b)		Rouletted (c)	
			Fine	Ave.	Fine	Ave.	Fine	Ave.
☐RB13	3¢	Orange	8.00	4.00	2.00	1.25	51.00	29.00
☐RB14	4¢	Red Brown	4.10	2.25	3.60	2.10	—	—
☐RB15	4¢	Red			3.60	2.10	62.00	40.00
☐RB16	5¢	Black	92.00	51.00	70.00	34.00	480.00	390.00
☐RB17	6¢	Violet Blue	19.00	12.00	12.00	7.00	142.00	85.00
☐RB18	6¢	Violet	—	—	18.00	11.00	170.00	95.00
☐RB19	10¢	Blue	—	—	200.00	115.00	—	—

Scott No.			Fine Un-cancelled Each	Ave. Un-cancelled Each	Fine Used Each	Ave. Used Each

1898. PROPRIETARY STAMPS—BATTLESHIP

			Fine Un-cancelled Each	Ave. Un-cancelled Each	Fine Used Each	Ave. Used Each
☐RB20	1/8¢	Yellow Green	.25	.22	.19	.16
☐RB21	1/4¢	Pale Green	.25	.22	.19	.16
☐RB22	3/8¢	Deep Orange	.26	.22	.19	.16
☐RB23	5/8¢	Deep Ultramarine	.26	.22	.19	.16
☐RB24	1¢	Dark Green	.41	.26	.24	.16
☐RB25	1 1/4¢	Violet	.26	.21	.21	.16
☐RB26	1 7/8¢	Dull Blue	2.75	1.90	.90	.48
☐RB27	2¢	Violet Brown	.41	.28	.26	.16
☐RB28	2 1/2¢	Lake	1.10	.60	.21	.16
☐RB29	3 3/4¢	Olive Gray	12.00	9.00	4.00	2.50
☐RB30	4¢	Purple	3.50	2.10	.90	.52
☐RB31	5¢	Brown Orange	3.50	2.10	1.00	.50

1914. BLACK PROPRIETARY STAMPS—S.L. WTMK.

☐RB32	1/8¢	Black	.26	.21	.21	.16
☐RB33	1/4¢	Black	1.20	.70	.90	.50
☐RB34	3/8¢	Black	.26	.21	.21	.16
☐RB35	1/2¢	Black	2.40	1.60	1.45	.90
☐RB36	1 1/4¢	Black	1.50	1.10	.75	.42
☐RB37	1 7/8¢	Black	24.00	14.00	14.00	9.00
☐RB38	2 1/4¢	Black	4.00	2.50	2.75	1.75
☐RB39	3 1/8¢	Black	60.00	38.00	42.00	26.00
☐RB40	3 3/4¢	Black	24.00	16.00	18.00	10.00
☐RB41	4¢	Black	40.00	23.00	24.00	12.50
☐RB42	4 3/8¢	Black	750.00	450.00	—	—
☐RB43	5¢	Black	84.00	50.00	54.00	32.00

1914. BLACK PROPRIETARY STAMPS—D.L. WTMK.

☐RB44	1/8¢	Black	.26	.21	.20	.16
☐RB45	1/4¢	Black	.26	.21	.20	.16
☐RB46	3/8¢	Black	.58	.36	.32	.21
☐RB47	1/2¢	Black	2.50	1.40	1.80	1.15
☐RB48	5/8¢	Black	.26	.22	.21	.16
☐RB49	1¢	Black	3.15	1.90	2.10	1.35
☐RB50	1 1/4¢	Black	.32	.22	.21	.16
☐RB51	1 1/2¢	Black	2.85	1.65	2.00	1.15
☐RB52	1 7/8¢	Black	.80	.50	.55	.36
☐RB53	2¢	Black	4.50	2.90	3.80	2.00

Scott No.			Fine Un-cancelled Each	Ave. Un-cancelled Each	Fine Used Each	Ave. Used Each
□RB54	2½¢	Black	1.20	.75	.95	.60
□RB55	3¢	Black	3.00	1.75	2.30	1.40
□RB56	3½¢	Black	3.50	2.10	2.70	1.60
□RB57	3¾¢	Black	8.10	5.00	6.50	4.00
□RB58	4¢	Black	.34	.22	.20	.16
□RB59	4¾¢	Black	10.00	5.50	6.50	4.00
□RB60	5¢	Black	2.40	1.15	2.00	1.10
□RB61	6¢	Black	42.00	25.00	34.00	20.00
□RB62	8¢	Black	12.00	7.00	10.00	6.00
□RB63	10¢	Black	8.50	5.50	6.00	3.75
□RB64	20¢	Black	16.00	10.00	12.00	8.00

1919. PROPRIETARY STAMPS

□RB65	1¢	Dark Blue	.26	.21	.16	.14
□RB66	2¢	Dark Blue	.26	.21	.16	.14
□RB67	3¢	Dark Blue	.90	.50	.50	.35
□RB68	4¢	Dark Blue	.90	.50	.52	.26
□RB69	5¢	Dark Blue	1.10	.62	.55	.36
□RB70	8¢	Dark Blue	10.00	6.00	7.10	4.60
□RB71	10¢	Dark Blue	2.60	1.75	1.85	1.15
□RB72	20¢	Dark Blue	4.10	3.00	2.60	1.50
□RB73	40¢	Dark Blue	24.00	14.00	9.00	5.50

1918–1934. FUTURE DELIVERY STAMPS

□RC1	2¢	Carmine Rose	1.35	.80	.21	.16
□RC2	3¢	Carmine Rose (cut 7.50)	26.00	16.00	19.00	12.00
□RC3	4¢	Carmine Rose	2.10	1.25	.21	.16
□RC3A	5¢	Carmine Rose	—	—	3.75	2.25
□RC4	10¢	Carmine Rose	4.75	2.90	.21	.16
□RC5	20¢	Carmine Rose	4.75	2.90	.22	.16
□RC6	25¢	Carmine Rose (cut .10)	15.00	10.00	.80	.46
□RC7	40¢	Carmine Rose (cut .10)	15.00	10.00	.48	.40
□RC8	50¢	Carmine Rose	3.80	2.40	.38	.16
□RC9	80¢	Carmine Rose (cut .75)	26.00	20.00	6.00	4.00
□RC10	$1	Green (cut .10)	—	—	.26	.16
□RC11	$2	Rose (cut .08)	—	—	.26	.16
□RC12	$3	Violet (cut .12)	—	—	1.15	.70
□RC13	$5	Dark Blue (cut .09)	—	—	.45	.26
□RC14	$10	Orange (cut .20)	—	—	.60	.40
□RC15	$20	Olive Bistre (cut .50)	—	—	3.50	2.00
□RC16	$30	Vermilion (cut .95)	—	—	3.00	1.85
□RC17	$50	Olive Green (cut .30)	—	—	.90	.60
□RC18	$60	Brown (cut .55)	—	—	1.85	1.10
□RC19	$100	Yellow Green (cut 5.00)	—	—	22.00	14.00
□RC20	$500	Blue (cut 3.00)	—	—	9.00	6.00
□RC21	$1000	Orange (cut 1.60)	—	1.00	4.00	3.00
□RC22	1¢	Carmine Rose Narrow Overprint	.60	.32	.19	.16
□RC23	80¢	Narrow Overprint (cut .20)	—	—	1.55	1.10

Scott No.			Fine Un-cancelled Each	Ave. Un-cancelled Each	Fine Used Each	Ave. Used Each
☐RC25	$1	Serif Overprint (cut .08)	7.50	4.50	.52	.40
☐RC26	$10	Serif Overprint (cut 4.50)			12.00	8.00

1918–1929. STOCK TRANSFER STAMPS—PERF. 11 OR 12

☐RD1	1¢	Carmine Rose, Perf. 11	.60	.36	.21	.16
☐RD2	1¢	Carmine Rose, Perf. 11	.25	.21	.21	.16
☐RD3	4¢	Carmine Rose, Perf. 11	.25	.21	.21	.16
☐RD4	5¢	Carmine Rose, Perf. 11	.25	.21	.21	.16
☐RD5	10¢	Carmine Rose, Perf. 11	.25	.21	.21	.16
☐RD6	20¢	Carmine Rose, Perf. 11	.36	.26	.21	.16
☐RD7	25¢	Carmine Rose, Perf. 12 (cut .07)	.72	.42	.21	.16
☐RD8	40¢	Carmine Rose, Perf. 11	.72	.41	.21	.16
☐RD9	50¢	Carmine Rose, Perf. 11	.45	.26	.21	.16
☐RD10	80¢	Carmine Rose, Perf. 11 (cut .07)	1.40	.95	.26	.18
☐RD11	$1	Green, perf. 11, Red Ovpt. (cut .40)	34.00	19.00	8.00	4.65
☐RD12	$1	Green, Perf. 11, Black Ovpt	1.40	.80	.21	.16
☐RD13	$2	Rose, Perf. 11	1.40	.80	.21	.16
☐RD14	$3	Violet, Perf. 11 (cut .17)	7.50	4.25	1.85	.75
☐RD15	$4	Y. Brown, Perf. 11 (cut .07)	4.00	2.25	.21	.16
☐RD16	$5	Blue, Perf. 11 (cut .07)	2.60	1.40	.21	.16
☐RD17	$10	Orange, Perf. 11 (cut .07)	4.00	2.75	.21	.16
☐RD18	$20	Bistre, Perf. 11 (cut 4.25	36.00	26.00	18.00	10.00
☐RD19	$30	Vermilion (cut 1.05)	13.00	9.00	4.00	2.65
☐RD20	$50	Olive Green (cut 9.75)	80.00	46.00	40.00	30.00
☐RD21	$60	Brown (cut 4.60)	50.00	33.00	18.00	12.00
☐RD22	$100	Green (cut 1.10)	20.00	12.00	4.50	3.00
☐RD23	$500	Blue (cut 38.00)	—	—	108.00	64.00
☐RD24	$1000	Orange (cut 10.00)	—	—	72.00	45.00
☐RD25	2¢	Carmine Rose, Perf. 10	.50	.30	.21	.14
☐RD26	4¢	Carmine Rose, Perf. 10	.50	.30	.21	.14
☐RD27	10¢	Carmine Rose, Perf. 10	.40	.26	.21	.14
☐RD28	20¢	Carmine Rose, Perf. 10	.40	.26	.21	.14
☐RD29	50¢	Carmine Rose, Perf. 10	1.00	.60	.21	.14
☐RD30	$1	Green, Perf. 10	2.25	1.10	.21	.14
☐RD31	$2	Carmine Rose, Perf. 10	2.25	1.10	.21	.14
☐RD32	$10	Orange, Perf. 10 (cut .07)	9.00	6.00	.21	.14

1919–1928.
STOCK TRANSFER STAMPS, SERIF OVERPRINT

☐RD33	2¢	Carmine Rose, Perf. 11	3.80	1.60	.55	.36
☐RD34	10¢	Carmine Rose, Perf. 11	.90	.24	.21	.15
☐RD35	20¢	Carmine Rose, Perf. 11	.90	.31	.22	.15
☐RD36	50¢	Carmine Rose, Perf. 11	1.80	.60	.30	.15
☐RD37	$1	Green, Perf. 11 (cut .11)	12.00	7.00	6.00	3.00
☐RD38	$2	Rose, Perf, 11 (cut .12)	11.00	6.00	5.50	3.00
☐RD39	2¢	Rose, Perf. 11 (cut .12)	3.00	1.50	.36	.21
☐RD40	10¢	Carmine Rose, Perf. 11	.80	.21	.21	.15
☐RD41	20¢	Carmine Rose, Perf. 10	1.15	.21	.21	.15

Scott No.			Fine Unused Block	Ave. Unused Block	Fine Unused Each	Ave. Unused Each	Fine Used Each	Ave. Used Each
CONFEDERATE STATES OF AMERICA STAMPS (N-H ADD 80%)								
☐1	5¢	J. Davis, Green	—	1200.00	132.00	90.00	100.00	56.00
☐2	10¢	Jefferson, Blue	—	1500.00	200.00	110.00	140.00	90.00
☐3	2¢	Jackson, Green	—	—	315.00	225.00	460.00	325.00
☐4	5¢	J. Davis, Blue	600.00	500.00	100.00	60.00	78.00	46.00
☐5	10¢	Jefferson, Rose	—	—	700.00	410.00	400.00	250.00
☐6	5¢	Davis, Lon. Print	95.00	80.00	8.00	6.00	16.00	11.00
☐7	5¢	Davis, Local Print	130.00	95.00	12.00	7.00	11.00	8.00
1863.								
☐8	2¢	Jackson, Br. Red	400.00	325.00	42.00	24.00	220.00	165.00
☐9	10¢	Davis (len)	—	—	600.00	400.00	415.00	260.00
☐10	10¢	Davis (w fr. lin.)	—	—	2100.00	1500.00	1100.00	700.00
☐11	10¢	Davis (no fr.)	78.00	62.00	9.00	7.00	11.00	7.00
☐12	10¢	Davis (fill. com)	90.00	84.00	9.50	7.00	11.00	7.00
☐13	20¢	Washington	380.00	300.00	32.00	25.00	300.00	200.00
1862.								
☐14	1¢	J.C. Calhoun	750.00	575.00	80.00	50.00	—	—

Scott No.			Fine Plate Block	Block	Fine Unused Each	Fine Used Each
1935. "FARLEY SPECIAL PRINTINGS"						
☐752	3¢	Newburgh	16.00	6.00	.21	.16
☐753	3¢	Byrd, Perf.	19.00	3.75	.58	.60
☐754	3¢	Mother's Day	20.00	3.75	.60	.50
☐755	3¢	Wisconsin	20.00	4.00	.65	.58
☐756	1¢	Park	6.00	1.60	.21	.16
☐757	2¢	Park	7.00	1.60	.28	.18
☐758	3¢	Park	18.00	6.00	.65	.60
☐759	4¢	Park	24.00	9.00	1.15	1.00
☐760	5¢	Park	30.00	15.00	2.20	1.80
☐761	6¢	Park	50.00	19.00	2.60	2.15
☐762	7¢	Park	40.00	17.00	2.00	1.80
☐763	8¢	Park	50.00	18.00	2.15	1.90
☐764	9¢	Park	60.00	21.00	2.25	2.00
☐765	10¢	Park	60.00	34.00	4.00	3.50
☐766a	1¢	Chicago	—	15.00	.80	.50
☐767a	3¢	Chicago	—	15.00	.80	.50
☐768a	3¢	Byrd	—	20.00	3.00	2.80
☐769a	1¢	Park	—	13.00	1.90	1.45
☐770a	3¢	Park	—	26.00	3.50	2.90
☐771	16¢	Air Spec. Del	90.00	—	3.00	2.70

Scott No.				Center Line Block	Fine Arrow Block	Block W/Vert. Line	Pair W/Vert. Line	Block W/Horiz. Line	Pair W/Horiz. Line
1935. FARLEY POSITION ON BLOCKS AND PAIRS									
☐752	3¢	Newburgh		49.00	26.00	18.00	8.00	9.00	4.25
☐753	3¢	Byrd		90.00	114.00	72.00	40.00	—	1.60
☐754	3¢	Mother's Day		9.00	16.00	4.00	1.50	4.50	1.70
☐755	3¢	Wisconsin		9.00	16.00	4.00	1.50	4.50	1.70
☐756	1¢	Park		4.00	10.00	1.70	.70	1.25	55
☐757	2¢	Park		6.00	10.00	1.60	.70	2.00	.80
☐758	3¢	Park		7.00	14.00	3.10	1.50	3.75	1.60
☐759	4¢	Park		10.00	40.00	6.00	2.50	6.00	3.00
☐760	5¢	Park		16.00	46.00	10.00	5.00	10.00	4.10
☐761	6¢	Park		19.00	75.00	15.00	6.00	11.00	7.00
☐762	7¢	Park		17.00	50.00	17.00	5.10	10.50	5.00
☐763	8¢	Park		19.00	55.00	19.00	6.00	14.00	5.00
☐764	9¢	Park		21.00	54.00	21.00	6.00	16.50	6.00
☐765	10¢	Park		30.00	152.00	29.00	10.00	27.00	10.00
☐766a	1¢	Chicago		14.00	—	15.00	8.50	12.00	6.75
☐767a	3¢	Chicago		14.00	—	15.00	8.50	11.00	6.75
☐768a	3¢	Byrd		18.00	—	17.00	7.50	14.50	6.75
☐769a	1¢	Park		11.00	—	14.00	5.00	10.00	5.00
☐770a	3¢	Park		24.00	—	21.00	11.00	19.00	12.00
☐771	16¢	Air Spec. Del		72.00	90.00	28.00	7.00	19.00	7.00

Scott No.				Fine Plate Block	Ave. Plate Block	Fine Unused Each	Ave. Unused Each	Fine Used Each	Ave. Used Each
HUNTING PERMIT STAMPS									
☐RW1 (1934)	$1	Blue		5000.00	3500.00	315.00	225.00	100.00	70.00
☐RW2 (1935)	$1	Rose Lake		5500.00	4500.00	315.00	215.00	130.00	90.00
☐RW3 (1936)	$1	Brown Blk		2600.00	2000.00	170.00	115.00	70.00	48.00
☐RW4 (1937)	$1	Lt. Green		1600.00	1200.00	125.00	88.00	42.00	27.00
☐RW5 (1938)	$1	Lt. Violet		1600.00	1200.00	141.00	100.00	48.00	28.00
☐RW6 (1939)	$1	Chocolate		1100.00	850.00	90.00	67.00	25.00	16.00
☐RW7 (1940)	$1	Sepia		950.00	800.00	90.00	67.00	25.00	16.00
☐RW8 (1941)	$1	Brn. Carmine		900.00	750.00	90.00	65.00	25.00	16.00
☐RW9 (1942)	$1	Violet Brn.		900.00	750.00	90.00	65.00	21.00	15.00
☐RW10 (1943)	$1	Deep Rose		350.00	215.00	40.00	27.00	21.00	15.00
☐RW11 (1944)	$1	Red Org.		310.00	210.00	40.00	27.00	21.00	15.00

Scott No.		Fine Plate Block	Ave. Plate Block	Fine Unused Each	Ave. Unused Each	Fine Used Each	Ave. Used Each
□RW12 (1945)	$1 Black	190.00	150.00	28.00	19.00	17.00	13.00
□RW13 (1946)	$1 Red Brn	190.00	150.00	28.00	19.00	15.00	10.00
□RW14 (1947)	$1 Black	190.00	150.00	28.00	19.00	14.00	10.00
□RW15 (1948)	$1 Brt. Blue	190.00	150.00	28.00	21.00	14.00	10.00
□RW16 (1949)	$2 Brt. Green	190.00	150.00	31.00	22.00	10.00	8.00
□RW17 (1950)	$1 Violet	200.00	160.00	36.00	24.00	10.00	8.00
□RW18 (1951)	$2 Gray Blk	200.00	160.00	36.00	24.00	8.50	6.00
□RW19 (1952)	$2 Ultramarine	200.00	160.00	36.00	24.00	8.50	6.00
□RW20 (1953)	$2 Dk. Rose Brn	200.00	160.00	36.00	24.00	8.50	6.00
□RW21 (1954)	$2 Black	200.00	160.00	36.00	24.00	8.50	6.00
□RW22 (1955)	$2 Dk. Blue	200.00	160.00	36.00	24.00	8.50	6.00
□RW23 (1956)	$2 Black	200.00	160.00	36.00	24.00	8.50	6.00
□RW24 (1957)	$2 Emerald	200.00	160.00	36.00	24.00	8.50	6.00
□RW25 (1958)	$2 Black	200.00	160.00	36.00	24.00	8.50	6.00
□RW26 (1959)	$3 Bl./Ochre/Blk	320.00	210.00	44.00	34.00	8.50	6.00
□RW27 (1960)	$3 Red Brn./Bl./Bist	320.00	210.00	44.00	34.00	8.50	8.00
□RW28 (1961)	$3 Bl./Bist./Brn	340.00	210.00	44.00	34.00	8.50	8.00
□RW29 (1962)	$3 Bl./Brn./Blk	400.00	240.00	54.00	34.00	12.00	9.00
□RW30 (1963)	$3 Blk./Bl. Yel./Grn	400.00	240.00	54.00	40.00	12.00	9.00
□RW31 (1964)	$3 Bl./Bl./Bist	1800.00	1400.00	54.00	40.00	12.00	9.00
□RW32 (1965)	$3 Grn./Blk./Brn	360.00	240.00	54.00	40.00	12.00	9.00
□RW33 (1966)	$3 Bl./Grn./Blk	360.00	240.00	54.00	40.00	12.00	9.00
□RW34 (1967)	$3 Multicolored	360.00	240.00	54.00	40.00	12.00	9.00
□RW35 (1968)	$3 Grn./Blk./Brn	210.00	160.00	40.00	30.00	8.00	9.00

Scott No.			Fine Plate Block	Ave. Plate Block	Fine Unused Each	Ave. Unused Each	Fine Used Each	Ave. Used Each
RW36 (1969)	$3	Multicolored	150.00	130.00	40.00	33 .00	8.00	6.00
RW37 (1970)	$3	Multicolored	150.00	130.00	38.00	30.00	8.00	6.00
RW38 (1971)	$3	Multicolored	150.00	130.00	30.00	24.00	8.00	6.00
RW39 (1972)	$5	Multicolored	100.00	80.00	22.00	19.00	6.00	5.00
RW40 (1973)	$5	Multicolored	90.00	80.00	21.00	18.00	6.00	5.00
RW41 (1974)	$5	Multicolored	75.00	46.00	16.50	12.00	6.00	5.00
RW42 (1975)	$5	Multicolored	60.00	46.00	14.00	11.00	6.00	5.00
RW43 (1976)	$5	Emerald & Blk.........	58.00	46.00	14.00	11.00	6.00	4.50
RW44 (1977)	$5	Multicolored	58.00	46.00	16.00	13.00	6.00	4.50
RW45 (1978)	$5	Multicolored	58.00	46.00	14.00	13.00	6.00	4.50
RW46 (1979)	$7.50	Multicolored	60.00	44.00	16.00	14.00	6.00	4.50
RW47 (1980)	$7.50	Multicolored	60.00	44.00	16.00	14.00	6.00	4.50
RW48 (1981)	$7.50	Multicolored	60.00	44.00	16.00	14.00	6.00	4.50
RW49 (1982)	$7.50	Multicolored	60.00	44.00	17.00	15.00	6.00	4.50
RW50 (1983)	$7.50	Multicolored	60.00	44.00	17.00	15.00	6.00	4.50
RW51 (1984)	$7.50	Multicolored	60.00	44.00	17.00	15.00	6.00	4.50
RW52 (1985)	$7.50	Multicolored	60.00	44.00	17.00	15.00	6.00	4.50
RW53 (1986)	$7.50	Multicolored	60.00	44.00	17.00	15.00	6.00	4.50
RW54 (1987)	$10.00	Multicolored	70.00	54.00	20.00	16.00	10.00	7.00
RW55 (1988)	$10.00	Multicolored	70.00	54.00	20.00	16.00	10.00	7.00
RW56 (1989)	$12.50	Multicolored	85.00	60.00	21.00	17.00	11.00	8.00
RW57 (1990)	$12.50	Multicolored	85.00	60.00	21.00	17.00	11.00	8.00
RW58 (1991)	$15.00	Multicolored	135.00	90.00	30.00	20.00	14.00	10.00
RW59 (1992)	$15.00	Multicolored	135.00	90.00	30.00	20.00	14.00	10.00

Scott No.			Fine Unused Each	Ave. Unused Each	Fine Used Each	Ave. Used Each
HAWAIIAN ISSUES						
1851–1952. "MISSIONARIES"						
☐1	2¢	Blue				
☐		On Cover	—	450,000.00	—	190,000.00
☐2	5¢	Blue				425,000.00
☐		On Cover	—	30,000.00	—	16,000.00
☐3	13¢	Blue				26,000.00
☐		On Cover	—	18,000.00	—	9,000.00
☐4	13¢	Blue				15,000.00
☐		On Cover	—	42,000.00	—	20,000.00
						28,000.00

NOTE: Prices on the above classic stamps of Hawaii vary greatly depending on the individual specimen and circumstances of sale.

NOTE: Beware of fake cancels on Hawaiian stamps, when the value is higher used than unused.

			Fine Unused Each	Ave. Unused Each	Fine Used Each	Ave. Used Each
1853. KING KAMEHAMEHA III						
☐5	5¢	Blue	—	600.00	—	450.00
☐6	13¢	Dark Red	—	400.00	—	350.00
☐7	5¢ on 13¢ Dark Red		—	4200.00	—	4800.00
1857.						
☐8	5¢	Blue	—	300.00	—	300.00
1861.						
☐9	5¢	Blue	—	120.00	—	115.00
1868. RE-ISSUE						
☐10	5¢	Blue	—	30.00	—	—
☐11	13¢	Rose	—	200.00	—	—
1869–1862.						
☐12	1¢	Light Blue	—	2600.00	—	2900.00
☐13	2¢	Light Blue	—	2300.00	—	1300.00
☐14	2¢	Black	—	3000.00	—	1400.00
1863.						
☐15	1¢	Black	—	275.00	—	325.00
☐16	2¢	Black	—	400.00	—	340.00
☐17	2¢	Dark Blue	—	3800.00	—	2200.00
☐18	2¢	Black	—	700.00	—	1000.00
1864–1865.						
☐19	1¢	Black				
☐20	2¢	Black	—	300.00	—	600.00
☐21	5¢	Blue	—	350.00	—	500.00
☐22	5¢	Blue	—	300.00	—	250.00
			—	250.00	—	300.00
1864. LAID PAPER						
☐23	1¢	Black	130.00	100.00	650.00	600.00
☐24	2¢	Black	130.00	100.00	650.00	500.00

Scott No.			Fine Unused Each	Ave. Unused Each	Fine Used Each	Ave. Used Each
1865. WOVE PAPER						
☐25	1¢	Blue	160.00	100.00	145.00	125.00
☐26	2¢	Blue	150.00	90.00	145.00	125.00
☐27	2¢	Rose	165.00	120.00	120.00	110.00
☐28	2¢	Rose Vert	165.00	120.00	120.00	110.00
1869. ENGRAVED						
☐29	2¢	Red	60.00	36.00	—	—
1864–1871.						
☐30	1¢	Purple	8.00	5.00	5.00	4.00
☐31	2¢	Vermilion	9.50	6.00	6.00	4.00
☐32	5¢	Blue	60.00	39.00	15.00	10.00
☐33	6¢	Green	15.00	10.00	6.00	4.00
☐34	18¢	Rose	80.00	42.00	20.00	8.50
1875.						
☐35	2¢	Brown	6.00	3.00	2.50	1.60
☐36	12¢	Black	36.00	24.00	19.00	11.00
☐37	1¢	Blue	4.00	3.00	5.50	4.00
☐38	2¢	Lilac Rose	72.00	46.00	27.00	17.00
☐39	5¢	Ultramarine	11.00	7.00	1.80	1.10
☐40	10¢	Black	21.00	14.00	15.00	9.00
☐41	15¢	Red Brown	36.00	21.00	20.00	12.00
1883–1886.						
☐42	1¢	Green	2.00	1.30	1.45	.80
☐43	2¢	Rose	3.50	2.00	.85	.50
☐44	10¢	Red Brown	16.00	10.00	7.00	4.00
☐45	10¢	Vermilion	21.00	11.00	11.00	8.00
☐46	12¢	Red Lilac	50.00	33.00	28.00	17.00
☐47	25¢	Dark Violet	78.00	48.00	38.00	22.00
☐48	50¢	Red	120.00	80.00	68.00	44.00
☐49	$1	Rose Red	190.00	115.00	84.00	50.00
☐50	2¢	Orange	115.00	92.00	—	—
☐51	2¢	Carmine	20.00	15.00	—	—
1890–1891.						
☐52	2¢	Dull Violet	6.00	2.50	1.25	.75
☐52c	5¢	Dark Blue	90.00	58.00	75.00	45.00
1893. PROVISIONAL GOVT. RED OVERPRINT						
☐53	1¢	Purple	4.00	2.50	4.00	2.10
☐54	1¢	Blue	4.00	2.50	6.00	3.00
☐55	1¢	Green	1.60	.85	2.50	1.50
☐56	2¢	Brown	4.50	2.60	9.00	6.00
☐57	2¢	Dull Violet	1.40	.90	1.25	.90
☐58	5¢	Dark Blue	9.00	5.00	15.00	10.00
☐59	5¢	Ultramarine	5.00	2.75	3.00	2.00

Scott No.			Fine Unused Each	Ave. Unused Each	Fine Used Each	Ave. Used Each
☐60	6¢	Green	9.00	5.00	18.00	10.00
☐61	10¢	Black	7.00	4.00	8.50	4.50
☐62	12¢	Black	7.00	4.10	11.00	7.00
☐63	12¢	Red Lilac	110.00	62.00	145.00	85.00
☐64	25¢	Dark Violet	20.00	11.00	24.00	16.00

BLACK OVERPRINT

☐65	2¢	Vermilion	44.00	28.00	43.00	29.00
☐66	2¢	Rose	1.15	.80	2.50	1.40
☐67	10¢	Vermilion	9.00	6.00	18.00	11.00
☐68	10¢	Red Brown	6.00	4.00	9.00	5.00
☐69	12¢	Red Lilac	200.00	115.00	270.00	180.00
☐70	15¢	Red Brown	15.00	10.00	27.00	16.00
☐71	18¢	Dull Rose	10.00	11.00	30.00	18.00
☐72	50¢	Red	48.00	28.00	76.00	42.00
☐73	$1	Rose Red	92.00	58.00	135.00	75.00
☐74	1¢	Yellow	2.00	1.10	1.30	.80
☐75	2¢	Brown	2.00	1.10	.75	.46
☐76	5¢	Rose Lake	3.90	2.10	1.75	1.10
☐77	10¢	Yellow Green	5.00	2.90	4.50	3.00
☐78	12¢	Blue	9.50	5.90	11.00	7.00
☐79	25¢	Deep Blue	9.50	6.00	11.00	7.00

1899.

☐80	1¢	Dark Green	1.60	.95	1.25	.80
☐81	2¢	Rose	1.60	.95	1.25	.80
☐82	5¢	Blue	4.50	2.80	3.15	2.00

1896. OFFICIAL STAMPS

☐O1	2¢	Green	30.00	17.00	17.00	11.00
☐O2	5¢	Dark Brown	30.00	17.00	17.00	11.00
☐O3	6¢	Deep Ultramarine	32.00	19.00	17.00	11.00
☐O4	10¢	Rose	29.00	16.00	17.00	11.00
☐O5	12¢	Orange	52.00	32.00	17.00	11.00
☐O6	25¢	Gray Violet	70.00	42.00	18.00	12.00

Scott No.		Single	Block Of 4
	FIRST DAY COVER ISSUES UNCACHETED		
□551	¹/₂¢ Hale	14.00	18.00
□552	1¢ Franklin	24.00	36.00
□553	1¹/₂¢ Harding	26.00	40.00
□554	2¢ Washington	36.00	52.00
□555	3¢ Lincoln	32.00	46.00
□556	4¢ Martha Washington	54.00	76.00
□557	5¢ Roosevelt	115.00	150.00
□558	6¢ Garfield	140.00	200.00
□559	7¢ McKinley	130.00	190.00
□560	8¢ Grant	130.00	180.00
□561	9¢ Jefferson	130.00	180.00
□562	10¢ Monroe	130.00	170.00
□563	11¢ Hayes	610.00	850.00
□564	12¢ Cleveland	160.00	220.00
□565	14¢ Indian	310.00	450.00
□566	15¢ Statue of Liberty	400.00	—
□568	25¢ Niagara Falls	550.00	750.00
□569	30¢ Bison	615.00	850.00
□570	50¢ Arlington	900.00	—
□571	$1 Lincoln Memorial	5000.00	—
□572	$2 U.S. Capitol	10,000.00	—
□573	$5 America	14,000.00	—
□576	1¹/₂¢ Harding	42.00	58.00
□581	1¢ Franklin	1800.00	—
□582	1¹/₂¢ Harding	36.00	50.00
□583a	2¢ Washington	42.00	—
□584	3¢ Lincoln	46.00	65.00
□585	4¢ Martha Washington	46.00	—
□586	5¢ Roosevelt	47.00	—
□587	6¢ Garfield	56.00	70.00
□588	7¢ McKinley	70.00	90.00
□589	8¢ Grant	60.00	—
□590	9¢ Jefferson	65.00	90.00
□591	10¢ Monroe	85.00	—
□597	1¢ Franklin	550.00	—
□598	1¹/₂¢ Harding	40.00	52.00
□599	2¢ Washington	700.00	—
□600	3¢ Lincoln	65.00	110.00
□602	5¢ Roosevelt	70.00	95.00
□603	10¢ Monroe	85.00	120.00

Scott No.		Single	Block Of 4
□604	1¢ Franklin	76.00	100.00
□605	1¹/₂¢ Harding	48.00	70.00
□606	2¢ Washington	26.00	40.00
□610	2¢ Harding	24.00	34.00
□611	2¢ Harding	73.00	100.00
□612	2¢ Harding	85.00	120.00
□614	1¢ Huguenot-Walloon	28.00	39.00
□615	2¢ Huguenot-Walloon	28.00	39.00
□616	5¢ Huguenot-Walloon	58.00	—
□617	1¢ Lexington-Concord	24.00	—
□618	2¢ Lexington Concord	30.00	—
□619	5¢ Lexington-Concord	72.00	—
□620	2¢ Norse-American	21.00	—
□621	5¢ Norse-American	24.00	—
□622	13¢ Harrison	16.00	—
□623	17¢ Wilson	17.00	—
□627	2¢ Sesquicenten-nial	9.00	14.00
□628	5¢ Erikson	13.00	17.00
□629	2¢ White Plains	6.00	10.00
□630	2¢ White Plains Sheet	11.00	—
□631	1¹/₂¢ Harding	32.00	80.00
□632	1¢ Franklin	42.00	58.00
□633	1¹/₂¢ Harding	42.00	58.00
□634	2¢ Washington	45.00	62.00
□635	3¢ Lincoln	40.00	55.00
□635a	3¢ Bright Violet	16.00	21.00
□636	4¢ Martha Washington	43.00	—
□637	5¢ Roosevelt	44.00	60.00
□638	6¢ Garfield	52.00	70.00
□639	7¢ McKinley	50.00	72.00
□640	8¢ Grant	55.00	76.00
□641	9¢ Jefferson	72.00	90.00
□642	10¢ Monroe	70.00	95.00
□643	2¢ Vermont	5.00	6.50
□644	2¢ Burgoyne	8.00	9.50
□645	2¢ Valley Forge	4.00	6.00
□646	2¢ Molly Pitcher	10.00	14.00
□647	2¢ Hawaii	13.00	18.00
□648	5¢ Hawaii	18.00	21.00
□649	2¢ Aero Conf.	6.00	8.00

Scott No.		Single	Block Of 4
☐650	5¢ Aero Conf.	8.00	11.00
☐651	2¢ Clark	5.00	8.00
☐653	½¢ Hale	28.00	36.00
☐654	2¢ Electric Light	8.00	11.00
☐655	2¢ Electric Light	70.00	90.00
☐656	2¢ Electric Light	110.00	—
☐657	2¢ Sullivan	4.00	6.00
☐658	1¢ Kansas	30.00	42.00
☐659	1½¢ Kansas	30.00	60.00
☐660	2¢ Kansas	32.00	61.00
☐661	3¢ Kansas	38.00	54.00
☐662	4¢ Kansas	43.00	62.00
☐663	5¢ Kansas	43.00	62.00
☐664	6¢ Kansas	55.00	65.00
☐665	7¢ Kansas	60.00	90.00
☐666	8¢ Kansas	75.00	110.00
☐667	9¢ Kansas	85.00	115.00
☐668	10¢ Kansas	100.00	140.00
☐669	1¢ Nebraska	30.00	40.00
☐670	1½¢ Nebraska	32.00	—
☐671	2¢ Nebraska	32.00	45.00
☐672	3¢ Nebraska	38.00	52.00
☐673	4¢ Nebraska	42.00	60.00
☐674	5¢ Nebraska	43.00	62.00
☐675	6¢ Nebraska	60.00	85.00
☐676	7¢ Nebraska	64.00	90.00
☐677	8¢ Nebraska	72.00	100.00
☐678	9¢ Nebraska	85.00	110.00
☐679	10¢ Nebraska	100.00	140.00
☐680	2¢ Fallen Timbers	3.10	5.00
☐681	2¢ Ohio River	3.10	5.00
☐682	2¢ Massachusetts Bay Colony	3.10	5.00
☐683	2¢ Carolina-Charleston	3.10	5.00
☐684	1½¢ Harding	4.00	5.50
☐685	4¢ Taft	5.50	7.50
☐686	1½¢ Harding	4.00	6.00
☐687	4¢ Taft	24.00	
☐688	2¢ Braddock	3.75	6.00
☐689	2¢ Von Steuben	3.40	5.00
☐690	2¢ Pulaski	3.50	5.00
☐692	11¢ Hayes	82.00	115.00
☐693	12¢ Cleveland	82.00	115.00
☐694	13¢ Harrison	82.00	115.00
☐695	14¢ Indian	90.00	125.00
☐696	15¢ Liberty	110.00	150.00
☐697	17¢ Wilson	290.00	—
☐698	20¢ Golden Gate	260.00	—

Scott No.		Single	Block Of 4
☐699	25¢ Niagara Falls	310.00	—
☐700	30¢ Bison	220.00	—
☐701	50¢ Arlington	350.00	—
☐702	2¢ Red Cross	3.00	4.00
☐703	2¢ Yorktown	3.00	5.00
☐704	½¢ Olive Brown	14.50	18.00
☐705	1¢ Green	14.50	18.00
☐706	1½¢ Brown	14.50	18.00
☐707	2¢ Carmine Rose	14.50	18.00
☐708	3¢ Deep Violet	14.50	18.00
☐709	4¢ Light Brown	14.50	18.00
☐710	5¢ Blue	14.50	18.00
☐711	6¢ Red Orange	14.50	18.00
☐712	7¢ Black	16.50	20.00
☐713	8¢ Olive Bistre	16.50	20.00
☐714	9¢ Pale Red	16.50	20.00
☐715	10¢ Orange Yellow	16.50	20.00
☐716	2¢ Olympic Winter Games	21.00	23.00
☐717	2¢ Arbor Day	16.00	21.00
☐718	3¢ Olympic Summer Games	21.00	26.00
☐719	5¢ Olympic Summer Games	23.00	35.00
☐720	3¢ Washington	33.00	42.00
☐721	3¢ Washington (coil)	34.00	—
☐722	3¢ Washington (coil)	34.00	—
☐723	6¢ garfield (coil)	34.00	—
☐724	3¢ William Penn	11.00	15.00
☐725	3¢ Daniel Webster	11.00	15.00
☐726	3¢ Gen. Oglethorpe	11.00	15.00
☐727	3¢ Peace Proclamation	12.00	16.00
☐728	1¢ Century of Progress	12.00	16.00
☐729	3¢ Century of Progress	12.00	16.00
☐730	1¢ American Philatelic Society, full sheet on cover	165.00	—
☐730a	1¢ American Philatelic Society	12.00	16.00
☐731	3¢ American Philatelic Society	150.00	—
☐731a	3¢ American Philatelic Society	12.00	16.00

Scott No.		Single	Block Of 4
☐732	3¢ National Recovery Administration	16.00	22.00
☐733	3¢ Byrd Antarctic	24.00	30.00
☐734	5¢ Kosciuszko	18.00	26.00
☐735	3¢ National Exhibition	48.00	—
☐735a	3¢ National Exhibition	16.00	—
☐736	3¢ Maryland Tercentenary	11.00	16.00
☐737	3¢ Mothers of America	11.00	16.00
☐738	3¢ Mothers of America	11.00	16.00
☐739	3¢ Wisconsin	11.00	16.00
☐740	1¢ Parks, Yosemite	11.00	16.00
☐741	2¢ Parks, Grand Canyon	11.00	16.00
☐742	3¢ Parks, Mt. Rainier	11.00	16.00
☐743	4¢ Parks, Mesa Verde	11.00	16.00
☐744	5¢ Parks, Yellowstone	11.00	16.00
☐745	6¢ Parks, Crater Lake	11.00	16.00
☐746	7¢ Parks, Acadia	11.00	16.00
☐747	8¢ Parks, Zion	11.00	16.00
☐748	9¢ Parks, Glacier Park	11.00	16.00
☐749	10¢ Parks, Smoky Mountains	11.00	16.00
☐750	3¢ American Philatelic Society, full sheet on cover	48.00	—
☐750a	3¢ American Philatelic Society	11.00	16.00
☐751	1¢ Trans-Mississippi Philatelic Expo, full sheet on cover	50.00	—
☐751a	1¢ Trans-Mississippi Philatelic Expo	11.00	16.00
☐752	3¢ Peace Commemoration	36.00	50.00
☐753	3¢ Byrd	36.00	50.00
☐754	3¢ Mothers of America	36.00	50.00
☐755	3¢ Wisconsin	36.00	50.00
☐756	1¢ Parks, Yosemite	21.00	26.00

Scott No.		Single	Block Of 4
☐757	2¢ Parks, Grand Canyon	21.00	25.00
☐758	3¢ Parks, Mount Ranier	21.00	25.00
☐759	4¢ Parks, Mesa Verde	21.00	25.00
☐760	5¢ Parks, Yellowstone	21.00	25.00
☐761	6¢ Parks, Crater Lake	24.00	32.00
☐762	7¢ Parks, Acadia	24.00	32.00
☐763	8¢ Parks, Zion	24.00	32.00
☐764	9¢ Parks, Glacier Park	24.00	32.00
☐765	10¢ Parks, Smoky Mountains	24.00	32.00
☐766a	1¢ Century of Progress	38.00	54.00
☐767a	3¢ Century of Progress	38.00	54.00
☐768a	3¢ Byrd	38.00	54.00
☐769a	1¢ Parks, Yosemite	38.00	54.00
☐770a	3¢ Parks, Mount Ranier	38.00	54.00
☐771	16¢ Airmail, special delivery	38.00	54.00

FIRST DAY COVER ISSUES CACHETED

Scott No.		Single	Block Of 4
☐610	2¢ Harding	650.00	—
☐617	1¢ Lexington-Concord	130.00	—
☐618	2¢ Lexington-Concord	130.00	—
☐619	5¢ Lexington-Concord	172.00	—
☐623	17¢ Wilson	280.00	—
☐627	2¢ Sesquicentennial	62.00	—
☐628	5¢ Erikson	425.00	- -
☐629	2¢ White Plains	48.00	—
☐630	2¢ White Plains Sheet	1200.00	—
☐635a	3¢ Bright Violet	42.00	—
☐643	2¢ Vermont	48.00	70.00
☐644	2¢ Burgoyne	52.00	80.00
☐645	2¢ Valley Forge	42.00	60.00

Scott No.		Single	Block Of 4
☐646	2¢ Molly Pitcher	82.00	—
☐647	2¢ Hawaii	52.00	70.00
☐648	5¢ Hawaii	62.00	85.00
☐649	2¢ Aero Conf.	32.00	45.00
☐650	5¢ Aero Conf.	34.00	42.00
☐651	2¢ Clark	29.00	42.00
☐654	2¢ Electric Light	29.00	42.00
☐655	2¢ Electric Light	166.00	—
☐656	2¢ Electric Light	250.00	—
☐657	2¢ Sullivan, Auburn N.Y.	28.00	43.00
☐680	2¢ Fallen Timbers	28.00	43.00
☐681	2¢ Ohio River	28.00	40.00
☐682	2¢ Massachusetts Bay Colony	32.00	46.00
☐683	2¢ California-Charleston	32.00	46.00
☐684	1½¢ Harding	32.00	46.00
☐685	4¢ Taft	42.00	60.00
☐686	1½¢ Harding	36.00	50.00
☐687	4¢ Taft	76.00	90.00
☐688	2¢ Braddock	29.00	42.00
☐689	2¢ Von Steuben	29.00	42.00
☐690	2¢ Pulaski	29.00	42.00
☐702	2¢ Red Cross	24.00	32.00
☐703	2¢ Yorktown	36.00	50.00
☐704	1½¢ Olive Brown	14.00	18.00
☐705	1¢ Green	14.00	18.00
☐706	1½¢ Brown	14.00	18.00
☐707	2¢ Carmine Rose	14.00	18.00
☐708	3¢ Deep Violet	14.00	18.00
☐709	4¢ Light Brown	14.00	18.00
☐710	5¢ Blue	14.00	18.00
☐711	6¢ Red Orange	14.00	18.00
☐712	7¢ Black	14.00	18.00
☐713	8¢ Olive Bistre	18.00	25.00
☐714	9¢ Pale Red	18.00	25.00
☐715	10¢ Orange Yellow	18.00	25.00
☐716	2¢ Olympic Winter Games	21.00	30.00
☐717	2¢ Arbor Day	16.00	24.00
☐718	3¢ Olympic Summer Games	21.00	30.00
☐719	5¢ Olympic Summer Games	21.00	30.00
☐720	3¢ Washington	34.00	42.00
☐720b	3¢ Booklet pane	140.00	—
☐721	3¢ Washington (coil)	36.00	—

Scott No.		Single	Block Of 4
☐722	3¢ Washington (coil)	36.00	—
☐723	6¢ Garfield (coil)	36.00	—
☐724	3¢ William Penn	16.00	22.00
☐725	3¢ Daniel Webster	16.00	22.00
☐726	3¢ Gen. Oglethorpe	16.00	22.00
☐727	3¢ Peace Proclamation	16.00	22.00
☐728	1¢ Century of Progress	16.00	22.00
☐729	3¢ Century of Progress	16.00	22.00
☐730	1¢ American Philatelic Society, full sheet on cover	170.00	—
☐730a	1¢ American Philatelic Society	15.00	21.00
☐731	3¢ American Philatelic Society	165.00	—
☐731a	3¢ American Philatelic Society	15.00	21.00
☐732	3¢ National Recovery Administration	16.00	22.00
☐733	3¢ Byrd Antarctic	26.00	36.00
☐734	5¢ Kosciuszko	21.00	29.00
☐735	3¢ National Exhibition	52.00	—
☐735a	3¢ National Exhibition	16.00	—
☐736	3¢ Maryland Tercentenary	11.00	15.00
☐737	3¢ Mothers of America	11.00	15.00
☐738	3¢ Mothers of America	11.00	15.00
☐739	2¢ Wisconsin	11.00	15.00
☐740	1¢ Parks, Yosemite	11.00	15.00
☐741	2¢ Parks, Grand Canyon	11.00	15.00
☐742	35¢ Parks, Mt. Ranier	11.00	15.00
☐743	4¢ Parks, Mesa Verde	11.00	15.00
☐744	5¢ Parks, Yellowstone	11.00	15.00
☐745	6¢ Parks, Crater Lake	11.00	15.00
☐746	7¢ Parks, Acadia	11.00	15.00
☐747	8¢ Parks, Zion	11.00	15.00

Scott No.			Single	Block Of 4
☐748	9¢	Parks, Glacier Park	11.00	15.00
☐749	10¢	Parks, Smoky Mountains	11.00	15.00
☐750	3¢	American Philatelic Society, full sheet on cover	48.00	—
☐750a	3¢	American Philatelic Society	12.00	17.00
☐751	1¢	Trans-Mississippi Philatelic Expo., full sheet on cover	48.00	—
☐751a	1¢	Trans-Mississippi Philatelic Expo.	12.00	17.00
☐752	3¢	Peace Commemoration	36.00	42.00
☐753	3¢	Byrd	36.00	42.00
☐754	3¢	Mothers of America	36.00	42.00
☐755	3¢	Wisconsin Tercentenary	34.00	40.00
☐756	1¢	Parks, Yosemite	21.00	28.00
☐757	2¢	Parks, Grand Canyon	21.00	28.00

Scott No.			Single	Block Of 4
☐758	3¢	Parks, Mount Rainier	21.00	28.00
☐759	4¢	Parks, Mesa Verde	21.00	28.00
☐760	5¢	Parks, Yellowstone	21.00	28.00
☐761	6¢	Parks, Crater Lake	21.00	28.00
☐762	7¢	Parks, Acadia	21.00	28.00
☐763	8¢	Parks, Zion	21.00	28.00
☐764	9¢	Parks, Glacier Park	21.00	28.00
☐765	10¢	Parks, Smoky Mountains	21.00	28.00
☐766a	1¢	Century of Progress	42.00	58.00
☐767a	3¢	Century of Progress	42.00	58.00
☐768a	3¢	Byrd	42.00	58.00
☐769a	1¢	Parks, Yosemite	42.00	58.00
☐770a	3¢	Parks, Mount Rainier	42.00	58.00
☐771	16¢	Airmail, special delivery	42.00	58.00

Scott No.			Single	Block	Plate Block
☐772	3¢	Connecticut Tercentenary	6.50	8.50	15.00
☐773	3¢	California Exposition	7.00	8.50	15.00
☐774	3¢	Boulder Dam	7.00	10.00	15.00
☐775	3¢	Michigan Centenary	6.50	8.50	15.00
☐776	3¢	Texas Centennial	10.00	14.00	20.00
☐777	3¢	Rhode Island Tercentenary	6.50	8.50	15.00
☐778	3¢	TIPEX	14.00	19.00	—
☐782	3¢	Arkansas Centennial	6.50	8.50	15.00
☐783	3¢	Oregon Territory	6.50	8.50	15.00
☐784	3¢	Susan B. Anthony	6.50	8.50	15.00
☐785	1¢	Army	5.00	7.00	11.00
☐786	2¢	Army	5.00	7.00	11.00
☐787	3¢	Army	5.00	7.00	11.00
☐788	5¢	Army	5.00	7.00	11.00
☐790	1¢	Navy	5.00	7.00	11.00
☐791	2¢	Navy	5.00	7.00	11.00
☐792	3¢	Navy	5.00	7.00	11.00
☐793	4¢	Navy	5.00	7.00	11.00
☐794	5¢	Navy	5.00	7.00	11.00
☐795	3¢	Ordinance of 1787	6.50	7.00	14.00
☐796	5¢	Virginia Dare	6.50	7.00	14.00
☐797	10¢	Souvenir Sheet	6.50	—	—

Scott No.			Single	Block	Plate Block
□798	3¢	Constitution	6.00	8.00	14.00
□799	3¢	Hawaii	6.00	8.00	14.00
□800	3¢	Alaska	6.00	8.00	14.00
□801	3¢	Puerto Rico	6.00	8.00	14.00
□802	3¢	Virgin Islands	6.00	8.00	14.00
□803	½¢	Franklin	2.50	3.00	5.50
□804	1¢	Washington	2.50	3.00	5.50
□805	1½¢	Martha Washington	2.35	3.00	5.50
□806	2¢	Adams	2.35	3.00	5.50
□807	3¢	Jefferson	2.35	3.00	5.50
□808	4¢	Madison	2.35	3.00	5.50
□809	4½¢	White House	2.35	3.50	5.50
□810	5¢	Monroe	2.35	3.50	5.50
□811	6¢	Adams	2.35	3.50	5.50
□812	7¢	Jackson	2.35	3.50	5.50
□813	8¢	VanBuren	2.35	3.50	5.50
□814	9¢	Harrison	2.35	3.50	5.50
□815	10¢	Tyler	2.35	4.10	6.25
□816	11¢	Polk	2.50	4.10	6.25
□817	12¢	Taylor	2.50	4.10	6.25
□818	13¢	Fillmore	2.50	4.10	6.25
□819	14¢	Pierce	2.50	4.10	6.25
□820	15¢	Buchanan	2.50	4.10	6.25
□821	16¢	Lincoln	3.50	4.10	7.50
□822	17¢	Johnson	3.50	4.10	7.50
□823	18¢	Grant	3.50	4.10	7.50
□824	19¢	Hayes	3.50	4.10	7.50
□825	20¢	Garfield	4.00	4.10	7.50
□826	21¢	Arthur	4.00	6.00	11.50
□827	22¢	Cleveland	4.00	6.00	11.50
□828	24¢	Harrison	4.00	6.00	11.50
□829	25¢	McKinley	6.00	7.25	13.00
□830	30¢	Roosevelt	13.00	16.00	25.00
□831	50¢	Taft	65.00	75.00	126.00
□832	$1	Wilson	32.00	43.00	72.00
□832c	$1	Wilson	120.00	185.00	250.00
□833	$2	Harding	200.00	225.00	360.00
□834	$5	Coolidge	5.50	8.00	11.50
□835	3¢	Constitution	5.50	8.00	11.50
□836	3¢	Swedes and Finns	5.50	8.00	11.50
□837	3¢	Northwest Sesquicentennial	5.50	8.00	11.50
□838	3¢	Iowa	5.50	8.00	11.50
□852	3¢	Golden Gate Expo	5.50	8.00	11.50
□853	3¢	N.Y. World's Fair	5.50	8.00	11.50
□854	3¢	Washington Inauguration	27.00	30.00	43.00
□855	3¢	Baseball Centennial	5.50	8.00	11.00
□856	3¢	Panama Canal	5.50	8.00	11.00
□857	3¢	Printing Tercentenary			

Scott No.			Single	Block	Plate Block
☐858	3¢	50th Statehood Anniversary	5.50	7.00	11.00
☐859	1¢	Washington Irving	2.50	3.50	5.00
☐860	2¢	James Fenimore Cooper	2.50	3.50	5.00
☐861	3¢	Ralph Waldo Emerson	2.50	3.50	5.00
☐862	5¢	Louisa May Alcott	3.50	4.00	5.50
☐863	10¢	Samuel L. Clemens	5.00	6.00	7.00
☐864	1¢	Henry W. Longfellow	2.50	3.50	5.00
☐865	2¢	John Greenleaf Whittier	2.50	3.50	5.00
☐866	3¢	James Russell Lowell	2.50	3.50	5.00
☐867	5¢	Walt Whitman	3.50	4.00	6.00
☐868	10¢	James Whitcomb Riley	6.00	7.50	12.00
☐869	1¢	Horace Mann	2.50	3.50	5.00
☐870	2¢	Mark Hopkins	2.50	3.50	5.00
☐871	3¢	Charles W. Eliot	2.50	3.50	5.00
☐872	5¢	Frances E. Willard	3.50	4.50	6.00
☐873	10¢	Booker T. Washington	8.50	11.00	16.00
☐874	1¢	John James Audubon	2.50	3.50	5.00
☐875	2¢	Dr. Crawford W. Long	2.50	3.50	5.00
☐876	3¢	Luther Burbank	2.50	3.50	5.00
☐877	5¢	Dr. Walter Reed	3.50	4.50	7.00
☐878	10¢	Jane Addams	5.50	8.50	11.00
☐879	1¢	Stephen Collins Foster	2.50	3.50	5.00
☐880	2¢	John Philip Sousa	2.50	3.50	5.00
☐881	3¢	Victor Herbert	2.50	3.50	5.00
☐882	5¢	Edward A. MacDowell	3.75	5.00	7.00
☐883	10¢	Ethelbert Nevin	4.50	8.00	11.00
☐884	1¢	Gilbert Charles Stuart	2.50	3.50	5.00
☐885	2¢	James A. McNeill Whistler	2.50	3.50	5.00
☐886	3¢	Augustus Saint-Gaudens	2.50	3.50	5.00
☐887	5¢	Daniel Chester French	3.50	4.50	7.00
☐888	10¢	Frederic Remington	4.50	8.00	11.00
☐889	1¢	Eli Whitney	2.50	3.50	5.00
☐890	2¢	Samuel F.B. Morse	2.50	3.50	5.00
☐891	3¢	Cyrus Hall McCormick	2.50	3.50	5.00
☐892	5¢	Elias Howe	3.50	4.50	7.50
☐893	10¢	Alexander Graham Bell	7.00	8.50	15.00
☐894	3¢	Pony Express	4.50	7.00	9.00
☐895	3¢	Pan American Union	4.50	7.00	9.00
☐896	3¢	Idaho Statehood	4.50	7.00	9.00
☐897	3¢	Wyoming Statehood	4.50	7.00	9.00
☐898	3¢	Coronado Expedition	4.50	7.00	9.00
☐899	1¢	Defense	3.50	4.50	7.00
☐900	2¢	Defense	3.50	4.50	7.00
☐901	3¢	Defense	3.50	4.50	7.00
☐902	3¢	Thirteenth Amendment	5.00	6.50	10.00
☐903	3¢	Vermont Statehood	4.50	6.00	9.00
☐904	3¢	Kentucky Statehood	3.50	4.50	7.00
☐905	3¢	"Win the War"	2.50	3.50	7.00

Scott No.			Single	Block	Plate Block
☐906	5¢	Chinese Commemorative	8.50	10.00	15.00
☐907	2¢	United Nations	3.50	5.00	7.00
☐908	1¢	Four Freedoms	4.50	5.00	10.00
☐909	5¢	Poland	4.50	5.25	11.00
☐910	5¢	Czechoslovakia	3.40	5.25	8.50
☐911	5¢	Norway	3.40	5.25	8.50
☐912	5¢	Luxembourg	3.40	5.25	8.50
☐913	5¢	Netherlands	3.40	5.25	8.50
☐914	5¢	Belgium	3.40	5.25	8.50
☐915	5¢	France	3.40	5.25	8.50
☐916	5¢	Greece	3.40	5.25	8.50
☐917	5¢	Yugoslavia	3.40	5.25	8.50
☐918	5¢	Albania	3.40	5.25	8.50
☐919	5¢	Austria	3.40	5.25	8.50
☐920	5¢	Denmark	3.40	5.25	8.50
☐921	5¢	Korea	3.40	5.25	8.50
☐922	3¢	Railroad	4.00	5.00	7.00
☐923	3¢	Steamship	3.00	4.50	7.00
☐924	3¢	Telegraph	3.00	4.50	7.00
☐925	3¢	Philippines	3.00	4.50	6.00
☐926	3¢	Motion Picture	3.00	4.50	6.00
☐927	3¢	Florida	3.00	4.50	6.00
☐928	5¢	United Nations Conference	5.00	6.00	9.50
☐929	3¢	Iwo Jima	2.90	4.50	5.50
☐930	1¢	Roosevelt	2.90	4.50	5.50
☐931	2¢	Roosevelt	2.90	4.50	5.50
☐932	3¢	Roosevelt	2.90	4.50	5.50
☐933	3¢	Roosevelt	2.90	4.50	5.50
☐934	3¢	Army	2.90	4.50	5.50
☐935	3¢	Navy	3.50	4.50	6.00
☐936	3¢	Coast Guard	3.50	4.50	6.00
☐937	3¢	Alfred E. Smith	3.50	4.50	6.00
☐938	3¢	Texas	2.90	4.50	6.00
☐939	3¢	Merchant Marine	2.90	4.50	6.00
☐940	3¢	Honorable Discharge	2.90	4.50	6.00
☐941	3¢	Tennessee	2.90	4.50	6.00
☐942	3¢	Iowa	2.90	4.50	6.00
☐943	3¢	Smithsonian	2.90	4.50	6.00
☐944	3¢	Santa Fe	2.90	4.50	6.00
☐945	3¢	Thomas A. Edison	2.90	4.50	6.00
☐946	3¢	Joseph Pulitzer	2.90	4.50	6.00
☐947	3¢	Stamp Centenary	2.90	4.50	6.00
☐948	5¢ and 10¢	Centenary Exhibition Sheet	3.50	—	—
☐949	3¢	Doctors	3.50	4.50	6.00
☐950	3¢	Utah	2.90	4.50	6.00
☐951	3¢	"Constitution"	3.50	4.50	6.00
☐952	3¢	Everglades Park	2.90	4.50	6.00
☐953	3¢	Carver	2.90	4.50	6.00

Scott No.			Single	Block	Plate Block
☐954	3¢	California Gold	2.25	3.75	4.50
☐955	3¢	Mississippi Territory	2.25	3.75	4.50
☐956	3¢	Four Chaplains	2.25	3.75	4.50
☐957	3¢	Wisconsin Centennial	2.25	3.75	4.50
☐958	5¢	Swedish Pioneers	2.25	3.75	4.50
☐959	3¢	Women's Progress	2.25	3.75	4.50
☐960	3¢	William Allen White	2.25	3.75	4.50
☐961	3¢	U.S.-Canada Friendship	2.25	3.75	4.50
☐962	3¢	Francis Scott Key	2.50	3.75	5.00
☐963	3¢	Salute to Youth	2.25	3.75	4.50
☐964	3¢	Oregon Territory	2.25	3.75	4.50
☐965	3¢	Harlan Fiske Stone	2.25	3.75	4.50
☐966	3¢	Palomar Observatory	2.50	3.75	4.50
☐967	3¢	Clara Barton	2.75	4.00	5.50
☐968	3¢	Poultry Industry	2.25	3.75	4.50
☐969	3¢	Gold Star Mothers	2.25	3.75	4.50
☐970	3¢	Volunteer Fireman	2.25	3.75	4.50
☐972	3¢	Indian Centennial	2.25	3.75	4.50
☐973	3¢	Rough Riders	2.25	3.50	4.50
☐974	3¢	Juliette Low	3.50	4.50	7.00
☐975	3¢	Will Rogers	2.25	3.50	4.50
☐976	3¢	Fort Bliss	3.00	4.75	6.00
☐977	3¢	Moina Michael	2.25	3.50	4.50
☐978	3¢	Gettysburg Address	3.00	3.50	6.00
☐979	3¢	American Turners Society	2.25	3.50	4.50
☐980	3¢	Joel Chandler Harris	2.25	3.50	4.50
☐981	3¢	Minnesota Territory	1.95	3.50	4.00
☐982	3¢	Washington and Lee University	1.95	3.50	4.00
☐983	3¢	Puerto Rico Election	1.95	3.50	4.00
☐984	3¢	Annapolis, Md.	1.95	3.50	4.00
☐985	3¢	G.A.R.	1.95	3.50	4.00
☐986	3¢	Edgar Allan Poe	2.25	3.75	4.50
☐987	3¢	American Bankers Association	1.95	3.50	4.00
☐988	3¢	Samuel Gompers	1.95	3.50	4.00
☐990	3¢	Nat. Capital Sesqui. (Executive)	1.95	3.50	4.00
☐991	3¢	Nat. Capital Sesqui. (Judicial)	1.95	3.50	4.00
☐992	3¢	Nat. Capital Sesqui. (Legislative)	1.95	3.50	4.00
☐993	3¢	Railroad Engineers	1.95	3.00	4.00
☐994	3¢	Kansas City Centenary	1.95	3.00	4.00
☐995	3¢	Boy Scout	3.50	4.00	7.00
☐996	3¢	Indiana Ter. Sesquicentennial	1.90	3.00	4.00
☐997	3¢	California Statehood	1.90	3.00	4.00
☐998	3¢	United Confederate Veterans	1.90	3.00	4.00
☐999	3¢	Nevada Centennial	1.90	3.00	4.00
☐1000	3¢	Landing of Cadillac	1.90	3.00	4.00
☐1001	3¢	Colorado Statehood	1.90	3.00	4.00
☐1002	3¢	American Chemical Society	1.90	3.00	4.00
☐1003	3¢	Battle of Brooklyn	1.90	3.00	4.00

Scott No.			Single	Block	Plate Block
☐1004	3¢	Betsy Ross	2.40	3.50	5.00
☐1005	3¢	4-H Clubs	1.90	3.50	4.00
☐1006	3¢	B & O Railroad	1.90	3.50	4.00
☐1007	3¢	American Automobile Assoc.	1.90	3.50	4.00
☐1008	3¢	NATO	1.90	3.50	4.00
☐1009	3¢	Grand Coulee Dam	1.90	3.50	4.00
☐1010	3¢	Lafayette	1.90	3.50	4.00
☐1011	3¢	Mt. Rushmore Memorial	1.90	3.50	4.00
☐1012	3¢	Civil Engineers	1.90	3.50	4.00
☐1013	3¢	Service Women	1.90	3.50	4.00
☐1014	3¢	Gutenberg Bible	1.90	3.50	4.00
☐1015	3¢	Newspaper boys	1.90	3.50	4.00
☐1016	3¢	Red Cross	1.90	3.50	4.00
☐1017	3¢	National Guard	1.90	3.50	4.00
☐1018	3¢	Ohio Sesquicentennial	1.90	3.50	4.00
☐1019	3¢	Washington Territory	1.90	3.50	4.00
☐1020	3¢	Louisiana Purchase	1.90	3.50	4.00
☐1021	5¢	Opening of Japan	1.90	3.50	4.00
☐1022	3¢	American Bar Association	1.90	3.50	4.00
☐1023	3¢	Sagamore Hill	1.90	3.50	4.00
☐1024	3¢	Future Farmers	1.90	3.50	4.00
☐1025	3¢	Trucking Industry	1.90	3.50	4.00
☐1026	3¢	Gen. G.S. Patton, Jr.	1.90	3.50	4.00
☐1027	3¢	New York City	1.90	3.50	4.00
☐1028	3¢	Gadsden Purchase	1.90	3.50	4.00
☐1029	3¢	Columbia University	1.90	3.50	4.00
☐1030	½¢	Franklin	1.90	3.50	4.00
☐1031	1¢	Washington	1.90	3.50	4.00
☐1031a	1¼¢	Palace	1.90	3.50	4.00
☐1032	1½¢	Mount Vernon	1.90	3.50	4.00
☐1033	2¢	Jefferson	1.90	3.50	4.00
☐1034	2½¢	Bunker Hill	1.90	3.50	4.00
☐1035	3¢	Statue of Liberty	1.90	3.50	4.00
☐1036	4¢	Lincoln	1.90	3.50	4.00
☐1037	4½¢	Hermitage	1.90	3.50	4.00
☐1038	5¢	Monroe	1.90	3.50	4.00
☐1039	6¢	Roosevelt	1.90	3.50	4.00
☐1040	7¢	Wilson	1.90	3.50	4.00
☐1041	8¢	Statue of Liberty	1.90	3.50	4.00
☐1042	8¢	Statue of Liberty	1.90	3.50	4.00
☐1042a	8¢	Pershing	3.00	4.50	6.00
☐1043	9¢	The Alamo	2.10	3.50	4.50
☐1044	10¢	Independence Hall	2.10	3.50	4.50
☐1045	12¢	Harrison	2.10	3.50	4.50
☐1046	15¢	John Jay	2.75	3.75	5.50
☐1046a	15¢	John Jay	2.30	3.60	5.00
☐1047	20¢	Monticello	2.75	3.60	5.50
☐1048	25¢	Paul Revere	2.75	3.60	5.50

Scott No.			Single	Block	Plate Block
☐1049	30¢	Robert E. Lee	3.00	4.00	6.00
☐1050	40¢	John Marshall	4.00	6.00	8.00
☐1051	50¢	Susan Anthony	5.00	7.00	10.00
☐1052	$1	Patrick Henry	7.50	10.00	16.00
☐1053	$5	Alexander Hamilton	48.00	75.00	100.00
☐1054	1¢	Washington	1.90	—	—
☐1055	2¢	Jefferson	1.90	—	—
☐1056	2½¢	Bunker Hill	1.90	—	—
☐1057	3¢	Statue of Liberty	1.90	—	—
☐1058	4¢	Lincoln	1.90	—	—
☐1059	4½¢	The Hermitage	1.90	—	—
☐1059a	25¢	Paul Revere	3.00	—	—
☐1059b	25¢	Tagged	24.00	—	—
☐1060	3¢	Nebraska Territory	1.90	3.00	4.00
☐1061	3¢	Kansas Territory	1.90	3.00	4.00
☐1062	3¢	George Eastman	1.90	3.00	4.00
☐1063	3¢	Lewis & Clark	1.90	3.00	4.00
☐1064	3¢	Pennsylvania Academy of the Fine Arts	1.90	3.00	4.00
☐1065	3¢	Land Grant Colleges	2.75	3.00	4.00
☐1066	8¢	Rotary International	2.75	3.00	4.00
☐1067	3¢	Armed Forces Reserve	2.10	3.00	4.00
☐1068	3¢	New Hampshire	1.90	3.00	4.00
☐1069	3¢	Soo Locks	1.90	3.00	4.00
☐1070	3¢	Atoms for Peace	1.90	3.00	4.00
☐1071	3¢	Fort Ticonderoga	1.90	3.00	4.00
☐1072	3¢	Andrew W. Mellon	1.90	3.00	4.00
☐1073	3¢	Benjamin Franklin	1.90	3.00	4.00
☐1074	3¢	Booker T. Washington	1.90	3.00	4.00
☐1075	3¢, 8¢	FIPEX Souvenir Sheet	4.50	3.00	4.00
☐1076	3¢	FIPEX	1.90	3.00	4.00
☐1077	3¢	Wildlife (Turkey)	1.90	3.00	4.00
☐1078	3¢	Wildlife (Antelope)	1.90	3.00	4.00
☐1079	3¢	Wildlife (Salmon)	1.90	3.00	4.00
☐1080	3¢	Pure Food and Drug Laws	1.90	3.00	4.00
☐1081	3¢	Wheatland	1.90	3.00	4.00
☐1082	3¢	Labor Day	1.90	3.00	4.00
☐1083	3¢	Nassau Hall	1.90	3.00	4.00
☐1084	3¢	Devils Tower	1.90	3.00	4.00
☐1085	3¢	Children	1.90	3.00	4.00
☐1086	3¢	Alexander Hamilton	1.90	3.00	4.00
☐1087	3¢	Polio	1.90	3.00	4.00
☐1088	3¢	Coast & Geodetic Survey	1.90	3.00	4.00
☐1089	3¢	Architects	1.90	3.00	4.00
☐1090	3¢	Steel Industry	1.90	3.00	4.00
☐1091	3¢	Naval Review	1.90	3.00	4.00
☐1092	3¢	Oklahoma Statehood	1.80	3.00	4.00
☐1093	3¢	School Teachers	1.80	3.00	4.00
☐1094	4¢	Flag			

Scott No.			Single	Block	Plate Block
☐1095	3¢	Shipbuilding	1.80	2.90	4.00
☐1096	8¢	Ramon Magsaysay	2.10	2.90	4.00
☐1097	3¢	Lafayette Bicentenary	1.80	2.90	4.00
☐1098	3¢	Wildlife (Whooping Crane)	1.80	2.90	4.00
☐1099	3¢	Religious Freedom	1.80	2.90	4.00
☐1100	3¢	Gardening Horticulture	1.80	2.90	4.00
☐1104	3¢	Brussels Exhibition	1.80	2.90	4.00
☐1105	3¢	James Monroe	1.80	2.90	4.00
☐1106	3¢	Minnesota Statehood	1.80	2.90	4.00
☐1107	3¢	International Geophysical Year	1.80	2.90	4.00
☐1108	3¢	Gunston Hall	1.80	2.90	4.00
☐1109	3¢	Mackinac Bridge	1.80	2.90	4.00
☐1110	4¢	Simon Bolivar	1.80	2.90	4.00
☐1111	8¢	Simon Bolivar	1.80	2.90	4.00
☐1112	4¢	Atlantic Cable	1.80	2.90	4.00
☐1113	1¢	Lincoln Sesquicentennial	1.80	2.90	4.00
☐1114	3¢	Lincoln Sesquicentennial	1.80	2.90	4.00
☐1115	4¢	Lincoln-Douglas Debates	1.80	2.90	4.00
☐1116	4¢	Lincoln Sesquicentennial	1.80	2.90	4.00
☐1117	4¢	Lajos Kossuth	1.80	2.90	4.00
☐1118	8¢	Lajos Kossuth	1.80	2.90	4.00
☐1119	4¢	Freedom of Press	1.80	2.90	4.00
☐1120	4¢	Overland Mail	1.80	2.90	4.00
☐1121	4¢	Noah Webster	1.80	2.90	4.00
☐1122	4¢	Forest Conservation	1.80	2.90	4.00
☐1123	4¢	Fort Duquesne	1.80	2.90	4.00
☐1124	4¢	Oregon Statehood	1.80	2.90	4.00
☐1125	4¢	San Martin	1.80	2.90	4.00
☐1126	8¢	San Martin	1.80	2.90	4.00
☐1127	4¢	NATO	1.80	2.90	4.00
☐1128	4¢	Arctic Explorations	1.80	2.90	4.00
☐1129	8¢	World Trade	1.80	2.90	4.00
☐1130	4¢	Silver Centennial	1.80	2.90	4.00
☐1131	4¢	St. Lawrence Seaway	1.80	2.90	4.00
☐1132	4¢	Flag	1.80	2.75	4.00
☐1133	4¢	Soil Conservation	1.80	2.75	4.00
☐1134	4¢	Petroleum Industry	1.80	2.75	4.00
☐1135	4¢	Dental Health	1.80	2.75	4.00
☐1136	4¢	Reuter	1.80	2.75	4.00
☐1137	8¢	Reuter	1.80	2.75	4.00
☐1138	4¢	Dr. Ephraim McDowell	1.80	2.75	4.00
☐1139	4¢	Washington "Credo"	1.80	2.75	4.00
☐1140	4¢	Franklin "Credo"	1.80	2.75	4.00
☐1141	4¢	Jefferson "Credo"	1.80	2.75	4.00
☐1142	4¢	Frances Scott Key "Credo"	1.80	2.75	4.00
☐1143	4¢	Lincoln "Credo"	1.80	2.75	4.00
☐1144	4¢	Patrick Henry "Credo"	1.80	2.75	4.00
☐1145	4¢	Boy Scouts	1.80	2.75	4.00

Scott No.			Single	Block	Plate Block
☐1146	4¢	Olympic Winter Games	1.65	2.90	3.90
☐1147	4¢	Masaryk	1.65	2.90	3.90
☐1148	8¢	Masaryk	1.65	2.90	3.90
☐1149	4¢	World Refugee Year	1.65	2.90	3.90
☐1150	4¢	Water Conservation	1.65	2.90	3.90
☐1151	4¢	SEATO	1.65	2.90	3.90
☐1152	4¢	American Woman	1.65	2.90	3.90
☐1153	4¢	50-Star Flag	1.65	2.90	3.90
☐1154	4¢	Pony Express Centennial	2.10	3.00	4.00
☐1155	4¢	Employ the Handicapped	1.65	2.90	3.90
☐1156	4¢	World Forestry Congress	1.65	2.90	3.90
☐1157	4¢	Mexican Independence	1.80	2.90	3.90
☐1158	4¢	U.S. Japan Treaty	1.65	2.90	3.90
☐1159	4¢	Paderewski	1.65	2.90	3.90
☐1160	8¢	Paderewski	1.65	2.90	3.90
☐1161	4¢	Robert A. Taft	1.65	2.90	3.90
☐1162	4¢	Wheels of Freedom	1.65	2.90	3.90
☐1163	4¢	Boys' Clubs	1.65	2.90	3.90
☐1164	4¢	Automated P.O.	1.65	2.90	3.90
☐1165	4¢	Mannerheim	1.65	2.90	3.90
☐1166	8¢	Mannerheim	1.65	2.90	3.90
☐1167	4¢	Camp Fire Girls	1.65	2.90	3.90
☐1168	4¢	Garibaldi	1.65	2.90	3.90
☐1169	8¢	Garibaldi	1.65	2.90	3.90
☐1170	4¢	Senator George	1.65	2.90	3.90
☐1171	4¢	Andrew Carnegie	1.65	2.90	3.90
☐1172	4¢	John Foster Dulles	1.65	2.90	3.90
☐1173	4¢	Echo I	1.65	2.90	3.90
☐1174	4¢	Gandhi	1.65	2.90	3.90
☐1175	8¢	Gandhi	1.65	2.90	3.90
☐1176	4¢	Range Conservation	1.65	2.90	3.90
☐1177	4¢	Horace Greeley	1.65	2.90	3.90
☐1178	4¢	Fort Sumter	2.10	3.00	4.00
☐1179	4¢	Battle of Shiloh	2.10	3.00	4.00
☐1180	5¢	Battle of Gettysburg	2.10	3.00	4.00
☐1181	5¢	Battle of Wilderness	2.10	3.00	4.00
☐1182	5¢	Appomattox	2.10	3.00	4.00
☐1183	4¢	Kansas Statehood	1.64	3.00	4.00
☐1184	4¢	Senator Norris	1.65	2.90	4.00
☐1185	4¢	Naval Aviation	1.65	2.90	4.00
☐1186	4¢	Workmen's Compensation	2.10	2.90	4.00
☐1187	4¢	Frederic Remington	2.50	3.25	5.00
☐1188	4¢	China Republic	3.50	4.00	6.00
☐1189	4¢	Naismith	3.50	4.00	6.00
☐1190	4¢	Nursing	2.50	3.75	5.00
☐1191	4¢	New Mexico Statehood	2.50	3.25	5.00
☐1192	4¢	Arizona Statehood	3.50	4.00	6.00
☐1193	4¢	Project Mercury			

Scott No.			Single	Block	Plate Block
☐1194	4¢	Malaria Eradication	1.65	2.90	3.90
☐1195	4¢	Charles Evans Hughes	1.65	2.90	3.90
☐1196	4¢	Seattle World's Fair	1.65	2.90	3.90
☐1197	4¢	Louisiana Statehood	1.65	2.90	3.90
☐1198	4¢	Homestead Act	1.65	2.90	3.90
☐1199	4¢	Girl Scouts	2.10	2.90	4.00
☐1200	4¢	Brien McMahon	1.65	2.90	3.90
☐1201	4¢	Apprenticeship	1.65	2.90	3.90
☐1202	4¢	Sam Rayburn	1.65	2.90	3.90
☐1203	4¢	Dag Hammarskjold	1.65	2.90	3.90
☐1204	4¢	Hammarskjold "Error"	4.50	8.50	11.00
☐1205	4¢	Christmas	1.65	3.25	3.90
☐1206	4¢	Higher Education	2.00	2.90	4.00
☐1207	4¢	Winslow Homer	2.00	2.90	4.00
☐1208	4¢	Flag	1.90	2.90	4.00
☐1209	4¢	Jackson	1.65	2.80	3.90
☐1213	5¢	Washington	1.65	2.80	3.90
☐1225	1¢	Jackson (coil)	1.65	2.50	2.90
☐1229	5¢	Washington (coil)	1.65	2.50	2.90
☐1230	5¢	Carolina Charter	1.65	2.75	3.90
☐1231	5¢	Food for Peace	1.65	2.75	3.90
☐1232	5¢	West Virginia Statehood	1.65	2.75	3.90
☐1233	5¢	Emancipation Proclamation	1.65	2.75	3.90
☐1234	5¢	Alliance for Progress	1.65	2.75	3.90
☐1235	5¢	Cordell Hull	1.65	2.75	3.90
☐1236	5¢	Eleanor Roosevelt	1.65	2.75	3.90
☐1237	5¢	Science	1.65	2.75	3.90
☐1238	5¢	City Mail Delivery	1.65	2.75	3.90
☐1239	5¢	Red Cross	1.65	2.75	3.90
☐1240	5¢	Christmas	1.65	2.75	3.90
☐1241	5¢	Audubon	1.65	2.75	3.90
☐1242	5¢	Sam Houston	1.65	2.75	3.90
☐1243	5¢	Charles Russell	5.00	3.50	5.00
☐1244	5¢	N.Y. World's Fair	1.65	2.75	3.90
☐1245	5¢	John Muir	1.65	2.75	3.90
☐1246	5¢	John F. Kennedy	2.10	3.00	4.00
☐1247	5¢	New Jersey Tercentenary	1.65	2.75	3.90
☐1248	5¢	Nevada Statehood	1.65	2.75	3.90
☐1249	5¢	Register & Vote	1.65	2.75	3.90
☐1250	5¢	Shakespeare	2.10	3.00	4.00
☐1251	5¢	Drs. Mayo	2.75	4.50	6.00
☐1252	5¢	American Music	1.65	2.75	3.90
☐1253	5¢	Homemakers	1.65	2.75	3.90
☐1254–57	5¢	Christmas	5.00	7.00	10.00
☐1258	5¢	Verrazano-Narrows Bridge	1.65	2.70	3.75
☐1259	5¢	Fine Arts	1.65	2.70	3.75
☐1260	5¢	Amateur Radio	2.10	3.00	4.00
☐1261	5¢	Battle of New Orleans	1.65	2.70	3.75

Scott No.			Single	Block	Plate Block
☐1262	5¢	Physical Fitness	2.10	3.00	4.00
☐1263	5¢	Cancer Crusade	2.75	3.50	6.00
☐1264	5¢	Churchill	1.60	2.60	3.60
☐1265	5¢	Magna Carta	1.60	2.60	3.60
☐1266	5¢	Intl. Cooperation Year	1.60	2.60	3.60
☐1267	5¢	Salvation Army	1.60	2.60	3.60
☐1268	5¢	Dante	1.60	2.60	3.60
☐1269	5¢	Herbert Hoover	1.60	2.60	3.60
☐1270	5¢	Robert Fulton	1.60	2.60	3.60
☐1271	5¢	Florida Settlement	1.60	2.60	3.60
☐1272	5¢	Traffic Safety	1.60	2.60	3.60
☐1273	5¢	Copley	1.60	2.60	3.60
☐1274	11¢	Intl. Telecommunication Union	1.60	2.60	3.60
☐1275	5¢	Adlai Stevenson	1.60	2.60	3.60
☐1276	5¢	Christmas	1.60	2.60	3.60
☐1278	1¢	Jefferson	1.60	2.60	3.60
☐1279	1¼¢	Gallatin	1.60	2.60	3.60
☐1280	2¢	Wright	1.60	2.60	3.60
☐1281	3¢	Parkman	1.60	2.60	3.60
☐1282	4¢	Lincoln	1.60	2.60	3.60
☐1283	5¢	Washington	1.60	2.60	3.60
☐1283B	5¢	Washington	1.60	2.60	3.60
☐1284	6¢	Roosevelt	1.60	2.60	3.60
☐1285	8¢	Einstein	2.10	3.00	4.00
☐1286	10¢	Jackson	1.90	2.65	3.75
☐1286a	12¢	Ford	1.90	2.65	3.75
☐1287	13¢	Kennedy	2.75	5.00	6.00
☐1288	15¢	Holmes	1.90	2.60	4.10
☐1289	20¢	Marshall	2.10	3.00	4.00
☐1290	25¢	Douglas	2.10	2.60	4.50
☐1291	30¢	Dewey	2.50	3.50	5.00
☐1292	40¢	Paine	2.75	5.00	6.00
☐1293	50¢	Stone	4.00	6.00	8.00
☐1294	$1	O'Neill	5.00	7.00	11.00
☐1295	$5	Moore	45.00	85.00	110.00
☐1304	5¢	Washington (coil)	—	pr. 1.50	lp. 3.00
☐1305	6¢	Roosevelt (coil)	—	pr. 1.50	lp. 3.00
☐1305C	$1	O'Neill (coil)	—	pr. 1.50	lp. 3.00
☐1306	5¢	Migratory Bird Treaty	1.60	2.50	3.65
☐1307	5¢	Humane Treatment of Animals	1.60	2.50	3.65
☐1308	5¢	Indiana Statehood	1.60	2.50	3.65
☐1309	5¢	Circus	1.60	2.50	3.65
☐1310	5¢	SIPEX	1.60	2.50	3.65
☐1311	5¢	SIPEX	1.60	2.50	3.65
☐1312	5¢	Bill of Rights	1.60	2.50	3.65
☐1313	5¢	Polish Millennium	1.60	2.50	3.65
☐1314	5¢	National Park Service	1.60	2.50	3.65
☐1315	5¢	Marine Corps Reserve	1.60	2.50	3.65

Scott No.			Single	Block	Plate Block
☐1316	5¢	Genl. Fed. of Women's Clubs	1.90	3.00	4.00
☐1317	5¢	Johnny Appleseed	1.60	2.70	3.60
☐1318	5¢	Beautification of America	1.60	2.70	3.60
☐1319	5¢	Great River Road	1.60	2.70	3.60
☐1320	5¢	Savings Bonds	1.90	3.00	4.00
☐1321	5¢	Christmas	1.90	3.00	4.00
☐1322	5¢	Mary Cassatt	1.60	2.70	3.60
☐1323	5¢	National Grange	1.60	2.70	3.60
☐1324	5¢	Canada Centenary	1.60	2.70	3.60
☐1325	5¢	Erie Canal	1.60	2.70	3.60
☐1326	5¢	Search for Peace	1.60	2.70	3.60
☐1327	5¢	Thoreau	1.60	2.70	3.60
☐1328	5¢	Nebraska Statehood	1.60	2.70	3.60
☐1329	5¢	Voice of America	1.60	2.70	3.60
☐1330	5¢	Davy Crockett	1.75	2.60	4.00
☐1331– 1332	5¢	Space Accomplishments	12.00pr.	20.00	24.00
☐1333	5¢	Urban Planning	1.60	2.60	3.60
☐1334	5¢	Finland Independence	1.60	2.60	3.60
☐1335	5¢	Thomas Eakins	1.60	2.60	3.60
☐1336	5¢	Christmas	1.90	3.00	4.00
☐1337	5¢	Mississippi Statehood	1.60	2.60	3.60
☐1338	6¢	Flag	1.60	2.60	3.60
☐1339	6¢	Illinois Statehood	1.60	2.60	3.60
☐1340	6¢	Hemis Fair '68	1.60	2.60	3.60
☐1341	$1	Airlift	8.00	12.00	17.00
☐1342	6¢	Youth-Elks	1.60	2.60	3.60
☐1343	6¢	Law and Order	3.00	4.50	6.00
☐1344	6¢	Register and Vote	1.60	2.60	3.60
☐1345– 1354	6¢	Historic Flag series of 10, all on one cover	11.00	—	—
☐1355	6¢	Disney	10.00	4.60	20.00
☐1356	6¢	Marquette	1.60	2.60	3.50
☐1357	6¢	Daniel Boone	1.60	2.60	3.50
☐1358	6¢	Arkansas River	1.60	2.60	3.50
☐1359	6¢	Leif Erikson	1.60	2.60	3.50
☐1360	6¢	Cherokee Strip	1.60	2.60	3.50
☐1361	6¢	John Trumbull	2.10	3.50	4.00
☐1362	6¢	Waterfowl Conservation	2.10	3.50	4.00
☐1363	6¢	Christmas	2.10	3.50	4.00
☐1364	6¢	American Indian	1.60	2.60	3.50
☐1365– 1368	6¢	Beautification of America	5.00	7.00	9.00
☐1369	6¢	American Legion	1.60	2.70	3.50
☐1370	6¢	Grandma Moses	1.60	2.70	3.50
☐1371	6¢	Apollo 8	3.50	5.00	7.00

NOTE: From number 1372 to date, most First Day Covers have a value of $1.50 to $2.00 for single stamps, $2.75 to $4.00 for blocks of four and $3.50 to $5.00 for plate blocks of four.

Start your U.S. collection with

SCOTT.

Stars and Stripes Album

48-page looseleaf album featuring stamps of the last 25 years. Pages can be integrated to next level album, the Pony Express.

176SAS0 .... **$8.95**

Pony Express Album

Housed in a padded leatherette binder, this 200-page album features spaces for thousands of stamps. Each space includes a brief story about the stamp.

178PEX0 .... **$24.95**

Minuteman Album

The classic American stamp album. All spaces identified with famous Scott Catalogue numbers. Pages feature brief story about stamps, providing a complete history of the U.S.

180AMM0 .... **$42.50**

Available at your local dealer or direct from:
Scott Publishing Co., P.O. Box 828, Sidney, OH 45365

The American Philatelic Society
to Really Enjoy Stamp Collecting

- 100-page Monthly Magazine
- Sales Circuit Approval Service
- Comprehensive Stamp Insurance
- Correspondence Courses/Seminars
- Library Borrowing & Copy Service

America's Best Stamp Monthly!

Call or write:

**APS P.O. Box 8000, Dept. HC
State College, PA 16803
(814) 237-3803**

Serving Stamp Collectors Since 1886

MEMBERSHIP IN THE ANA COULD BE YOUR BEST INVESTMENT THIS YEAR.

As a rare coin collector or hobbyist, you continually deal with a variety of questions. How can you know that the coin you're about to purchase is not counterfeit? How can you find the detailed, current information you need to build your collection? There is no authority to help you solve all these problems. Unless you belong to the American Numismatic Association.

Coin Certification and Grading. ANA experts examine rare coins for authenticity to help safeguard against counterfeiting and misrepresentation. ANA now offers the ANACS Grading Service—third party expert opinions as to the condition of U.S. coins submitted for examination, and will issue certificates of authenticity.

Library Service. The largest circulating numismatic library in the world is maintained by the ANA. Its sole purpose is to provide you with free access to invaluable information that can't be found anywhere else.

The Numismatist. The Association's fully-illustrated magazine, considered *the* outstanding publication devoted exclusively to all phases of numismatics, is mailed free to all members.

And there are more benefits available through the ANA. Like coin insurance, special seminars, free booklets and photographic services. You can't find benefits like these anywhere else. Don't you owe it to yourself to join today?

I want some recognition!
Make me an ANA Member.

Check One:

☐ Regular $26 plus $6 first-year
   processing fee
☐ Junior $11 (age 17 or younger)
☐ Senior $22 plus $6 first-year
   processing fee (age 65 or older)
☐ 5-Year $120
☐ Life $750
☐ Foreign $28 plus $6 first-year
   processing fee

☐ Mr.   ☐ Mrs.   ☐ Ms.

Name _____
         Please Print

Street _____

City _____

State _____ Zip _____

Birthdate _____ / _____ / _____

I agree to abide by the American
Numismatic Association's bylaws and
Code of Ethics which require the
publication of each applicant's name
and state.

_____
Signature of Applicant

_____
Signature of Parent or Guardian
(required for Junior applicant)

☐ Check here if you DO NOT want
   your name and address forwarded
   to an ANA Club Representative in
   your area.

☐ Check here if you want your name
   provided to numismatic-related
   companies.

☐ Check   ☐ Money Order
☐ MasterCard   ☐ VISA
☐ AmExpress

_____
Credit Card Account No.
Expiration Date _____

_____
Signature of Cardholder (required)
SPONSOR _____ ANA No. _____
(optional)

Foreign applications must be
accompanied by U.S. Funds drawn on
a U.S. bank.

OR JOIN BY PHONE:
Use your VISA, MasterCard or
American Express Card.
      Call 719-632-2646

Return application with payment to:
American Numismatic Association
818 N. Cascade Ave.
Colorado Springs, CO 80903-3279

THE BLACKBOOKS!

The leading authorities on U.S. coins, paper money, and postage stamps!
All national bestsellers, these dynamic books are the proven annual guides for collectors in these fields for more than two decades!
- **COINS** — Every U.S. coin evaluated. . . features the American Numismatic Association Official Grading System!
- **PAPER MONEY**— Every government-issued note covered!
- **POSTAGE STAMPS** — Every U.S. stamp detailed. . . features a full-color, fast-find photo index arranged by the Scott numbering system!

DON'T LEAVE HOME WITHOUT THEM!

HOUSE OF COLLECTIBLES
201 East 50th Street, New York, New York 10022

Please send me the following:

☐ The Official Blackbook Price Guide of U.S. Coins, 33rd Ed.   0-876-37936-6 / $6.00
☐ The Official Blackbook Price Guide of U.S. Postage Stamps, 17th Ed.
0-876-37930-7 / $6.00
☐ The Official Blackbook Price Guide of U.S. Paper Money, 27th Ed.
0-876-37933-1 / $6.00

I am enclosing $_____ (add $2 for the first book and 50¢ for each additional copy to cover postage and handling). Send check or money order—no cash or C.O.D.'s, please. Prices and numbers are subject to change without notice.

Name_____

Address_____

City_____ State_____ Zip Code_____

Allow at least 4 weeks for delivery.

**TO ERR IS HUMAN
—AND PROFITABLE!**

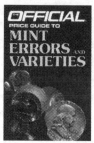

The Official® Identification and Price Guide to Minting Varieties and Errors, by leading expert Alan Herbert, is an incomparable reference for both investors and collectors.

- Every class and variety represented—the most complete classification ever published

- Step-by-step explanations of the minting process

- How to avoid counterfeits

- A helpful glossary, plus over 250 photos and classification index

---

HOUSE OF COLLECTIBLES
201 East 50th Street
New York, New York 10022

Please send me *The Official® Identification and Price Guide to Minting Varieties and Errors*, 5th Ed. . . . 0-876-37825-4 . . . $12.95. I am enclosing $_____$(add $2 for the first book and 50¢ for each additional copy to cover postage and handling). Send check or money order—no cash or C.O.D.'s, please. Prices and numbers are subject to change without notice.

Name_____

Address_____

City_____State_____Zip Code_____

Allow at least 4 weeks for delivery.